Parallel Lives Vol. 1

Parallel Lives Vol. 1

by Plutarch

Wilder Publications, LLC.
PO Box 3005
Radford VA 24143-3005

ISBN 10: 1-61720-651-2
ISBN 13: 978-1-61720-651-1

Table of Contents:

Preface.

No apologies are needed for a new edition of so favourite an author as Plutarch. From the period of the revival of classical literature in Europe down to our own times, his writings have done more than those of any other single author to familiarise us with the greatest men and the greatest events of the ancient world.

The great Duke of Marlborough, it is said, confessed that his only knowledge of English history was derived from Shakespeare's historical plays, and it would not be too much to say that a very large proportion of educated men, in our own as well as in Marlborough's times, have owed much of their knowledge of classical antiquity to the study of Plutarch's Lives. Other writers may be read with profit, with admiration, and with interest; but few, like Plutarch, can gossip pleasantly while instructing solidly; can breathe life into the dry skeleton of history, and show that the life of a Greek or Roman worthy, when rightly dealt with, can prove as entertaining as a modern novel. No one is so well able as Plutarch to dispel the doubt which all schoolboys feel as to whether the names about which they read ever belonged to men who were really alive; his characters are so intensely human and lifelike in their faults and failings as well as in their virtues, that we begin to think of them as of people whom we have ourselves personally known.

His biographies are numerous and short. By this, he avoids one of the greatest faults of modern biographers, that namely of identifying himself with some one particular personage, and endeavouring to prove that all his actions were equally laudable. Light and shade are as necessary to a character as to a picture, but a man who devotes his energies for years to the study of any single person's life, is insensibly led into palliating or explaining away his faults and exaggerating his excellencies until at last he represents him as an impossible monster of virtue. Another advantage which we obtain by his method is that we are not given a complete chronicle of each person's life, but only of the remarkable events in it, and such incidents as will enable us to judge of his character. This also avoids what is the dreariest part of all modern biographies, those chapters I mean which describe the slow decay of their hero's powers, his last illness, and finally his death. This subject, which so many writers of our own time seem to linger lovingly upon, is dismissed by Plutarch in a few lines, unless any circumstance of note attended the death of the person described.

Without denying that Plutarch is often inaccurate and often diffuse; that his anecdotes are sometimes absurd, and his metaphysical speculations not unfrequently ridiculous, he is nevertheless generally admitted to be one of the most readable authors of antiquity, while all agree that his morality is of the purest and loftiest type.

The first edition of the Greek text of Plutarch's Lives appeared at Florence in the year 1517, and two years afterwards it was republished by Aldus. Before this, however, about the year 1470, a magnificent Latin version by various hands appeared at Rome. From this, from the Greek text, and also from certain MSS. to which he had access, Amyot in the year 1559 composed his excellent translation, of which it has been well said: "Quoique en vieux Gaulois, elle a un air de fraicheur qui la fait rejeunir de jour en jour."

Amyot's spirited French version was no less spiritedly translated by Sir Thomas North. His translation was much read and admired in its day; a modern reviewer even goes so far as to say that it is "still beyond comparison the best version of Parallel Lives which the English tongue affords." Be this as it may, the world will ever be deeply indebted to North's translation, for it is to Shakespeare's perusal of that work that we owe 'Coriolanus,' 'Antony and Cleopatra,' and 'Julius Caesar.'

North's translation was followed by that known as Dryden's. This work, performed by many different hands, is of unequal merit. Some Lives are rendered into a racy and idiomatic, although somewhat archaic English, while others fall far short of the standard of Sir Thomas North's work. Dryden's version has during the last few years been re-edited by A.H. Clough, Fellow of Oriel College, Oxford.

The translation by which Plutarch is best known at the present day is that of the Langhornes. Their style is certainly dull and commonplace, and is in many instances deserving of the harsh epithets which have been lavished upon it. We must remember, however, before unsparingly condemning their translation, that the taste of the age for which they wrote differed materially from that of our own, and that people who could read the 'Letters of Theodosius and Constantia' with interest, would certainly prefer Plutarch in the translation of the Langhornes to the simpler phrases of North's or Dryden's version. All events, comic or tragic, important or commonplace, are described with the same inflated monotony which was mistaken by them for the dignity of History. Yet their work is in many cases far more correct as a translation, and the author's meaning is sometimes much more clearly expressed, than in Dryden's earlier version. Langhorne's Plutarch was re-edited by Archdeacon Wrangham in the year 1819.

In 1844, thirteen Lives were translated by that eminent scholar the late Mr. George Long; and it is by way of complement to these Lives that the present version was undertaken with his consent and his approval.

Those translated by Mr. Long were selected by him as illustrating a period of Roman history in which he was especially interested, and will therefore be found to be more fully annotated than the others. It has seemed to me unnecessary to give information in the notes which can at the present day be obtained in a more convenient form in Dr. Smith's Classical Dictionary and Dictionary of Antiquities, many of the articles in which are written by Mr. Long himself. The student of classical literature will naturally prefer the exhaustive essays to be found in these works to any notes appended to Plutarch's text, while to those who read merely "for the story," the notes prove both troublesome and useless.

In deciding on the spelling of the Greek proper names, I have felt great hesitation. To make a Greek speak of Juno or Minerva seems as absurd as to make a Roman swear by Herakles or Ares. Yet both Greek and Roman divinities are constantly mentioned. The only course that seemed to avoid absolute absurdity appeared to me to be that which I have adopted, namely to speak of the Greek divinities by their Greek, and the Latin ones by their Latin names. In substituting a k for the more usual c, I have followed the example of Grote, who in his History spells all Greek names exactly as they are written, with the exception of those with which we are so familiar in their Latin form as to render this practically impossible; as for instance in the case of Cyprus or Corinth, or of a name like Thucydides, where a return to the Greek k would be both pedantic and unmeaning.

The text, which I have followed throughout, is that of C. Sintenis, Leipsic, 1873.

AUBREY STEWART.

Preface to the Civil Wars of Rome.

Among the extant Lives of Plutarch there are thirteen Lives of Romans which belong to the most eventful period of Roman history. They are the lives of the brothers Tiberius and Caius Sempronius Gracchus, of Caius Marius, Lucius Cornelius Sulla, Quintus Sertorius, Marcus Licinius Crassus, Cneius Pompeius Magnus, Marcus Porcius Cato the Younger, Marcus Tullius Cicero, Lucius Licinius Lucullus, Caius Julius Caesar, Marcus Junius Brutus, and Marcus Antonius. From the year of the death of Tiberius Gracchus, B.C. 133, to the death of Marcus Antonius, B.C. 30, a period of about one hundred years, the Roman State was convulsed by revolutions which grew out of the contest between the People and the Nobility, or rather, out of the contests between the leaders of these two bodies. This period is the subject of Appian's History of the Civil Wars of the Romans, in Five Books. Appian begins with the Tribunate and legislation of Tiberius Gracchus, from which he proceeds to the Dictatorship of Sulla, and then to the quarrels between Pompeius and Caesar, and Caesar's Dictatorship and assassination. He then proceeds to the history of the Triumvirate formed after Caesar's death by his great nephew Caius Julius Caesar Octavianus, Marcus Antonius, and Lepidus, the quarrels of the Triumviri, the downfall of Lepidus, who was reduced to the condition of a private person, and the death of Sextus Pompeius, the last support of the party in whose cause his father, Cneius Pompeius, lost his life. The remainder of this History, which is lost, carried the narration down to the quarrels of Octavianus and Marcus Antonius, which ended in the defeat of Antonius in the battle of Actium, B.C. 31, and his death in Egypt, B.C. 30. The victory over Antonius placed all the power in the hands of Octavianus, who, in the year B.C. 27, received from the Roman Senate the title of Augustus, or the Sacred, by which name he is commonly known as the first of the long series of Roman Emperors. "He made himself," says Appian (Civil Wars, i. 5), "like Caius Julius Caesar, and still more than Caesar, governor of his country and of all the nations under it, without needing either election or the popular votes, or any show of such things. After his government had subsisted for a long time, and been maintained with vigour, fortunate in all his measures, and feared, he left behind him descendants and successors who kept the power that he transmitted to them. In this way, after various civil commotions, the Roman State was restored to tranquillity, and the government became a Monarchy. And how this came about I have explained, and brought together all the events, which are well worth the study of those who wish to become acquainted with ambition of men unbounded, love of power excessive, endurance unwearied, and forms of suffering infinite." Thus, the historian's object was to trace the establishment of the Imperial power in Rome back to its origin, to show that the contests of the rival heads of parties involved the State in endless calamities, which resulted in a dissolution of all the bonds that held society together, and rendered the assumption of supreme power by one man a healing and a necessary event.

As already observed, it happens that thirteen of Plutarch's extant Lives are the lives of the most distinguished of the Romans who lived during this eventful period; and though Plutarch's Lives severally are not histories of the times to which they respectively refer, nor collectively form a History of any given time, yet they are valuable as portraits of illustrious men, and help us to form a better judgment of those who make so conspicuous a figure in History.

Plutarch was a native of the town of Chaeroneia, in Boeotia; the times of his birth and death are not exactly known, but we learn from his own works that he was a young student at Delphi, in the thirteenth year of the reign of the Emperor Nero, A.D. 66. He visited both Italy and Rome, and probably resided at Rome for some time. He wrote his Life of Demosthenes, at least after his return to Chaeroneia: he says (Life of Demosthenes, c. 2), that he had not time to exercise himself in the Latin Language during his residence at Rome, being much occupied with public business, and giving lessons in philosophy. Accordingly it was late before he began to read the Latin writers; and we may infer from his own words that he never acquired a very exact knowledge of the language. He observes that it happened in his case, that in his study of the Latin writers he did not so much learn and understand the facts from the words, as acquire the meaning of the words from the facts, of which he had already some knowledge. We may perhaps conclude from this, that Plutarch wrote all his Roman lives in Chaeroneia, after he had returned there from Rome. The statement that Plutarch was the preceptor of the Emperor Trajan, and was raised to the consular rank by him, is not supported by sufficient evidence. Plutarch addressed to Trajan his Book of Apophthegms, or Sayings of Kings and Commanders; but this is all that is satisfactorily ascertained as to the connection between the Emperor and Philosopher. Trajan died A.D. 117.

"The plan of Plutarch's Biographies is briefly explained by himself in the introduction to the Life of Alexander the Great, where he makes an apology for the brevity with which he is compelled to treat of the numerous events in the Lives of Alexander and Caesar. 'For,' he says, 'I do not write Histories, but

Lives; nor do the most conspicuous acts of necessity exhibit a man's virtue or his vice, but oftentimes some slight circumstance, a word, or a jest, shows a man's character better than battles with the slaughter of tens of thousands, and the greatest arrays of armies and sieges of cities. Now, as painters produce a likeness by a representation of the countenance and the expression of the eyes, without troubling themselves about the other parts of the body, so I must be allowed to look rather into the signs of a man's character, and thus give a portrait of his life, leaving others to describe great events and battles.' The object then of Plutarch in his Biographies was a moral end, and the exhibition of the principal events in a man's life was subordinate to this his main design; and though he may not always have adhered to the principle which he laid down, it cannot be denied that his view of what biography should be, is much more exact than that of most persons who have attempted this style of composition. The life of a statesman or of a general, when written with a view of giving a complete history of all the public events in which he was engaged, is not biography, but history. This extract from Plutarch will also in some measure be an apology for the want of historical order observable in many of his Lives. Though altogether deficient in that critical sagacity which discerns truth from falsehood, and distinguishes the intricacies of confused and conflicting statements, Plutarch has preserved in his Lives a vast number of facts which would otherwise have been unknown to us. He was a great reader, and must have had access to large libraries. It is said that he quotes two hundred and fifty writers, a great part of whose works are now entirely lost." (Penny Cyclopaedia, art. "Plutarch," by the writer of this Preface.)

The lively portraitures of men drawn in Plutarch's Lives have made them favourite reading in all ages. Whether Plutarch has succeeded in drawing the portraits true, we cannot always determine, because the materials for such a judgment are sometimes wanting. But when we can compare his Lives with other extant authorities, we must admit, that though he is by no means free from error as to his facts, he has generally selected those events in a man's life which most clearly show his temper, and that on the whole, if we judge of a man by Plutarch's measure, we shall form a just estimate of him. He generally wrote without any predilections or any prejudices. He tells us of a man's good and bad acts, of his good and bad qualities; he makes no attempt to conceal the one or the other; he both praises and blames as the occasion may arise; and the reader leaves off with a mixed opinion about Plutarch's Greeks and Romans, though the favourable or the unfavourable side always predominates. The benevolent disposition of Plutarch, and his noble and elevated character, have stamped themselves on all that he has written. A man cannot read these Lives without being the better for it: his detestation of all that is mean and disingenuous will be increased; his admiration of whatever is truthful and generous will be strengthened and exalted.

The translation of these Lives is difficult. Plutarch's text is occasionally corrupted; and where it is not corrupted, his meaning is sometimes obscure. Many of the sentences are long and ill-constructed; the metaphors often extravagant; and the just connection of the parts is sometimes difficult to discover. Many single words which are or ought to be pertinent in Plutarch, and which go towards a description of character in general or of some particular act, can hardly be rendered by any English equivalent; and a translator often searches in vain for something which shall convey to the reader the exact notion of the original. Yet Plutarch's narrative is lively and animated; his anecdotes are appropriately introduced and well told; and if his taste is sometimes not the purest, which in his age we could not expect it to be, he makes amends for this by the fulness and vigour of his expression. He is fond of poetical words, and they are often used with striking effect. His moral reflections, which are numerous, have the merit of not being unmeaning and tiresome, because he is always in earnest and has got something to say, and does not deal in commonplaces. When the reflection is not very profound, it is at least true; and some of his remarks show a deep insight into men's character.

I have attempted to give Plutarch's meaning in plain language; to give all his meaning, and neither more nor less. If I have failed in any case, it is because I could do no better. But, though I have not always succeeded in expressing exactly what I conceive to be the meaning of the original, I have not intentionally added to it or detracted from it. It may be that there are passages in which I have mistaken the original; and those who have made the experiment of rendering from one language into another, know that this will sometimes happen even in an easy passage. A difficult passage attracts more than usual of a translator's attention, and if he fails there, it is either because the difficulty cannot be overcome, or because he cannot overcome it. Mere inadvertence or sleepiness may sometimes cause a translator to blunder, when he would not have blundered if any friend had been by to keep him awake.

The best thing that a man can do to avoid these and other errors is to compare his translation, when he has finished it, with some other. The translation which I have compared with mine is the German translation of Kaltwasser, Magdeburg, 1799, which is generally correct. Kaltwasser in his Preface speaks of the way in which he used the German translations of two of his predecessors, J. Christopher Kind, Leipzig, 1745-1754, and H. v. Schirach, 1776-1780, and some others. He says, "These two translations, with the French translations above mentioned, I have duly used, for it is the duty of a translator to compare himself with his predecessors; but I lay my labour before the eyes of the public, without fearing that I shall be accused of copying or of close imitation. First of all, I carefully studied the text of my author and translated him as well as I could: then, and not before, I compared the labour of my predecessors, and where I found a more suitable expression or a happier turn, I made use of it without hesitation. In this way, every fault, every deviation of the old translators must be apparent; the most striking of them I have remarked on in the notes, but I have more frequently amended such things silently, as a comparison will show the reader." The translator has not compared his version with any English version. The translation of North, which has great merit in point of expression, is a version of Amyot's French version, from which, however, it differs in some passages, where it is decidedly wrong and Amyot's version is right. Indeed, it is surprising to find how correct this old French translation generally is. The translation of 'Plutarch's Lives from the Greek by several hands,' was published at London in 1683-86. It was dedicated by Dryden to James Butler, the first Duke of Ormond, in a fulsome panegyric. It is said that forty-one translators laboured at the work. Dryden did not translate any of the Lives; but he wrote the Life of Plutarch which is prefixed to this translation. The advertisement prefixed to the translation passes under the name and character of the bookseller (Jacob Tonson), but, as Malone observes, it may from internal evidence be safely attributed to Dryden. The bookseller says, "You have here the first volume of Plutarch's Lives turned from the Greek into English; and give me leave to say, the first attempt of doing it from the originals." This is aimed at North's version, of which Dryden remarks in his Life of Plutarch: "As that translation was only from the French, so it suffered this double disadvantage; first, that it was but a copy of a copy, and that too but lamely taken from the Greek original; secondly, that the English language was then unpolished, and far from the perfection which it has since attained; so that the first version is not only ungrammatical and ungraceful, but in many places almost unintelligible." There is another English version, by the Langhornes, which has often been reprinted; there is an edition of it with notes by Wrangham. I have compared my translation carefully with the German of Kaltwasser, and sometimes with the French of Amyot, and I have thus avoided some errors into which I should have fallen. There are errors both in the versions of Amyot and Kaltwasser which I have avoided; but I may have fallen into others.

The translation of Kaltwasser contains some useful notes. Those which I have added to this translation are intended to explain so much as needs explanation to a person who is not much acquainted with Roman history and Roman usages; but they will also be useful to others. The notes of Kaltwasser have often reminded me of the passages where some note would be useful, and have occasionally furnished materials also. But as I have always referred to the original authorities, I do not consider it necessary to make more than this general acknowledgment. The notes added to this translation are all my own, and contain my own opinions and observations.

This translation has been made from the edition of C. Sintenis, Leipzig, 1839, and I have compared the text of Sintenis with that of G.H. Schaefer, Leipzig, 1826, which has been severely criticized: this edition contains, however, some useful notes. I have very seldom made any remarks on the Greek text, as such kind of remark would not have suited the plan and design of this version, which is not intended for verbal critics.

I shall explain by two brief extracts what is my main design in this version and in the notes, which must be my apology for not affecting a learned commentary, and my excuse to those who shall not find here the kind of remarks that are suitable to a critical edition of an ancient author. I have had another object than to discuss the niceties of words and the forms of phrases, a labour which is well in its place, if it be done well, but is not what needs to be done to such an author as Plutarch to render him useful. A man who was a great reader of Plutarch, a just and solid thinker above the measure of his age, and not surpassed in his way by any writer in our own, Montaigne, observes in his 'Essay of the Education of Children'—"Let him enquire into the manners, revenues, and alliances of princes, things in themselves very pleasant to learn, and very useful to know. In this conversing with men, I mean, and principally those who only live in the records of history, he shall by reading those books, converse with those great and heroic souls of former and better ages. 'Tis an idle and vain study, I confess, to those who make it so, by doing it after a negligent manner, but to those who do it with care and observation, 'tis a study of inestimable fruit and value; and the only one, as Plato reports, the Lacedaemonians reserved to themselves. What profit shall he not reap as to the business of men, by reading the Lives of Plutarch? But withal, let my governor remember to what end his instructions are principally directed, and that he do not so much imprint in his pupil's memory the date of the ruin of Carthage, as the manners of Hannibal and Scipio; not so much where Marcellus died, as why it was unworthy of his duty that he died there. That he do not teach him so much the narrative part, as the business of history. The reading of which, in my opinion, is a thing that of all others we apply ourselves unto with the most differing and uncertain measures." North, in his address to the Reader, says: "The profit of stories, and the praise of the Author, are sufficiently declared by Amiot, in his Epistle to the Reader: so that I shall not need to make many words thereof. And indeed if you will supply the defects of this translation, with your own diligence and good understanding: you shall not need to trust him, you may prove yourselves, that there is no prophane study better than Plutarch. All other learning is private, fitter for Universities than Cities, fuller of contemplation than experience, more commendable in students themselves, than profitable unto others. Whereas stories are fit for every place, reach to all persons, serve for all times, teach the living, revive the dead, so far excelling all other books, as it is better to see learning in Noblemen's lives, than to read it in Philosophers' writings."

GEORGE LONG.

Life of Plutarch.

Plutarch was born probably between A.D. 45 and A.D. 50, at the little town of Chaeronea in Boeotia. His family appears to have been long established in this place, the scene of the final destruction of the liberties of Greece, when Philip defeated the Athenians and Boeotian forces there in 338 B.C. It was here also that Sulla defeated Mithridates, and in the great civil wars of Rome we again hear, this time from Plutarch himself, of the sufferings of the citizens of Chaeronea. Nikarchus, Plutarch's great-grandfather, was, with all the other citizens, without any exception, ordered by a lieutenant of Marcus Antonius to transport a quantity of corn from Chaeronea to the coast opposite the island of Antikyra. They were compelled to carry the corn on their shoulders, like slaves, and were threatened with the lash if they were remiss. After they had performed one journey, and were preparing their burdens for a second, the welcome news arrived that Marcus Antonius had lost the battle of Actium, whereupon both the officers and soldiers of his party stationed in Chaeronea at once fled for their own safety, and the provisions thus collected were divided among the inhabitants of the city.

When Plutarch was born, however, no such warlike scenes as these were to be expected. Nothing more than the traditions of war remained on the shores of the Mediterranean. Occasionally some faint echo of strife would make itself heard from the wild tribes on the Danube, or in the far Syrian deserts, but over nearly all the world known to the ancients was established the Pax Romana. Battles were indeed fought, and troops were marched upon Rome, but this was merely to decide who was to be the nominal head of the vast system of the Empire, and what had once been independent cities, countries, and nations submitted unhesitatingly to whoever represented that irresistible power. It might be imagined that a political system which destroyed all national individuality, and rendered patriotism in its highest sense scarcely possible, would have reacted unfavourably on the literary character of the age. Yet nothing of the kind can be urged against the times which produced Epictetus, Dio Chrysostom and Arrian; while at Rome, Pliny the Younger, Tacitus, Martial, and Juvenal were reviving the memories of the Augustan age.

From several passages in Plutarch's writings we gather that he studied under a master named Ammonius, at Athens. For instance, at the end of his Life of Themistokles, he mentions a descendant of that great man who was his fellow-student at the house of Ammonius the philosopher. Again, he tells us that once Ammonius, observing at his afternoon lecture that some of his class had indulged too freely in the pleasures of the table, ordered his own son to be flogged, "because," he said, "the young gentleman cannot eat his dinner without pickles," casting his eye at the same time upon the other offenders so as to make them sensible that the reproof applied to them also.

By way of completing his education he proceeded to visit Egypt. The "wisdom of the Egyptians" always seems to have had a fascination for the Greeks, and at this period Alexandria, with its famous library and its memories of the Ptolemies, of Kallimachus and of Theokritus, was an important centre of Greek intellectual activity. Plutarch's treatise on Isis and Osiris is generally supposed to be a juvenile work suggested by his Egyptian travels. In all the Graeco-Egyptian lore he certainly became well skilled, although we have no evidence as to how long he remained in Egypt. He makes mention indeed of a feast given in his honour by some of his relatives on the occasion of his return home from Alexandria, but we can gather nothing from the passage as to his age at that time.

One anecdote of his early life is as follows:—"I remember," he says, "that when I was still a young man, I was sent with another person on a deputation to the Proconsul; my colleague, as it happened, was unable to proceed, and I saw the Proconsul and performed the commission alone. When I returned I was about to lay down my office and to give a public account of how I had discharged it, when my father rose in the public assembly and enjoined me not to say I went, but we went, nor to say that I said, but we said, throughout my story, giving my colleague his share."

The most important event in the whole of Plutarch's pious and peaceful life is undoubtedly his journey to Italy and to Rome; but here again we know little more than that he knew but little Latin when he went thither, and was too busy when there to acquire much knowledge of that tongue. His occupation at Rome, besides antiquarian researches which were afterwards worked up into his Roman Lives, was the delivery of lectures on philosophical and other subjects, a common practice among the learned Greeks of his day. Many of these lectures, it is conjectured, were afterwards recast by him into the numerous short treatises on various subjects now included under the general name of Moralia. Plutarch's visit to Rome and business there is admirably explained in the following passage of North's 'Life of Plutarch':—"For my part, I think Plutarch was drawn to Rome by meanes of some friends he had there, especially by Sossius Senecio, that had been a Consull, who was of great estimation at that time, and namely under the Empire of Trajan. And that which maketh me think so, is because of Plutarch's own words, who saith in the beginning of his first book of his discourse at the table, that he gathered together all his reasons and discourses made here and there, as well in Rome with Senecio, as in Greece with Plutarch and others. Not being likely that he would have taken the pains to have made so long a voyage, and to have come to such a city where he understood not their vulgar tongue, if he had not been drawn thither by Senecio, and such other men; as also in acknowledgement of the good turnes and honour he had received by such men, he dedicated diverse of his bookes unto them, and among others, the Lives unto Senecio, and the nine volumes of his discourse at the table, with the treaty, How a man may know that he profiteth in vertue. Now for the time, considering what he saith in the end of his book against curiosity, I suppose that he taught in Rome in the time of Titus and of Domitian: for touching this point, he maketh mention of a nobleman called Rusticus, who being one day at his lecture, would not open a letter which was brought him from the Emperor, nor interrupt Plutarch, but attended to the end of his declamation, and until all the hearers were gone away; and addeth also, that Rusticus was afterwards put to death by the commandment of Domitian. Furthermore, about the beginning of the Life of Demosthenes, Plutarch saith, that whilst he remained in Italy and at Rome, he had no leizure to study the Latine tongue; as well for that he was busied at that time with matters he had in hand, as also to satisfie those that were his followers to learne philosophie of him."

A list of all Plutarch's writings would be a very long one. Besides the Lives, which is the work on which his fame chiefly rests, he wrote a book of 'Table Talk,' which may have suggested to Athenaeus the plan of his 'Symposium.'

The most remarkable of his minor works is that 'On the Malignity of Herodotus.' Grote takes this treatise as being intended seriously as an attack upon the historian, and speaks of the "honourable frankness which Plutarch calls his malignity." But it is probably merely a rhetorical exercise, in which Plutarch has endeavoured to see what could be said against so favourite and well-known a writer.

He was probably known as an author before he went to Rome. Large capitals have always had a natural attraction for literary genius, as it is in them alone that it can hope to be appreciated. And if this be the case at the present day, how much more must it have been so before the invention of printing, at a time when it was more usual to listen to books read aloud than to read them oneself? Plutarch journeyed to Rome just as Herodotus went to Athens, or as he is said to have gone to the Olympian festival, in search of an intelligent audience of educated men. Whether his object was merely praise, or whether he was influenced by ideas of gain, we cannot say. No doubt his lectures were not delivered gratis, and that they were well attended seems evident from Plutarch's own notices of them, and from the names which have been preserved of the eminent men who used to frequent them. Moreover, strange though it may appear to us, the demand for books seems to have been very brisk even though they were entirely written by hand.

The epigrams of Martial inform us of the existence of a class of slaves whose occupation was copying books, and innumerable allusions in Horace, Martial, &c., to the Sosii and others prove that the trade of a bookseller at Rome was both extensive and profitable. Towards the end of the Republic it became the fashion for Roman nobles to encourage literature by forming a library, and this taste was given immense encouragement by Augustus, who established a public library in the Temple of Apollo on the Mount Palatine, in imitation of that previously founded by Asinius Pollio. There were other libraries besides these, the most famous of which was the Ulpian library, founded by Trajan, who called it so from his own name, Ulpius. Now Trajan was a contemporary of our author, and this act of his clearly proves that there must have been during Plutarch's lifetime a considerable reading public, and consequent demand for books at Rome.

Of Plutarch's travels in Italy we know next to nothing. He mentions incidentally that he had seen the bust or statue of Marius at Ravenna, but never gives us another hint of how far he explored the country about which he wrote so much. No doubt his ignorance of the Latin language must not be taken as a literal statement, and probably means that he was not skilled in it as a spoken tongue, for we can scarcely imagine that he was without some acquaintance with it when he first went to Rome, and he certainly afterwards became well read in the literature of Rome. In some cases he has followed Livy's narrative with a closeness which proves that he must have been acquainted with that author either in the original or in a translation, and the latter alternative is, of the two, the more improbable.

It seems to be now generally thought that his stay at Rome was a short one. Clough, in his excellent Preface, says on this subject, "The fault which runs through all the earlier biographies, from that of Rualdus downwards, is the assumption, wholly untenable, that Plutarch passed many years, as many perhaps as forty, at Rome. The entire character of his life is of course altered by such an impression." He then goes on to say that in consequence of this mistaken idea, it is not worth while for him to quote Dryden's 'Life of Plutarch,' which was originally prefixed to the translations re-edited by himself. Yet I trust I may be excused if I again quote North's 'Life of Plutarch,' as the following passage seems to set vividly before us the quiet literary occupation of his later days.

"For Plutarch, though he tarried a long while in Italy, and in Rome, yet that tooke not away the remembrance of the sweet aire of Greece, and of the little towne where he was borne; but being touched from time to time with a sentence of an ancient poet, who saith that,

"'In whatsoever countrey men are bred (I know not by what sweetnesse of it led), They nourish in their minds a glad desire, Unto their native homes for to retire,'

"he resolved to go back into Greece againe, there to end the rest of his daies in rest and honour among his citizens, of whom he was honourably welcomed home. Some judge that he left Rome after the death of Trajan, being then of great yeares, to leade a more quiet life. So being then at rest, he earnestly took in hand that which he had long thought of before, to wit, the Lives, and tooke great pains with it until he had brought his worke to perfection, as we have done at this present; although that some Lives, as those of Scipio African, of Metellus Numidicus, and some other are not to be found. Now himselfe confesseth in some place, that when he began this worke, at the first it was but to profit others; but that afterwards it was to profit himselfe, looking upon those histories, as if he had looked in a glasse, and seeking to reform his life in some sort, and to forme it in the mould of the vertues of these great men; taking this fashion of searching their manners, and writing the Lives of these noble men, to be a familiar haunting and frequenting of them. Also he thought, [said he himselfe] that he lodged these men one after another in his house, entering into consideration of their qualities, and that which was great in either of them, choosing and principally taking that which was to be noted, and most worthy to be knowne in their sayings and deeds."

Of Plutarch in his domestic relations we gather much information from his own writings. The name of his father has not been preserved, but it was probably Nikarchus, from the common habit of Greek families to repeat a name in alternate generations. His brothers Timon and Lamprias are frequently mentioned in his essays and dialogues, where Timon is spoken of in the most affectionate terms. Rualdus has ingeniously recovered the name of his wife, Timoxena, from internal evidence afforded by his writings. A touching letter is still extant, addressed by Plutarch to his wife, bidding her not give way to excessive grief at the death of their only daughter, who was named Timoxena after her mother. The number of his sons we cannot exactly state. Autobulus and Plutarch are especially spoken of as his sons, since the treatise on the Timaeus of Plato is dedicated to them, and the marriage of his son Autobulus is the occasion of one of the dinner-parties recorded in the 'Table Talk.' Another person, one Soklarus, is spoken of in terms which seem to imply that he was Plutarch's son, but this is nowhere definitely stated. His treatise also on Marriage Questions, addressed to Eurydike and Pollianus, seems to speak of her as having been recently an inmate of his house, but without enabling us to form an opinion whether she was his daughter or not. A modern writer well describes his maturer years by the words: "Plutarch was well born, well taught, well conditioned; a self-respecting amiable man, who knew how to better a good education by travels, by devotion to affairs private and public; a master of ancient culture, he read books with a just criticism: eminently social, he was a king in his own house, surrounded himself with select friends, and knew the high value of good conversation; and declares in a letter written to his wife that 'he finds scarcely an erasure, as in a book well written, in the happiness of his life.'"

He was an active member of the little community of Chaeronea, being archon of that town. Whether this dignity was annual or for life we do not know, but it was probably the former, and very likely he served it more than once. He speaks of his devotion to the duties of his office as causing him to incur the ridicule of some of his fellow-citizens, when they saw him engaged in the humblest duties. "But," he says, in Clough's version, "the story told about Antisthenes comes to my assistance. When some one expressed surprise at his carrying home some pickled fish from market in his own hands, It is, he answered, for myself. Conversely, when I am reproached with standing by and watching while tiles are measured out, and stone and mortar brought up, This service, I say, is not for myself, it is for my country."

Plutarch was for many years a priest of Apollo at Delphi. The scene of some of his 'Table Talk' is laid there, when he in his priestly capacity gives a dinner party in honour of the victor in the poetic contest at the Pythian games. Probably this office was a source of considerable income, and as the journey from Chaeronea to Delphi, across Mount Parnassus, is a very short one, it interfered but little with his literary and municipal business. In his essay on "Whether an old man should continue to take part in public life," he says, "You know, Euphanes, that I have for many Pythiads (that is, periods of four years elapsing between the Pythian festivals), exercised the office of Priest of Apollo: yet I think you would not say to me, 'Plutarch, you have sacrificed enough; you have led processions and dances enough; it is time, now that you are old, to lay aside the garland from your head, and to retire as superannuated from the oracle.'"

Thus respected and loved by all, Plutarch's old age passed peacefully away. "Notwithstanding," as North says, "that he was very old, yet he made an end of the Lives.... Furthermore, Plutarch, having lived alwaies honourably even to old age, he died quietly among his children and friends in the city of Chaeronea, leaving his writings, an immortal savour of his name, unto posterity. Besides the honour his citizens did him, there was a statue set up for him by ordinance of the people of Rome, in memory of his virtues. Now furthermore, though time hath devoured some part of the writings of this great man, and minished some other: neverthelesse those which remaine, being a great number, have excellent use to this day among us."

Life of Theseus.

I. As in books on geography, Sossius Senecio, the writers crowd the countries of which they know nothing into the furthest margins of their maps, and write upon them legends such as, "In this direction lie waterless deserts full of wild beasts;" or, "Unexplored morasses;" or, "Here it is as cold as Scythia;" or, "A frozen sea;" so I, in my writings on Parallel Lives, go through that period of time where history rests on the firm basis of facts, and may truly say, "All beyond this is portentous and fabulous, inhabited by poets and mythologers, and there is nothing true or certain."

When I had written the lives of Lykurgus the lawgiver and Numa the king, it appeared to me natural to go back to Romulus also, as I was engaged on the history of times so close to his. So when I was reflecting, in the words of Aeschylus,

"Against this chieftain, who can best contend? Whom shall I match in fight, what trusty friend?"

it occurred to me to compare the founder of the fair and famous city of Athens with him, and to contrast Theseus with the father of unconquered glorious Rome. Putting aside, then, the mythological element, let us examine his story, and wherever it obstinately defies probability, and cannot be explained by natural agency, let us beg the indulgence of our readers, who will kindly make allowance for tales of antiquity.

II. Theseus appears to have several points of resemblance to Romulus. Both were unacknowledged illegitimate children, and were reputed to descend from the Gods.

"Both warriors, well we all do know,"

and both were wise as well as powerful. The one founded Rome, while the other was the joint founder of Athens; and these are two of the most famous of cities. Both carried off women by violence, and neither of them escaped domestic misfortune and retribution, but towards the end of their lives both were at variance with their countrymen, if we may put any trust in the least extravagant writings upon the subject.

III. Theseus traced his descent on the father's side from Erechtheus and the original Autochthones, while on the mother's side he was descended from Pelops. For Pelops surpassed all the other princes of the Peloponnesus in the number of his children as well as in wealth; and of these he gave many of his daughters in marriage to the chief men of the country, and established many of his sons as rulers in various cities. One of these, Pittheus, the grandfather of Theseus, founded Troezen, which is indeed but a little state, though he had a greater reputation than any man of his time for eloquence and wisdom. The nature of this wisdom of his seems to have been much of the same kind as that which made the reputation of Hesiod, in the collection of maxims known as the 'Works and Days.' One of these maxims is indeed ascribed to Pittheus:

"Let promised pay be truly paid to friends."

At any rate, this is what Aristotle the philosopher has recorded; and also Euripides, when he speaks of Hippolytus as "child of holy Pittheus," shows the prevailing opinion about Pittheus. Now Aegeus desired to have children, and the Oracle at Delphi is said to have given him the well-known response, forbidding him to have intercourse with any woman before he reached Athens, but not appearing to explain this clearly. Consequently, on his way home, he went to Troezen, and asked the advice of Pittheus about the response of the God, which ran thus:

"Great chief, the wine-skin's foot must closed remain, Till thou to Athens art returned again."

Pittheus clearly perceived what the oracle must mean, and persuaded or cheated Aegeus into an intrigue with Aethra. Afterwards, when he discovered that he had conversed with the daughter of Pittheus, as he imagined that she might prove with child, he left behind him his sword and sandals hidden under a great stone, which had a hollow inside it exactly fitting them. This he told to Aethra alone, and charged her if a son of his should be born, and on growing to man's estate should be able to lift the stone and take from under it the deposit, that she should send him at once with these things to himself, in all secrecy, and as far as possible concealing his journey from observation. For he greatly feared the sons of Pallas, who plotted against him, and despised him on account of his childlessness, they themselves being fifty brothers, all the sons of Pallas.

IV. When Aethra's child was born, some writers say that he was at once named Theseus, from the tokens placed under the stone; others say that he was afterwards so named at Athens, when Aegeus acknowledged him as his son. He was brought up by his grandfather Pittheus, and had a master and tutor, Konnidas, to whom even to the present day, the Athenians sacrifice a ram on the day before the feast of Theseus, a mark of respect which is much more justly due to him, than those which they pay to Silanion and Parrhasius, who have only made pictures and statues of Theseus.

V. As it was at that period still the custom for those who were coming to man's estate to go to Delphi and offer to the god the first-fruits of their hair (which was then cut for the first time), Theseus went to Delphi, and they say

that a place there is even to this day named after him. But he only cut the front part of his hair, as Homer tells us the Abantes did, and this fashion of cutting the hair was called Theseus's fashion because of him. The Abantes first began to cut their hair in this manner, not having, as some say, been taught to do so by the Arabians, nor yet from any wish to imitate the Mysians, but because they were a warlike race, and met their foes in close combat, and studied above all to come to a hand-to-hand fight with their enemy, as Archilochus bears witness in his verses:
"They use no slings nor bows, Euboea's martial lords, But hand to hand they close And conquer with their swords."

So they cut their hair short in front, that their enemies might not grasp it. And they say that Alexander of Macedon for the same reason ordered his generals to have the beards of the Macedonians shaved, because they were a convenient handle for the enemy to grasp.

VI. Now while he was yet a child, Aethra concealed the real parentage of Theseus, and a story was circulated by Pittheus that his father was Poseidon. For the people of Troezen have an especial reverence for Poseidon; he is their tutelar deity; to him they offer first-fruits of their harvest, and they stamp their money with the trident as their badge. But when he was grown into a youth, and proved both strong in body and of good sound sense, then Aethra led him to the stone, told him the truth about his father, and bade him take the tokens from beneath it and sail to Athens with them. He easily lifted the stone, but determined not to go to Athens by sea, though the voyage was a safe and easy one, and though his mother and his grandfather implored him to go that way. By land it was a difficult matter to reach Athens, as the whole way was infested with robbers and bandits. That time, it seems, produced men of great and unwearied strength and swiftness, who made no good use of these powers, but treated all men with overbearing insolence, taking advantage of their strength to overpower and slay all who fell into their hands, and disregarding justice and right and kindly feeling, which they said were only approved of by those who dared not do injury to others, or feared to be injured themselves, while men who could get the upper hand by force might disregard them. Of these ruffians, Herakles in his wanderings cut off a good many, but others had escaped him by concealing themselves, or had been contemptuously spared by him on account of their insignificance. But Herakles had the misfortune to kill Iphitus, and thereupon sailed to Lydia and was for a long time a slave in that country under Omphale, which condition he had imposed upon himself as a penance for the murder of his friend. During this period the country of Lydia enjoyed peace and repose; but in

Greece the old plague of brigandage broke out afresh, as there was now no one to put it down. So that the journey overland to Athens from Peloponnesus was full of peril; and Pittheus, by relating to Theseus who each of these evildoers was, and how they treated strangers, tried to prevail upon him to go by sea. But it appears that Theseus had for a long time in his heart been excited by the renown of Herakles for courage: he thought more of him than of any one else, and loved above all to listen to those who talked of him, especially if they had seen and spoken to him. Now he could no longer conceal that he was in the same condition as Themistokles in later times, when he said that the trophy of Miltiades would not let him sleep. Just so did the admiration which Theseus conceived for Herakles make him dream by night of his great exploits, and by day determine to equal them by similar achievements of his own.

VII. As it happened, they were connected, being second cousins; for Aethra was the daughter of Pittheus, and Alkmena the daughter of Lysidike, and Lysidike and Pittheus were brother and sister, being the children of Pelops and Hippodameia. So Theseus thought that it would be a great and unbearable disgrace to him that his cousin should go everywhere and clear the sea and land of the brigands who infested them, and he should refuse to undertake the adventures that came in his way; throwing discredit upon his reputed father by a pusillanimous flight by sea, and upon his real father by bringing him only the sandals and an unfleshed sword, and not proving his noble birth by the evidence of some brave deed accomplished by him. In this spirit he set out on his journey, with the intention of doing wrong to no one, but of avenging himself on any one who offered wrong to him.

VIII. And first in Epidaurus he slew Periphetes, who used a club as his weapon, and on this account was called the club-bearer, because he laid hands upon him and forbade him to proceed farther on his way. The club took his fancy, and he adopted it as a weapon, and always used it, just as Herakles used his lion's skin; for the skin was a proof of how huge a beast the wearer had overcome, while the club, invincible in the hands of Theseus, had yet been worsted when used against him. At the Isthmus he destroyed Sinis the Pine-bender by the very device by which he had slain so many people, and that too without having ever practised the art, proving that true valour is better than practice and training. Sinis had a daughter, a tall and beautiful girl, named Perigoune. When her father fell she ran and hid herself. Theseus sought her everywhere, but she fled into a place where wild asparagus grew thick, and with a simple child-like faith besought the plants to conceal her, as if they could understand her words, promising that if they did so she never would destroy or burn them. However, when Theseus called to her, pledging himself to take care of her and do her no hurt, she came out, and afterwards bore Theseus a son, named Melanippus. She afterwards was given by Theseus in marriage to Deïoneus, the son of Eurytus of Oechalia. Ioxus, a son of Melanippus, and Theseus's grandchild, took part in Ornytus's settlement in Caria; and for this reason the descendants of Ioxus have a family custom not to burn the asparagus plant, but to reverence and worship it.

IX. Now the wild sow of Krommyon, whom they called Phaia, was no ordinary beast, but a fierce creature and hard to conquer. This animal he turned out of his way to destroy, that it might not be thought that he performed his exploits of necessity. Besides, he said, a brave man need only punish wicked men when they came in his way, but that in the case of wild beasts he must himself seek them out and attack them. Some say that Phaia was a murderous and licentious woman who carried on brigandage at Krommyon, and was called a sow from her life and habits, and that Theseus put her to death.

X. Before coming to Megara he slew Skeiron by flinging him down a precipice into the sea, so the story runs, because he was a robber, but some say that from arrogance he used to hold out his feet to strangers and bid them wash them, and that then he kicked the washers into the sea. But Megarian writers, in opposition to common tradition, and, as Simonides says, "warring with all antiquity," say that Skeiron was not an arrogant brigand, but repressed brigandage, loved those who were good and just, and was related to them. For, they point out, Aeakus is thought to have been the most righteous of all the Greeks, and Kychreus of Salamis was worshipped as a god, and the virtue of Peleus and Telamon is known to all. Yet Skeiron was the son-in-law of Kychreus, and father-in-law of Aeakus, and grandfather of Peleus and Telamon, who were both of them sons of Endeis, the daughter of Skeiron and his wife Chariklo. It is not then reasonable to suppose that these, the noblest men of their time, would make alliances with a malefactor, and give and receive from him what they prized most dearly. But they say that Theseus slew Skeiron, not when he first went to Athens, but that afterwards he took the town of Eleusis which belonged to the Megarians, by dealing treacherously with Diokles, who was the chief magistrate there, and that on that occasion he killed Skeiron. This is what tradition says on both sides.

XI. At Eleusis Theseus overcame Kerkyon of Arcadia in wrestling and killed him, and after journeying a little farther he killed Damastes, who was surnamed Prokroustes, by compelling him to fit his own body to his bed, just as he used to fit the bodies of strangers to it. This he did in imitation of

Herakles; for he used to retort upon his aggressors the same treatment which they intended for him. Thus Herakles offered up Busiris as a sacrifice, and overcame Antaeus in wrestling, and Kyknus in single combat, and killed Termerus by breaking his skull. This is, they say, the origin of the proverb, "A Termerian mischief," for Termerus, it seems, struck passers-by with his head, and so killed them. So also did Theseus sally forth and chastise evildoers, making them undergo the same cruelties which they practised on others, thus justly punishing them for their crimes in their own wicked fashion.

XII. As he proceeded on his way, and reached the river Kephisus, men of the Phytalid race were the first to meet and greet him. He demanded to be purified from the guilt of bloodshed, and they purified him, made propitiatory offerings, and also entertained him in their houses, being the first persons from whom he had received any kindness on his journey. It is said to have been on the eighth day of the month Kronion, which is now called Hekatombeion, that he came to his own city. On entering it he found public affairs disturbed by factions, and the house of Aegeus in great disorder; for Medea, who had been banished from Corinth, was living with Aegeus, and had engaged by her drugs to enable Aegeus to have children. She was the first to discover who Theseus was, while Aegeus, who was an old man, and feared every one because of the disturbed state of society, did not recognise him. Consequently she advised Aegeus to invite him to a feast, that she might poison him. Theseus accordingly came to Aegeus's table. He did not wish to be the first to tell his name, but, to give his father an opportunity of recognising him, he drew his sword, as if he meant to cut some of the meat with it, and showed it to Aegeus. Aegeus at once recognised it, overset the cup of poison, looked closely at his son and embraced him. He then called a public meeting and made Theseus known as his son to the citizens, with whom he was already very popular because of his bravery. It is said that when the cup was overset the poison was spilt in the place where now there is the enclosure in the Delphinium, for there Aegeus dwelt; and the Hermes to the east of the temple there they call the one who is "at the door of Aegeus."

XIII. But the sons of Pallas, who had previously to this expected that they would inherit the kingdom on the death of Aegeus without issue, now that Theseus was declared the heir, were much enraged, first that Aegeus should be king, a man who was merely an adopted child of Pandion, and had no blood relationship to Erechtheus, and next that Theseus, a stranger and a foreigner, should inherit the kingdom. They consequently declared war. Dividing themselves into two bodies, the one proceeded to march openly upon the city from Sphettus, under the command of Pallas their father, while the other lay in ambush at Gargettus, in order that they might fall upon their opponents on two sides at once. But there was a herald among them named Leos, of the township of Agnus, who betrayed the plans of the sons of Pallas to Theseus. He suddenly attacked those who were in ambush, and killed them all, hearing which the other body under Pallas dispersed. From this time forth they say that the township of Pallene has never intermarried with that of Agnus, and that it is not customary amongst them for heralds to begin a proclamation with the words "Acouete Leo," (Oyez) for they hate the name of Leo because of the treachery of that man.

XIV. Now Theseus, who wished for employment and also to make himself popular with the people, went to attack the bull of Marathon, who had caused no little trouble to the inhabitants of Tetrapolis. He overcame the beast, and drove it alive through the city for all men to see, and then sacrificed it to Apollo of Delphi. Hekale, too, and the legend of her having entertained Theseus, does not seem altogether without foundation in fact; for the people of the neighbouring townships used to assemble and perform what was called the Hekalesian sacrifice to Zeus Hekalus, and they also used to honour Hekale, calling her by the affectionate diminutive Hekaline, because she also, when feasting Theseus, who was very young, embraced him in a motherly way, and used such like endearing diminutives. She also made a vow on Theseus's behalf, when he was going forth to battle, that if he returned safe she would sacrifice to Zeus; but as she died before he returned, she had the above-mentioned honours instituted by command of Theseus, as a grateful return for her hospitality. This is the legend as told by Philochorus.

XV. Shortly after this the ship from Crete arrived for the third time to collect the customary tribute. Most writers agree that the origin of this was, that on the death of Androgeus, in Attica, which was ascribed to treachery, his father Minos went to war, and wrought much evil to the country, which at the same time was afflicted by scourges from Heaven (for the land did not bear fruit, and there was a great pestilence and the rivers sank into the earth). So that as the oracle told the Athenians that, if they propitiated Minos and came to terms with him, the anger of Heaven would cease and they should have a respite from their sufferings, they sent an embassy to Minos and prevailed on him to make peace, on the condition that every nine years they should send him a tribute of seven youths and seven maidens. The most tragic of the legends states these poor children when they reached Crete were thrown into the Labyrinth, and there either were devoured by the Minotaur or else perished with hunger, being unable to find the way out. The Minotaur, as Euripides tells us, was

"A form commingled, and a monstrous birth, Half man, half bull, in twofold shape combined."

XVI. Philochorus says that the Cretans do not recognise this story, but say that the Labyrinth was merely a prison, like any other, from which escape was impossible, and that Minos instituted gymnastic games in honour of Androgeus, in which the prizes for the victors were these children, who till then were kept in the Labyrinth. Also they say that the victor in the first contest was a man of great power in the state, a general of the name of Taurus, who was of harsh and savage temper, and ill-treated the Athenian children. And Aristotle himself, in his treatise on the constitution of the Bottiaeans, evidently does not believe that the children were put to death by Minos, but that they lived in Crete as slaves, until extreme old age; and that one day the Cretans, in performance of an ancient vow, sent first-fruits of their population to Delphi. Among those who were thus sent were the descendants of the Athenians, and, as they could not maintain themselves there, they first passed over to Italy, and there settled near Iapygium, and from thence again removed to Thrace, and took the name of Bottiaeans. For this reason, the Bottiaean maidens when performing a certain sacrifice sing "Let us go to Athens." Thus it seems to be a terrible thing to incur the hatred of a city powerful in speech and song; for on the Attic stage Minos is always vilified and traduced, and though he was called "Most Kingly" by Hesiod, and "Friend of Zeus" by Homer, it gained him no credit, but the playwrights overwhelmed him with abuse, styling him cruel and violent. And yet Minos is said to have been a king and a lawgiver, and Rhadamanthus to have been a judge under him, carrying out his decrees.

XVII. So when the time of the third payment of the tribute arrived, and those fathers who had sons not yet grown up had to submit to draw lots, the unhappy people began to revile Aegeus, complaining that he, although the author of this calamity, yet took no share in their affliction, but endured to see them left childless, robbed of their own legitimate offspring, while he made a foreigner and a bastard the heir to his kingdom. This vexed Theseus, and determining not to hold aloof, but to share the fortunes of the people, he came forward and offered himself without being drawn by lot. The people all admired his courage and patriotism, and Aegeus finding that his prayers and entreaties had no effect on his unalterable resolution, proceeded to choose the rest by lot. Hellanikus says that the city did not select the youths and maidens by lot, but that Minos himself came thither and chose them, and that he picked out Theseus first of all, upon the usual conditions, which were that the Athenians should furnish a ship, and that the youths should embark in it and sail with him, not carrying with them any weapon of war; and that when the Minotaur was slain, the tribute should cease. Formerly, no one had any hope of safety; so they used to send out the ship with a black sail, as if it were going to a certain doom; but now Theseus so encouraged his father, and boasted that he would overcome the Minotaur, that he gave a second sail, a white one, to the steersman, and charged him on his return, if Theseus were safe, to hoist the white one, if not, the black one as a sign of mourning. But Simonides says that it was not a white sail which was given by Aegeus, but "a scarlet sail embrued in holm oak's juice," and that this was agreed on by him as the signal of safety. The ship was steered by Phereklus the son of Amarsyas, according to Simonides.

But Philochorus says that Theseus had one Nausithous sent him from Skirus of Salamis, to steer the ship, and Phaeax to act as look-out, as the Athenians had not yet turned their attention to the sea.

One of the youths chosen by lot was Menestheos the son of Skirus's daughter. The truth of this account is attested by the shrines of Nausithous and Phaeax, which Theseus built at Phalerum, and by the feast called the Kybernesia or pilot's festival, which is held in their honour.

XVIII. When the lots were drawn Theseus brought the chosen youths from the Prytaneum, and proceeding to the temple of the Delphian Apollo, offered the suppliants' bough to Apollo on their behalf. This was a bough of the sacred olive-tree bound with fillets of white wool. And after praying he went to sea on the sixth day of the month Munychion, on which day even now they send maidens as suppliants to the temple of the Delphian Apollo. And there is a legend that the Delphian oracle told him that Aphrodite would be his guide and fellow-traveller, and that when he was sacrificing a she-goat to her by the seaside, it became a he-goat; wherefore the goddess is called Epitragia.

XIX. When they reached Crete, according to most historians and poets, Ariadne fell in love with him, and from her he received the clue of string, and was taught how to thread the mazes of the Labyrinth. He slew the Minotaur, and, taking with him Ariadne and the youths, sailed away. Pherekydes also says that Theseus also knocked out the bottoms of the Cretan ships, to prevent pursuit. But Demon says that Taurus, Minos's general, was slain in a sea-fight in the harbour, when Theseus sailed away. But according to Philochorus, when Minos instituted his games, Taurus was expected to win every prize, and was grudged this honour; for his great influence and his unpopular manners made him disliked, and scandal said, that he was too intimate with Pasiphae. On this account, when Theseus offered to contend with him, Minos agreed. And, as it was the custom in Crete for women as well

as men to be spectators of the games, Ariadne was present, and was struck
with the appearance of Theseus, and his strength, as he conquered all
competitors. Minos was especially pleased, in the wrestling match, at Taurus's
defeat and shame, and, restoring the children to Theseus, remitted the tribute
for the future. Kleidemus tells the story in his own fashion and at unnecessary
length, beginning much farther back. There was, he says, a decree passed by
all the Greeks, that no ship should sail from any post with more than five
hands on board, but Jason alone, the master of the great ship Argo, should
cruise about, and keep the sea free of pirates. Now when Daedalus fled to
Athens, Minos, contrary to the decree, pursued him in long war galleys, and
being driven to Sicily by a storm, died there. When his son Deukalion sent a
warlike message to the Athenians, bidding them give up Daedalus to him, or
else threatening that he would put to death the children whom Minos had
taken as hostages, Theseus returned him a gentle answer, begging for the life
of Daedalus, who was his own cousin and blood relation, being the son of
Merope, the daughter of Erechtheus. But he busied himself with building a
fleet, some of it in Attica, in the country of the Thymaitadae, far from any
place of resort of strangers, and some in Troezen, under the management of
Pittheus, as he did not wish his preparations to be known. But when the ships
were ready to set sail, having with him as pilots, Daedalus himself and some
Cretan exiles, as no one knew that he was coming, and the Cretans thought
that it was a friendly fleet that was advancing, he seized the harbour, and
marched at once to Knossus before his arrival was known. Then he fought a
battle at the gates of the Labyrinth, and slew Deukalion and his body-guard.
As Ariadne now succeeded to the throne, he made peace with her, took back
the youths, and formed an alliance between the Cretans and the Athenians,
in which each nation swore that it would not begin a war against the other.

XX. There are many more stories about these events, and about Ariadne,
none of which agree in any particulars. Some say that she hanged herself
when deserted by Theseus, and some, that she was taken to Naxos by his
sailors, and there dwelt with Oenarus, the priest of Dionysus, having been
deserted by Theseus, who was in love with another.

"For Aegle's love disturbed his breast."

This line, we are told by Hereas of Megara, was struck out of Hesiod's
poems by Peisistratus; and again he says that he inserted into Homer's
description of the Shades,

"Peirithous and Theseus, born of gods,"

to please the Athenians. Some writers say that Theseus had by Ariadne two sons, Staphylus and Oenopion, whom Ion of Chios follows when he speaks of his own native city as that

"Which erst Oenopion stablished, Theseus' son."

The pleasantest of these legends are in nearly every one's mouth. But Paeon of Amathus gives an account peculiar to himself, that Theseus was driven by a storm to Cyprus, and that Ariadne, who was pregnant, suffered much from the motion of the ship, and became so ill, that she was set on shore, but Theseus had to return to take charge of the ship, and was blown off to sea. The women of the country took care of Ariadne, and comforted her in her bereavement, even bringing forged letters to her as if from Theseus, and rendering her assistance during her confinement; and when she died in childbirth, they buried her. Theseus, on his return, grieved much, and left money to the people of the country, bidding them sacrifice to Ariadne; he also set up two little statues, one of silver, and the other of brass. And at this sacrifice, which takes place on the second day of the month Gorpiaeus, one of the young men lies down on the ground, and imitates the cries of a woman in travail; and the people of Amathus call that the grove of Ariadne Aphrodite, in which they show her tomb.

But some writers of Naxos tell a different story, peculiar to themselves, that there were two Minoses and two Ariadnes, of whom one, they say, was married to Dionysus in Naxos, and was the mother of Staphylus and his brother, while the younger was carried off by Theseus, and came to Naxos after he deserted her; and a nurse called Korkyne came with her, whose tomb they point out. Then Naxians also says that this Ariadne died there, and is honoured, but not so much as the elder; for at the feast in honour of the elder, there are merriment and revelry, but at that of the younger gloomy rites are mingled with mirth.

XXI. Theseus, when he sailed away from Crete, touched at Delos; here he sacrificed to the god and offered up the statue of Aphrodite, which Ariadne had given him; and besides this, he and the youths with him danced a measure which they say is still practised by the people of Delos to this day, being an imitation of the turnings and windings of the Labyrinth expressed by complicated evolutions performed in regular order. This kind of dance is called by the Delians "the crane dance," according to Dikaearchus. It was danced round the altar of the Horns, which is all formed of horns from the left side. They also say that he instituted games at Delos, and that then for the first time a palm was given by him to the victor.

XXII. As he approached Attica, both he and his steersman in their delight forgot to hoist the sail which was to be a signal of their safety to Aegeus; and he in his despair flung himself down the cliffs and perished. Theseus, as soon as he reached the harbour, performed at Phalerum the sacrifices which he had vowed to the gods if he returned safe, and sent off a herald to the city with the news of his safe return. This man met with many who were lamenting the death of the king, and, as was natural, with others who were delighted at the news of their safety, and who congratulated him and wished to crown him with garlands. These he received, but placed them on his herald's staff, and when he came back to the seashore, finding that Theseus had not completed his libation, he waited outside the temple, not wishing to disturb the sacrifice. When the libation was finished he announced the death of Aegeus, and then they all hurried up to the city with loud lamentations: wherefore to this day, at the Oschophoria, they say that it is not the herald that is crowned, but his staff, and that at the libations the bystanders cry out, "Eleleu, Iou, Iou;" of which cries the first is used by men in haste, or raising the paean for battle, while the second is used by persons in surprise and trouble.

Theseus, after burying his father, paid his vow to Apollo, on the seventh day of the month Pyanepsion; for on this day it was that the rescued youths went up into the city. The boiling of pulse, which is customary on this anniversary, is said to be done because the rescued youths put what remained of their pulse together into one pot, boiled it all, and merrily feasted on it together. And on this day also, the Athenians carry about the Eiresione, a bough of the olive tree garlanded with wool, just as Theseus had before carried the suppliants' bough, and covered with first-fruits of all sorts of produce, because the barrenness of the land ceased on that day; and they sing, "Eiresione, bring us figs And wheaten loaves, and oil, And wine to quaff, that we may all Host merrily from toil."

However, some say that these ceremonies are performed in memory of the Herakleidae, who were thus entertained by the Athenians; but most writers tell the tale as I have told it.

XXIII. Now the thirty-oared ship, in which Theseus sailed with the youths, and came back safe, was kept by the Athenians up to the time of Demetrius Phalereus. They constantly removed the decayed part of her timbers, and renewed them with sound wood, so that the ship became an illustration to philosophers of the doctrine of growth and change, as some argued that it remained the same, and others, that it did not remain the same. The feast of the Oschophoria, or of carrying boughs, which to this day the Athenians celebrate, was instituted by Theseus. For he did not take with him all the maidens who were drawn by lot, but he chose two youths, his intimate friends, who were feminine and fair to look upon, but of manly spirit; these by warm baths and avoiding the heat of the sun and careful tending of their hair and skin he completely metamorphosed, teaching them to imitate the voice and carriage and walk of maidens. These two were then substituted in the place of two of the girls, and deceived every one; and when they returned, he and these two youths walked in procession, dressed as now those who carry boughs at the Oschophoria are dressed. They carry them in honour of Dionysus and Ariadne, because of the legend, or rather because they returned home when the harvest was being gathered in. And the women called supper-carriers join in carrying them and partake of the sacrifice, in imitation of the mothers of those who were drawn by lot; for they used continually to bring their children food. Also, old tales are told, because these women used to tell their children such ones, to encourage and amuse them.

These things are related by the historian Demus. Moreover, a sacred enclosure was dedicated to Theseus, and those families out of whom the tribute of the children had been gathered were bidden to contribute to sacrifices to him. These sacrifices were presided over by the Phytalidae, which post Theseus bestowed upon them as a recompense for their hospitality towards him.

XXIV. After the death of Aegeus, Theseus conceived a great and important design. He gathered together all the inhabitants of Attica and made them citizens of one city, whereas before they had lived dispersed, so as to be hard to assemble together for the common weal, and at times even fighting with one another.

He visited all the villages and tribes, and won their consent; the poor and lower classes gladly accepting his proposals, while he gained over the more powerful by promising that the new constitution should not include a king, but that it should be a pure commonwealth, with himself merely acting as general of its army and guardian of its laws, while in other respects it would allow perfect freedom and equality to every one. By these arguments he convinced some of them, and the rest knowing his power and courage chose rather to be persuaded than forced into compliance. He therefore destroyed the prytaneia, the senate house, and the magistracy of each individual township, built one common prytaneum and senate house for them all on the site of the present acropolis, called the city Athens, and instituted the Panathenaic festival common to all of them. He also instituted a festival for the resident aliens, on the sixteenth of the month, Hekatombeion, which is still kept up. And having, according to his promise, laid down his sovereign power, he arranged the new constitution under the auspices of the gods; for he made inquiry at Delphi as to how he should deal with the city, and received the following answer:

"Thou son of Aegeus and of Pittheus' maid, My father hath within thy city laid The bounds of many cities; weigh not down Thy soul with thought; the bladder cannot drown."

The same thing they say was afterwards prophesied by the Sibyl concerning the city, in these words:

"The bladder may be dipped, but cannot drown."

XXV. Wishing still further to increase the number of his citizens, he invited all strangers to come and share equal privileges, and they say that the words now used, "Come hither all ye peoples," was the proclamation then used by Theseus, establishing as it were a commonwealth of all nations. But he did not permit his state to fall into the disorder which this influx of all kinds of people would probably have produced, but divided the people into three classes, of Eupatridae or nobles, Geomori or farmers, Demiurgi or artisans. To the Eupatridae he assigned the care of religious rites, the supply of magistrates for the city, and the interpretation of the laws and customs sacred or profane, yet he placed them on an equality with the other citizens, thinking that the nobles would always excel in dignity, the farmers in usefulness, and the artisans in numbers. Aristotle tells us that he was the first who inclined to democracy, and gave up the title of king; and Homer seems to confirm this view by speaking of the people of the Athenians alone of all the states mentioned in his catalogue of ships. Theseus also struck money with the figure of a bull, either alluding to the bull of Marathon, or Taurus, Minos' general, or else to encourage farming among the citizens. Hence they say came the words, "worth ten," or "worth a hundred oxen." He permanently annexed Megara to Attica, and set up the famous pillar on the Isthmus, on which he wrote the distinction between the countries in two trimeter lines, of which the one looking east says,

"This is not Peloponnesus, but Ionia,"

and the one looking west says,

"This is Peloponnesus, not Ionia."

And also he instituted games there, in emulation of Herakles; that, just as Herakles had ordained that the Greeks should celebrate the Olympic games in honour of Zeus, so by Theseus's appointment they should celebrate the Isthmian games in honour of Poseidon.

The festival which was previously established there in honour of Melikerta used to be celebrated by night, and to be more like a religious mystery than a great spectacle and gathering. Some writers assert that the Isthmian games were established in honour of Skeiron, and that Theseus wished to make them an atonement for the murder of his kinsman; for Skeiron was the son of Kanethus and of Henioche the daughter of Pittheus. Others say that this festival was established in honour of Sinis, not of Skeiron. Be this as it may, Theseus established it, and stipulated with the Corinthians that visitors from Athens who came to the games should have a seat of honour in as large a space as could be covered by a sail of the public ship which carried them, when stretched out on the ground. This we are told by Hellanikus and Andron of Halikarnassus.

XXVI. Besides this, according to Philochorus and other writers, he sailed with Herakles to the Euxine, took part in the campaign against the Amazons, and received Antiope as the reward for his valour; but most historians, among whom are Pherekydes, Hellanikus, and Herodorus, say that Theseus made an expedition of his own later than that of Herakles, and that he took the Amazon captive, which is a more reasonable story. For no one of his companions is said to have captured an Amazon; while Bion relates that he caught this one by treachery and carried her off; for the Amazons, he says, were not averse to men, and did not avoid Theseus when he touched at their coast, but even offered him presents. He invited the bearer of these on board his ship; and when she had embarked he set sail. But one, Menekrates, who has written a history of the town of Nikaea in Bithynia, states that Theseus spent a long time in that country with Antiope, and that there were three young Athenians, brothers, who were his companions in arms, by name Euneon, Thoas, and Soloeis. Soloeis fell in love with Antiope, and, without telling his brothers, confided his passion to one of his comrades. This man laid the matter before Antiope, who firmly rejected his pretensions, but treated him quietly and discreetly, telling Theseus nothing about it. Soloeis, in despair at his rejection, leaped into a river and perished; and Theseus then at length learned the cause of the young man's death. In his sorrow he remembered and applied to himself an oracle he had received from Delphi. It had been enjoined upon him by the Pythia that whenever he should be struck down with special sorrow in a foreign land, he should found a city in that place and leave some of his companions there as its chiefs. In consequence of this the city which he founded was called Pythopolis, in honour of the Pythian Apollo, and the neighbouring river was called Soloeis, after the youth who died in it. He left there the brothers of Soloeis as the chiefs and lawgivers of the new city, and together, with them one Hermus, an Athenian Eupatrid. In consequence of this, the people of Pythopolis call a certain place in their city the house of Hermes, by a mistaken accentuation transferring the honour due to their founder, to their god Hermes.

XXVII. This was the origin of the war with the Amazons; and it seems to have been carried on in no feeble or womanish spirit, for they never could have encamped in the city nor have fought a battle close to the Pnyx and the Museum unless they had conquered the rest of the country, so as to be able to approach the city safely. It is hard to believe, as Hellanikus relates, that they crossed the Cimmerian Bosphorus on the ice; but that they encamped almost in the city is borne witness to by the local names, and by the tombs of the fallen. For a long time both parties held aloof, unwilling to engage; but at last Theseus, after sacrificing to Phobos (Fear), attacked them. The battle took place in the month Boedromion, on the day on which the Athenians celebrate the feast Boedromia. Kleidemus gives us accurate details, stating that the left wing of the Amazons stood at the place now called the Amazoneum, while the right reached up to the Pnyx, at the place where the gilded figure of Victory now stands. The Athenians attacked them on this side, issuing from the Museum, and the tombs of the fallen are to be seen along the street which leads to the gate near the shrine of the hero Chalkodus, which is called the Peiraeic gate. On this side the women forced them back as far as the temple of the Eumenides, but on the other side those who assailed them from the temple of Pallas, Ardettus, and the Lyceum, drove their right wing in confusion back to their camp with great slaughter. In the fourth month of the war a peace was brought about by Hippolyte; for this writer names the wife of Theseus Hippolyte, not Antiope. Some relate that she was slain fighting by the side of Theseus by a javelin hurled by one Molpadia, and that the column which stands beside the temple of Olympian Earth is sacred to her memory. It is not to be wondered at that history should be at fault when dealing with such ancient events as these, for there is another story at variance with this, to the effect that Antiope caused the wounded Amazons to be secretly transported to Chalkis, where they were taken care of, and some of them were buried there, at what is now called the Amazoneum. However, it is a proof of the war having ended in a treaty of peace, that the place near the temple of Theseus where they swore to observe it, is still called Horeomosium, and that the sacrifice to the Amazons always has taken place before the festival of Theseus. The people of Megara also show a burying-place of the Amazons, as one goes from the market-place to what they call Rhus, where the lozenge-shaped building stands. It is said that some others died at Chaeronea, and were buried by the little stream which it seems was anciently called Thermodon, but now is called Haemon, about which we have treated in the life of Demosthenes. It would appear that the Amazons did not even get across Thessaly without trouble, for graves of them are shown to this day at Skotussa and Kynoskephalae.

XXVIII. The above is all that is worthy of mention about the Amazons; for, as to the story which the author of the 'Theseid' relates about this attack of the Amazons being brought about by Antiope to revenge herself upon Theseus for his marriage with Phaedra, and how she and her Amazons fought, and how Herakles slew them, all this is clearly fabulous. After the death of Antiope, Theseus married Phaedra, having a son by Antiope named Hippolytus, or Demophoon, according to Pindar. As for his misfortunes with this wife and son, as the account given by historians does not differ from that which appears in the plays of the tragic poets, we must believe them to have happened as all these writers say.

XXIX. However, there are certain other legends about Theseus' marriage which have never appeared on the stage, which have neither a creditable beginning nor a prosperous termination: for it is said that he carried off one Anaxo, a Troezenian girl, and after slaying Sinis and Kerkyon he forced their daughters, and that he married Periboea the mother of Ajax and also Phereboea and Iope the daughter of Iphikles: and, as has been told already, it was on account of his love for Aegle the daughter of Panopeus that he deserted Ariadne, which was a shameful and discreditable action. And in addition to all this he is charged with carrying off Helen, which brought war upon Attica, and exile and destruction on himself; about which we shall speak presently. But, though many adventures were undertaken by the heroes of those times, Herodorus is of opinion that Theseus took no part in any of them, except with the Lapithae in their fight with the Centaurs; though other writers say that he went to Kolchis with Jason and took part with Meleager in the hunt of the Kalydonian boar.

From these legends arises the proverb, "Not without Theseus;" also he by himself without any comrades performed many glorious deeds, from which the saying came into vogue, "This is another Herakles."

Theseus, together with Adrastus, effected the recovery of the bodies of those who fell under the walls of the Cadmea at Thebes, not after conquering the Thebans, as Euripides puts it in his play, but by a truce and convention, according to most writers. Philochorus even states that this was the first occasion on which a truce was made for the recovery of those slain in battle. But we have shown in our 'Life of Herakles' that he was the first to restore the corpses of the slain to the enemy. The tombs of the rank and file are to be seen at Eleutherae, but those of the chiefs at Eleusis, by favour of Theseus to

Adrastus. Euripides's play of the 'Suppliants' is contradicted by that of Aeschylus, the 'Eleusinians,' in which Theseus is introduced giving orders for this to be done.

XXX. His friendship for Peirithous is said to have arisen in the following manner: He had a great reputation for strength and courage; Peirithous, wishing to make trial of these, drove his cattle away from the plain of Marathon, and when he learned that Theseus was pursuing them, armed, he did not retire, but turned and faced him. Each man then admiring the beauty and courage of his opponent, refrained from battle, and first Peirithous holding out his hand bade Theseus himself assess the damages of his raid upon the cattle, saying that he himself would willingly submit to whatever penalty the other might inflict. Theseus thought no more of their quarrel, and invited him to become his friend and comrade; and they ratified their compact of friendship by an oath. Hereupon, Peirithous, who was about to marry Deidameia, begged Theseus to come and visit his country and meet the Lapithae. He also had invited the Centaurs to the banquet; and as they in their drunken insolence laid hands upon the women, the Lapithae attacked them. Some of them they slew, and the rest they overcame, and afterwards, with the assistance of Theseus, banished from their country. Herodorus, however, says that this is not how these events took place, but that the war was going on, and that Theseus went to help the Lapithae and while on his way thither first beheld Herakles, whom he made a point of visiting at Trachis, where he was resting after his labours and wanderings; and that they met with many compliments and much good feeling on both sides. But one would more incline to those writers who tell us that they often met, and that Herakles was initiated by Theseus's desire, and was also purified before initiation at his instance, which ceremony was necessary because of some reckless action.

XXXI. Theseus was fifty years old, according to Hellanikus, when he carried off Helen, who was a mere child. For this reason some who wish to clear him of this, the heaviest of all the charges against him, say that it was not he who carried off Helen, but that Idas and Lynkeus carried her off and deposited her in his keeping. Afterwards the Twin Brethren came and demanded her back, but he would not give her up; or even it is said that Tyndareus himself handed her over to him, because he feared that Enarsphorus the son of Hippocoon would take her by force, she being only a child at the time. But the most probable story and that which most writers agree in is the following: The two friends, Theseus and Peirithous, came to Sparta, seized the maiden, who was dancing in the temple of Artemis Orthia, and carried her off. As the pursuers followed no farther than Tegea, they felt no alarm, but leisurely travelled through Peloponnesus, and made a compact that whichever of them should win Helen by lot was to have her to wife, but must help the other to a marriage. They cast lots on this understanding, and Theseus won. As the maiden was not yet ripe for marriage he took her with him to Aphidnae, and there placing his mother with her gave her into the charge of his friend Aphidnus, bidding him watch over her and keep her presence secret. He himself in order to repay his obligation to Peirithous went on a journey with him to Epirus to obtain the daughter of Aidoneus the king of the Molossians, who called his wife Persephone, his daughter Kore, and his dog Cerberus. All the suitors of his daughter were bidden by him to fight this dog, and the victor was to receive her hand. However, as he learned that Peirithous and his friend were come, not as wooers, but as ravishers, he cast them into prison. He put an end to Peirithous at once, by means of his dog, but only guarded Theseus strictly.

XXXII. Now at this period Mnestheus, the son of Peteus, who was the son of Orneus, who was the son of Erechtheus, first of all mankind they say took to the arts of a demagogue, and to currying favour with the people. This man formed a league of the nobles, who had long borne Theseus a grudge for having destroyed the local jurisdiction and privileges of each of the Eupatrids by collecting them all together into the capital, where they were no more than his subjects and slaves; and he also excited the common people by telling them that although they were enjoying a fancied freedom they really had been deprived of their ancestral privileges and sacred rites, and made to endure the rule of one foreign despot, instead of that of many good kings of their own blood.

While he was thus busily employed, the invasion of Attica by the sons of Tyndareus greatly assisted his revolutionary scheme; so that some say that it was he who invited them to come. At first they abstained from violence, and confined themselves to asking that their sister Helen should be given up to them; but when they were told by the citizens that she was not in their hands, and that they knew not where she was, they proceeded to warlike measures. Akademus, who had by some means discovered that she was concealed at Aphidnae, now told them where she was; for which cause he was honoured by the sons of Tyndareus during his life, and also the Lacedaemonians, though they often invaded the country and ravaged it unsparingly, yet never touched the place called the Akademeia, for Akademus's sake. Dikaearchus says that Echemus and Marathus, two Arcadians, took part in that war with the sons of Tyndareus; and that from the first the place now called

Akademeia was then named Echedemia, and that from the second the township of Marathon takes its names, because he in accordance with some oracle voluntarily offered himself as a sacrifice there in the sight of the whole army.

However, the sons of Tyndareus came to Aphidnae, and took the place after a battle, in which it is said that Alykus fell, the son of Skeiron, who then was fighting on the side of the Dioskuri. In memory of this man it is said that the place in the territory of Megara where his remains lie is called Alykus. But Hereas writes that Alykus was slain by Theseus at Aphidnae, and as evidence he quotes this verse about Alykus,
"Him whom Theseus slew in the spacious streets of Aphidnae, Fighting for fair-haired Helen."

But it is not likely that if Theseus had been there, his mother and the town of Aphidnae would have been taken.

XXXIII. After the fall of Aphidnae, the people of Athens became terrified, and were persuaded by Mnestheus to admit the sons of Tyndareus to the city, and to treat them as friends, because, he said, they were only at war with Theseus, who had been the first to use violence, and were the saviours and benefactors of the rest of mankind. These words of his were confirmed by their behaviour, for, victorious as they were, they yet demanded nothing except initiation into the mysteries, as they were, no less than Herakles, connected with the city. This was permitted them, and they were adopted by Aphidnus, as Herakles had been by Pylius. They received divine honours, being addressed as "Anakes," either because of the cessation of the war, or from the care they took, when they had such a large army within the walls of Athens, that no one should be wronged; for those who take care of or guard anything are said to do it "anakos," and perhaps for this reason kings are called "Anaktes." Some say that they were called Anakas because of the appearance of their stars in the heavens above, for the Attics called "above" "anekas."

XXXIV. It is said that Aethra, the mother of Theseus, was carried off as a captive to Lacedaemon, and thence to Troy with Helen, and Homer supports this view, when he says that there followed Helen,
      "Aithra the daughter of Pittheus and large-eyed Klymene."

Others reject this verse, and the legend about Mounychus, who is said to have been the bastard son of Laodike, by Demophoon, and to have been brought up in Troy by Aithra. But Istrus, in his thirteenth book of his 'History of Attica,' tells quite a different and peculiar story about Aithra, that he had heard that Paris was conquered by Achilles and Patroklus near the river

Spercheius, in Thessaly, and that Hector took the city of Troezen by storm, and amongst the plunder carried off Aithra, who had been left there. But this seems impossible.

XXXV. Now Aidoneus the Molossian king chanced to be entertaining Herakles, and related to him the story of Theseus and Peirithous, what they had intended to do, and how they had been caught in the act and punished. Herakles was much grieved at hearing how one had perished ingloriously, and the other was like to perish. He thought that nothing would be gained by reproaching the king for his conduct to Peirithous, but he begged for the life of Theseus, and pointed out that the release of his friend was a favour which he deserved. Aidoneus agreed, and Theseus, when set free, returned to Athens, where he found that his party was not yet overpowered. Whatever consecrated grounds had been set apart for him by the city, he dedicated to Herakles, and called Heraklea instead of Thesea, except four, according to Philochorus. But, as he at once wished to preside and manage the state as before, he was met by factious opposition, for he found that those who had been his enemies before, had now learned not to fear him, while the common people had become corrupted, and now required to be specially flattered instead of doing their duty in silence.

He endeavoured to establish his government by force, but was overpowered by faction; and at last, despairing of success, he secretly sent his children to Euboea, to Elephenor, the son of Chalkodous; and he himself, after solemnly uttering curses on the Athenians at Gargettus, where now is the place called Araterion, or the place of curses, set sail for Skyros, where he was, he imagined, on friendly terms with the inhabitants, and possessed a paternal estate in the island. At that time Lykomedes was king of Skyros; so he proceeded to demand from him his lands, in order to live there, though some say that he asked him to assist him against the Athenians. Lykomedes, either in fear of the great reputation of Theseus, or else to gain the favour of Mnestheus, led him up to the highest mountain top in the country, on the pretext of showing him his estate from thence, and pushed him over a precipice. Some say that he stumbled and fell of himself, as he was walking after supper, according to his custom. As soon as he was dead, no one thought any more of him, but Mnestheus reigned over the Athenians, while Theseus's children were brought up as private citizens by Elephenor, and followed him to Ilium. When Mnestheus died at Ilium, they returned home and resumed their rightful sovereignty. In subsequent times, among many other things which led the Athenians to honour Theseus as a hero or demi-god, most remarkable was his appearance at the battle of Marathon, where his spirit was seen by many, clad in armour, leading the charge against the barbarians.

XXXVI. After the Persian war, in the archonship of Phaedo, the Athenians were told by the Delphian Oracle to take home the bones of Theseus and keep them with the greatest care and honour. There was great difficulty in obtaining them and in discovering his tomb, on account of the wild and savage habits of the natives of the island. However, Kimon took the island, as is written in my history of his Life, and making it a point of honour to discover his tomb, he chanced to behold an eagle pecking with its beak and scratching with its talons at a small rising ground. Here he dug, imagining that the spot had been pointed out by a miracle. There was found the coffin of a man of great stature, and lying beside it a brazen lance-head and a sword. These relics were brought to Athens by Kimon, on board of his trireme, and the delighted Athenians received them with splendid processions and sacrifices, just as if the hero himself were come to the city. He is buried in the midst of the city, near where the Gymnasium now stands, and his tomb is a place of sanctuary for slaves, and all that are poor and oppressed, because Theseus, during his life, was the champion and avenger of the poor, and always kindly hearkened to their prayers. Their greatest sacrifice in his honour takes place on the eighth of the month of Pyanepsion, upon which day he and the youths came back from Crete. But besides this they hold a service in his honour on the eighth of all the other months, either because it was on the eighth day of Hekatombeion that he first arrived in Athens from Troezen, as is related by Diodorus the topographer, or else thinking that number to be especially his own, because he is said to have been the son of Poseidon, and Poseidon is honoured on the eighth day of every month. For the number eight is the first cube of an even number, and is double the first square, and therefore peculiarly represents the immovable abiding power of that god whom we address as "the steadfast," and the "earth upholder."

Life of Romulus.

I. Historians are not agreed upon the origin and meaning of the famous name of Rome, which is so celebrated through all the world. Some relate that the Pelasgi, after wandering over the greater part of the world, and conquering most nations, settled there, and gave the city its name from their own strength in battle. Others tell us that after the capture of Troy some fugitives obtained ships, were carried by the winds to the Tyrrhenian or Tuscan coast, and cast anchor in the Tiber. There the women, who had suffered much from the sea voyage, were advised by one who was accounted chief among them for wisdom and noble birth, Roma by name, to burn the ships. At first the men were angry at this, but afterwards, being compelled to settle round about the Palatine Hill, they fared better than they expected, as they found the country fertile and the neighbours hospitable; so they paid great honour to Roma, and called the city after her name. From this circumstance, they say, arose the present habit of women kissing their male relatives and connections; because those women, after they had burned the ships, thus embraced and caressed the men, trying to pacify their rage.

II. Some say that Roma, who gave the name to the city, was the daughter of Italus and Leucaria, or of Telephus the son of Hercules, and the wife of Aeneas, while others say that she was the daughter of Ascanius the son of Aeneas. Others relate that Romanus, the son of Odysseus and Circe, founded the city, or that it was Romus, the son of Hemathion, who was sent from Troy by Diomedes; or Romis the despot of the Latins, who drove out of his kingdom the Tyrrhenians, who, starting from Thessaly, had made their way to Lydia, and thence to Italy. And even those who follow the most reasonable of these legends, and admit that it was Romulus who founded the city after his own name, do not agree about his birth; for some say that he was the son of Aeneas and Dexithea the daughter of Phorbas, and with his brother Romus was brought to Italy when a child, and that as the river was in flood, all the other boats were swamped, but that in which the children were was carried to a soft bank and miraculously preserved, from which the name of Rome was given to the place. Others say that Roma, the daughter of that Trojan lady, married Latinus the son of Telemachus and bore a son, Romulus; while others say that his mother was Aemilia the daughter of Aeneas and Lavinia, by an intrigue with Mars; while others give a completely legendary account of his birth, as follows:

In the house of Tarchetius, the king of the Albani, a cruel and lawless man, a miracle took place. A male figure arose from the hearth, and remained there for many days. Now there was in Etruria an oracle of Tethys, which told Tarchetius that a virgin must be offered to the figure; for there should be born of her a son surpassing all mankind in strength, valour, and good fortune. Tarchetius hereupon explained the oracle to one of his daughters, and ordered her to give herself up to the figure; but she, not liking to do so, sent her servant-maid instead. Tarchetius, when he learned this, was greatly incensed, and cast them both into prison, meaning to put them to death. However, in a dream, Vesta appeared to him, forbidding him to slay them. In consequence of this he locked them up with a loom, telling them that when they had woven the piece of work upon it they should be married. So they wove all day, and during the night other maidens sent by Tarchetius undid their work again. Now when the servant-maid was delivered of twins, Tarchetius gave them to one Teratius, and bade him destroy them. He laid them down near the river; and there they were suckled by a she-wolf, while all sorts of birds brought them morsels of food, until one day a cowherd saw them. Filled with wonder he ventured to come up to the children and bear them off. Saved from death in this manner they grew up, and then attacked and slew Tarchetius. This is the legend given by one Promathion, the compiler of a history of Italy.

III. But the most credible story, and that has most vouchers for its truth, is that which was first published in Greece by Diokles of Peparethos, a writer whom Fabius Pictor has followed in most points. There are variations in this legend also; but, generally speaking, it runs as follows:

The dynasty established by Aeneas at Alba Longa, came down to two brothers, Numitor and Amulius. Amulius offered his brother the choice between the sovereign power and the royal treasure, including the gold brought from Troy. Numitor chose the sovereign power. But Amulius, possessing all the treasure, and thereby having more power than his brother, easily dethroned him, and, as he feared his brother's daughter might have children who would avenge him, he made her a priestess of Vesta, sworn to celibacy for ever. This lady is named by some Ilia, by others Rhea or Silvia. After no long time she was found to be with child, against the law of the Vestals. Her life was saved by the entreaties of Antho, the king's daughter, but she was closely imprisoned, that she might not be delivered without Amulius's knowledge. She bore two children of remarkable beauty and size, and Amulius, all the more alarmed at this, bade an attendant take them and expose them. Some say that this man's name was Faustulus, while others say that this was not his name, but that of their rescuer. However, he placed the infants in a cradle, and went down to the river with the intention of throwing them into it, but seeing it running strong and turbulently, he feared to approach it, laid down the cradle near the bank and went away. The river, which was in flood, rose, and gently floated off the cradle, and carried it down to a soft place which is now called Cermalus, but anciently, it seems, was called Germanus, because brothers are called germani.

IV. Near this place was a fig-tree, which they called Ruminalius, either from Romulus, as most persons imagine, or because cattle came to ruminate in its shade, or, more probably, because of the suckling of the children there, for the ancients called the nipple rouma. Moreover, they call the goddess who appears to have watched over the children Roumilia, and to her they sacrifice offerings without wine, and pour milk as a libation upon her altar.

It is said that while the infants were lying in this place, the she-wolf suckled them, and that a woodpecker came and helped to feed and watch over them. Now these animals are sacred to the god Mars; and the Latins have a peculiar reverence and worship for the woodpecker. These circumstances, therefore, did not a little to confirm the tale of the mother of the children, that their father was Mars, though some say that she was deceived by Amulius himself, who, after condemning her to a life of virginity, appeared before her dressed in armour, and ravished her. Others say that the twofold meaning of the name of their nurse gave rise to this legend, for the Latins use the word lupa for she-wolves, and also for unchaste women, as was the wife of Faustulus, who brought up the children, Acca Laurentia by name. To her also the Romans offer sacrifice, and in the month of April the priest of Mars brings libations to her, and the feast is called Laurentia.

V. The Romans also worship another Laurentia, for this reason: The priest of Hercules, weary with idleness, proposed to the god to cast the dice on the condition that, if he won, he should receive something good from the god, while if he lost, he undertook to provide the god with a bountiful feast and a fair woman to take his pleasure with. Upon these conditions he cast the dice, first for the god, and then for himself, and was beaten. Wishing to settle his wager properly, and making a point of keeping his word, he prepared a feast for the god, and hired Laurentia, then in the pride of her beauty, though not yet famous. He feasted her in the temple, where he had prepared a couch, and after supper he locked her in, that the god might possess her. And, indeed, the god is said to have appeared to the lady, and to have bidden her go early in the morning into the market-place, and to embrace the first man she met, and make him her friend. There met her a citizen far advanced in years, possessing a fair income, childless, and unmarried. His name was Tarrutius. He took Laurentia to himself, and loved her, and upon his death left her heiress to a large and valuable property, the greater part of which she left by will to the city. It is related of her, that after she had become famous, and was thought to enjoy the favour of Heaven, she vanished near the very same spot where the other Laurentia lay buried. This place is now called Velabrum, because during the frequent overflowings of the river, people used there to be ferried over to the market-place; now they call ferrying velatura. Some say that the road from the market-place to the circus, starting from this point, used to be covered with sails or awnings by those who treated the people to a spectacle; and in the Latin tongue a sail is called velum. This is why the second Laurentia is honoured by the Romans.

VI. Now Faustulus, the swineherd of Amulius, kept the children concealed from every one, though some say that Numitor knew of it, and shared the expense of their education. They were sent to Gabii to learn their letters, and everything else that well-born children should know; and they were called Romulus and Remus, because they were first seen sucking the wolf. Their noble birth showed itself while they were yet children, in their size and beauty; and when they grew up they were manly and high-spirited, of invincible courage and daring. Romulus, however, was thought the wiser and more politic of the two, and in his discussions with the neighbours about pasture and hunting, gave them opportunities of noting that his disposition was one which led him to command rather than to obey. On account of these qualities they were beloved by their equals and the poor, but they despised the king's officers and bailiffs as being no braver than themselves, and cared neither for their anger nor their threats. They led the lives and followed the pursuits of nobly born men, not valuing sloth and idleness, but exercise and hunting, defending the land against brigands, capturing plunderers, and avenging those who had suffered wrong. And thus they became famous.

VII. Now a quarrel arose between the herdsmen of Numitor and those of Amulius, and cattle were driven off by the former. Amulius's men, enraged at this, fought and routed the others, and recovered a great part of the booty. They cared nothing for Numitor's anger, but collected together many needy persons and slaves, and filled them with a rebellious spirit. While Romulus was absent at a sacrifice (for he was much addicted to sacrifices and divination), the herdsmen of Numitor fell in with Remus, accompanied by a small band, and fought with him. After many wounds had been received on both sides, Numitor's men conquered and took Remus alive. Remus was brought before Numitor, who did not punish him, as he feared his brother's temper, but went to his brother and begged for justice, saying that he had suffered wrong at the hands of the king his brother's servants. As all the people of Alba sympathised with Remus, and feared that he would be unjustly put to death, or worse, Amulius, alarmed at them, handed over Remus to his brother Numitor, to deal with as he pleased. Numitor took him, and as soon as he reached home, after admiring the bodily strength and stature of the youth, which surpassed all the rest, perceiving in his looks his courageous and fiery spirit, undismayed by his present circumstances, and having heard that his deeds corresponded to his appearance, and above all, as seems probable, some god being with him and watching over the first beginnings of great events, he was struck by the idea of asking him to tell the truth as to who he was, and how he was born, giving him confidence and encouragement by his kindly voice and looks. The young man boldly said, "I will conceal nothing from you, for you seem more like a king than Amulius. You hear and judge before you punish, but he gives men up to be punished without a trial. Formerly we (for we are twins) understood that we were the sons of Faustulus and Laurentia, the king's servants; but now that we are brought before you as culprits, and are falsely accused and in danger of our lives, we have heard great things about ourselves. Whether they be true or not, we must now put to the test. Our birth is said to be a secret, and our nursing and bringing up is yet stranger, for we were cast out to the beasts and the birds, and were fed by them, suckled by a she-wolf, and fed with morsels of food by a woodpecker as we lay in our cradle beside the great river. Our cradle still exists, carefully preserved, bound with brazen bands, on which is an indistinct inscription, which hereafter will serve as a means by which we may be recognised by our parents, but to no purpose if we are dead." Numitor, considering the young man's story, and reckoning up the time from his apparent age, willingly embraced the hope which was dawning on his mind, and considered how he might obtain a secret interview with his daughter and tell her of all this; for she was still kept a close prisoner.

VIII. Faustulus, when he heard of Remus being captured and delivered up to Numitor, called upon Romulus to help him, and told him plainly all about his birth; although previously he had hinted so much, that any one who paid attention to his words might have known nearly all about it; and he himself with the cradle ran to Numitor full of hopes and fears, now that matters had come to a critical point. He was viewed with suspicion by the guards at the king's gate, and while they were treating him contemptuously, and confusing him by questions, they espied the cradle under his cloak. Now it chanced that one of them had been one of those who had taken the children to cast them away, and had been present when they were abandoned. This man, seeing the cradle and recognising it by its make and the inscription on it, suspected the truth, and at once told the king and brought the man in to be examined. Faustulus, in those dire straits, did not altogether remain unshaken, and yet did not quite allow his secret to be wrung from him. He admitted that the boys were alive, but said that they were living far away from Alba, and that he himself was bringing the cradle to Ilia, who had often longed to see and touch it to confirm her belief in the life of her children. Now Amulius did what men generally do when excited by fear or rage. He sent in a great hurry one who was a good man and a friend of Numitor, bidding him ask Numitor whether he had heard anything about the survival of the children. This man on arrival, finding Numitor all but embracing Remus, confirmed his belief that he was his grandson, and bade him take his measures quickly, remaining by him himself to offer assistance. Even had they wished it, there was no time for delay; for Romulus was already near, and no small number of the citizens, through hatred and fear of Amulius, were going out to join him. He himself brought no small force, arrayed in companies of a hundred each. Each of these was led by a man who carried a bundle of sticks and straw upon a pole. The Latins called these manipla; and from this these companies are even at the present day called maniples in the Roman army. Now as Remus raised a revolt within, while Romulus assailed the palace without, the despot was captured and put to death without having been able to do anything, or take any measures for his own safety.

The greater part of the above story is told by Fabius Pictor and Diokles of Peparethos, who seem to have been the first historians of the foundation of Rome. The story is doubted by many on account of its theatrical and artificial form, yet we ought not to disbelieve it when we consider what wondrous works are wrought by chance, and when, too, we reflect on the Roman Empire, which, had it not had a divine origin, never could have arrived at its present extent.

IX. After the death of Amulius, and the reorganisation of the kingdom, the twins, who would not live in Alba as subjects, and did not wish to reign there during the life of their grandfather, gave up the sovereign power to him, and, having made a suitable provision for their mother, determined to dwell by themselves, and to found a city in the parts in which they themselves had been reared; at least, this is the most probable of the various reasons which are given. It may also have been necessary, as many slaves and fugitives had gathered round them, either that they should disperse these men and so lose their entire power, or else go and dwell alone amongst them. It is clear, from the rape of the Sabine women, that the citizens of Alba would not admit these outcasts into their own body, since that deed was caused, not by wanton insolence, but by necessity, as they could not obtain wives by fair means; for after carrying the women off they treated them with the greatest respect. Afterwards, when the city was once founded, they made it a sanctuary for people in distress to take refuge in, saying that it belonged to the god Asylus; and they received in it all sorts of persons, not giving up slaves to their masters, debtors to their creditors, or murderers to their judges, but saying that, in accordance with a Pythian oracle, the sanctuary was free to all; so that the city soon became full of men, for they say that at first it contained no less than a thousand hearths. Of this more hereafter. When they were proceeding to found the city, they at once quarrelled about its site. Romulus fixed upon what is now called Roma Quadrata, a square piece of ground, and wished the city to be built in that place; but Remus preferred a strong position on Mount Aventino, which, in memory of him, was called the Remonium, and now is called Rignarium.

They agreed to decide their dispute by watching the flight of birds, and having taken their seats apart, it is said that six vultures appeared to Remus, and afterwards twice as many to Romulus. Some say that Remus really saw his vultures, but that Romulus only pretended to have seen them, and when Remus came to him, then the twelve appeared to Romulus; for which reason the Romans at the present day draw their auguries especially from vultures. Herodorus of Pontus says that Hercules delighted in the sight of a vulture, when about to do any great action. It is the most harmless of all creatures, for it injures neither crops, fruit, nor cattle, and lives entirely upon dead corpses. It does not kill or injure anything that has life, and even abstains from dead birds from its relationship to them. Now eagles, and owls, and falcons, peck and kill other birds, in spite of Aeschylus's line,

"Bird-eating bird polluted e'er must be."

Moreover, the other birds are, so to speak, ever before our eyes, and continually remind us of their presence; but the vulture is seldom seen, and it is difficult to meet with its young, which has suggested to some persons the strange idea that vultures come from some other world to pay us their rare visits, which are like those occurrences which, according to the soothsayers, do not happen naturally or spontaneously, but by the interposition of Heaven.

X. When Remus discovered the deceit he was very angry, and, while Romulus was digging a trench round where the city wall was to be built, he jeered at the works, and hindered them. At last, as he jumped over it, he was struck dead either by Romulus himself, or by Celer, one of his companions.

In this fight, Faustulus was slain, and also Pleistinus, who is said to have been Faustulus's brother and to have helped him in rearing Romulus and his brother. Celer retired into Tyrrhenia, and from him the Romans call quick sharp men Celeres; Quintus Metellus, who, when his father died, in a very few days exhibited a show of gladiators, was surnamed Celer by the Romans in their wonder at the short time he had spent in his preparations.

XI. Romulus, after burying Remus and his foster-parents in the Remurium, consecrated his city, having fetched men from Etruria, who taught him how to perform it according to sacred rites and ceremonies, as though they were celebrating holy mysteries. A trench was dug in a circle round what is now the Comitium, and into it were flung first-fruits of all those things which are honourable and necessary for men. Finally each man brought a little of the earth of the country from which he came, and flung it into one heap and mixed it all together. They call this pit by the same name as the heavens, Mundus. Next, they drew the outline of the city in the form of a circle, with this place as its centre. And then the founder, having fitted a plough with a brazen ploughshare, and yoked to it a bull and a cow, himself ploughs a deep furrow round the boundaries. It is the duty of his attendants to throw the clods inwards, which the plough turns up, and to let none of them fall outwards. By this line they define the extent of the fortifications, and it is called by contraction, Pomoerium, which means behind the walls or beyond the walls (post moenia). Wherever they intend to place a gate they take off the ploughshare, and carry the plough over, leaving a space. After this ceremony they consider the entire wall sacred, except the gates; but if they were sacred also, they could not without scruple bring in and out necessaries and unclean things through them.

XII. It is agreed that the foundation of the city took place on the eleventh day before the Kalends of May (the 21st of April). And on this day the Romans keep a festival which they call the birthday of the city. At this feast, originally, we are told, they sacrificed nothing that has life, but thought it right to keep the anniversary of the birth of the city pure and unpolluted by blood. However, before the foundation of the city, they used to keep a pastoral feast called Palilia. The Roman months at the present day do not in any way correspond to those of Greece; yet they (the Greeks) distinctly affirm that the day upon which Romulus founded the city was the 30th of the month. The Greeks likewise tell us that on that day an eclipse of the sun took place, which they think was that observed by Antimachus of Teos, the epic poet, which occurred in the third year of the sixth Olympiad. In the time of Varro the philosopher, who of all the Romans was most deeply versed in

Roman history, there was one Taroutius, a companion of his, a philosopher and mathematician, who had especially devoted himself to the art of casting nativities, and was thought to have attained great skill therein. To this man Varro proposed the task of finding the day and hour of Romulus's birth, basing his calculations on the influence which the stars were said to have had upon his life, just as geometricians solve their problems by the analytic method; for it belongs, he argued, to the same science to predict the life of a man from the time of his birth, and to find the date of a man's birth if the incidents of his life are given. Taroutius performed his task, and after considering the things done and suffered by Romulus, the length of his life, the manner of his death, and all such like matters, he confidently and boldly asserted that Romulus was conceived by his mother in the first year of the second Olympiad, at the third hour of the twenty-third day of the month which is called in the Egyptian calendar Choiac, at which time there was a total eclipse of the sun. He stated that he was born on the twenty-first day of the month Thouth, about sunrise. Rome was founded by him on the ninth day of the month Pharmouthi, between the second and third hour; for it is supposed that the fortunes of cities, as well as those of men, have their certain periods which can be discovered by the position of the stars at their nativities. The quaint subtlety of these speculations may perhaps amuse the reader more than their legendary character will weary him.

XIII. When the city was founded, Romulus first divided all the able-bodied males into regiments, each consisting of three thousand infantry and three hundred cavalry. These were named legions, because they consisted of men of military age selected from the population. The rest of the people were now organised. They were called Populus, and a hundred of the noblest were chosen from among them and formed into a council. These he called Patricians, and their assembly the Senate. This word Senate clearly means assembly of old men; and the members of it were named Patricians, according to some, because they were the fathers of legitimate offspring; according to others, because they were able to give an account of who their own fathers were, which few of the first colonists were able to do. Others say that it was from their Patrocinium, as they then called, and do at the present day call, their patronage of their clients. There is a legend that this word arose from one Patron, a companion of Evander, who was kind and helpful to his inferiors. But it is most reasonable to suppose that Romulus called them by this name because he intended the most powerful men to show kindness to their inferiors, and to show the poorer classes that they ought not to fear the great nor grudge them their honours, but be on friendly terms with them, thinking of them and addressing them as fathers (Patres). For, up to the present day, foreigners address the senators as Lords, but the Romans call them Conscript Fathers, using the most honourable and least offensive of their titles. Originally they were merely called the Fathers, but afterwards, as more were enrolled, they were called Conscript Fathers. By this more dignified title Romulus distinguished the Senate from the People; and he introduced another distinction between the powerful and the common people by naming the former patrons, which means defenders, and the latter clients, which means dependants. By this means he implanted in them a mutual good feeling which was the source of great benefits, for the patrons acted as advocates for their clients in law suits, and in all cases became their advisers and friends, while the clients not only respected their patrons but even assisted them, when they were poor, to portion their daughters or pay their creditors. No law or magistrate could compel a patron to bear witness against his client, nor a client against his patron. Moreover, in later times, although all their other rights remained unimpaired, it was thought disgraceful for a patron to receive money from a client. So much for these matters.

XIV. In the fourth month after the city was founded, we are told by Fabius, the reckless deed of carrying off the women took place. Some say that Romulus himself naturally loved war, and, being persuaded by some prophecies that Rome was fated to grow by wars and so reach the greatest prosperity, attacked the Sabines without provocation; for he did not carry off many maidens, but only thirty, as though it was war that he desired more than wives for his followers. This is not probable: Romulus saw that his city was newly-filled with colonists, few of whom had wives, while most of them were a mixed multitude of poor or unknown origin, who were despised by the neighouring states, and expected by them shortly to fall to pieces. He intended his violence to lead to an alliance with the Sabines, as soon as the damsels became reconciled to their lot, and set about it as follows: First he circulated a rumour that the altar of some god had been discovered, hidden in the earth. This god was called Census, either because he was the god of counsel (for the Romans to this day call their assembly Concilium, and their chief magistrates consuls, as it were those who take counsel on behalf of the people), or else it was the equestrian Neptune. The altar stands in the greater hippodrome, and is kept concealed except during the horse-races, when it is uncovered. Some say that, as the whole plot was dark and mysterious, it was natural that the god's altar should be underground. When it was brought out, he proclaimed a splendid sacrifice in its honour, and games and shows open to all men. Many people assembled to see them, and Romulus sat among his nobles, dressed in a purple robe. The signal for the assault was that he should rise, unfold his cloak, and then again wrap it around him. Many men armed with swords stood round him, and at the signal they drew their swords, rushed forward with a shout, and snatched up the daughters of the Sabines, but allowed the others to escape unharmed. Some say that only thirty were carried off, from whom the thirty tribes were named, but Valerius of Antium says five hundred and twenty-seven, and Juba six hundred and eighty-three, all maidens. This is the best apology for Romulus; for they only carried off one married woman, Hersilia, which proved that it was not through insolence or wickedness that they carried them off, but with the intention of forcibly effecting a union between the two races. Some say that Hersilia married Hostilius, one of the noblest Romans, others that she married Romulus himself, and that he had children by her; one daughter, called Prima from her being the first-born, and one son, whom his father originally named Aollius, because of the assembling of the citizens, but whom they afterwards named Avillius. This is the story as told by Zenodotus of Troezen, but many contradict it.

XV. Among the ravishers they say there were some men of low condition who had seized a remarkably tall and beautiful maiden. When any of the nobles met them and endeavoured to take her away from them, they cried out that they were taking her to Talasius, a young man of good family and reputation. Hearing this, all agreed and applauded, and some even turned and accompanied them, crying out the name of Talasius through their friendship for him. From this circumstance the Romans up to the present day call upon Talasius in their marriage-songs, as the Greeks do upon Hymen; for Talasius is said to have been fortunate in his wife. Sextius Sulla of Carthage, a man neither deficient in learning or taste, told me that this word was given by Romulus as the signal for the rape, and so that all those who carried off maidens cried "Talasio." But most authors, among whom is Juba, think that it is used to encourage brides to industry and spinning wool (talasia), as at that time Greek words had not been overpowered by Latin ones. But if this be true, and the Romans at that time really used this word "talasia" for wool-spinning, as we do, we might make another more plausible conjecture about it. When the treaty of peace was arranged between the Romans and the Sabines, a special provision was made about the women, that they were to do no work for the men except wool-spinning. And thus the custom remained for the friends of those who were married afterwards to call upon Talasius in jest, meaning to testify that the bride was to do no other work than spinning. To the present day the custom remains in force that the bride must not step over the threshold into her house, but be lifted over it and carried in, because the Sabine maidens were carried in forcibly, and did not walk in.

Some add that the parting of the bride's hair with the point of a spear is done in memory of the first Roman marriage having been effected by war and battle; on which subject we have enlarged further in our treatise on Causes.

The rape of the Sabines took place upon the eighteenth day of the month Sextilis, which is now called August, on which day the feast of the Consualia is kept.

XVI. The Sabines were a numerous and warlike tribe, dwelling in unwalled villages, as though it was their birthright as a Lacedaemonian colony to be brave and fearless. Yet when they found themselves bound by such hostages to keep the peace, and in fear for their daughters, they sent an embassy to propose equitable and moderate terms, that Romulus should give back their daughters to them, and disavow the violence which had been used, and that afterwards the two nations should live together in amity and concord. But when Romulus refused to deliver up the maidens, but invited the Sabines to accept his alliance, while the other tribes were hesitating and considering what was to be done, Acron, the king of the Ceninetes, a man of spirit and renown in the wars, who had viewed Romulus first proceeding in founding a city with suspicion, now, after what he had done in carrying off the women, declared that he was becoming dangerous, and would not be endurable unless he were chastised. He at once began the war, and marched with a great force; and Romulus marched to meet him. When they came in sight of each other they each challenged the other to fight, the soldiers on both sides looking on. Romulus made a vow that if he should overcome and kill his enemy he would himself carry his spoils to the temple of Jupiter and offer them to him. He overcame his adversary, and slew him, routed his army and captured his city. He did not harm the inhabitants, except that he ordered them to demolish their houses and follow him to Rome, to become citizens on equal terms with the rest. This is the policy by which Rome grew so great, namely that of absorbing conquered nations into herself on terms of equality.

Romulus, in order to make the fulfilment of his vow as pleasing to Jupiter, and as fine a spectacle for the citizens as he could, cut down a tall oak-tree at his camp, and fashioned it into a trophy, upon which he hung or fastened all the arms of Acron, each in its proper place. Then he girded on his own clothes, placed a crown of laurel upon his long hair, and, placing the trophy upright on his right shoulder, marched along in his armour, singing a paean of victory, with all the army following him. At Rome the citizens received him with admiration and delight; and this procession was the origin of all the subsequent triumphs and the model which they imitated. The trophy itself was called an offering to Jupiter Feretrius; for the Romans call to strike, ferire, and Romulus prayed that he might strike down his enemy. The spoils were called spolia opima, according to Varro, because opim means excellence. A more plausible interpretation would be from the deed itself, for work is called in Latin opus. This dedication of spolia opima is reserved as a privilege for a general who has slain the opposing general with his own hand. It has only been enjoyed by three Roman generals, first by Romulus, who slew Acron, king of the Ceninetes, second by Cornelius Cossus, who slew the Tyrrhenian Tolumnius, and, above all, by Claudius Marcellus, who killed Britomart, the king of the Gauls. Now Cossus and Marcellus drove into the city in chariots and four, carrying the trophies in their own hands; but Dionysius is in error when he says that Romulus used a chariot and four, for the historians tell us that Tarquinius, the son of Demaratus, was the first of the kings who introduced this pomp into his triumphs. Others say that Poplicola was the first to triumph in a chariot. However, the statues of Romulus bearing the trophy, which are to be seen in Rome, are all on foot.

XVII. After the capture of the Ceninete tribe, while the rest of the Sabines were still engaged in preparation for war, the inhabitants of Fidenae and Crustumerium and Antemna attacked the Romans. A battle took place in which they were all alike worsted, after which they permitted Romulus to take their cities, divide their lands, and incorporate them as citizens. Romulus divided all the lands among the citizens, except that which was held by the fathers of any of the maidens who had been carried off, which he allowed them to retain.

The remainder of the Sabines, angry at these successes, chose Tatius as their general and marched against Rome. The city was hard to attack, as the Capitol stood as an advanced fort to defend it. Here was placed a garrison, and Tarpeius was its commander, not the maiden Tarpeia, as some write, who make out Romulus a fool; but it was this Tarpeia, the daughter of the captain of the garrison, who betrayed the capital to the Sabines, for the sake of the golden bracelets which she saw them wearing. She asked as the price of her treachery that they should give her what they wore on their left arms. After making an agreement with Tatius, she opened a gate at night and let in the Sabines. Now it appears that Antigonus was not singular when he said that he loved men when they were betraying, but hated them after they had betrayed; as also Caesar said, in the case of Rhymitalkes the Thracian, that he loved the treachery but hated the traitor; but this seems a common reflection about bad men by those who have need of them, just as we need the poison of certain venomous beasts; for they appreciate their value while they are making use of them, and loathe their wickedness when they have done with them. And that was how Tarpeia was treated by Tatius. He ordered the Sabines to remember their agreement, and not to grudge her what was on their left arms. He himself first of all took off his gold armlet, and with it flung his great oblong shield. As all the rest did the like, she perished, being pelted with the gold bracelets and crushed by the number and weight of the shields. Tarpeius also was convicted of treachery by Romulus, according to Juba's version of the history of Sulpicius Galba. The other legends about Tarpeia are improbable; amongst them that which is told by Antigonus, that she was the daughter of Tatius the Sabine leader, abducted by Romulus, and treated by her father as is related above. Simylus the poet talks utter nonsense when he says that it was not the Sabines but the Gauls to whom Tarpeia betrayed the Capitol, because she was in love with their king. His verses run as follows: "And near Tarpeia, by the Capitol That dwelt, betrayer of the walls of Rome. She loved the chieftain of the Gauls too well, To guard from treachery her father's home."

And a little afterwards he speaks of her death.

"Her did the Boians and the Celtic tribes Bury, but not beside the stream of Po; From off their warlike arms their shields they flung, And what the damsel longed for laid her low."

XVIII. However, as Tarpeia was buried there, the hill was called the Tarpeian hill until King Tarquinius, when he dedicated the place to Jupiter, removed her remains and abolished the name of Tarpeia. But even to this day they call the rock in the Capitol the Tarpeian Rock, down which malefactors used to be flung. When the Sabines held the citadel, Romulus in fury challenged them to come down and fight. Tatius accepted his challenge with confidence, as he saw that if overpowered his men would have a strong place of refuge to retreat to. All the intermediate space, in which they were about to engage, was surrounded by hills, and so seemed to make a desperate battle necessary, as there were but narrow outlets for flight or pursuit. It chanced, also, that the river had been in flood a few days before, and had left a deep muddy pool of water upon the level ground where the Forum now stands; so that men's footing was not certain, but difficult and treacherous. Here a piece of good fortune befell the Sabines as they heedlessly pressed forward. Curtius, one of their chiefs, a man with a reputation for dashing courage, rode on horseback far before the rest. His horse plunged into this morass, and he, after trying to extricate him, at last finding it impossible, left him there and saved himself. This place, in memory of him, is still called the Gulf of Curtius.

Warned of their danger, the Sabines fought a stout and indecisive battle, in which many fell, amongst them Hostilius. He is said to have been the husband of Hersilia and the grandfather of Hostilius, who became king after the reign of Numa. Many combats took place in that narrow space, as we may suppose; and especial mention is made of one, which proved the last, in which Romulus was struck on the head by a stone and like to fall, and unable to fight longer. The Romans now gave way to the Sabines, and fled to the Palatine hill, abandoning the level ground. Romulus, now recovered from the blow, endeavoured to stay the fugitives, and with loud shouts called upon them to stand firm and fight. But as the stream of fugitives poured on, and no one had the courage to face round, he lifted his hands to heaven and prayed to Jupiter to stay the army and not to allow the tottering state of Rome to fall, but to help it. After his prayer many were held back from flight by reverence for the king, and the fugitives suddenly resumed their confidence. They made their first stand where now is the temple of Jupiter Stator, which one may translate "He who makes to stand firm;" and then forming their ranks once more they drove back the Sabines as far as what is now called the Palace, and the Temple of Vesta.

XIX. While they were preparing to fight as though the battle was only now just begun, they were restrained by a strange spectacle, beyond the power of words to express. The daughters of the Sabines who had been carried off were seen rushing from all quarters, with loud shrieks and wailings, through the ranks and among the dead bodies, as though possessed by some god. Some of them carried infant children in their arms, and others wore their hair loose and dishevelled. All of them kept addressing the Romans and the Sabines alternately by the most endearing names. The hearts of both armies were melted, and they fell back so as to leave a space for the women between them. A murmur of sorrow ran through all the ranks, and a strong feeling of pity was excited by the sight of the women, and by their words, which began with arguments and upbraidings, but ended in entreaties and tears. "What wrong have we done to you," said they, "that we should have suffered and should even now suffer such cruel treatment at your hands? We were violently and wrongfully torn away from our friends, and after we had been carried off we were neglected by our brothers, fathers, and relatives for so long a time, that now, bound by the closest of ties to our enemies, we tremble for our ravishers and wrongers when they fight, and weep when they fall. Ye would not come and tear us from our ravishers while we were yet maidens, but now ye would separate wives from their husbands, and mothers from their children, a worse piece of service to us than your former neglect. Even if it was not about us that you began to fight, you ought to cease now that you have become fathers-in-law, and grandfathers, and relatives one of another. But if the war is about us, then carry us off with your sons-in-law and our children, and give us our fathers and relatives, but do not take our husbands and children from us. We beseech you not to allow us to be carried off captive a second time." Hersilia spoke at length in this fashion, and as the other women added their entreaties to hers, a truce was agreed upon, and the chiefs met in conference. Hereupon the women made their husbands and children known to their fathers and brothers, fetched food and drink for such as needed it, and took the wounded into their own houses to be attended to there. Thus they let their friends see that they were mistresses of their own houses, and that their husbands attended to their wishes and treated them with every respect.

In the conference it was accordingly determined that such women as chose to do so should continue to live with their husbands, free, as we have already related, from all work and duties except that of spinning wool (talasia); that the Romans and the Sabines should dwell together in the city, and that the city should be called Rome, after Romulus, but the Romans be called Quirites after the native city of Tatius; and that they should both reign and command the army together. The place where this compact was made is even to this day called the Comitium, for the Romans call meeting coire.

XX. Now that the city was doubled in numbers, a hundred more senators were elected from among the Sabines, and the legions were composed of six thousand infantry and six hundred cavalry. They also established three tribes, of which they named one Rhamnenses, from Romulus, another Titienses from Tatius, and the third Lucerenses, after the name of a grove to which many had fled for refuge, requiring asylum, and had been admitted as citizens. They call a grove lucus. The very name of tribe and tribune show that there were three tribes. Each tribe was divided into ten centuries, which some say were named after the women who were carried off; but this seems to be untrue, as many of them are named after places. However, many privileges were conferred upon the women, amongst which were that men should make way for them when they walked out, to say nothing disgraceful in their presence, or appear naked before them, on pain of being tried before the criminal court; and also that their children should wear the bulla, which is so called from its shape, which is like a bubble, and was worn round the neck, and also the broad purple border of their robe (praetexta).

The kings did not conduct their deliberations together, but each first took counsel with his own hundred senators, and then they all met together. Tatius dwelt where now is the temple of Juno Moneta, and Romulus by the steps of the Fair Shore, as it is called, which are at the descent from the Palatine hill into the great Circus. Here they say the sacred cornel-tree grew, the legend being that Romulus, to try his strength, threw a spear, with cornel-wood shaft, from Mount Aventine, and when the spear-head sunk into the ground, though many tried, no one was able to pull it out. The soil, which was fertile, suited the wood, and it budded, and became the stem of a good-sized cornel-tree. After the death of Romulus this was preserved and reverenced as one of the holiest objects in the city. A wall was built round it, and whenever any one thought that it looked inclined to droop and wither he at once raised a shout to tell the bystanders, and they, just as if they were assisting to put out a fire, called for water, and came from all quarters carrying pots of water to the place. It is said that when Gaius Caesar repaired the steps, and the workmen were digging near it, they unintentionally damaged the roots, and the tree died.

XXI. The Sabines adopted the Roman system of months, and all that is remarkable about them will be found in the 'Life of Numa.' But Romulus adopted the large oblong Sabine shield, and gave up the round Argolic shields which he and the Romans had formerly carried. The two nations shared each other's festivals, not abolishing any which either had been wont to celebrate, but introducing several new ones, among which are the Matronalia, instituted in honour of the women at the end of the war, and that of the Carmentalia. It is thought by some that Carmenta is the ruling destiny which presides over a man's birth, wherefore she is worshipped by mothers. Others say that she was the wife of Evander the Arcadian, a prophetess who used to chant oracles in verse, and hence surnamed Carmenta (for the Romans call verses carmina); whereas it is generally admitted that her right name was Nicostrate. Some explain the name of Carmenta more plausibly as meaning that during her prophetic frenzy she was bereft of intellect; for the Romans call to lack, carcre; and mind, mentem.

We have spoken before of the feast of the Palilia. That of the Lupercalia would seem, from the time of its celebration, to be a ceremony of purification; for it is held during the ominous days of February, a month whose name one might translate by Purification; and that particular day was originally called Febraté. The name of this feast in Greek signifies that of wolves, and it is thought, on this account, to be very ancient, and derived from the Arcadians who came to Italy with Evander. Still this is an open question, for the name may have arisen from the she-wolf, as we see that the Luperci start to run their course from the place where Romulus is said to have been exposed. The circumstances of the ritual are such as to make it hard to conjecture their meaning. They slaughter goats, and then two youths of good family are brought to them. Then some with a bloody knife mark the foreheads of the youths, and others at once wipe the blood away with wool dipped in milk. The youths are expected to laugh when it is wiped away. After this they cut the skins of the goats into strips and run about naked, except a girdle round the middle, striking with the thongs all whom they meet. Women in the prime of life do not avoid being struck, as they believe that it assists them in childbirth and promotes fertility. It is also a peculiarity of this festival that the Luperci sacrifice a dog. One Bontes, who wrote an elegiac poem on the origin of the Roman myths, says that when Romulus and his party had killed Amulius, they ran back in their joy to the place where the she-wolf suckled them when little, and that the feast is typical of this, and that the young nobles run, "As, smiting all they met, that day From Alba Romulus and Remus ran."

The bloody sword is placed upon their foreheads in token of the danger and slaughter of that day, and the wiping with the milk is in remembrance of their nurse. Caius Acilius tells us that, before the foundation of Rome, the cattle of Romulus and Remus were missing, and they, after invoking Faunus, ran out to search for them, naked, that they might not be inconvenienced by sweat; and that this is the reason that the Luperci ran about naked. As for the dog, one would say that if the sacrifice is purificatory, it is sacrificed on behalf of those who use it. The Greeks, in their purificatory rites, sacrifice dogs, and often make use of what is called Periskylakismos. But if this feast be in honour of the she-wolf, in gratitude for her suckling and preserving of Romulus, then it is very natural to sacrifice a dog, for it is an enemy of wolves; unless, indeed, the beast is put to death to punish it for hindering the Luperci when they ran their course.

XXII. It is said also that Romulus instituted the service of the sacred fire of Vestae, and the holy virgins who keep it up, called Vestals. Others attribute this to Numa, though they say that Romulus was a very religious prince, and learned in divination, for which purpose he used to carry the crooked staff called lituus, with which to divide the heavens into spaces for the observation of the flight of birds. This, which is preserved in the Palatium, was lost when the city was taken by the Gauls; but afterwards, when the barbarians had been repulsed, it was found unharmed in a deep bed of ashes, where everything else had been burned or spoiled. He also enacted some laws, the most arbitrary of which is that a wife cannot obtain a divorce from her husband, but that a husband may put away his wife for poisoning her children, counterfeiting keys, or adultery. If any one put away his wife on other grounds than these, he enacted that half his property should go to his wife, and half to the temple of Ceres. A man who divorced his wife was to make an offering to the Chthonian gods. A peculiarity of his legislation is that, while he laid down no course of procedure in case of parricide, he speaks of all murder by the name of parricide, as though the one were an abominable, but the other an impossible crime. And for many years it appeared that he had rightly judged, for no one attempted anything of the kind at Rome for nearly six hundred years; but it is said that the first parricide was that of Lucius Hostilius, which he committed after the war with Hannibal. Enough has now been said upon these subjects.

XXIII. In the fifth year of the reign of Tatius, some of his relatives fell in with ambassadors from Laurentum, on their way to Rome, and endeavoured to rob them. As the ambassadors would not submit to this, but defended themselves, they slew them. Romulus at once gave it as his opinion that the authors of this great and audacious crime ought to be punished, but Tatius hushed the matter up, and enabled them to escape. This is said to have been the only occasion upon which they were openly at variance, for in all other matters they acted with the greatest possible unanimity. The relatives, however, of the murdered men, as they were hindered by Tatius from receiving any satisfaction, fell upon him when he and Romulus were offering sacrifice at Lavinium, and slew him, but respected Romulus, and praised him as a just man. He brought home the body of Tatius, and buried it honourably. It lies near what is called the Armilustrium, on Mount Aventine.

But Romulus neglected altogether to exact any satisfaction for the murder. Some writers say that the city of Lavinium, in its terror, delivered up the murderers of Tatius, but that Romulus allowed them to depart, saying that blood had been atoned for by blood. This speech of his gave rise to some suspicion that he was not displeased at being rid of his colleague. However, it caused no disturbance in the state, and did not move the Sabines to revolt, but partly out of regard for Romulus, and fear of his power, and belief in his divine mission, they continued to live under his rule with cheerfulness and respect. Many foreign tribes also respected Romulus, and the more ancient Latin races sent him ambassadors, and made treaties of friendship and alliance.

He took Fidenae, a city close to Rome, according to some authorities, by sending his cavalry thither on a sudden, and ordering them to cut the pivots of the city gates, and then unexpectedly appearing in person. Others say that the people of Fidenae first invaded the Roman territory, drove off plunder from it, and insulted the neighbourhood of the city itself, and that Romulus laid an ambush for them, slew many, and took their city. He did not destroy it, but made it a Roman colony, and sent two thousand five hundred Romans thither as colonists on the Ides of April.

XXIV. After this a pestilence fell upon Rome, which slew men suddenly without previous sickness, and afflicted the crops and cattle with barrenness. A shower of blood also fell in the city, so that religious terror was added to the people's sufferings. As a similar visitation befell the citizens of Laurentum, it became evident that the wrath of the gods was visiting these cities because of the unavenged murders of Tatius and of the ambassadors. The guilty parties were delivered up on both sides, and duly punished, after which the plague was sensibly mitigated. Romulus also purified the city with lustrations, which, they say, are even now practised at the Ferentine gate. But before the plague ceased, the people of Camerium attacked the Romans, supposing that they would be unable to defend themselves on account of their misfortune, and overran their country. Nevertheless, Romulus instantly marched against them, slew six hundred of them in battle, and took their city. Half the survivors he transplanted to Rome, and settled twice as many Romans as the remainder at Camerium, on the Kalends of Sextilis. So many citizens had he to spare after he had only inhabited Rome for about sixteen years. Among the other spoils, he carried off a brazen four-horse chariot from Camerium; this he dedicated in the temple of Vulcan, having placed in it a figure of himself being crowned by Victory.

XXV. As the city was now so flourishing, the weaker of the neighbouring states made submission, and were glad to receive assurance that they would be unharmed; but the more powerful, fearing and envying Romulus, considered that they ought not to remain quiet, but ought to check the growth of Rome. First the Etruscans of Veii, a people possessed of wide lands and a large city, began the war by demanding the surrender to them of Fidenae, which they claimed as belonging to them. This demand was not only unjust, but absurd, seeing that they had not assisted the people of Fidenae when they were fighting and in danger, but permitted them to be destroyed, and then demanded their houses and lands, when they were in the possession of others. Receiving a haughty answer from Romulus, they divided themselves into two bodies, with one of which they attacked Fidenae, and with the other went to meet Romulus. At Fidenae they conquered the Romans, and slew two thousand; but they were defeated by Romulus, with a loss of eight thousand men. A second battle now took place at Fidenae, in which all agree that Romulus took the most important part, showing the greatest skill and courage, and a strength and swiftness more than mortal. But some accounts are altogether fabulous, such as that fourteen hundred were slain, more than half of whom Romulus slew with his own hand. The Messenians appear to use equally inflated language about Aristomenes, when they tell us that he thrice offered sacrifice for having slain a hundred Lacedaemonians. After the victory, Romulus did not pursue the beaten army, but marched straight to the city of Veii. The citizens, after so great a disaster, made no resistance, but at their own request were granted a treaty and alliance for a hundred years, giving up a large portion of their territory, called the Septem Pagi, or seven districts, and their saltworks by the river, and handing over fifty of their leading men as hostages.

For his success at Veii, Romulus enjoyed another triumph, on the Ides of October, when he led in his train many captives, amongst whom was the Veientine general, an old man, who was thought to have mismanaged matters foolishly and like a boy. On this account to this day, when a sacrifice is made for victory, they lead an old man through the Forum and up to the Capitol, dressed in a boy's robe with wide purple border, and with a child's bulla hung round his neck; and the herald calls out "Sardinians for sale." For the Tyrrhenians or Tuscans are said to be of Sardinian origin, and Veii is a Tyrrhenian city.

XXVI. This was Romulus's last war. After it, he, like nearly all those who have risen to power and fame by a great and unexpected series of successes, became filled with self-confidence and arrogance, and, in place of his former popular manners, assumed the offensive style of a despot. He wore a purple tunic, and a toga with a purple border, and did business reclining instead of sitting on a throne; and was always attended by the band of youths called Celeres, from their quickness in service. Others walked before him with staves to keep off the crowd, and were girt with thongs, with which to bind any one whom he might order into custody. The Latins used formerly to call to bind ligare, and now call it alligare; wherefore the staff-bearers are called lictors, and their staves are called bacula, from the rods which they then carried. It is probable that these officers now called lictors by the insertion of the c, were originally called litors, that is, in Greek, leitourgoi (public officials). For to this day the Greeks call a town-hall leitus, and the people laos.

XXVII. When Romulus' grandfather Numitor died in Alba, although he was evidently his heir, yet through a desire for popularity he left his claim unsettled, and contented himself with appointing a chief magistrate for the people of Alba every year; thus teaching the Roman nobles to desire a freer constitution, which should not be so much encroached upon by the king. For at Rome now even the so-called Fathers took no part in public affairs, but had merely their name and dignity, and were called into the Senate House more for form's sake than to express their opinions. When there, they listened in silence to Romulus's orders, and the only advantage which they possessed over the commons was that they knew the king's mind sooner than they. Worst of all was, that he of his own authority divided the land which was obtained in war amongst the soldiers, and restored the hostages to the Veientines, against the will of the Senate and without consulting it, by which he seemed purposely to insult it. On this account the Senate was suspected, when shortly after this he miraculously disappeared. His disappearance took place on the Nones of the month now called July, but then Quintilis, leaving nothing certain or agreed on about his end except the date. Even now things happen in the same fashion as then; and we need not wonder at the uncertainty about the death of Romulus, when that of Scipio Africanus, in his own house after supper, proved so inexplicable, some saying that it arose from an evil habit of body, some that he had poisoned himself, some that his enemies had suffocated him during the night. And yet the corpse of Scipio lay openly exposed for all to see, and gave all who saw it some ground for their conjectures; whereas Romulus suddenly disappeared, and no morsel of his body or shred of his garments were ever seen again. Some supposed that the Senators fell upon him in the Temple of Vulcan, and, after killing him cut his body in pieces and each of them carried off one in the folds of his robe. Others think that his disappearance took place neither in the Temple of Vulcan, nor yet in the presence of the Senators alone, but say that Romulus was holding an assembly without the city, near a place called the Goat's Marsh, when suddenly strange and wonderful things took place in the heavens, and marvellous changes; for the sun's light was extinguished, and night fell, not calm and quiet, but with terrible thunderings, gusts of wind, and driving spray from all quarters. Hereupon the people took to flight in confusion, but the nobles collected together by themselves. When the storm was over, and the light returned, the people returned to the place again, and searched in vain for Romulus, but were told by the nobles not to trouble themselves to look for him, but to pray to Romulus and reverence him, for he had been caught up into heaven, and now would be a propitious god for them instead of a good king.

The people believed this story, and went their way rejoicing, and praying to him with good hope; but there were some who discussed the whole question in a harsh and unfriendly spirit, and blamed the nobles for encouraging the people to such acts of folly when they themselves were the murderers of the king.

XXVIII. Now Julius Proculus, one of the noblest patricians, and of good reputation, being one of the original colonists from Alba, and a friend and companion of Romulus, came into the Forum, and there upon his oath, and touching the most sacred things, stated before all men that as he was walking along the road Romulus appeared, meeting him, more beautiful and taller than he had ever appeared before, with bright and glittering arms. Astonished at the vision he had spoken thus: "O king, for what reason or with what object have you left us exposed to an unjust and hateful suspicion, and left the whole city desolate and plunged in the deepest grief?" He answered, "It pleased the gods, Proculus, that I should spend thus much time among mankind, and after founding a city of the greatest power and glory should return to heaven whence I came. Fare thee well; and tell the Romans that by courage and self-control they will attain to the highest pitch of human power. I will ever be for you the kindly deity Quirinus."

This tale was believed by the Romans from the manner of Proculus in relating it and from his oath: indeed a religious feeling almost amounting to ecstasy seems to have taken hold of all present; for no one contradicted him, but all dismissed their suspicions entirely from their minds and prayed to Quirinus, worshipping him as a god.

This account resembles the Greek legends of Aristeas of Proconnesus, and that of Kleomedes of Astypalaea. The story goes that Aristeas died in a fuller's shop, and that when his friends came to fetch his body it had disappeared; then some persons who had just returned from travel said that they had met Aristeas walking along the road to Kroton. Kleomedes, we are told, was a man of unusual size and strength, but stupid and half-crazy, who did many deeds of violence, and at last in a boy's school struck and broke in two the column that supported the roof, and brought it down. As the boys were killed, Kleomedes, pursued by the people, got into a wooden chest, and shut down the lid, holding in inside so that many men together were not able to force it open. They broke open the chest, and found no man in it, dead or alive. Astonished at this, they sent an embassy to the oracle at Delphi, to whom the Pythia answered,

"Last of the heroes is Kleomedes of Astypalaea."

And it also related that the corpse of Alkmena when it was being carried out for burial, disappeared, and a stone was found lying on the bier in its place. And many such stories are told, in which, contrary to reason, the earthly parts of our bodies are described as being deified together with the spiritual parts. It is wicked and base to deny that virtue is a spiritual quality, but again it is foolish to mix earthly with heavenly things.

We must admit, speaking with due caution, that, as Pindar has it, the bodies of all men follow overpowering Death, but there remains a living spirit, the image of eternity, for it alone comes from heaven. Thence it comes, and thither it returns again, not accompanied by the body, but only when it is most thoroughly separated and cleansed from it, and become pure and incorporeal. This is the pure spirit which Herakleitus calls the best, which darts through the body like lightning through a cloud, whereas that which is clogged by the body is like a dull, cloudy exhalation, hard to loose and free from the bonds of the body. There is no reason, therefore, for supposing that the bodies of good men rise up into heaven, which is contrary to nature; but we must believe that men's virtues and their spirits most certainly, naturally and rightly proceed from mankind to the heroes, and from them to the genii, and from thence, if they be raised above and purified from all mortal and earthly taint, even as is done in the holy mysteries, then, not by any empty vote of the senate, but in very truth and likelihood they are received among the gods, and meet with the most blessed and glorious end.

XXIX. Some say that the name Quirinus, which Romulus received, means Mars; others that it was because his people were called Quirites. Others, again, say that the spear-head or spear was called by the ancients Quiris, and that the statue of Juno leaning on a spear is called Juno Quirites, and that the dart which is placed in the Regia is addressed as Mars, and that it is customary to present with a spear those who have distinguished themselves in war, and therefore that it was as a warrior, or god of war, that Romulus was called Quirinus. A temple dedicated to him is built on the Quirinal Hill which bears his name, and the day of his translation is called the People's Flight, and the Nonae Caprotinae, because they go out of the city to the Goat's Marsh on that day to sacrifice, for in Latin a goat is called Capra. And as they go to the sacrifice they call out many of the names of the country, as Marcus, Lucius, Caius, with loud shouts, in imitation of their panic on that occasion, and their calling to each other in fear and confusion. But some say that this is not an imitation of terror, but of eagerness, and that this is the reason of it: after the Gauls had captured Rome and been driven out by Camillus, and the city through weakness did not easily recover itself, an army of Latins, under one Livius Postumius, marched upon it. He halted his army not far from Rome, and sent a herald to say that the Latins were willing to renew their old domestic ties, which had fallen into disuse, and to unite the races by new intermarriage. If, therefore, the Romans would send out to them all their maidens and unmarried women, they would live with them on terms of peace and friendship, as the Romans had long before done with the

Sabines. The Romans, when they heard this, were afraid of going to war, yet thought that the surrender of their women was no better than captivity. While they were in perplexity, a female slave named Philotis, or according to some Tutola, advised them to do neither, but by a stratagem to avoid both war and surrender of the women. This stratagem was that they should dress Philotis and the best looking of the other female slaves like free women, and send them to the enemy; then at night Philotis said she would raise a torch, and the Romans should come under arms and fall upon the sleeping enemy. This was done, and terms were made with the Latins. Philotis raised the torch upon a certain fig-tree with leaves which spread all round and behind, in such a manner that the light could not be seen by the enemy, but was clearly seen by the Romans. When they saw it, they immediately rushed out, calling frequently for each other at the various gates in their eagerness. As they fell unexpectedly upon the enemy, they routed them, and keep the day as a feast. Therefore the Nones are called Caprotinae because of the fig-tree, which the Romans call caprificus, and the women are feasted out of doors, under the shade of fig-tree boughs. And the female slaves assemble and play, and afterwards beat and throw stones at each other, as they did then, when they helped the Romans to fight. These accounts are admitted by but few historians, and indeed the calling out one another's names in the daytime, and walking down to the Goats' Marsh seems more applicable to the former story, unless, indeed, both of these events happened on the same day.

Romulus is said to have been fifty-four years old, and to be in the thirty-eighth year of his reign when he disappeared from the world.

Comparison of Theseus and Romulus.

I. The above are all the noteworthy particulars which we have been able to collect about Theseus and Romulus. It seems, in the first place, that Theseus of his own free will, and without any compulsion, when he might have reigned peacefully in Troezen, where he was heir to the kingdom, no mean one, longed to accomplish heroic deeds: whereas Romulus was an exile, and in the position of a slave; the fear of death was hanging over him if unsuccessful, and so, as Plato says, he was made brave by sheer terror, and through fear of suffering death and torture was forced into doing great exploits. Moreover, Romulus's greatest achievement was the slaying of one man, the despot of Alba, whereas Skeiron, Sinis, Prokrustes, and Korynetes were merely the accompaniments and prelude to the greater actions of Theseus, and by slaying them he freed Greece from terrible scourges, before those whom he saved even knew who he was. He also might have sailed peacefully over the sea to Athens, and had no trouble with those brigands, whereas Romulus could not be free from trouble while Amulius lived. And it is a great argument in favour of Theseus that he attacked those wicked men for the sake of others, having himself suffered no wrong at their hands; whereas the twins were unconcerned at Amulius's tyranny so long as it did not affect themselves. And although it may have been a great exploit to receive a wound in fighting the Sabines, and to slay Acron, and to kill many enemies in battle, yet we may compare with these, on Theseus's behalf, his battle with the Centaurs and his campaign against the Amazons. As for the courage which Theseus showed in the matter of the Cretan tribute, when he voluntarily sailed to Crete with the youths and maidens, whether the penalty was to be given to the Minotaur to eat, or be sacrificed at the tomb of Androgeus, or even to be cast into dishonoured slavery under an insolent enemy, which is the least miserable fate mentioned by any writer, what a strength of mind, what public spirit and love of fame it shows! In this instance it seems to me that philosophers have truly defined love as a "service designed by the gods for the care and preservation of the young." For the love of Ariadne seems to have been specially intended by Heaven to save Theseus; nor need we blame her for her passion, but rather wonder that all men and women did not share it. If she alone felt it, then I say she deserved the love of a god, because of her zeal for all that is best and noblest.

II. Both were born statesmen, yet neither behaved himself as a king should do, but, from similar motives, the one erred on the side of democracy, the other on that of despotism. The first duty of a king is to preserve his crown; and this can be effected as well by refraining from improperly extending his rights as by too great eagerness to keep them. For he who either gives up or overstrains his prerogative ceases to be a king or constitutional ruler, but becomes either a despot or demagogue; and in the one case is feared, in the other despised by his subjects. Still the one is the result of kindliness of disposition, and the other that of selfishness and ferocity.

III. If we are not to attribute their misfortunes to chance, but to peculiarities of disposition, then we cannot acquit Romulus of blame in his treatment of his brother, nor Theseus in that of his son; but the greatest excuse must be made for the one who acted under the greatest provocation. One would not have thought that Romulus would have flown into such a passion during a grave deliberation on matters of state; while Theseus was misled, in his treatment of his son, by love and jealousy and a woman's slander, influences which few men are able to withstand. And what is more, Romulus's fury resulted in actual deeds of unfortunate result; whereas the anger of Theseus spent itself in words and an old man's curses, and the youth seems to have owed the rest of his suffering to chance; so here, at any rate, one would give one's vote for Theseus.

IV. Romulus, however, has the credit of having started with the most slender resources, and yet of having succeeded. The twins were called slaves and the sons of a swineherd before they achieved their liberty; yet they freed nearly all the Latin race, and at one and the same time gained those titles which are the most glorious among men, of slayers of their enemies, preservers of their own house, kings of their own nation, and founders of a new city, not by transferring the population of old ones, as Theseus did, when he brought together many towns into one, and destroyed many cities that bore the names of kings and heroes of old. Romulus did this afterwards, when he compelled his conquered enemies to cast down and obliterate their own dwellings, and become fellow-citizens with their conquerors; yet at first he did not change the site of his city nor increase it, but starting with nothing to help him, he obtained for himself territory, patrimony, sovereignty, family, marriage, and relatives, and he killed no one, but conferred great benefits on those who, instead of homeless vagrants, wished to become a people and inhabitants of a city. He slew no brigands or robbers, but he conquered kingdoms, took cities, and triumphed over kings and princes.

V. As for the misfortune of Remus, it seems doubtful whether Romulus slew him with his own hand, as most writers attribute the act to others. He certainly rescued his mother from death, and gloriously replaced his grandfather, whom he found in an ignoble and servile position, on the throne of Aeneas. He did him many kindnesses, and never harmed him even against his will. But I can scarcely imagine that Theseus's forgetfulness and carelessness in hoisting the black sail can, by any excuses or before the mildest judges, come much short of parricide: indeed, an Athenian, seeing how hard it is even for his admirers to exculpate him, has made up a story that Aegeus, when the ship was approaching, hurriedly ran up to the acropolis to view it, and fell down, as though he were unattended, or would hurry along the road to the shore without servants.

VI. The crimes of Theseus in carrying off women are without any decent excuse; first, because he did it so often, for he carried off Ariadne and Antiope and Anaxo of Troezen, and above all when he was an old man he carried off Helen, when she was not yet grown up, and a mere child, though he was past the age for even legitimate marriage. Besides, there was no reason for it, for these Troezenian, Laconian, and Amazonian maidens, besides their not being betrothed to him, were no worthier mothers for his children than the Athenian daughters of Erechtheus and Kekrops would have been, so we must suspect that these acts were done out of mere riotous wantonness.

Now Romulus, though he carried off nearly eight hundred women, yet kept only one, Hersilia, for himself, and distributed the others among the unmarried citizens; and afterwards, by the respect, love, and justice with which he treated them, proved that his wrongful violence was the most admirable and politic contrivance for effecting the union of the two nations. By means of it he welded them into one, and made it the starting-point of harmony at home and strength abroad. The dignity, love, and permanence with which he invested the institution of marriage is proved by the fact that during two hundred and thirty years no man separated from his wife or woman from her husband; but, just as in Greece, very exact persons can mention the first instance of parricide or matricide, so all the Romans know that Spurius Carvilius was the first who put away his wife, upon a charge of barrenness. Events also testify to the superior wisdom of Romulus, for, in consequence of that intermarriage, the two kings and the two races shared the empire, whereas, from the marriage of Theseus, the Athenians obtained no alliance or intercourse with any nation, but only hatreds and wars and deaths of citizens and at last the destruction of Aphidnae, and they themselves escaped from the fate which Paris brought upon Troy, only by the mercy of their enemies and their own entreaties and supplications. The mother of Theseus, not nearly but quite, suffered the fate of Hekuba, who was abandoned and given up by her son, unless the story of her captivity is false, as I hope it is, together with much of the rest.

Also the religious part of their histories makes a great distinction between them. For Romulus's success was due to the great favour of Heaven, whereas the oracle given to Aegeus, to refrain from all women in foreign parts, seems to argue that the birth of Theseus took place contrary to the will of the gods.

Life of Lykurgus.

I. With regard to Lykurgus the lawgiver there is nothing whatever that is undisputed; as his birth, his travels, his death, and, besides all this, his legislation, have all been related in various ways; and also the dates of his birth do not in any way accord. Some say that he was contemporary with Iphitus, and with him settled the conditions of the Olympic truce; and among these is Aristotle the philosopher, who adduces as a proof of it the quoit which is at Olympia, on which the name of Lykurgus is still preserved. Others, among them Eratosthenes and Apollodorus, by computing the reigns of the kings of Sparta, prove that he must have lived many years before the first Olympiad. Timaeus conjectures that there were two men of the name of Lykurgus in Sparta at different times, and that the deeds of both are attributed to one of them, on account of his celebrity. The elder, he thinks, must have lived not far off the time of Homer; indeed some say that he came into the presence of Homer. Xenophon gives an idea of his antiquity when he speaks of him as living in the time of the Herakleidae. By descent of course the last kings of Sparta are Herakleidae, but he appears to mean by Herakleid-ae the earliest of all, who were next to Herakles himself.

However, in spite of these discrepancies, we will endeavour, by following the least inconsistent accounts and the best known authorities, to write the history of his life. Simonides the poet tells us that the father of Lykurgus was not Eunomus, but Prytanis. But most writers do not deduce his genealogy thus, but say that Soüs was the son of Prokles, and grandson of Aristodemus, and that Soüs begat Euripus; Euripus, Prytanis, and Prytanis, Eunomus. Eunomus had two sons, Polydektes by his first wife, and Lykurgus by his second wife Dionassa, which makes him, according to Dieutychides, sixth in descent from Prokles, and eleventh from Herakles.

II. The most remarkable of his ancestors was Soüs, in whose reign the Spartans enslaved the Helots, and annexed a large portion of Arcadia. It is said that Soüs once was besieged by the Kleitorians, in a fort where there was no water, and was compelled to conclude a treaty to restore the territory in dispute, if he and his men were permitted to drink at the nearest spring. After this had been agreed upon, he called his men together, and offered his kingdom to any one who could refrain from drinking. But as no one could do this, but all drank, last of all he himself came down to the spring, and in the presence of the enemy merely sprinkled his face with the water, and marched off, refusing to restore the disputed territory, on the ground that all did not drink. But though he gained great fame by this, yet it was not he but his son Eurypon who gave the name of Eurypontidae to the family, because Eurypon was the first to relax the despotic traditions of his family and render his government more popular with the people. But as a consequence of this the people were encouraged to demand more freedom, and great confusion and lawlessness prevailed in Sparta for a long time, because some of the kings opposed the people and so became odious, while others were found to yield to them, either to preserve their popularity, or from sheer weakness of character. It was during this period of disorder that the father of Lykurgus lost his life. He was endeavouring to part two men who were quarrelling, and was killed by a blow from a cook's chopper, leaving the kingdom to his elder son Polydektes.

III. He also died after a short time, and, as all thought, Lykurgus ought to have been the next king. And he did indeed reign until his brother's wife was found to be pregnant; but as soon as he heard this, he surrendered the crown to the child, if it should be a boy, and merely administered the kingdom as guardian for the child. The Lacedaemonian name for the guardian of a royal orphan is prodikus. Now the queen made a secret proposal to him, that she should destroy her infant and that they should live together as king and queen. Though disgusted at her wickedness, he did not reject the proposal, but pretended to approve of it. He said that she must not risk her life and injure her health by procuring abortion, but that he would undertake to do away with the child. Thus he deluded her until her confinement, at which time he sent officials and guards into her chamber with orders to hand the child over to the women if it was a girl, and to bring it to him, whatever he might be doing, if it was a boy. He happened to be dining with the archons when a male child was born, and the servants brought it to him. He is said to have taken the child and said to those present, "A king is born to you, O Spartans," and to have laid him down in the royal seat and named him Charilaus, because all men were full of joy admiring his spirit and justice. He was king for eight months in all; and was much looked up to by the citizens, who rendered a willing obedience to him, rather because of his eminent virtues than because he was regent with royal powers. There was, nevertheless, a faction which grudged him his elevation, and tried to oppose him, as he was a young man.

They consisted chiefly of the relatives and friends of the queen-mother, who considered that she had been insultingly treated, and her brother Leonidas once went so far in his abusive language as to hint to Lykurgus that he knew that he meant to be king, throwing the suspicion upon Lykurgus, if anything should happen to the child, that he would be supposed to have managed it. This sort of language was used by the queen-mother also, and he, grieved and alarmed, decided to avoid all suspicion by leaving the country and travelling until his nephew should be grown up and have an heir born to succeed him.

IV. With this intention he set sail, and first came to Crete, where he studied the constitution and mixed with the leading statesmen. Some part of their laws he approved and made himself master of, with the intention of adopting them on his return home, while with others he was dissatisfied. One of the men who had a reputation there for learning and state-craft he made his friend, and induced him to go to Sparta. This was Thales, who was thought to be merely a lyric poet, and who used this art to conceal his graver acquirements, being in reality deeply versed in legislation. His poems were exhortations to unity and concord in verse, breathing a spirit of calm and order, which insensibly civilised their hearers and by urging them to the pursuit of honourable objects led them to lay aside the feelings of party strife so prevalent in Sparta; so that he may be said in some degree to have educated the people and prepared them to receive the reforms of Lykurgus.

From Crete Lykurgus sailed to Asia Minor, wishing, it is said, to contrast the thrifty and austere mode of life of the Cretans with the extravagance and luxury of the Ionians, as a physician compares healthy and diseased bodies, and to note the points of difference in the two states. There, it seems, he first met with the poems of Homer, which were preserved by the descendants of Kreophylus, and observing that they were no less useful for politics and education than for relaxation and pleasure, he eagerly copied and compiled them, with the intention of bringing them home with him. There was already some dim idea of the existence of these poems among the Greeks, but few possessed any portions of them, as they were scattered in fragments, but Lykurgus first made them known. The Egyptians suppose that Lykurgus visited them also, and that he especially admired their institution of a separate caste of warriors. This he transferred to Sparta, and, by excluding working men and the lower classes from the government, made the city a city indeed, pure from all admixture. Some Greek writers corroborate the Egyptians in this, but as to Lykurgus having visited Libya and Iberia, or his journey to India and meeting with the Gymnosophists, or naked philosophers, there, no one that we know of tells this except the Spartan Aristokrates, the son of Hipparchus.

V. During Lykurgus's absence the Lacedaemonians regretted him and sent many embassies to ask him to return, telling him that their kings had indeed the royal name and state, but nothing else to distinguish them from the common people, and that he alone had the spirit of a ruler and the power to influence men's minds. Even the kings desired his presence, as they hoped that he would assist in establishing their authority and would render the masses less insolent. Returning to a people in this condition, he at once began alterations and reforms on a sweeping scale, considering that it was useless and unprofitable to do such work by halves, but that, as in the case of a diseased body, the original cause of the disorder must be burned out or purged away, and the patient begin an entirely new life. After reflecting on this, he made a journey to Delphi. Here he sacrificed to the god, and, on consulting the oracle, received that celebrated answer in which the Pythia speaks of him as beloved by the gods, and a god rather than a man, and when he asked for a good system of laws, answered that the god gives him what will prove by far the best of all constitutions. Elated by this he collected the leading men and begged them to help him, first by talking privately to his own friends, and thus little by little obtaining a hold over more men and banding them together for the work. When the time was ripe for the attempt, he bade thirty of the nobles go into the market-place early in the morning completely armed, in order to overawe the opposition. The names of twenty of the most distinguished of these men have been preserved by Hermippus, but the man who took the greatest part in all Lykurgus's works, and who helped him in establishing his laws, was Arthmiades. At first King Charilaus was terrified at the confusion, imagining that a revolt had broken out against himself, and fled for refuge to the temple of Minerva of the Brazen House; but, afterward reassured and having received solemn pledges for his safety, returned and took part in their proceedings. He was of a gentle nature, as is proved by the words of his colleague, King Archelaus, who, when some were praising the youth, said, "How can Charilaus be a good man, if he is not harsh even to wicked men?"

Of Lykurgus's many reforms, the first and most important was the establishment of the Council of Elders, which Plato says by its admixture cooled the high fever of royalty, and, having an equal vote with the kings on vital points, gave caution and sobriety to their deliberations. For the state, which had hitherto been wildly oscillating between despotism on the one hand and democracy on the other, now, by the establishment of the Council of the Elders, found a firm footing between these extremes, and was able to preserve a most equable balance, as the eight-and-twenty elders would lend the kings their support in the suppression of democracy, but would use the people to suppress any tendency to despotism. Twenty-eight is the number of

Elders mentioned by Aristotle, because of the thirty leading men who took the part of Lykurgus two deserted their post through fear. But Sphairus says that those who shared his opinions were twenty-eight originally. A reason may be found in twenty-eight being a mystic number, formed by seven multiplied by four, and being the first perfect number after six, for like that, it is equal to all its parts. But I think that he probably made this number of elders, in order that with the two kings the council might consist of thirty members in all.

VI. Lykurgus was so much interested in this council as to obtain from Delphi an oracle about it, called the rhetra, which runs as follows: "After you have built a temple to Zeus of Greece and Athene of Greece, and have divided the people into tribes and obes, you shall found a council of thirty, including the chiefs, and shall from season to season apellazein the people between Babyka and Knakion, and there propound measures and divide upon them, and the people shall have the casting vote and final decision." In these words tribes and obes are divisions into which the people were to be divided; the chiefs mean the kings; apellazein means to call an assembly, in allusion to Apollo, to whom the whole scheme of the constitution is referred. Babyka and Knakion they now call Oinous; but Aristotle says that Knakion is a river and Babyka a bridge. Between these they held their assemblies, without any roof or building of any kind; for Lykurgus did not consider that deliberations were assisted by architecture, but rather hindered, as men's heads were thereby filled with vain unprofitable fancies, when they assemble for debate in places where they can see statues and paintings, or the proscenium of a theatre, or the richly ornamented roof of a council chamber. When the people were assembled, he permitted no one to express an opinion; but the people was empowered to decide upon motions brought forward by the kings and elders. But in later times, as the people made additions and omissions, and so altered the sense of the motions before them, the kings, Polydorus and Theopompus, added these words to the rhetra, "and if the people shall decide crookedly, the chiefs and elders shall set it right." That is, they made the people no longer supreme, but practically excluded them from any voice in public affairs, on the ground that they judged wrongly. However these kings persuaded the city that this also was ordained by the god. This is mentioned by Tyrtaeus in the following verses:

"They heard the god, and brought from Delphi home, Apollo's oracle, which thus did say: That over all within fair Sparta's realm The royal chiefs in council should bear sway, The elders next to them, the people last; If they the holy rhetra would obey."

VII. Though Lykurgus had thus mixed the several powers of the state, yet his successors, seeing that the powers of the oligarchy were unimpaired, and that it was, as Plato calls it, full of life and vigour, placed as a curb to it the power of the Ephors. The first Ephors, of whom Elatus was one, were elected about a hundred and thirty years after Lykurgus, in the reign of Theopompus. This king is said to have been blamed by his wife because he would transmit to his children a less valuable crown than he had received, to which he answered: "Nay, more valuable, because more lasting." In truth, by losing the odium of absolute power, the King of Sparta escaped all danger of being dethroned, as those of Argos and Messene were by their subjects, because they would abate nothing of their despotic power. The wisdom of Lykurgus became clearly manifest to those who witnessed the revolutions and miseries of the Argives and Messenians, who were neighbouring states and of the same race as the Spartans, who, originally starting on equal terms with them, and indeed seeming in the allotment of their territories to have some advantage, yet did not long live happily, but the insolent pride of the kings and the unruly temper of the people together resulted in a revolution, which clearly proved that the checked and balanced constitution established among the Spartans was a divine blessing for them. But of this more hereafter.

VIII. The second and the boldest of Lykurgus's reforms was the redistribution of the land. Great inequalities existed, many poor and needy people had become a burden to the state, while wealth had got into a very few hands. Lykurgus abolished all the mass of pride, envy, crime, and luxury which flowed from those old and more terrible evils of riches and poverty, by inducing all land-owners to offer their estates for redistribution, and prevailing upon them to live on equal terms one with another, and with equal incomes, striving only to surpass each other in courage and virtue, there being henceforth no social inequalities among them except such as praise or blame can create.

Putting his proposals immediately into practice, he divided the outlying lands of the state among the Perioeki, in thirty thousand lots, and that immediately adjoining the metropolis among the native Spartans, in nine thousand lots, for to that number they then amounted. Some say that Lykurgus made six thousand lots, and that Polydorus added three thousand afterwards; others that he added half the nine thousand, and that only half was allotted by Lykurgus.

Each man's lot was of such a size as to supply a man with seventy medimni of barley, and his wife with twelve, and oil and wine in proportion; for thus much he thought ought to suffice them, as the food was enough to maintain them in health, and they wanted nothing more. It is said that, some years afterwards, as he was returning from a journey through the country at harvest-time, when he saw the sheaves of corn lying in equal parallel rows, he smiled, and said to his companions that all Laconia seemed as if it had just been divided among so many brothers.

IX. He desired to distribute furniture also, in order completely to do away with inequality; but, seeing that actually to take away these things would be a most unpopular measure, he managed by a different method to put an end to all ostentation in these matters. First of all he abolished the use of gold and silver money, and made iron money alone legal; and this he made of great size and weight, and small value, so that the equivalent for ten minae required a great room for its stowage, and a yoke of oxen to draw it. As soon as this was established, many sorts of crime became unknown in Lacedaemon. For who would steal or take as a bribe or deny that he possessed or take by force a mass of iron which he could not conceal, which no one envied him for possessing, which he could not even break up and so make use of; for the iron when hot was, it is said, quenched in vinegar, so as to make it useless, by rendering it brittle and hard to work?

After this, he ordered a general expulsion of the workers in useless trades. Indeed, without this, most of them must have left the country when the ordinary currency came to an end, as they would not be able to sell their wares: for the iron money was not current among other Greeks, and had no value, being regarded as ridiculous; so that it could not be used for the purchase of foreign trumpery, and no cargo was shipped for a Laconian port, and there came into the country no sophists, no vagabond soothsayers, no panders, no goldsmiths or workers in silver plate, because there was no money to pay them with. Luxury, thus cut off from all encouragement, gradually became extinct; and the rich were on the same footing with other people, as they could find no means of display, but were forced to keep their money idle at home. For this reason such things as are useful and necessary, like couches and tables and chairs, were made there better than anywhere else, and the Laconian cup, we are told by Kritias, was especially valued for its use in the field. Its colour prevented the drinker being disgusted by the look of the dirty water which it is sometimes necessary to drink, and it was contrived that the dirt was deposited inside the cup and stuck to the bottom, so as to make the drink cleaner than it would otherwise have been. These things were due to the lawgiver; for the workmen, who were not allowed to make useless things, devoted their best workmanship to useful ones.

X. Wishing still further to put down luxury and take away the desire for riches, he introduced the third and the most admirable of his reforms, that of the common dining-table. At this the people were to meet and dine together upon a fixed allowance of food, and not to live in their own homes, lolling on expensive couches at rich tables, fattened like beasts in private by the hands of servants and cooks, and undermining their health by indulgence to excess in every bodily desire, long sleep, warm baths, and much repose, so that they required a sort of daily nursing like sick people. This was a great advantage, but it was a greater to render wealth valueless, and, as Theophrastus says, to neutralise it by their common dining-table and the simplicity of their habits. Wealth could not be used, nor enjoyed, nor indeed displayed at all in costly apparatus, when the poor man dined at the same table with the rich; so that the well-known saying, that "wealth is blind and lies like a senseless log," was seen to be true in Sparta alone of all cities under heaven. Men were not even allowed to dine previously at home, and then come to the public table, but the others, watching him who did not eat or drink with them, would reproach him as a sensual person, too effeminate to eat the rough common fare.

For these reasons it is said that the rich were bitterly opposed to Lykurgus on this question, and that they caused a tumult and attacked him with shouts of rage. Pelted with stones from many hands, he was forced to run out of the market-place, and take sanctuary in a temple. He outstripped all his pursuers except one, a hot-tempered and spirited youth named Alkander, who came up with him, and striking him with a club as he turned round, knocked out his eye. Lykurgus paid no heed to the pain, but stood facing the citizens and showed them his face streaming with blood, and his eye destroyed. All who saw him were filled with shame and remorse. They gave up Alkander to his mercy, and conducted him in procession to his own house, to show their sympathy. Lykurgus thanked them and dismissed them, but took Alkander home with him. He did him no harm and used no reproachful words, but sent away all his servants and bade him serve him. Alkander, being of a generous nature, did as he was ordered, and, dwelling as he did with Lykurgus, watching his kind unruffled temper, his severe simplicity of life, and his unwearied labours, he became enthusiastic in his admiration of him, and used to tell his friends and acquaintances that Lykurgus, far from being harsh or overbearing, was the kindest and gentlest of men. Thus was Alkander tamed and subdued, so that he who had been a wicked and insolent youth was made into a modest and prudent man.

As a memorial of his misfortune, Lykurgus built the temple of Athene, whom he called Optilitis, for the Dorians in that country call the eyes optiloi.

Some writers, however, among whom is Dioskorides, who wrote an 'Account of the Spartan Constitution,' say that Lykurgus was struck upon the eye, but not blinded, and that he built this temple as a thank-offering to the goddess for his recovery.

At any rate, it was in consequence of his mishap that the Spartans discontinued the habit of carrying staffs when they met in council.

XI. The Cretans call this institution of taking meals in common andreia, which means men's repast; but the Lacedaemonians call it phiditia, which can either be explained as another form of philia, friendship, putting a d for an l, from the friendly feelings which prevailed at them, or else because it accustomed them to frugality, which is called pheido. Possibly the first letter was an addition, and the word may have originally been editia, from edodé, food.

They formed themselves into messes of fifteen, more or less. Each member contributed per month a medimnus of barley, eight measures of wine, five minas' weight of cheese, and half as much of figs; and in addition to this a very small sum of money to buy fish and other luxuries for a relish to the bread. This was all, except when a man had offered a sacrifice, or been hunting, and sent a portion to the public table. For persons were allowed to dine at home whenever they were late for dinner in consequence of a sacrifice or a hunting expedition, but the rest of the company had to be present. This custom of eating in common lasted for very many years. When King Agis returned from his victorious campaign against the Athenians, and wished to dine at home with his wife, he sent for his share of the public dinner, and the polemarchs refused to let him have it. As next day, through anger, he did not offer the customary sacrifice, they fined him. Boys were taken to the public tables, as though they were schools of good manners; and there they listened to discourses on politics, and saw models of gentlemanly behaviour, and learned how to jest with one another, joking without vulgarity, and being made the subjects of jokes without losing their temper. Indeed, it was considered peculiarly Laconian to be able to take a joke; however, if the victim could not, he was entitled to ask that it should go no farther. As they came in, the eldest present said to each man, pointing to the door, "Through this no tale passes."

It is said that they voted for a new member of a mess in this manner. Each man took a piece of bread crumb and threw it in silence into a vessel, which a servant carried on his head. Those who voted for the new member threw in their bread as it was, those who voted against, crushed it flat in their hands. If even one of these crushed pieces be found, they rejected the candidate, as they wished all members of the society to be friendly. The candidate was said to be rejected by the kaddichus, which is their name for the bowl into which the bread is thrown.

The "black broth" was the most esteemed of their luxuries, insomuch that the elder men did not care for any meat, but always handed it over to the young, and regaled themselves on this broth. It is related that, in consequence of the celebrity of this broth, one of the kings of Pontus obtained a Laconian cook, but when he tasted it he did not like it. His cook thereupon said, "O king, those who eat this broth must first bathe in the Eurotas." After drinking wine in moderation the guests separate, without any torches; for it is not permitted to walk with a light on this or any other occasion, in order that they may accustom themselves to walk fearlessly and safely in the dark. This then is the way in which the common dining-tables are managed.

XII. Lykurgus did not establish any written laws; indeed, this is distinctly forbidden by one of the so-called Rhetras.

He thought that the principles of most importance for the prosperity and honour of the state would remain most securely fixed if implanted in the citizens by habit and training, as they would then be followed from choice rather than necessity; for his method of education made each of them into a lawgiver like himself. The trifling conventions of everyday life were best left undefined by hard-and-fast laws, so that they might from time to time receive corrections or additions from men educated in the spirit of the Lacedaemonian system. On this education the whole scheme of Lykurgus's laws depended. One rhetra, as we have seen, forbade the use of written laws. Another was directed against expenditure, and ordered that the roof of every house should consist of beams worked with the axe, and that the doors should be worked with the saw alone, and with no other tools. Lykurgus was the first to perceive the truth which Epameinondas is said in later times to have uttered about his own table, when he said that "such a dinner has no room for treachery." He saw that such a house as that has no place for luxury and expense, and that there is no man so silly and tasteless as to bring couches with silver feet, purple hangings, or golden goblets into a simple peasant's house, but that he would be forced to make his furniture match the house, and his clothes match his furniture, and so on. In consequence of this it is said that the elder Leotychides when dining in Corinth, after looking at a costly panelled ceiling, asked his host whether the trees grew square in that country. A third rhetra of Lykurgus is mentioned, which forbids the Spartans to make war frequently with the same people, lest by constant practice they too should become warlike. And this especial accusation was subsequently brought against King Agesilaus in later times, that, by his frequent and long-continued invasions of Boeotia, he made the Thebans a match for the Lacedaemonians; for which cause Antalkidas, when he saw him wounded, said, "The Thebans pay you well for having taught them to fight, which they were neither willing nor able to do before."

Maxims of this sort they call rhetras, which are supposed to have a divine origin and sanction.

XIII. Considering education to be the most important and the noblest work of a lawgiver, he began at the very beginning, and regulated marriages and the birth of children. It is not true that, as Aristotle says, he endeavoured to regulate the lives of the women, and failed, being foiled by the liberty and habits of command which they had acquired by the long absences of their husbands on military expeditions, during which they were necessarily left in sole charge at home, wherefore their husbands looked up to them more than was fitting, calling them Mistresses; but he made what regulations were necessary for them also. He strengthened the bodies of the girls by exercise in running, wrestling, and hurling quoits or javelins, in order that their children might spring from a healthy source and so grow up strong, and that they themselves might have strength, so as easily to endure the pains of childbirth. He did away with all affectation of seclusion and retirement among the women, and ordained that the girls, no less than the boys, should go naked in processions, and dance and sing at festivals in the presence of the young men. The jokes which they made upon each man were sometimes of great value as reproofs for ill-conduct; while, on the other hand, by reciting verses written in praise of the deserving, they kindled a wonderful emulation and thirst for distinction in the young men: for he who had been praised by the maidens for his valour went away congratulated by his friends; while, on the other hand, the raillery which they used in sport and jest had as keen an edge as a serious reproof; because the kings and elders were present at these festivals as well as all the other citizens. This nakedness of the maidens had in it nothing disgraceful, as it was done modestly, not licentiously, producing simplicity, and teaching the women to value good health, and to love honour and courage no less than the men. This it was that made them speak and think as we are told Gorgo, the wife of Leonidas, did. Some foreign lady, it seems, said to her, "You Laconian women are the only ones that rule men." She answered, "Yes; for we alone bring forth men."

XIV. These were also incentives to marriage, I mean these processions, and strippings, and exercises of the maidens in the sight of the young men, who, as Plato says, are more swayed by amorous than by mathematical considerations; moreover, he imposed certain penalties on the unmarried men. They were excluded from the festival of the Gymnopaedia, in honour of Athene; and the magistrates ordered them during winter to walk naked round the market-place, and while doing so to sing a song written against themselves, which said that they were rightly served for their disobedience to the laws; and also they were deprived of the respect and observance paid by the young to the elders.

Thus it happened that no one blamed the young man for not rising before Derkyllidas, famous general as he was. This youth kept his seat, saying, "You have not begotten a son to rise before me."

Their marriage custom was for the husband to carry off his bride by force. They did not carry off little immature girls, but grown up women, who were ripe for marriage. After the bride had been carried off the bridesmaid received her, cut her hair close to her head, dressed her in a man's cloak and shoes, and placed her upon a couch in a dark chamber alone. The bridegroom, without any feasting and revelry, but as sober as usual, after dining at his mess, comes into the room, looses her virgin zone, and, after passing a short time with her, retires to pass the night where he was wont, with the other young men. And thus he continued, passing his days with his companions, and visiting his wife by stealth, feeling ashamed and afraid that any one in the house should hear him, she on her part plotting and contriving occasions for meeting unobserved. This went on for a long time, so that some even had children born to them before they ever saw their wives by daylight. These connections not only exercised their powers of self-restraint, but also brought them together with their bodies in full vigour and their passions unblunted by unchecked intercourse with each other, so that their passion and love for each other's society remained unextinguished.

Having thus honoured and dignified the married state, he destroyed the vain womanish passion of jealousy, for, while carefully avoiding any disorder or licentiousness, he nevertheless permitted men to associate worthy persons with them in the task of begetting children, and taught them to ridicule those who insisted on the exclusive possession of their wives, and who were ready to fight and kill people to maintain their right. It was permitted to an elderly husband, with a young wife, to associate with himself any well-born youth whom he might fancy, and to adopt the offspring as his own.

And again, it was allowable for a respectable man, if he felt any admiration for a virtuous mother of children, married to some one else, to induce her husband to permit him to have access to her, that he might as it were sow seed in a fertile field, and obtain a fine son from a healthy stock. Lykurgus did not view children as belonging to their parents, but above all to the state; and therefore he wished his citizens to be born of the best possible parents; besides the inconsistency and folly which he noticed in the customs of the rest of mankind, who are willing to pay money, or use their influence with the owners of well-bred stock, to obtain a good breed of horses or dogs, while they lock up their women in seclusion and permit them to have children by none but themselves, even though they be mad, decrepit, or diseased; just as if the good or bad qualities of children did not depend entirely upon their parents, and did not affect their parents more than any one else.

But although men lent their wives in order to produce healthy and useful citizens, yet this was so far from the licence which was said to prevail in later times with respect to women, that adultery was regarded amongst them as an impossible crime. A story is told of one Geradas, a very old Spartan, who, when asked by a stranger what was done to adulterers among them, answered, "Stranger, there are no adulterers with us." "And if there were one?" asked the stranger. "Then," said Geradas, "he would have to pay as compensation a bull big enough to stand on Mount Täygetus and drink from the river Eurotas." The stranger, astonished, asked "Where can you find so big a bull?" "Where can you find an adulterer in Sparta?" answered Geradas. This is what is said about their marriage ceremonies.

XV. A father had not the right of bringing up his offspring, but had to carry it to a certain place called Lesché, where the elders of the tribe sat in judgment upon the child. If they thought it well-built and strong, they ordered the father to bring it up, and assigned one of the nine thousand plots of land to it; but if it was mean-looking or misshapen, they sent it away to the place called the Exposure, a glen upon the side of Mount Täygetus; for they considered that if a child did not start in possession of health and strength, it was better both for itself and for the state that he should not live at all. Wherefore the women used to wash their newborn infants with wine, not with water, to make trial of their constitution. It was thought that epileptic or diseased children shrank from the wine and fell into convulsions, while healthy ones were hardened and strengthened by it. A certain supervision was exercised over the nurses, making them bring up the children without swaddling clothes, so as to make their movements free and unconfined, and also to make them easily satisfied, not nice as to food, not afraid in the dark, not frightened at being alone, not peevish and fretful. For this reason, many foreigners used to obtain Lacedaemonian nurses for their children, and it is said that Amykla, the nurse of Alkibiades, was a Lacedaemonian. But Plato tells us that Perikles put him under the care of one Zopyrus, who was no better than the other slaves; whereas Lykurgus would not intrust the Spartan boys to any bought or hired servants, nor was each man allowed to bring up and educate his son as he chose, but as soon as they were seven years of age he himself received them from their parents, and enrolled them in companies. Here they lived and messed in common, and were associated for play and for work. However, a superintendent of the boys was appointed, one of the best born and bravest men of the state, and they themselves in their troops chose as leader him who was wisest, and fiercest in fight. They looked to him for orders, obeyed his commands, and endured his punishments, so that even in childhood they learned to obey. The elder men watched them at their play, and by instituting fights and trials of strength, carefully learned which was the bravest and most enduring. They learned their letters, because they are necessary, but all the rest of their education was meant to teach them to obey with cheerfulness, to endure labours, and to win battles. As they grew older their training became more severe; they were closely shorn, and taught to walk unshod and to play naked. They wore no tunic after their twelfth year, but received one garment for all the year round. They were necessarily dirty, as they had no warm baths and ointments, except on certain days, as a luxury. They slept all together in troops and companies, on beds of rushes which they themselves had picked on the banks of the Eurotas with their hands, for they were not allowed to use a knife. In winter they mixed the herb called lycophon with the rushes, as it is thought to possess some warmth.

XVI. At this age the elder men took even greater interest in them, frequenting the gymnasia where they were, and listening to their repartees with each other, and that not in a languid careless manner, but just as if each thought himself the father, instructor, and captain of them all.

Thus no time was left unemployed, and no place was left without some one to give good advice and punish wrong-doing; although a regular superintendent of the boys was appointed from the leading men of the city, and they had their own chiefs, who were the wisest and bravest of the Eirenes. This is a name given to those who have begun their second year after ceasing to be children, and the eldest of the children are called Melleirenes. This Eiren, who is twenty years old, commands his company in their battles, and in the house uses them as his servants to prepare dinner. He orders the bigger boys to carry logs of wood, and the little ones to gather pot herbs. They also bring him what they steal, which they do, some from the gardens, and some from the men's dining-tables, where they rush in very cleverly and cautiously; for if one be taken, he is severely scourged for stealing carelessly and clumsily. They also steal what victuals they can, learning to take them from those who are asleep or off their guard. Whoever is caught is punished by stripes and starvation. Their meals are purposely made scanty, in order that they may exercise their ingenuity and daring in obtaining additions to them. This is the main object of their short commons, but an incidental advantage is the growth of their bodies, for they shoot up in height when not weighed down and made wide and broad by excess of nutriment. This also is thought to produce beauty of figure; for lean and slender frames develop vigour in the limbs, whereas those which are bloated and over-fed cannot attain this, from their weight. This we see in the case of women who take purgatives during pregnancy, whose children are thin, but well-shaped and slender, because from their slight build they receive more distinctly the impress of their mother's form. However, it may be that the cause of this phenomenon is yet to be discovered.

XVII. The boys steal with such earnestness that there is a story of one who had taken a fox's cub and hidden it under his cloak, and, though his entrails were being torn out by the claws and teeth of the beast, persevered in concealing it until he died. This may be believed from what the young men in Lacedaemon do now, for at the present day I have seen many of them perish under the scourge at the altar of Diana Orthias.

After dinner the Eiren would recline, and bid one of the boys sing, and ask another some questions which demand a thoughtful answer, such as "Who is the best among men?" or "How is such a thing done?" By this teaching they began even in infancy to be able to judge what is right, and to be interested in politics; for not to be able to answer the questions, "Who is a good citizen?" or "Who is a man of bad repute?" was thought to be the sign of a stupid and unaspiring mind. The boy's answer was required to be well reasoned, and put into a small compass; he who answered wrongly was punished by having his thumb bitten by the Eiren. Often when elders and magistrates were present the Eiren would punish the boys; if only he showed that it was done deservedly and with method, he never was checked while punishing, but when the boys were gone, he was called to account if he had done so either too cruelly or too remissly.

The lovers of the boys also shared their honour or disgrace; it is said that once when a boy in a fight let fall an unmanly word, his lover was fined by the magistrates. Thus was love understood among them; for even fair and honourable matrons loved young maidens, but none expected their feelings to be returned. Rather did those who loved the same person make it a reason for friendship with each other, and vie with one another in trying to improve in every way the object of their love.

XVIII. The boys were taught to use a sarcastic yet graceful style of speaking, and to compress much thought into few words; for Lykurgus made the iron money have little value for its great size, but on the other hand he made their speech short and compact, but full of meaning, teaching the young, by long periods of silent listening, to speak sententiously and to the point. For those who allow themselves much licence in speech seldom say anything memorable. When some Athenian jeered at the small Laconian swords, and said that jugglers on the stage could easily swallow them, King Agis answered, "And yet with these little daggers we can generally reach our enemies." I think that the Laconian speech, though it seems so short, yet shows a great grasp of the subject and has great power over the listeners. Lykurgus himself seems to have been short and sententious, to judge from what has been preserved of his sayings; as, for instance, that remark to one who proposed to establish a democracy in the state, "First establish a democracy in your own household." And when he was asked why he ordained the sacrifices to be so small and cheap, he answered, "It is in order that we may never be forced to omit them." So too in gymnastic exercises, he discouraged all those which are not performed with the hand closed.

The same class of answers are said to have been made by him to his fellow-countrymen in his letters. When they asked how they should keep off their enemies, he answered, "By remaining poor, and not each trying to be a greater man than the other." Again, about walls, he said, "that cannot be called an open town which has courage, instead of brick walls to defend it." As to the authenticity of these letters, it is hard to give an opinion.

XIX.—The following anecdotes show their dislike of long speeches. When some one was discoursing about matters useful in themselves at an unfitting time, King Leonidas said, "Stranger, you speak of what is wanted when it is not wanted." Charilaus the cousin of Lykurgus, when asked why they had so few laws answered, that men of few words required few laws. And Archidamidas, when some blamed Hekataeus the Sophist for having said nothing during dinner, answered, "He who knows how to speak knows when to speak also." The following are some of those sarcastic sayings which I before said are not ungrateful. Demaratus, when some worthless fellow pestered him with unreasonable queries, and several times inquired, "Who is the best man in Sparta?" answered, "He who is least like you." When some were praising the magnificence and justice with which the Eleans conducted the Olympian games, Agis said, "What is there so very remarkable in the people of Elis acting justly on one day in every five years?"

A stranger was vaunting his admiration of them, and was saying that in his own city he was called a lover of Sparta. Theopompus observed, "It would be more to your credit to be called a lover of your own city." Pleistoanax the son of Pausanias, when an Athenian orator reproached the Lacedaemonians for ignorance, observed, "What you say is quite true, for we are the only Greeks who have not learned some mischief from you."

When a stranger asked Archidamidas how many Spartans there were, he answered, "Enough to keep off bad men."

One may also discover their peculiarities in their jokes; for they are taught never to talk at random, nor to utter a syllable that does not contain some thought. As, when one of them was invited to hear a man imitate the nightingale, he answered, "I have heard the original;" and the man who read this epigram—
"These men, to quench a tyrant's pride, Before Selinus fought and died."

"These men," said he, "deserved to die; for, instead of quenching it, they should have let it burn itself out." When a young man was promised a present of cocks that would fight till they died, he said, "I had rather have some that will fight and kill their foes." This was the style of their talk; so that some have well said that philosophy is more truly Laconian than gymnastic exercises.

XX.—Their education in poetry and music was no less carefully watched over than their cleverness and purity of speech, but their songs were such as rouse men's blood and stir them to deeds of prowess, written in plain unaffected language, upon noble and edifying subjects. For the most part they consisted of panegyrics upon those who had been happy enough to die for their country, reproaches of cowards for living a miserable life, and encouragement to bravery suitable to those of all ages. A good instance of this is that on festivals when there are three choruses, that of the old men first sang—
"We once were lusty youths and tall."

Then that of the young men sang—
"We still are stout; come, try a fall,"
and the third, that of the children, rejoined—
"But we'll be stronger than you all."

Indeed, if one pays any attention to such Laconian poetry as is still extant, and to the march music which was played on the flutes when they were going to meet their enemies, it becomes clear that Terpander and Pindar were right in connecting poetry with bravery. The former speaks thus of the Lacedaemonians:

"Where the youths are bold with the spear, And the voice of the muse is clear, And justice to all is dear."

And Pindar says of them—

"Where the old are wise in council, And the young are brave in fight; Where song and dance are honoured On many a festal night."

For they represent them as being most warlike and at the same time most poetical.

"The sword with song full well combines,"

as the Laconian poet says. Even in their battles the king first sacrificed to the Muses, to remind them, it would appear, of their education and their former contests, that they may be bold in danger, and do deeds worthy of record in the fight.

XXI.—In time of war, too, they relaxed their strict rules and allowed their young men to dress their hair and ornament their shields and costumes, taking a pride in them such as one does in high-mettled horses. For this reason, although they all let their hair grow long after the age of puberty, yet it was especially in time of danger that they took pains to have it smooth and evenly parted, remembering a saying of Lykurgus about the hair, that it made a well-looking man look handsomer, and an ugly man look more ferocious.

During a campaign they made the young men perform less severe gymnastic exercises, and allowed them to live a freer life in other respects, so that, for them alone of all mankind, war was felt as a relief from preparation for war. When their array was formed and the enemy were in sight, the king used to sacrifice a kid, and bid them all put on garlands, and the pipers to play the hymn to Kastor; then he himself began to sing the paean for the charge, so that it was a magnificent and terrible spectacle to see the men marching in time to the flutes, making no gap in their lines, with no thought of fear, but quietly and steadily moving to the sound of the music against the enemy. Such men were not likely to be either panic-stricken or over-confident, but had a cool and cheerful confidence, believing that the gods were with them.

With the king used to march into battle a Spartan who had won a crown in the public games of Greece. It is said that one of them was offered a mighty bribe at Olympia, but refused to take it, and with great trouble threw his adversary in the wrestling-match. Some one then asked him, "Laconian, what have you gained by your victory?" The man, smiling with delight, answered, "I shall fight in front of the king in the wars." After they had routed their enemy and gained the victory, they were wont to pursue so far as to render their success secure, and then to draw off, as they did not think it manly or befitting a Greek to cut down and butcher those who could fight no longer.

This was not merely magnanimous, but very useful to them, for their enemies, knowing that they slew those who resisted, but spared those who gave way, often judged it better for themselves to flee than to stand their ground.

XXII. The sophist Hippias states that Lykurgus himself was a great warrior and took part in many campaigns; and Philostephanus even attributed to Lykurgus the division of the cavalry into the troops called oulamos. This, according to him, consisted of a troop of fifty horsemen drawn up in a square. Demetrius Phalereus, on the other hand, says that he had no experience in war, and arranged the whole constitution in time of peace. Moreover the institution of the Olympic truce seems to be the idea of a man of gentle and peaceful temperament, some however say, according to Hermippus, that Lykurgus had at first no communication with Iphitus, but happened to be present in the crowd; that he then heard a voice as it were of a man behind him blaming him and wondering why he did not encourage his fellow-citizens to take part in the festival. As, when he turned round, there was no one who could have said so, he concluded that it was a divine warning, and, at once joining Iphitus and assisting him in regulating the festival, he rendered it both more splendid and more lasting.

XXIII. The training of the Spartan youth continued till their manhood. No one was permitted to live according to his own pleasure, but they lived in the city as if in a camp, with a fixed diet and fixed public duties, thinking themselves to belong, not to themselves, but to their country. Those who had nothing else to do, either looked after the young, and taught them what was useful, or themselves learned such things from the old. For ample leisure was one of the blessings with which Lykurgus provided his countrymen, seeing that they were utterly forbidden to practise any mechanical art, while money-making and business were unnecessary, because wealth was disregarded and despised. The Helots tilled the ground, and produced the regular crops for them. Indeed, a Spartan who was at Athens while the courts were sitting, and who learned that some man had been fined for idleness, and was leaving the court in sorrow accompanied by his grieving friends, asked to be shown the man who had been punished for gentlemanly behaviour. So slavish did they deem it to labour at trade and business. In Sparta, as was natural, lawsuits became extinct, together with money, as the people had neither excess nor deficiency, but all were equally well off, and enjoyed abundant leisure by reason of their simple habits. All their time was spent in dances, feasting, hunting or gymnastic exercises and conversation, when they were not engaged in war.

XXIV. Those who were less than thirty years old never came into the market-place at all, but made their necessary purchases through their friends and relations. And it was thought discreditable to the older men to be seen there much, and not to spend the greater part of the day in the gymnasium and the lesches or places for conversation. In these they used to collect together and pass their leisure time, making no allusions to business or the affairs of commerce, but their chief study being to praise what was honourable, and contemn what was base in a light satiric vein of talk which was instructive and edifying to the hearers. Nor was Lykurgus himself a man of unmixed austerity: indeed, he is said by Sosibius to have set up the little statue of the god of laughter, and introduced merriment at proper times to enliven their wine-parties and other gatherings. In a word, he trained his countrymen neither to wish nor to understand how to live as private men, but, like bees, to be parts of the commonwealth, and gather round their chief, forgetting themselves in their enthusiastic patriotism, and utterly devoted to their country. This temper of theirs we can discern in many of their sayings. Paidaretus, when not elected into the three hundred, went away rejoicing that the city possessed three hundred better men than himself. Polykratidas, when he went with some others on a mission to the generals of the great king, was asked by them, if he and his party came as private persons or as ambassadors? He answered, "As ambassadors, if we succeed; as private men, if we fail."

And when some citizens of Amphipolis came to Lacedaemon, and went to see the mother of Brasidas, Argileonis, she asked them whether Brasidas died bravely and worthily of Sparta. When they praised him to excess, and said that he had not left his like behind, she said, "Say not so, strangers; Brasidas was a noble and a gallant man, but Sparta has many better than he."

XXV. Lykurgus himself composed his senate, as we have seen, of the persons who took part in his plot; and in future be ordained that vacancies should be filled up by those men, upwards of sixty years of age, who were adjudged to be the most worthy.

This seemed the greatest prize in the world, and also the most difficult to obtain; for it was not merely that a man should be adjudged swiftest of the swift, or strongest of the strong, but he had to be chosen as the best and wisest of all good and wise men, and, as a prize, was to obtain power to regulate the morals of the state, as he was intrusted with powers of life and death, and disfranchisement, and with all the highest penalties.

The elections took place as follows: The citizens were all assembled, and certain men were placed in a building close by, where they could neither see nor be seen, but merely hear the shouts of the general assembly. They decided these, as indeed they did other contests, by shouts of approval, not of all at once, but lots were cast, and each candidate in the order denoted by his lot came forward and silently walked through the assembly. The men locked up in the building had writing materials, and noted down who was cheered most loudly, not knowing who each man was, beyond that he was first, second, third, and so on, of the candidates. They then told the number of the man for whom there had been most voices, and he crowned himself with a garland and offered sacrifice to the gods, followed by many of the young men, who congratulated him, and by many women, who sang songs praising his virtues and his felicity. As he went from one temple to another, each of his relatives used to offer him food, saying, "The state honours you with this banquet." But he would pass by them all, and go to his usual mess-table. Here nothing uncommon took place, except that he was given a second ration, which he took away with him; and after dinner, the women of his own family being at the doors of the mess-room, he would call for the one whom he wished to honour, and give her his portion, saying that he had received it as a prize, and gave it to her as such. This caused her to be greatly envied by the other women.

XXVI.—Moreover, he made excellent regulations about funerals. In the first place, he abolished all silly superstition, and raised no objections to burial in the city, and to placing tombs near the temples, in order to accustom the young to such sights from their infancy, so that they might not feel any horror of death, or have any notion about being defiled by touching a dead body, or walking among tombs. Next, he permitted nothing to be buried with the dead, but they placed the body in the grave, wrapped in a purple cloth and covered with olive-leaves. It was not permitted to inscribe the name of the deceased upon his tomb, except in the case of men who had fallen in war, or of women who had been priestesses. A short time was fixed for mourning, eleven days; on the twelfth they were to sacrifice to Demeter (Ceres) and cease from their grief. For, in Sparta, nothing was left without regulation, but, with all the necessary acts of life, Lykurgus mingled some ceremony which might enkindle virtue or discourage vice; indeed he filled his city with examples of this kind, by which the citizens were insensibly moulded and impelled towards honourable pursuits. For this reason he would not allow citizens to leave the country at pleasure, and to wander in foreign lands, where they would contract outlandish habits, and learn to imitate the untrained lives and ill-regulated institutions to be found abroad. Also, he banished from Lacedaemon all strangers who were there for no useful purpose; not, as Thucydides says, because he feared they might imitate his constitution, and learn something serviceable for the improvement of their own countries, but rather for fear that they might teach the people some mischief. Strangers introduce strange ideas; and these lead to discussions of an unsuitable character, and political views which would jar with the established constitution, like a discord in music. Wherefore he thought that it was more important to keep out evil habits than even to keep the plague from coming into the city.

XXVII. In all these acts of Lykurgus, we cannot find any traces of the injustice and unfairness which some complain of in his laws, which they say are excellent to produce courage, but less so for justice. And the institution called Krypteia, if indeed it is one of the laws of Lykurgus, as Aristotle tells us, would agree with the idea which Plato conceived about him and his system. The Krypteia was this: the leaders of the young men used at intervals to send the most discreet of them into different parts of the country, equipped with daggers and necessary food; in the daytime these men used to conceal themselves in unfrequented spots, and take their rest, but at night they would come down into the roads and murder any Helots they found. And often they would range about the fields, and make away with the strongest and bravest Helots they could find. Also, as Thucydides mentions in his History of the Peloponnesian War, those Helots who were especially honoured by the Spartans for their valour were crowned as free men, and taken to the temples with rejoicings; but in a short time they all disappeared, to the number of more than two thousand, and in such a way that no man, either then or afterwards, could tell how they perished. Aristotle says that the Ephors, when they first take office, declare war against the Helots, in order that it may be lawful to destroy them. And much other harsh treatment used to be inflicted upon them; and they were compelled to drink much unmixed wine, and then were brought into the public dining-halls, to show the young what drunkenness is.

They were also forced to sing low songs, and to dance low dances, and not to meddle with those of a higher character. It is said that when the Thebans made their celebrated campaign in Lacedaemon, they ordered the Helots whom they captured to sing them the songs of Terpander, and Alkman, and Spendon the Laconian; but they begged to be excused, for, they said, "the masters do not like it." So it seems to have been well said that in Lacedaemon, the free man was more free, and the slave more a slave than anywhere else. This harsh treatment, I imagine, began in later times, especially after the great earthquake, when they relate that the Helots joined the Messenians, ravaged the country, and almost conquered it. I cannot impute this wicked act of the

Krypteia to Lykurgus, when I consider the gentleness and justice of his general behaviour, which also we know was inspired by Heaven.

XXVIII. When the leading men of the city were thoroughly imbued with the spirit of his institutions, and the newly constituted state was able to walk by itself without leading-strings, and bear its own weight alone, then, as Plato says of God, that he was pleased with the world that he had created, when it first began to live and move, so was it with Lykurgus. He admired the spectacle of his laws in operation, and, as far as was possible by human prudence, he desired to leave it eternal and unchangeable. He assembled all the citizens, and told them that the city was now fairly well provided with materials for happiness and virtue, but that he would not bestow upon them the most valuable gift of all, until he had taken counsel with Heaven. It was therefore their duty to abide by the already established laws, and to change and alter nothing till he returned from Delphi; on his return, he would do whatever the god commanded. They all assented, and bade him depart, and he, after making first the kings and elders, and then the rest of the citizens, swear that they would keep their existing constitution till Lykurgus came back, set out for Delphi. Upon reaching the temple he sacrificed to the god, and inquired whether his laws were good, and sufficient for the prosperity and happiness of his country. Receiving answer from the oracle that his laws were indeed good, and that the city would become famous if it kept the constitution of Lykurgus, he wrote down this prophecy and sent it to Sparta. But he himself, after offering a second sacrifice to the god, and having embraced his friends and his son, determined not to release his countrymen from their oath, but to put an end to his own life, being at an age when, though life was still pleasant, it seemed time to go to his rest, after having excellently arranged all his people's affairs. He departed by starvation, as he thought that a true statesman ought to make even his death of service to the state, and not like that of a private person, the useless end of an idle life. His death came in the fulness of time, after he had done an excellent work, and it was left as the guardian of all the good that he had done, because the citizens had sworn that they would abide by his constitution until he returned to them. Nor was he deceived in his expectations; for the state was by far the most celebrated in Greece, for good government at home and renown abroad, during a period of five hundred years, under his constitution, which was kept unaltered by fourteen kings, counting from himself down to Agis the son of Archidamus. For the institution of Ephors was not a relaxation, but a strengthening of the original scheme, and while it seemed popular it really confirmed the power of the oligarchy.

XXIX. But in the reign of Agis money found its way into Sparta, and, after money, selfishness and greed for gain came in, on account of Lysander, who, though himself incorruptible, yet filled his country with luxury and love of gold, as he brought back gold and silver from the wars, and disregarded the laws of Lykurgus. Before this, when those laws were in force, Sparta was like a wise and practised warrior more than a city, or rather, she with her simple staff and cloak, like Herakles with his lion-skin and club, ruled over a willing Greece, deposed bad kings or factions, decided wars, and crushed revolutions; and that, too, often without moving a single soldier, but merely by sending a commissioner, who was at once obeyed, even as bees collect and rank themselves in order when their queen appears. Sparta then had so much order and justice as to be able to supply her neighbours; and I cannot understand those who say that the Lacedaemonians "knew how to obey, but not how to rule;" nor that story of some one who said to king Theopompus that the safety of Sparta lay in her kings knowing how to rule. "Rather," he answered, "in her citizens knowing how to obey."

They would not brook an incapable commander: their very obedience is a lesson in the art of command; for a good leader makes good followers, and just as it is the object of the horse-breaker to turn out a gentle and tractable horse, so it is the object of rulers to implant in men the spirit of obedience. But the Lacedaemonians produced a desire in other states to be ruled by them and to obey them; for they used to send embassies and ask not for ships or money or troops, but for one Spartan for a leader; and when they obtained him, they respected him and feared him, as, for instance, the Sicilians had Gylippus as a general, the people of Chalkidike had Brasidas, while Lysander and Kallikratidas and Agesilaus were made use of by all the Greeks in Asia Minor. These men were called Regulators and Pacificators in each several state, and the whole city of Sparta was regarded as a school and example of orderly public life and of settled political institutions. This was alluded to by Stratonikus when he said in jest that the Athenians ought to conduct mysteries and shows, the Eleans to be stewards at the games, and the Lacedaemonians to be beaten if the others did not do right. This was not spoken seriously; but Antisthenes, the Sokratic philosopher, was serious when he said of the Thebans, who were in high spirits after their victory at Leuktra, that they were as pleased as schoolboys who had beaten their master.

XXXI. Not that this was Lykurgus's main object, that his country should dominate over as many other states as possible; but seeing that, in states as in individuals, happiness is derived from virtue and single-mindedness, he directed all his efforts to implant in his countrymen feelings of honour, self-reliance, and self-control. These were also taken as the basis of their constitution by Plato, Diogenes, Zeno, and all who have written with any success upon this subject. But they have left mere dissertations; Lykurgus produced an inimitable constitution, confuted those who complained of the unreality of the 'Essay on the True Philosopher,' by showing them the spectacle of an entire city acting like philosophers, and thereby obtained for himself a greater reputation than that of any other Greek legislator at any period. For this reason Aristotle says that he has less honour in Lacedaemon than he deserves, although his memory is greatly respected; for he has a temple, and they sacrifice to him every year as if he was a god. It is also said that after his remains were carried home, his tomb was struck by lightning. This distinction befell scarcely any other man of note except Euripides, who died long after him, and was buried at Arethusa in Macedonia. It was considered a great proof and token of his fame by the admirers of Euripides, that this should happen to him after his death which happened before to the especial favourite of Heaven. Some say that Lykurgus died at Kirrha, but Apollothemis says that he was taken to Elis and died there, and Timaeus and Aristoxenus say that he ended his days in Crete. Aristoxenus even says that the Cretans show his tomb in what is called the Strangers' Road in Pergamia. He is said to have left one son, Antiorus, who died childless, and so ended the family. His companions and relatives and their descendants kept up the practice of meeting together for a long period; and the days when they met were called Lykurgids. Aristokrates the son of Hipparchus says that when Lykurgus died in Crete, his friends burned his body and threw the ashes into the sea, at his own request, as he feared that if any remains of him should be brought back to Lacedaemon, they would think themselves absolved from their oath, and change the constitution. This is the story of Lykurgus.

Life of Numa.

I. There is a considerable conflict of opinion about the time of King Numa's reign, although several pedigrees seem to be accurately traced to him. One Clodius, in a book on the verification of dates, insists that all these old records were destroyed during the Gaulish troubles, and that those which are now extant were composed by interested persons, by whose means men who had no right to such honours claimed descent from the noblest families. Though Numa is said to have been a friend of Pythagoras, yet some deny that he had any tincture of Greek learning, arguing that either he was born with a natural capacity for sound learning, or that he was taught by some barbarian. Others say that Pythagoras was born much later, some five generations after the times of Numa, but that Pythagoras the Spartan, who won the Stadium race at Olympia on the thirteenth Olympiad, wandered into Italy, and there meeting Numa, assisted him in the establishment of his constitution; and that from this cause, the Roman constitution in many points resembles the Laconian. The Olympic games were instituted in the third year of Numa's reign. Another story is that Numa was a Sabine by birth, and the Sabines consider themselves to be of Lacedaemonian origin. It is hard to reconcile the dates, especially those which refer to Olympiads, the table of which is said to have been made out by Hippias of Elis, on no trustworthy basis. However, what things I have heard about Numa that are worthy of mention I shall proceed to relate, beginning from a starting-point of my own.

II. Rome had been founded, and Romulus had reigned, for thirty-seven years, when upon the fifth day of the month of July, which day is now called nonae caprotinae, he was performing a public sacrifice outside the gates, at a place called the Goat's Marsh, in the presence of the Senate and most of the people. Suddenly a great commotion began in the air, thick clouds covered the earth, with violent gusts and showers. The people fled in terror, and Romulus disappeared. His body could never be found, but suspicion fell upon the patricians, and a report was current among the populace that they had long been jealous of his power as king, and had determined to get it into their own hands. Indeed, he had dealt with them very harshly and tyrannically. Fearing this suspicion, they gave out that he was not dead, but had been caught up into heaven; and Proclus, a man of mark, swore that he saw Romulus ascend into heaven in his armour as he was, and that he heard a voice ordering that he should be called Quirinus. Another disturbance took place in Rome about the election of the next king, because the new citizens were not yet thoroughly amalgamated with the old ones, the people were unquiet, and the patricians suspicious of one another. Nevertheless they all determined that they would have a king, but they disagreed not merely about who, but of what race he should be.

Romulus's original colonists thought it a monstrous thing that the Sabines, because they had been admitted to a share of the city and the country, should propose to rule over it; while the Sabines not unreasonably urged that because, after the death of Tatius, they had acquiesced in Romulus reigning alone, now in their turn they ought to furnish a king of their own nation. They had not, they said, been adopted by a more powerful race than themselves, but had, by their combination with the Romans, greatly raised the power and renown of their city.

The two races were at issue on these points. The patricians, fearing that confusion might arise if the state were left without a head, made one of their own number every day assume the insignia of royalty, perform the usual sacrifices to the gods, and transact business for six hours by day, and six by night. This equal division of their periods of rule was not only just for those in office, but prevented any jealousy of them being felt by the populace, each day and night, because they saw one who had been a king become a private person. This form of government the Romans call an interregnum.

III. But, although they appeared to manage things so smoothly, suspicions and threatenings of disturbance arose, for men said that they meditated altering the form of government to an oligarchy, in order to keep all political power in their own hands, and would not therefore elect a king. Hereupon the two factions agreed that one should select a king from the ranks of the other. This, they thought, would both put an end to their quarrels for the present, and also ensure the candidate who should be chosen being impartial, because he would be friendly to the one party because it had chosen him, and to the other because he belonged to it by birth. The Sabines gave the Romans their choice which they would do; and they decided that it would be better to choose a Sabine king themselves, than to be ruled by a Roman chosen by the Sabines. After deliberation amongst themselves, they chose Numa Pompilius, a man who was not one of those Sabines who had settled in Rome, but whose excellence was so well-known to all, that the Sabines, as soon as they heard his name, were even more eager for him than the Romans who had chosen him. When they had informed the people of their decision, they sent an embassy to Numa, composed of the leading men of both parties, to beg of him to come to Rome and assume the crown.

Numa belonged to a celebrated Sabine city, Cures, from which the united Romans and Sabines called themselves Quirites. He was the son of Pomponius, an honourable citizen, and was the youngest of four brothers. By a miraculous coincidence he was born on the very day on which Romulus founded Rome; that is, the tenth day before the Calends of May. His naturally good disposition had been so educated by sorrow and philosophic pursuits, that he rose superior not merely to commonplace vices, but even to the worship of brute force, so common among barbarians, and considered true courage to consist in the conquest of his own passions. Accordingly he banished all luxury and extravagance from his house, and was known as a trusty friend and counsellor, both by his countrymen and by strangers. When at leisure, he disregarded sensual enjoyments and money-getting, but devoted himself to the service of the gods and to speculations about their nature and power, so that he obtained great celebrity. Indeed Tatius, when he was acting as joint-king with Romulus, chose him for the husband of his only daughter Tatia. But Numa was not elated by his marriage, and did not remove to the town where his father-in-law was king, but stayed where he was in Cures, among the Sabines, tending his aged father; while Tatia also preferred the quiet of a private citizen's life to the pomp which she might have enjoyed in Rome. She is said to have died in the thirteenth year after her marriage.

IV. Now Numa was in the habit of leaving the city and passing much of his time in the country, wandering alone in the sacred groves and dwelling in desert places. Hence the story first arose that it was not from any derangement of intellect that he shunned human society, but because he held converse with higher beings, and had been admitted to marriage with the gods, and that, by passing his time in converse with the nymph Egeria, who loved him, he became blessed, and learned heavenly wisdom. It is evident that this is the same as many ancient myths; such as that told by the Phrygians about Attis, that of the Bithynians about Herodotus, that of the Arcadians about Endymion, and many others. Yet it seems probable that a god, who loves man better than bird or beast, should take pleasure in conversing with those men who are remarkable for goodness, and not despise nor disdain to hold communion with the wise and righteous. But it is hard to believe that a god or deity could feel the passion of love for a human form; although the Egyptians not unreasonably say, that a woman may be impregnated by the spirit of a god, but that a man can have no material union with a god. However it is very right to believe that a god can feel friendship for a man, and from this may spring a love which watches over him and guides him in the path of virtue. There is truth in the myths of Phorbas, of Hyacinthus, and of Admetus, who were all loved by Apollo, as was also Hippolytus of Sicyon. It is said that whenever he set sail from Sikyon to Kirrha on the opposite coast, the Pythia would recite the verse,

    "Now goes our dear Hippolytus to sea,"

as if the god knew that he was coming and rejoiced at it.

There is also a legend that Pan loved Pindar and his verses; and for the Muse's sake, Hesiod and Archilochus were honoured after their deaths; while Sophokles during his life is said, by a legend which remains current at the present day, to have become the friend of Aesculapius, and on his death to have had the rites of burial supplied by the care of another god.

If, then, we believe the legends which are told about these persons, why should we doubt that Zaleukus, Minos, Zoroaster, Numa, and Lykurgus were inspired by Heaven, when they governed their kingdoms and gave them laws? We may suppose that the gods, when in an earnest mood, would hold converse with such men as these, the best of their kind, to talk with and encourage them, just as they visit the poets, if they do at all, when inclined for pleasure. However, if any one thinks differently, as Bacchylides says, "The way is broad."

The other view, which some take about Lykurgus and Numa and such men, seems very plausible, that they, having to deal with an obstinate and unmanageable people when introducing great political changes, invented the idea of their own divine mission as a means of safety for themselves.

V. It was in Numa's fortieth year that the envoys came from Rome to ask him to be king. Their spokesmen were Proculus and Velesius, one of whom had very nearly been elected king, for the Romulus people inclined much to Proculus, and those of Tatius were equally in favour of Velesius. These men made a short speech, imagining that Numa would be delighted with his fortune; but it appears that it took much hard pleading to induce a man who had lived all his life in peace to take the command of a city which owed its origin and its increase alike to war. He said, in the presence of his father and of Marcius, one of his relations, "Every change in a man's life is dangerous; and when a man is not in want of anything needful, and has no cause for being dissatisfied with his lot, it is sheer madness for him to change his habits and way of life; for these, at any rate, have the advantage of security, while in the new state all is uncertain. Not even uncertain are the perils of royalty, judging from Romulus himself, who was suspected of having plotted against his partner Tatius, and whose peers were suspected of having assassinated him. Yet these men call Romulus the child of the gods, and tell how he had a divinely sent nurse, and was preserved by a miracle while yet a child; while

I was born of mortal parents, and brought up by people whom you all know: even the points which you praise in my character are far from those which make a good king, being love of leisure and of unprofitable speculation, and also a great fondness for peace and unwarlike matters, and for men who meet together for the glory of the gods or for cheerful converse with one another, and who at other times plough their fields and feed their cattle at home. But you Romans have very likely many wars left upon your hands by Romulus, for the conduct of which the state requires a vigorous warrior in the prime of life. The people too, from their successes, are accustomed to and eager for war, and are known to be longing for fresh conquests and possessions; so that they would ridicule me when I told them to honour the gods and act justly, and if I tried to instil a hatred of wars and of brute force into a city which wants a general more than a king."

VI. As he refused the offered crown in such terms, the Romans used every kind of entreaty to induce him to accept it, begging him not to plunge the state again into civil war, because there was no other man whom the two parties would agree to receive as their king. In their absence, his father and Marcius begged him not to refuse so great and marvellous an offer. "If," they said, "you do not desire wealth, because of your simple life, and do not care for the glory of royalty, because you derive more glory from your own virtue, yet think that to be king is to serve God, who gives you this office and will not allow your righteousness to lie idle, useful only to yourself. Do not therefore shrink from assuming this office, which gives you an opportunity to conduct the solemn ceremonials of religion with due pomp, and to civilise the people and turn their hearts, which can be effected more easily by a king than by any one else. This people loved Tatius, though he was a foreigner, and they respect the memory of Romulus as if he was a god. And who knows, if the people, although victorious, may not have had enough of wars, and, sated with triumphs and spoils, may not be desirous of a gentle and just ruler under whom they may enjoy rest and peace. If, however, they are madly bent upon war, is it not better that you should hold the reins, and direct their fury elsewhere, becoming yourself a bond of union and friendship between the Sabine nation and this powerful and flourishing city?" Besides these arguments, it is said that the omens were favourable, and that the people of the city, as soon as they heard of the embassy, came and besought him to go and become king, and thus unite and combine the two races.

VII. When he had made up his mind, he sacrificed to the gods, and started for Rome. The Senate and people met him and showed great affection for him; the matrons also greeted him, and there were sacrifices in the temples, and every one was as joyous as if he had received a kingdom instead of a king. When they came into the Forum, the interrex or temporary king, Spurius Vettius, put it to the vote, and all the people voted for Numa. When they offered him the insignia of royalty, he bade them stop, saying that he wished to have his crown confirmed to him by God as well as by man. Taking the prophets and priests he ascended the Capitol, which the Romans at that time called the Tarpeian Hill. There the chief of the prophets made him turn towards the south, covered his head, and then standing behind him with his hand laid upon his head, he prayed, and looked for a sign or omen sent from the gods in every quarter of the heavens. A strange silence prevailed among the people in the Forum, as they watched him eagerly, until a prosperous omen was observed. Then Numa received the royal robes and came down from the hill among the people. They received him with cheers and congratulations, as the most pious of men, and as beloved of Heaven. When he became king, his first act was to disband the body-guard of three hundred men, whom Romulus always had kept about his person, who were called Celeres, that is, swift; for Numa would not distrust a loyal people nor reign over a disloyal one. Next he instituted a third high priest, in addition to the existing priests of Jupiter and Mars, whom, in honour of Romulus, he called the Flamen Quirinalis. The elder priests are called Flamens from the skull-caps which they wear, and the word is derived from the Greek word for felt; for at that time Greek words were mingled with Latin ones more than now. For instance, the laena worn by the priests is said by Juba to be the Greek chlaina, and the boy, whose parents must be both alive, who is servant to the priest of Jupiter, is called Camillus, just as the Greeks sometimes call Hermes (Mercury) Cadmilus, from his being the servant of the gods.

VIII. Numa, after confirming his popularity by these measures, proceeded at once to attempt to convert the city from the practice of war and the strong hand, to that of right and justice, just as a man tries to soften and mould a mass of iron. The city at that time was indeed what Plato calls "inflamed and angry," for it owed its very existence to the reckless daring by which it had thrust aside the most warlike races of the country, and had recruited its strength by many campaigns and ceaseless war, and, as carpentry becomes more fixed in its place by blows, so the city seemed to gain fresh power from its dangers. Thinking that it would be a very difficult task to change the habits of this excited and savage people, and to teach them the arts of peace, he looked to the gods for help, and by sacrifices, processions, and choral dances, which he himself organised and arranged, he awed, interested, and softened the manners of the Romans, artfully beguiling them out of their

warlike ferocity. Sometimes he spoke of supernatural terrors, evil omens, and unpropitious voices, so as to influence them by means of superstition. These measures proved his wisdom, and showed him a true disciple of Pythagoras, for the worship of the gods was an important part of his state policy, as it is of Pythagoras's system of philosophy. His love of outward show and stratagem was also said to be derived from Pythagoras, for as the latter tamed an eagle and made it alight upon him, and when walking through the crowd at Olympia showed his golden thigh, and did all the other surprising devices which made Timon of Phlius write the epigram—
"Pythagoras by magic arts, And mystic talk deludes men's hearts,"
    so did Numa invent the story of his amour with a wood-nymph and his secret converse with her, and of his enjoying the society of the Muses. He referred most of his prophetic utterances to the Muses, and taught the Romans to worship one of them especially, whom he called Tacita, which means silent or dumb. This seems to have been done in imitation of Pythagoras, who especially revered silence. His legislation about images was also connected with the Pythagorean doctrine, which says that first principles cannot be touched or seen, but are invisible spiritual essences; for Numa forbade the Romans to worship any likenesses of men or of beasts. Among them there was no image of a god, either carved or moulded, in the early times. For a hundred and seventy years they built temples, and placed shrines in them, but made no image of any living thing, considering that it was wrong to make the worse like the better, and that God cannot be comprehended otherwise than by thought. Their sacrifices also were connected with the Pythagorean doctrine; they were for the most part bloodless, and performed with flour, libations of wine, and all the commonest things. But besides these, there are other distinct proofs of the connection of these two men with one another. One of these is that the Romans enrolled Pythagoras as a citizen, as we are told by Epicharmus the comic poet, in a letter which he wrote to Antenor. He was a man who lived in old times and underwent the Pythagorean training. Another proof is that of his four sons, King Numa named one Mamercus after the son of Pythagoras; from whom sprung the ancient patrician house of the Aemilii. This name was originally given him in sport by the king, who used to call him aimulos or wily. I myself have heard many Romans narrate that an oracle once bade the Romans establish the wisest and the bravest of the Greeks in their own city, and that in consequence of it they set up two brazen statues in the Forum, one of Alkibiades and one of Pythagoras. But all this can be so easily disputed that it is not worth while to pursue it farther or to put any trust in it.

IX. To Numa also is referred the institution of the Pontifices, or high priests; and he himself is said to have been one of the first. The Pontifices are so called, according to some authorities, because they worship the gods, who are powerful and almighty; for powerful in Latin is potens. Others say that it refers to an exception made in favour of possibilities, meaning that the legislator ordered the priests to perform what services lay in their power, and did not deny that there are some which they cannot. But the most usually received and most absurd derivation is that the word means nothing more than bridge builders, and that they were so named from the sacrifices which are offered upon the sacred bridge, which are of great sanctity and antiquity. The Latins call a bridge pontem. This bridge is intrusted to the care of the priests, like any other immovable holy relic; for the Romans think that the removal of the wooden bridge would call down the wrath of Heaven. It is said to be entirely composed of wood, in accordance with some oracle, without any iron whatever.

The stone bridge was built many years afterwards, when Aemilius was Quaestor. However, it is said that the wooden bridge itself does not date from the time of Numa, but that it was finished by Marcius, the grandson of Numa, when he was king.

The chief priest, or Pontifex Maximus, is an interpreter and prophet or rather expounder of the will of Heaven. He not only sees that the public sacrifices are properly conducted, but even watches those who offer private sacrifices, opposes all departure from established custom, and points out to each man how to honour the gods and how to pray to them. He also presides over the holy maidens called vestals.

The consecration of the vestal virgins, and the worship and watching of the eternal flame by them, are entirely attributed to Numa, and explained either by the pure and uncorruptible essence of fire being intrusted to the keeping of those who are stainless and undefiled, or by that which is barren and without fruit being associated with maidens.

Indeed, in Greece, wherever an eternal fire is kept up, as at Delphi and Athens, it is not maidens, but widows, past the age to wed, that tend it. When any of these fires chance to go out, as, for instance, the sacred lamp went out at Athens when Aristion was despot, and the fire went out at Delphi when the temple was burned by the Persians, and at Rome in the revolutions during the time of the wars with King Mithridates the fire, and even the altar upon which it burned, was swept away; then they say that it must not be lighted from another fire, but that an entirely new fire must be made, lighted by a pure and undefiled ray from the sun. They usually light it with mirrors made by hollowing the surface of an isosceles right-angled triangle, which conducts all the rays of light into one point. Now when it is placed opposite to the sun, so that all the rays coming from all quarters are collected together into that point, the ray thus formed passes through the thin air, and at once lights the dryest and lightest of the objects against which it strikes, for that ray has the strength and force of fire itself.

Some say that the only duty of the vestal virgins is to watch that eternal fire, but others say they perform certain secret rites, about which we have written as much as it is lawful to divulge, in the Life of Camillus.

X. The first maidens who were consecrated by Numa were named Gegania and Verenia; and afterwards Canuleia and Tarpeia were added. Servius subsequently added two more to their number, which has remained six ever since his reign. Numa ordained that the maidens should observe celibacy for thirty years, during the first ten years of which they were to learn their duties, during the next perform them, and during the last to teach others. After this period any of them who wished might marry and cease to be priestesses; but it is said that very few availed themselves of this privilege, and that those few were not happy, but, by their regrets and sorrow for the life they had left, made the others scruple to leave it, prefer to remain virgins till their death. They had great privileges, such as that of disposing of their property by will when their fathers were still alive, like women who have borne three children. When they walk abroad they are escorted by lictors with the fasces; and if they happen to meet any criminal who is being taken to execution, he is not put to death; but the vestal must swear that she met him accidentally, and not on purpose. When they use a litter, no one may pass under it on pain of death. The vestals are corrected by stripes for any faults which they commit, sometimes by the Pontifex Maximus, who flogs the culprit without her clothes, but with a curtain drawn before her. She that breaks her vow of celibacy is buried alive at the Colline Gate, at which there is a mound of earth which stretches some way inside the city wall. In it they construct an underground chamber, of small size, which is entered from above. In it is a bed with bedding, and a lamp burning; and also some small means of supporting life, such as bread, a little water in a vessel, milk, and oil, as though they wished to avoid the pollution of one who had been consecrated with such holy ceremonies dying of hunger. The guilty one is placed in a litter, covered in, and gagged with thongs so that she cannot utter a sound. Then they carry her through the Forum. All make way in silence, and accompany her passage with downcast looks, without speaking. There is no more fearful sight than this, nor any day when the city is plunged into deeper mourning. When the litter reaches the appointed spot, the servants loose her bonds, and the chief priest, after private prayer and lifting his hands to Heaven before his dreadful duty, leads her out, closely veiled, places her upon a ladder which leads down into the subterranean chamber. After this he turns away with the other priests; the ladder is drawn up after she has descended, and the site of the chamber is obliterated by masses of earth which are piled upon it, so that the place looks like any other part of the mound. Thus are the vestals punished who lose their chastity.

XI. Numa is said to have built the Temple of Vesta, which was to contain the sacred fire, in a circular form, imitating thereby not the shape of the earth, but that of the entire universe, in the midst of which the Pythagoreans place the element of fire, which they call Vesta and the Unit. The earth they say is not motionless, and not in the centre of its orbit, but revolves round the central fire, occupying by no means the first or the most honourable place in the system of the universe. These ideas are said to have been entertained by Plato also in his old age; for he too thought that the earth was in a subordinate position, and that the centre of the universe was occupied by some nobler body.

XII. The Pontifices also explain, to those who inquire of them, the proper ceremonies at funerals. For Numa taught them not to think that there was any pollution in death, but that we must pay due honours to the gods below, because they will receive all that is noblest on earth. Especially he taught them to honour the goddess Libitina, the goddess who presides over funeral rites, whether she be Proserpine, or rather Venus, as the most learned Romans imagine, not unnaturally referring our birth and our death to the same divinity.

He also defined the periods of mourning, according to the age of the deceased. He allowed none for a child under three years of age, and for one older the mourning was only to last as many months as he lived years, provided those were not more than ten. The longest mourning was not to continue above ten months, after which space widows were permitted to marry again; but she that took another husband before that term was out was obliged by his decree to sacrifice a cow with calf.

Of Numa's many other institutions I shall only mention two, that of the Salii and of the Feciales, which especially show his love of justice. The Feciales are, as it were, guardians of peace, and in my opinion obtain their name from their office; for they were to act as mediators, and not to permit an appeal to arms before all hope of obtaining justice by fair means had been lost. The Greeks call it peace when two states settle their differences by negotiation and not by arms; and the Roman Feciales frequently went to states that had done wrong and begged them to think better of what they had done. If they rejected their offers, then the Feciales called the gods to witness, invoked dreadful curses upon themselves and their country, if they were about to fight in an unjust cause, and so declared war. Against the will of the Feciales, or without their approval, no Roman, whether king or common soldier, was allowed to take up arms, but the general was obliged first to have it certified to him by the Feciales that the right was on his side, and then to take his measures for a campaign. It is said that the great disaster with the Gauls befell the city in consequence of this ceremony having been neglected. The barbarians were besieging Clusium; Fabius Ambustus was sent as an ambassador to their camp to make terms on behalf of the besieged. His proposals met with a harsh reply, and he, thinking that his mission was at an end, had the audacity to appear before the ranks of the men of Clusium in arms, and to challenge the bravest of the barbarians to single combat. He won the fight, slew his opponent and stripped his body; but the Gauls recognised him, and sent a herald to Rome, complaining that Fabius had broken faith and not kept his word, and had waged war against them without its being previously declared. Hereupon the Feciales urged the Senate to deliver the man up to the Gauls, but he appealed to the people, and by their favour escaped his just doom. Soon after the Gauls came and sacked Rome, except the Capitol. But this is treated of more at length in the 'Life of Camillus.'

XIII. The priests called Salii are said to owe their origin to the following circumstances: In the eighth year of Numa's reign an epidemic raged throughout Italy, and afflicted the city of Rome. Now amidst the general distress it is related that a brazen shield fell from heaven into the hands of Numa. Upon this the king made an inspired speech, which he had learned from Egeria and the Muses. The shield, he said, came for the salvation of the city, and they must guard it, and make eleven more like it, so that no thief could steal the one that fell from heaven, because he could not tell which it was. Moreover the place and the meadows round about it, where he was wont to converse with the Muses, must be consecrated to them, and the well by which it was watered must be pointed out as holy water to the vestal virgins, that they might daily take some thence to purify and sprinkle their temple. The truth of this is said to have been proved by the immediate cessation of the plague. He bade workmen compete in imitating the shield, and, when all others refused to attempt it, Veturius Mamurius, one of the best workmen of the time, produced so admirable an imitation, and made all the shields so exactly alike, that even Numa himself could not tell which was the original.

He next appointed the Salii to guard and keep them. These priests were called Salii, not, as some say, after a man of Samothrace or of Mantinea named Salius, who first taught the art of dancing under arms, but rather from the springing dance itself, which they dance through the city when they carry out the shields in the month of March, dressed in scarlet tunics, girt with brazen girdles, with brazen helmets on their heads and little daggers with which they strike the shields. The rest of their dance is done with their feet; they move gracefully, whirling round, swiftly and airily counter-changing their positions with light and vigorous motions according to rhythm and measure. The shields are called ancilia, because of their shape; for they are not round, nor with a perfect circumference, but are cut out of a wavy line, and curl in at the thickest part towards each other; or they may be called ancilia after the name of the elbow, ankon, on which they are carried; at least so Juba conjectures in his endeavours to find a Greek derivation for the word. The name may be connected with the fall of the shield from above (anekathen), or with the healing (akesis) of the plague, and the cessation of that terrible calamity, if we must refer the word to a Greek root.

It is related that, to reward Mamurius for his workmanship, his name is mentioned in the song which the Salii sing while they dance their Pyrrhic dance; others, however, say that it is not Veturium Mamurium that they say, but Veterem Memoriam, which means ancient memory.

XIV. After he had arranged all religious ceremonies, he built, near the temple of Vesta, the Regia, as a kind of royal palace; and there he spent most of his time, engaged in religious duties, instructing the priests, or awaiting some divine colloquy. He had also another house on the hill of Quirinus, the site of which is even now pointed out.

In all religious processions through the city the heralds went first to bid the people cease their work, and attend to the ceremony; for just as the Pythagoreans are said to forbid the worship of the gods in a cursory manner, and to insist that men shall set out from their homes with this purpose and none other in their minds, so Numa thought it wrong that the citizens should see or hear any religious ceremony in a careless, half-hearted manner, and made them cease from all worldly cares and attend with all their hearts to the most important of all duties, religion; so he cleared the streets of all the hammering, and cries, and noises which attend the practice of ordinary trades and handicrafts, before any holy ceremony. Some trace of this custom still survives in the practice of crying out Hoc age when the consul is taking the auspices or making a sacrifice. These words mean "Do this thing," and are used to make the bystanders orderly and attentive. Many of his other precepts are like those of the Pythagoreans; for just as they forbid men to sit upon a quart measure, or to stir the fire with a sword, or to turn back when they set out upon a journey, and bid them sacrifice an odd number to the gods above, and an even one to those below, all of which things had a mystical meaning, which was hidden from the common mass of mankind, so also some of Numa's rites can only be explained by reference to some secret legend, such as his forbidding men to make a libation to the gods with wine made from an unpruned vine, and his ordering that no sacrifice should be made without flour, and that men should turn round while worshipping and sit after they had worshipped. The first two of these seem to point to cultivation of the fruits of the earth, as a part of righteousness; the turning round of the worshippers is said to be in imitation of the revolution of the globe, but it seems more probable that, as all temples look towards the east, the worshipper who enters with his back to the sun turns round towards this god also, and begs of them both, as he makes his circuit, to fulfil his prayer. Unless indeed there is an allusion to the symbolical wheel of the Egyptians, and the change of posture means that nothing human is constant, and that, however God may turn about our lives, it is our duty to be content. The act of sitting after prayer was said to portend that such as were good would obtain a solid and lasting fulfilment of their prayers. Or again, this attitude of rest marks the division between different periods of prayer; so that after the end of one prayer they seat themselves in the presence of the gods, in order that under their auspices they may begin the next. This fully agrees with what has been said above, and shows that the lawgiver intended to accustom his countrymen not to offer their prayers in a hurry, or in the intervals of doing something else, but when they were at leisure and not pressed for time.

XV. By this religious training the city became so easily managed by Numa, and so impressed by his power, as to believe stories of the wildest character about him, and to think nothing incredible or impossible if he wished to do it. For instance, it is related that once he invited many of the citizens to dine with him, and placed before them common vessels and poor fare; but, as they were about to begin dinner, he suddenly said that his familiar goddess was about to visit him, and at once displayed abundance of golden cups and tables covered with costly delicacies. The strangest story of all is that of his conversation with Jupiter. The legend runs that Mount Aventine was not at this time enclosed within the city, but was full of fountains and shady glens, and haunted by two divinities, Picus and Faunus, who may be compared to Satyrs or to Pan, and who, in knowledge of herbs and magic, seem equal to what the Greeks call the Daktyli of Mount Ida. These creatures roamed about

Italy playing their tricks, but Numa caught them by filling the spring at which they drank with wine and honey. They turned into all kinds of shapes, and assumed strange and terrible forms, but when they found that they were unable to escape, they told Numa much of the future, and showed him how to make a charm against thunder-bolts, which is used to this day, and is made of onions and hair and sprats. Some say that it was not these deities who told him the charm, but that they by magic arts brought down Jupiter from heaven, and he, in a rage, ordered Numa to make the charm of "Heads"; and when Numa added, "Of onions," he said "Of men's"—"Hair," said Numa, again taking away the terrible part of the imprecation. When then Jupiter said "With living"—"Sprats," said Numa, answering as Egeria had taught him. The god went away appeased, and the place was in consequence called Ilicius. This was how the charm was discovered.

These ridiculous legends show the way in which the people had become accustomed to regard the gods. Indeed Numa is said to have placed all his hopes in religion, to such an extent that even when a message was brought him, saying, "The enemy are approaching," he smiled and said, "And I am sacrificing."

XVI. The first temples that he founded are said to have been those of Fides or Faith, and Terminus. Fides is said to have revealed to the Romans the greatest of all oaths, which they even now make use of; while Terminus is the god of boundaries, to whom they sacrifice publicly, and also privately at the divisions of men's estates; at the present time with living victims, but in old days this was a bloodless sacrifice, for Numa argued that the god of boundaries must be a lover of peace, and a witness of righteousness, and therefore averse to bloodshed.

Indeed Numa was the first king who defined the boundaries of the country, since Romulus was unwilling, by measuring what was really his own, to show how much he had taken from other states: for boundaries, if preserved, are barriers against violence; if disregarded, they become standing proofs of lawless injustice. The city had originally but a small territory of its own, and Romulus gained the greater part of its possessions by the sword. All this Numa distributed among the needy citizens, thereby removing the want which urged them to deeds of violence, and, by turning the people's thoughts to husbandry, he made them grow more civilised as their land grew more cultivated. No profession makes men such passionate lovers of peace as that of a man who farms his own land; for he retains enough of the warlike spirit to fight fiercely in defence of his own property, but has lost all desire to despoil and wrong his neighbours. It was for this reason that Numa encouraged agriculture among the Romans, as a spell to charm away war, and loved the art more because of its influence on men's minds than because of the wealth which it produced. He divided the whole country into districts, which he called pagi, and appointed a head man for each, and a patrol to guard it. And sometimes he himself would inspect them, and, forming an opinion of each man's character from the condition of his farm, would raise some to honours and offices of trust, and blaming others for their remissness, would lead them to do better in future.

XVII. Of his other political measures, that which is most admired is his division of the populace according to their trades. For whereas the city, as has been said, originally consisted of two races, which stood aloof one from the other and would not combine into one, which led to endless quarrels and rivalries, Numa, reflecting that substances which are hard and difficult to combine together, can nevertheless be mixed and formed into one mass if they are broken up into small pieces, because then they more easily fit into each other, determined to divide the whole mass of the people of Rome into many classes, and thus, by creating numerous petty rivalries, to obliterate their original and greatest cause of variance.

His division was according to their trades, and consisted of the musicians, the goldsmiths, the builders, the dyers, the shoemakers, the carriers, the coppersmiths, and the potters. All the other trades he united into one guild. He assigned to each trade its special privileges, common to all the members, and arranged that each should have its own times of meeting, and worship its own special patron god, and by this means he did away with that habit, which hitherto had prevailed among the citizens, of some calling themselves Sabines, and some Romans; one boasting that they were Tatius's men, and other Romulus's. So this division produced a complete fusion and unity. Moreover he has been much praised for another of his measures, that, namely, of correcting the old law which allows fathers to sell their sons for slaves. He abolished this power in the case of married men, who had married with their father's consent; for he thought it a monstrous injustice that a woman, who had married a free man, should be compelled to be the wife of a slave.

XVIII. He also dealt with astronomical matters, not with perfect accuracy, and yet not altogether without knowledge. During the reign of Romulus the months had been in a state of great disorder, some not containing twenty days, some five-and-thirty, and some even more, because the Romans could not reconcile the discrepancies which arise from reckoning by the sun and the moon, and only insisted upon one thing, that the year should consist of three hundred and sixty days.

Numa reckoned the variation to consist of eleven days, as the lunar year contains three hundred and fifty-four days, and the solar year three hundred and sixty-five. He doubled these eleven days and introduced them every other year, after February, as an intercalary month, twenty-two days in duration, which was called by the Romans Mercedinus. This was a remedy for the irregularities of the calendar which itself required more extensive remedies.

He also altered the order of the months, putting March, which used to be the first month, third, and making January the first, which in the time of Romulus had been the eleventh, and February the second, which then had been the twelfth. There are many writers who say that these months, January and February, were added to the calendar by Numa, and that originally there had only been ten months in the year, just as some barbarians have three, and in Greece the Arcadians have four, and the Acarnanians six. The Egyptians originally had but one month in their year, and afterwards are said to have divided it into four mouths; wherefore, though they live in the newest of all countries, they appear to be the most ancient of all nations, and in their genealogies reckon an incredible number of years, because they count their months as years.

XIX. One proof that the Romans used to reckon ten months and not twelve in the year is the name of the last month; for up to the present day it is called December, the tenth, and the order of the months shows that March was the first, for the fifth month from it they called Quintilis, the fifth; and the sixth month Sextilis, and so on for the others, although, by their putting January and February before March, it resulted that the month which they number fifth is really seventh in order. Moreover, there is a legend that the month of March, being the first, was dedicated by Romulus to Mars, and the second, April, to Aphrodité (Venus); in which month they sacrifice to this goddess, and the women bathe on the first day of it crowned with myrtle. Some, however, say that April is not named after Aphrodité, because the word April does not contain the letter h, and that it comes from the Latin word aperio, and means the month in which the spring-time opens the buds of plants; for that is what the word signifies. Of the following months, May is named after Maia, the mother of Hermes or Mercury, for it is dedicated to her, and June from Juno. Some say that these names signify old age and youth, for old men are called by the Latins majores, and young men juniores. The remaining months they named, from the order in which they came, the fifth, sixth, seventh, eighth, ninth, tenth: Quintilis, Sextilis, September, October,

November, December. Then Quintilis was called Julius after Julius Caesar, who conquered Pompeius; and Sextilis was called Augustus, after the second of the Roman Emperors. The next two months Domitian altered to his own titles, but not for any long time, as after his death they resumed their old names of September and October. The last two alone have preserved their original names without change. Of the months, added or altered by Numa, Februarius means the month of purification, for that is as nearly as possible the meaning of the word, and during it they sacrifice to the dead, and hold the festival of the Lupercalia, which resembles a ceremony of purification. The first month, Januarius, is named after Janus. My opinion is, that Numa moved the month named after Mars from its precedence, wishing the art of good government to be honoured before that of war. For Janus in very ancient times was either a deity or a king, who established a social polity, and made men cease from a savage life like that of wild beasts. And for this reason his statues are made with a double face, because he turned men's way of life from one form to another.

XX. There is a temple to him in Rome, which has two doors, and which they call the gate of war. It is the custom to open the temple in time of war, and to close it during peace. This scarcely ever took place, as the empire was almost always at war with some state, being by its very greatness continually brought into collision with the neighbouring tribes. Only in the time of Caesar Augustus, after he had conquered Antonius, it was closed; and before that, during the consulship of Marcus Atilius and Titus Manlius, for a short time, and then was almost immediately reopened, as a new war broke out. But during Numa's reign no one saw it open for a single day, and it remained closed for forty-three years continuously, so utterly had he made wars to cease on all sides. Not only was the spirit of the Romans subdued and pacified by the gentle and just character of their king, but even the neighbouring cities, as if some soothing healthful air was breathed over them from Rome, altered their habits and longed to live quiet and well-governed, cultivating the earth, bringing up their families in peace, and worshipping the gods. And gay festivals and entertainments, during which the people of the various states fearlessly mixed with one another, prevailed throughout Italy, for Numa's knowledge of all that was good and noble was shed abroad like water from a fountain, and the atmosphere of holy calm by which he was surrounded spread over all men. The very poets when they wrote of that peaceful time were unable to find adequate expressions for it, as one writes—

"Across the shields are cobwebs laid, Rust eats the lance and keen edged blade; No more we hear the trumpets bray. And from our eyes no more is slumber chased away."

No war, revolution, or political disturbance of any kind is recorded during Numa's reign, neither was there any envy or hatred of him or any attempt by others to obtain the crown; but either fear of the gods who visibly protected him, or reverence for his virtues, or the special grace of Heaven, made men's lives innocent and untainted with evil, and formed a striking proof of the truth of what Plato said many years afterwards, that the only escape from misery for men is when by Divine Providence philosophy is combined with royal power, and used to exalt virtue over vice. Blessed indeed is the truly wise man, and blessed are they who hear the words of his mouth. Indeed his people require no restraints or punishments, but seeing a plain example of virtue in the life of their chief, they themselves of their own accord reform their lives, and model them upon that gentle and blessed rule of love and just dealing one with another which it is the noblest work of politicians to establish. He is most truly a king who can teach such lessons as these to his subjects, and Numa beyond all others seems to have clearly discerned this truth.

XXI. Historians differ in their accounts of his wives and children. Some say that he married Tatia alone, and was the father of one daughter only, named Pompilia; but others, besides her, assign to him four sons, named Pompo, Pinus, Calpus, and Mamercus, from whom descended the four noble families of the Pomponii, Pinarii, Calphurnii, and Mamerci, which for this reason took the title of Rex, that is, king. Others again say that these pedigrees were invented to flatter these families, and state that the Pompilian family descends not from Tatia, but from Lucretia, whom he married after he became king. All, however, agree that Pompilia married Marcius, the son of that Marcius who encouraged Numa to accept the crown. This man accompanied Numa to Rome, was made a member of the Senate, and after Numa's death laid claim to the crown, but was worsted by Tullus Hostilius and made away with himself. His son Marcius, who married Pompilia, remained in Rome, and became the father of Ancus Marcius, who was king after Tullus Hostilius, and who was only five years old when Numa died.

We are told by Piso that Numa died, not by a sudden death, but by slow decay from sheer old age, having lived a little more than eighty years.

XXII. He was enviable even in death, for all the friendly and allied nations assembled at his funeral with national offerings. The senators bore his bier, which was attended by the chief priests, while the crowd of men, women and children who were present, followed with such weeping and wailing, that one would have thought that, instead of an aged king, each man was about to bury his own dearest friend, who had died in the prime of life. At his own wish, it is said, the body was not burned, but placed in two stone coffins and buried on the Janiculum Hill. One of these contained his body, and the other the sacred books which he himself had written, as Greek legislators write their laws upon tablets. During his life he had taught the priests the contents of these books, and their meaning and spirit, and ordered them to be buried with his corpse, because it was right that holy mysteries should be contained, not in soulless writings, but in the minds of living men. For the same reason they say that the Pythagoreans never reduced their maxims to writing, but implanted them in the memories of worthy men; and when some of their difficult processes in geometry were divulged to some unworthy men, they said that Heaven would mark its sense of the wickedness which had been committed by some great public calamity; so that, as Numa's system so greatly resembled that of Pythagoras, we can easily pardon those who endeavour to establish a connection between them.

Valerius of Antium says that twelve sacred books and twelve books of Greek philosophy were placed in the coffin. Four hundred years afterwards, when Publius Cornelius and Marcus Baebius were consuls, a great fall of rain took place, and the torrent washed away the earth and exposed the coffins. When the lids were removed, one of the coffins was seen by all men to be empty, and without any trace of a corpse in it; the other contained the books, which were read by Petilius the praetor, who reported to the Senate that in his opinion it was not right that their contents should be made known to the people, and they were therefore carried to the Comitium and burned there.

All good and just men receive most praise after their death, because their unpopularity dies with them or even before them; but Numa's glory was enhanced by the unhappy reigns of his successors. Of five kings who succeeded him, the last was expelled and died an exile, and of the other four, not one died a natural death, but three were murdered by conspirators, and Tullus Hostilius, who was king next after Numa, and who derided and insulted his wise ordinances, especially those connected with religion, as lazy and effeminate, and who urged the people to take up arms, was cut down in the midst of his boastings by a terrible disease, and became subject to superstitious fears in no way resembling Numa's piety. His subjects were led to share these terrors, more especially by the manner of his death, which is said to have been by the stroke of a thunderbolt.

Comparison of Numa with Lykurgus.

I. Now that we have gone through the lives of Numa and Lykurgus, we must attempt, without being daunted by difficulties, to reconcile the points in which they appear to differ from each other. Much they appear to have had in common, as, for example, their self-control, their piety, and their political and educational ability; and while the peculiar glory of Numa is his acceptance of the throne, that of Lykurgus is his abdication. Numa received it without having asked for it; Lykurgus when in full possession gave it up. Numa, though a private man and not even a Roman, was chosen by the Romans as their king; but Lykurgus from being a king reduced himself to a private station. It is honourable to obtain a crown by righteousness, but it is also honourable to prefer righteousness to a crown. Numa's virtue made him so celebrated that he was judged worthy to be king, Lykurgus' made him so great that he did not care to be king.

Again, like those who tune the strings of a lyre, Lykurgus drew tighter the relaxed and licentious Sparta, while Numa merely slackened the highly strung and warlike Rome, so that here Lykurgus had the more difficult task. He had to persuade his countrymen, not to take off their armour and lay aside their swords, but to leave off using gold and silver, and to lay aside costly hangings and furniture; he had not to make them exchange wars for sacrifices and gay festivals, but to cease from feasts and drinking-parties, and work hard both in the field and in the palaestra to train themselves for war.

For this reason, Numa was able to effect his purpose without difficulty, and without any loss of popularity and respect; while Lykurgus was struck and pelted, and in danger of his life, and even so could scarcely carry out his reforms. Yet the genius of Numa was kindly and gentle, and so softened and changed the reckless fiery Romans that they became peaceful, law-abiding citizens; and if we must reckon Lykurgus' treatment of the Helots as part of his system, it cannot be denied that Numa was a far more civilised lawgiver, seeing that he allowed even to actual slaves some taste of liberty, by his institution of feasting them together with their masters at the festival of Saturn.

For this custom of allowing the labourers to share in the harvest-feast is traced to Numa. Some say that this is in remembrance of the equality which existed in the time of Saturn, when there was neither master nor slave, but all were kinsmen and had equal rights.

II. Both evidently encouraged the spirit of independence and self-control among their people, while of other virtues, Lykurgus loved bravery, and Numa loved justice best; unless indeed we should say that, from the very different temper and habits of the two states, they required to be treated in a different manner. It was not from cowardice, but because he scorned to do an injustice, that Numa did not make war; while Lykurgus made his countrymen warlike, not in order that they might do wrong, but that they might not be wronged. Each found that the existing system required very important alterations to check its excesses and supply its defects. Numa's reforms were all in favour of the people, whom he classified into a mixed and motley multitude of goldsmiths and musicians and cobblers; while the constitution introduced by Lykurgus was severely aristocratic, driving all handicrafts into the hands of slaves and foreigners, and confining the citizens to the use of the spear and shield, as men whose trade was war alone, and who knew nothing but how to obey their leaders and to conquer their enemies. In Sparta a free man was not permitted to make money in business, in order that he might be truly free.

Each thing connected with the business of making money, like that of preparing food for dinner, was left in the hands of slaves and helots. Numa made no regulations of this kind, but, while he put an end to military plundering, raised no objection to other methods of making money, nor did he try to reduce inequalities of fortune, but allowed wealth to increase unchecked, and disregarded the influx of poor men into the city and the increase of poverty there, whereas he ought at the very outset, like Lykurgus, while men's fortunes were still tolerably equal, to have raised some barrier against the encroachments of wealth, and to have restrained the terrible evils which take their rise and origin in it. As for the division of the land among the citizens, in my opinion, Lykurgus cannot be blamed for doing it, nor yet can Numa for not doing it. The equality thus produced was the very foundation and corner-stone of the Lacedaemonian constitution, while Numa had no motive for disturbing the Roman lands, which had only been recently distributed among the citizens, or to alter the arrangements made by Romulus, which we may suppose were still in force throughout the country.

III. With regard to a community of wives and children, each took a wise and statesman-like course to prevent jealousy, although the means employed by each were different. A Roman who possessed a sufficient family of his own might be prevailed upon by a friend who had no children to transfer his wife to him, being fully empowered to give her away, by divorce, for this purpose; but a Lacedaemonian was accustomed to lend his wife for intercourse with a friend, while she remained living in his house, and without the marriage being thereby dissolved. Many, we are told, even invited those who, they thought, would beget fine and noble children, to converse with their wives. The distinction between the two customs seems to be this: the Spartans affected an unconcern and insensibility about a matter which excites most men to violent rage and jealousy; the Romans modestly veiled it by a legal contract which seems to admit how hard it is for a man to give up his wife to another. Moreover Numa's regulations about young girls were of a much more feminine and orderly nature, while those of Lykurgus were so highflown and unbecoming to women, as to have been the subject of notice by the poets, who call them Phainomerides, that is with bare thighs, as Ibykus says; and they accuse them of lust, as Euripides says—

"They stay not, as befits a maid, at home, But with young men in shameless dresses roam."

For in truth the sides of the maiden's tunic were not fastened together at the skirt, and so flew open and exposed the thigh as they walked, which is most clearly alluded to in the lines of Sophokles—

"She that wanders nigh, With scanty skirt that shows the thigh, A Spartan maiden fair and free, Hermione."

On this account they are said to have become bolder than they should be, and to have first shown this spirit towards their husbands, ruling uncontrolled over their households, and afterwards in public matters, where they freely expressed their opinions upon the most important subjects. On the other hand, Numa preserved that respect and honour due from men to matrons which they had met with under Romulus, who paid them these honours to atone for having carried them off by force, but he implanted in them habits of modesty, sobriety, and silence, forbidding them even to touch wine, or to speak even when necessary except in their husbands' presence. It is stated that once, because a woman pleaded her own cause in the Forum, the Senate sent to ask the oracle what this strange event might portend for the state.

A great proof of the obedience and modesty of the most part of them is the way in which the names of those who did any wrong is remembered. For, just as in Greece, historians record the names of those who first made war against their own kindred or murdered their parents, so the Romans tell us that the first man who put away his wife was Spurius Carvilius, nothing of the kind having happened in Rome for two hundred and thirty years from its foundation; and that the wife of Pinarius, Thalaea by name, was the first to quarrel with her mother-in-law Gegania in the reign of Tarquinius Superbus—so well and orderly were marriages arranged by this lawgiver.

IV. The rest of their laws for the training and marriage of maidens agree with one another, although Lykurgus put off the time of marriage till they were full-grown, in order that their intercourse, demanded as it was by nature, might produce love and friendship in the married pair rather than the dislike often experienced by an immature child towards her husband, and also that their bodies might be better able to support the trials of child-bearing, which he regarded as the sole object of marriage; whereas the Romans gave their daughters in marriage at the age of twelve years or even younger, thinking thus to hand over a girl to her husband pure and uncorrupt both in body and mind. It is clear that the former system is best for the mere production of children, and the latter for moulding consorts for life. But by his superintendence of the young, his collecting them into companies, his training and drill, with the table and exercises common to all, Lykurgus showed that he was immensely superior to Numa, who, like any commonplace lawgiver, left the whole training of the young in the hands of their fathers, regulated only by their caprice or needs; so that whoever chose might bring up his son as a shipwright, a coppersmith, or a musician, as though the citizens ought not from the very outset to direct their attention to one object, but were like people who have embarked in the same ship for various causes, who only in time of danger act together for the common advantage of all, and at other times pursue each his own private ends. Allowance must be made for ordinary lawgivers, who fail through want of power or of knowledge in establishing such a system; but no such excuse can be made for Numa, who was a wise man, and who was made king of a newly-created state which would not have opposed any of his designs. What could be of greater importance than to regulate the education of the young and so to train them that they might all become alike in their lives and all bear the same impress of virtue? It was to this that Lykurgus owed the permanence of his laws; for he could not have trusted to the oaths which he made them take, if he had not by education and training so steeped the minds of the young in the spirit of his laws, and by his method of bringing them up implanted in them such a love for the state, that the most important of his enactments remained in force for more than five hundred years; for the lives of all Spartans seem to have been coloured by these laws. That which was the aim and end of Numa's policy, that Rome should be at peace and friendly with her neighbours, ceased immediately upon his death; at once the double-gated temple, which he kept closed as if he really kept war locked up in it, had both its gates thrown open and filled Italy with slaughter. His excellent and righteous policy did not last for a moment, for the people were not educated to support it, and therefore it could not be lasting. But, it may be asked, did not Rome flourish by her wars? It is hard to answer such a question, in an age which values wealth, luxury, and dominion more than a gentle peaceful life that wrongs no one and suffices for itself. Yet this fact seems to tell for Lykurgus, that the Romans gained such an enormous increase of power by departing from Numa's policy, while the Lacedaemonians, as soon as they fell away from the discipline of Lykurgus, having been the haughtiest became the most contemptible of Greeks, and not only lost their supremacy, but had even to struggle for their bare existence. On the other hand, it was truly glorious for Numa that he was a stranger and sent for by the Romans to be their king; that he effected all his reforms without violence, and ruled a city composed of discordant elements without any armed force such as Lykurgus had to assist him, winning over all men and reducing them to order by his wisdom and justice.

Life of Solon.

I. Didymus the grammarian, in the book about Solon's laws which he wrote in answer to Asklepiades, quotes a saying of one Philokles, that Solon was the son of Euphorion, which is quite at variance with the testimony of all other writers who have mentioned Solon: for they all say that he was the son of Exekestides, a man whose fortune and power were only moderate, but whose family was of the noblest in Athens; for he was descended from Kodrus the last Athenian king. Herakleides of Pontus relates that the mother of Solon was first cousin to the mother of Peisistratus. The two boys, we are told, were friends when young, and when in after years they differed in politics they still never entertained harsh or angry feelings towards one another, but kept alive the sacred flame of their former intimate friendship. Peisistratus is even said to have dedicated the statue of Love in the Academy where those who are going to run in the sacred torch-race light their torches.

II. According to Hermippus, Solon, finding that his father had by his generosity diminished his fortune, and feeling ashamed to be dependent upon others, when he himself was come of a house more accustomed to give than to receive, embarked in trade, although his friends were eager to supply him with all that he could wish for. Some, however, say that Solon travelled more with a view to gaining experience and learning than to making money. He was indeed eager to learn, as he wrote when an old man,

"Old to grow, but ever learning,"

but disregarded wealth, for he wrote that he regarded as equally rich the man who owned

"Gold and broad acres, corn and wine; And he that hath but clothes and food, A wife, and youthful strength divine."

Yet elsewhere he has written, but

"I long for wealth, not by fraud obtained, For curses wait on riches basely gained."

There is no reason for an upright statesman either to be over anxious for luxuries or to despise necessaries. At that period, as Hesiod tells us, "Work was no disgrace," nor did trade carry any reproach, while the profession of travelling merchant was even honourable, as it civilised barbarous tribes, and gained the friendship of kings, and learned much in many lands. Some merchants founded great cities, as, for example, Protis, who was beloved by the Gauls living near the Rhone, founded Marseilles. It is also said that Thales the sage, and Hippocrates the mathematician, travelled as merchants, and that Plato defrayed the expenses of his journey to Egypt by the oil which he disposed of in that country.

III. Solon's extravagance and luxurious mode of life, and his poems, which treat of pleasure more from a worldly than a philosophic point of view, are attributed to his mercantile training; for the great perils of a merchant's life require to be paid in corresponding pleasures. Yet it is clear that he considered himself as belonging to the class of the poor, rather than that of the rich, from the following verses:

"The base are rich, the good are poor; and yet Our virtue for their gold we would not change; For that at least is ours for evermore, While wealth we see from hand to hand doth range."

His poetry was originally written merely for his own amusement in his leisure hours; but afterwards he introduced into it philosophic sentiments, and interwove political events with his poems, not in order to record them historically, but in some cases to explain his own conduct, and in others to instruct, encourage, or rebuke the Athenians. Some say that he endeavoured to throw his laws into an epic form, and tell us that the poem began—

"To Jove I pray, great Saturn's son divine, To grant his favour to these laws of mine."

Of ethical philosophy, he, like most of the sages of antiquity, was most interested in that branch which deals with political obligations. As to natural science, his views are very crude and antiquated, as we see from the following verses:

"From clouds the snow and hail descend, And thunderbolts the lightnings send; The waves run high when gales do blow, Without the wind they're still enow."

Indeed, of all the sages of that time, Thales alone seems to have known more of physics than was necessary to supply man's every-day needs; all the others having gained their reputation for political wisdom.

IV. These wise men are said to have met at Delphi, and again at Corinth, where they were entertained by the despot Periander. Their reputation was greatly increased by the tripod which was sent to all of them and refused by all with a gracious rivalry. The story goes that some men of Cos were casting a net, and some strangers from Miletus bought the haul of them before it reached the surface.

The net brought up a golden tripod, the same which, it is said, Helen threw into the sea at that spot, in accordance with some ancient oracle, when she was sailing away from Troy. A dispute arose at first between the strangers and the fishermen; afterwards it was taken up by their respective cities, who even came to blows about it. Finally they consulted the oracle at Delphi, which ordered it to be given to the wisest. Now it was first sent to Miletus, to Thales, as the men of Cos willingly gave it to that one man, although they had fought with all the Milesians together about it. Thales said that Bias was wiser than himself, and sent it to him; and by him it was again sent to another man, as being wiser yet. So it went on, being sent from one to another until it came to Thales a second time, and at last was sent from Miletus to Thebes and consecrated to Apollo Ismenius. As Theophrastus tells the story, the tripod was first sent to Bias at Priéne, and secondly to Thales at Miletus, and so on through all of the wise men until it again reached Bias, and was finally offered at Delphi. This is the more common version of the story, although some say that it was not a tripod but a bowl sent by Croesus, others that it was a drinking-cup left behind by one Bathykles.

V. Anacharsis is said to have met Solon, and afterwards Thales in private, and to have conversed with them. The story goes that Anacharsis came to Athens, went to Solon's door, and knocked, saying that he was a stranger and had come to enter into friendship with him. When Solon answered that friendships were best made at home, Anacharsis said, "Well then, do you, who are at home, enter into friendship with me." Solon, admiring the man's cleverness, received him kindly, and kept him for some time in his house. He was at this time engaged in politics, and was composing his laws. Anacharsis, when he discovered this, laughed at Solon's undertaking, if he thought to restrain the crimes and greed of the citizens by written laws, which he said were just like spiders' webs; for, like them, they caught the weaker criminals, but were broken through by the stronger and more important.

To this Solon answered, that men keep covenants, because it is to the advantage of neither party to break them; and that he so suited his laws to his countrymen, that it was to the advantage of every one to abide by them rather than to break them. Nevertheless, things turned out more as Anacharsis thought than as Solon wished. Anacharsis said too, when present at an assembly of the people, that he was surprised to see that in Greece wise men spoke upon public affairs, and ignorant men decided them.

VI. When Solon went to Thales at Miletus, he expressed his wonder at his having never married and had a family. Thales made no answer at the time, but a few days afterwards arranged that a man should come to him and say that he left Athens ten days before. When Solon inquired of him, whether anything new had happened at Athens, the man answered, as Thales had instructed him, that "there was no news, except the death of a young man who had been escorted to his grave by the whole city. He was the son, they told him, of a leading citizen of great repute for his goodness, but the father was not present, for they said he had been travelling abroad for some years." "Unhappy man," said Solon, "what was his name?" "I heard his name," answered the man, "but I cannot remember it; beyond that there was much talk of his wisdom and justice." Thus by each of his answers he increased Solon's alarm, until he at last in his excitement asked the stranger whether it were not Solon's son that was dead. The stranger said that it was. Solon was proceeding to beat his head and show all the other marks of grief, when Thales stopped him, saying with a smile, "This, Solon, which has the power to strike down so strong a man as you, has ever prevented my marrying and having children. But be of good courage, for this tale which you have been told is untrue." This story is said by Hermippus to have been told by Pataikos, he who said that he had inherited the soul of Aesop.

VII. It is a strange and unworthy feeling that prompts a man not to claim that to which he has a right, for fear that he may one day lose it; for by the same reasoning he might refuse wealth, reputation, or wisdom, for fear of losing them hereafter. We see even virtue, the greatest and most dear of all possessions, can be destroyed by disease or evil drugs; and Thales by avoiding marriage still had just as much to fear, unless indeed he ceased to love his friends, his kinsmen, and his native land. But even he adopted his sister's son Kybisthus; for the soul has a spring of affection within it, and is formed not only to perceive, to reflect, and to remember, but also to love. If it finds nothing to love at home, it will find something abroad; and when affection, like a desert spot, has no legitimate possessors, it is usurped by bastard children or even servants, who when they have obtained our love, make us fear for them and be anxious about them. So that one may often see men, in a cynical temper, inveighing against marriage and children, who themselves shortly afterwards will be plunged into unmanly excesses of grief, at the loss of their child by some slave or concubine. Some have even shown terrible grief at the death of dogs and horses; whereas others, who have lost noble sons, made no unusual or unseemly exhibition of sorrow, but passed the remainder of their lives calmly and composedly. Indeed it is weakness, not affection, which produces such endless misery and dread to those who have not learned to take a rational view of the uncertainty of life, and who cannot enjoy the presence of their loved ones because of their constant agony for fear of losing them. We should not make ourselves poor for fear of losing our property, nor should we guard ourselves against a possible loss of friends by making none; still less ought we to avoid having children for fear that our child might die. But we have already dwelt too much upon this subject.

VIII. After a long and harassing war with the Megarians about the possession of the Island of Salamis, the Athenians finally gave up in sheer weariness, and passed a law forbidding any one for the future, either to speak or to write in favour of the Athenian claim to Salamis, upon pain of death. Solon, grieved at this dishonour, and observing that many of the younger men were eager for an excuse to fight, but dared not propose to do so because of this law, pretended to have lost his reason. His family gave out that he was insane, but he meanwhile composed a poem, and when he had learned it by heart, rushed out into the market-place wearing a small felt cap, and having assembled a crowd, mounted the herald's stone and recited the poem which begins with the lines—
"A herald I from Salamis am come, My verse will tell you what should there be done."

The name of this poem is Salamis; it consists of a hundred beautifully written lines. After he had sung it, his friends began to commend it, and Peisistratus made a speech to the people, which caused such enthusiasm that they abrogated the law and renewed the war, with Solon as their leader. The common version of the story runs thus: Solon sailed with Peisistratus to Kolias, where he found all the women of the city performing the customary sacrifice to Demeter (Ceres). At the same time, he sent a trusty man to Salamis, who represented himself as a deserter, and bade the Megarians follow him at once to Kolias, if they wished to capture all the women of the first Athenian families. The Megarians were duped, and sent off a force in a ship. As soon as Solon saw this ship sail away from the island, he ordered the women out of the way, dressed up those young men who were still beardless in their clothes, headdresses, and shoes, gave them daggers, and ordered them to dance and disport themselves near the seashore until the enemy landed, and their ship was certain to be captured. So the Megarians, imagining them to be women, fell upon them, struggling which should first seize them, but they were cut off to a man by the Athenians, who at once sailed to Salamis and captured it.

IX. Others say that the island was not taken in this way, but that first of all Solon received the following oracular response from Apollo at Delphi:
"Appease the land's true lords, the heroes blest, Who near Asopia's fair margin rest, And from their tombs still look towards the West."

After this, Solon is said to have sailed by night, unnoticed by the Megarians, and to have sacrificed to the heroes Periphemus and Kychreus. His next act was to raise five hundred Athenian volunteers, who by a public decree were to be absolute masters of the island if they could conquer it. With these he set sail in a number of fishing-boats, with a triaconter or ship of war of thirty oars, sailing in company, and anchored off a certain cape which stretches towards Euboea. The Megarians in Euboea heard an indistinct rumour of this, and at once ran to arms, and sent a ship to reconnoitre the enemy. This ship, when it came near Solon's fleet, was captured and its crew taken prisoners. On board of it Solon placed some picked men, and ordered them to make sail for the city of Salamis, and to conceal themselves as far as they could. Meanwhile he with the remaining Athenians attacked the Megarian forces by land; and while the battle was at its hottest, the men in the ship succeeded in surprising the city.

This story appears to be borne out by the proceedings which were instituted in memory of the capture. In this ceremony an Athenian ship used to sail to Salamis, at first in silence, and then as they neared the shore with warlike shouts. Then a man completely armed used to leap out and run, shouting as he went, up to the top of the hill called Skiradion, where he met those who came by land. Close by this place stands the temple of Ares, which Solon built; for he conquered the Megarians in the battle, and sent away the survivors with a flag of truce.

X. However, as the Megarians still continued the war, to the great misery of both sides, they agreed to make the Lacedaemonians arbitrators and judges between them. Most writers say that Solon brought the great authority of Homer's 'Iliad' to his aid, by interpolating in the catologue of ships the two verses—

"Ajax from Salamis twelve vessels good Brought, and he placed them where the Athenians stood,"

which he had read as evidence before the court.

The Athenians, however, say that all this is nonsense, but that Solon proved to the arbitrators that Philaeus and Eurysakes, the sons of Ajax, when they were enrolled as Athenian citizens, made over the island to Athens, and dwelt, one at Brauron, in Attica, and the other at Melité; moreover, there is an Athenian tribe which claims descent from Philaeus, to which Peisistratus belonged. Wishing, however, yet more thoroughly to prove his case against the Megarians, he based an argument on the tombs in the island, in which the corpses were buried, not in the Megarian, but in the Athenian manner. For the Megarians bury their dead looking towards the east, and the Athenians towards the west. But Hereas of Megara denies this, and says that the Megarians also bury their dead looking towards the west, and moreover, that each Athenian had a coffin to himself, while the Megarians place two or three bodies in one coffin. However, Solon supported his case by quoting certain oracles from Delphi, in which the god addresses Salamis as Ionian. The Spartan arbitrators were five in number, their names being Kritolaidas, Amompharetus, Hypsichidas, Anaxilos, and Kleomenes.

XI. Solon's reputation and power were greatly increased by this, but he became much more celebrated and well-known in Greece by his speeches on behalf of the temple at Delphi, in which he urged the necessity of checking the insolent conduct of the people of Kirrha towards the temple, and of rallying in defence of the god. The Amphiktyons, prevailed upon by his eloquence, declared war, as we learn from Aristotle, among other writers, in his book about the winners of the prize at the Pythian games, in which he attributes this decision to Solon. However, he was not made general in that war, as Hermippus relates, quoting from Evanthes of Samos; for Aeschines the orator does not mention him, and, in the records of Delphi, Alkmaeon, not Solon, is mentioned as general of the Athenians on that occasion.

XII. Athens had long been suffering from the anger of the gods, which it had incurred by the treatment of Kylon's party. These conspirators took sanctuary in Athene's temple, but were induced by Megakles the archon to quit it and stand their trial. They fastened a thread to the shrine of the goddess, and kept hold of it so as still to be under her protection. But as they were coming down from the Acropolis, just beside the temple of the Furies, the string broke, and Megakles and the other archons, thinking that the goddess rejected their appeal, seized them. Some of them were stoned to death outside the temple, and some who had fled for sanctuary to the altars were slain there. Only those who fell as suppliants at the feet of the archons' wives were spared. After this the archons were called accursed, and were viewed with horror; moreover, the survivors of Kylon's party regained strength, and continued their intrigues against Megakles and the archons. At the time of which we are speaking these dissensions had reached their height, and the city was divided into two factions, when Solon, who was already a man of great reputation, came forward with some of the noblest Athenians, and by his entreaties and arguments prevailed upon those magistrates who were called accursed, to stand trial and be judged by a jury of three hundred citizens selected from the best families. Myron of Phlya prosecuted, and the archons were found guilty, and forced to leave the country. The bodies of such of them as had died were dug up, and cast out beyond the borders of Attica.

During these disorders the Athenians were again attacked by the Megarians, and lost Nisaea, and were again driven out of Salamis. The city was also a prey to superstitious terrors, and apparitions were seen, so that the prophets, after inspecting their victims, said that the city was polluted and under a curse, and that it required purification. Upon this they sent for Epimenides the Phaestian, of Crete, who is reckoned among the seven wise men of Greece, by some of those who do not admit Periander into their number. He was thought to enjoy the favour of Heaven, and was skilled in all the lore of the sacred mysteries, and in the sources of divine inspiration; wherefore he was commonly reported to be the child of the nymph Balte, and to be one of the old Curetes of Crete revived. He came to Athens and was a friend to Solon, assisting him greatly in his legislation. He remodelled their religious rites, and made their mourning more moderate, introducing certain sacrifices shortly after the funeral, and abolishing the harsh and barbarous treatment which women were for the most part subject to before in times of mourning. Above all, by purifications and atoning sacrifices, and the erection of new temples, he so sanctified and hallowed the city as to make the minds of the people obedient to the laws, and easily guided into unity and concord. It is said that he saw Munychia, and viewed it carefully for some time in silence. Then he said to the bystanders, "How blind is man to the future. The Athenians would eat this place up with their teeth if they knew what misfortunes it will bring upon them?" A prophetic saying of the same kind is attributed to Thales. He bade his friends bury him in a low and neglected quarter of Miletus, telling them that one day it would be the market-place of the city. Epimenides was greatly honoured by the Athenians, and was offered large sums of money by them, and great privileges, but he refused them all, and only asked for a branch of the sacred olive-tree, which he received and went his way.

XIII. When the troubles about Kylon were over, and the accursed men cast out of the country, the Athenians relapsed into their old dispute about the constitution. The state was divided into as many factions as there were parts of the country, for the Diakrii, or mountaineers, favoured democracy; the Pedioei, oligarchy; while those who dwelt along the seashore, called Parali, preferred a constitution midway between these two forms, and thus prevented either of the other parties from carrying their point. Moreover, the state was on the verge of revolution, because of the excessive poverty of some citizens, and the enormous wealth of others, and it appeared that the only means of putting an end to these disorders was by establishing an absolute despotism. The whole people were in debt to a few wealthy men; they either cultivated their farms, in which case they were obliged to pay one-sixth of the profit to their creditors, and were called Hektemori, or servants, or else they had raised loans upon personal security, and had become the slaves of their creditors, who either employed them at home, or sold them to foreigners. Many were even compelled to sell their own children, which was not illegal, and to leave the country because of the harshness of their creditors.

The greater part, and those of most spirit, combined together, and encouraged one another not to suffer such oppression any longer, but to choose some trustworthy person to protect their interests, to set free all enslaved debtors, redistribute the land, and, in a word, entirely remodel the constitution.

XIV. In this position of affairs, the most sensible men in Athens perceived that Solon was a person who shared the vices of neither faction, as he took no part in the oppressive conduct of the wealthy, and yet had sufficient fortune to save him from the straits to which the poor were reduced. In consequence of this, they begged him to come forward and end their disputes. But Phanias of Lesbos says that Solon deceived both parties, in order to save the state, promising the poor a redistribution of lands, and the rich a confirmation of their securities. However, Solon himself tells us that it was with reluctance that he interfered, as he was threatened by the avarice of the one party, and the desperation of the other. He was chosen archon next after Philombrotus, to act as an arbitrator and lawgiver at once, because the rich had confidence in him as a man of easy fortune, and the poor trusted him as a good man. It is said also that a saying which he had let fall some time before, that "equality does not breed strife," was much circulated at the time, and pleased both parties, because the rich thought it meant that property should be distributed according to merit and desert, while the poor thought it meant according to rule and measure. Both parties were now elate with hope, and their leaders urged Solon to seize the supreme power in the state, of which he was practically possessed, and make himself king. Many even of the more moderate class of politicians, who saw how weary and difficult a task it would be to reform the state by debates and legislative measures, were quite willing that so wise and honest a man should undertake the sole management of affairs. It is even said that Solon received an oracle as follows:
"Take thou the helm, the vessel guide, Athens will rally to thy side."

His intimate friends were loudest in their reproaches, pointing out that it was merely the name of despot from which he shrunk, and that in his case his virtues would lead men to regard him as a legitimate hereditary sovereign; instancing also Tunnondas, who in former times had been chosen by the Euboeans, and, at the present time, Pittakus, who had been chosen king of Mitylene. But nothing could shake Solon's determination. He told his friends

that monarchy is indeed a pleasant place, but there is no way out of it; and he inserted the following verses in answer to Phokus, in one of his poems:
"But if I spared My country, and with dread tyrannic sway, Forbore to stain and to pollute my glory; I feel no shame at this; nay rather thus, I think that I excel mankind."

From which it is clear that he possessed a great reputation even before he became the lawgiver of Athens.

In answer to the reproaches of many of his friends at his refusal to make himself despot, he wrote as follows:
"Not a clever man was Solon, not a calculating mind, For he would not take the kingdom, which the gods to him inclined, In his net he caught the prey, but would not draw it forth to land, Overpowered by his terrors, feeble both of heart and hand; For a man of greater spirit would have occupied the throne, Proud to be the Lord of Athens, though 'twere for a day alone, Though the next day he and his into oblivion were thrown."

XV. This is the way in which he says the masses, and low-minded men, spoke of him. He, however, firmly rejecting the throne, proceeded quietly to administer public affairs, in laying down his laws without any weak yielding to the powerful, or any attempt to court popularity. Such as were good, he did not meddle with, fearing that if he

"Disturbed and overset the state,"

he might not have sufficient power to

"Reconstitute and organise again,"

in the best way. He carried out his measures by persuasion, and, where he thought he could succeed, by force; in his own words,

"Combining Force and Justice both together."

Being afterwards asked whether he had composed the best possible laws for the Athenians, he answered, "The best that they would endure." And the habit of Athenians of later times, who soften down harsh words by using politer equivalents, calling harlots "mistresses," taxes "contributions," garrisons of cities "protectors," and the common prison "the house," was, it seems, first invented by Solon, who devised the name of "relief from burdens" for his measure to abolish all debts.

This was his first measure; namely, to put an end to all existing debts and obligations, and to forbid any one in future to lend money upon security of the person of the debtor. Some writers, among whom is Androtion, say that he benefited the poor, not by the absolute extinction of debt, but by establishing a lower rate of interest; and that this measure was called "Relief from burdens," and together with it the two other measures for the enlargement of measures and of the value of money, which were passed about the same time. For he ordered a mina, which was before constituted of seventy three drachmas, to contain a hundred, so that, though they paid the same amount, yet the value was less; thus those who had much to pay were benefited, and still their creditors were not cheated. But most writers say that the "Relief from burdens" meant the extinction of all securities whatever, and this agrees best with what we read in his poems. For Solon prides himself in these upon having

"Taken off the mortgages, which on the land were laid, And made the country free, which was formerly enslaved."

While he speaks of bringing back Athenian citizens who had been sold into slavery abroad,

"In distant lands who roam, Their native tongue forgot, Or here endure at home A slave's disgraceful lot,"

and of making them free men again.

It is said that in consequence of this measure he met with the greatest trouble of his life. As he was meditating how he might put an end to debt, and what words and preambles were best for the introduction of this law, he took counsel with his most intimate friends, such as Konon and Kleinias and Hipponikus, informing them that he had no intention of interfering with the tenure of land, but that he intended to abolishing all existing securities. They instantly took time by the forelock, borrowed large sums from the wealthy, and bought up a great extent of land. Presently the decree came forth, and they remained in enjoyment of these estates, but did not repay their loan to their creditors. This brought Solon into great discredit, for the people believed that he had been their accomplice. But he soon proved that this must be false, by remitting a debt of five talents which he himself had lent; and some state the sum at fifteen talents, amongst whom is Polyzelus of Rhodes. However, his friends were for ever afterwards called "The Swindlers."

XVI. By this measure he pleased neither party, but the rich were dissatisfied at the loss of their securities, and the poor were still more so because the land was not divided afresh, as they hoped it would be, and because he had not, like Lykurgus, established absolute equality.

But Lykurgus was eleventh in direct descent from Herakles, and had reigned in Lacedaemon for many years, and had his own great reputation, friends, and interest to assist him in carrying out his reforms: and although he chose to effect his purpose by violence, so that his eye was actually knocked out, yet he succeeded in carrying that measure, so valuable for the safety and concord of the state, by which it was rendered impossible for any citizen to be either rich or poor. Solon's power could not reach this height, as he was only a commoner and a moderate man; yet he did all that was in his power, relying solely upon the confidence and goodwill of his countrymen.

It is clear that they were disappointed, and expected more from his legislation, from his own verses—
"Once they speculated gaily, what good luck should them befall, Now they look upon me coldly, as a traitor to them all."

Yet he says, if any one else had been in his position,
"He ne'er would have desisted from unsettling the laws, Till he himself got all the cream."

However, not long afterwards, they perceived the public benefits which he had conferred upon them, forgot their private grievances, and made a public sacrifice in honour of the Seisachtheia, or "Relief from burdens." Moreover, they constituted Solon supreme reformer and lawgiver, not over some departments only, but placing everything alike in his hands; magistracies, public assemblies, senate, and law-courts. He had full powers to confirm or abolish any of these, and to fix the proper qualifications for members of them, and their numbers and times of meeting.

XVII. First of all, then, he repealed all the laws of Drakon, except those relating to murder, because of their harshness and the excessive punishments which they awarded. For death was the punishment for almost every offence, so that even men convicted of idleness were executed, and those who stole pot-herbs or fruits suffered just like sacrilegious robbers and murderers. So that Demades afterwards made the joke that Drakon's laws were not written with ink, but with blood. It is said that Drakon himself, when asked why he had fixed the punishment of death for most offences, answered that he considered these lesser crimes to deserve it, and he had no greater punishment for more important ones.

XVIII. In the next place, Solon, who wished to leave all magistracies as he found them, in the hands of the wealthy classes, but to give the people a share in the rest of the constitution, from which they were then excluded, took a census of the wealth of the citizens, and made a first class of those who had an annual income of not less than five hundred medimni of dry or liquid produce; these he called Pentakosiomedimni. The next class were the Hippeis, or knights, consisting of those who were able to keep a horse, or who had an income of three hundred medimni. The third class were the Zeugitae, whose property qualification was two hundred medimni of dry or liquid produce; and the last class were the Thetes, whom Solon did not permit to be magistrates, but whose only political privilege was the right of attending the public assemblies and sitting as jurymen in the law courts. This privilege was at first insignificant, but afterwards became of infinite importance, because most disputes were settled before a jury. Even in those cases which he allowed the magistrates to settle, he provided a final appeal to the people.

Solon moreover is said to have purposely worded his laws vaguely and with several interpretations, in order to increase the powers of these juries, because persons who could not settle their disputes by the letter of the law were obliged to have recourse to juries of the people, and to refer all disputes to them, as being to a certain extent above the laws. He himself notices this in the following verses:

"I gave the people all the strength they needed, Yet kept the power of the nobles strong; Thus each from other's violence I shielded, Not letting either do the other wrong."

Thinking that the weakness of the populace required still further protection, he permitted any man to prosecute on behalf of any other who might be ill-treated. Thus if a man were struck or injured, any one else who was able and willing might prosecute on his behalf, and the lawgiver by this means endeavoured to make the whole body of citizens act together and feel as one. A saying of his is recorded which quite agrees with the spirit of this law. Being asked, what he thought was the best managed city? "That," he answered, "in which those who are not wronged espouse the cause of those who are, and punish their oppressors."

XIX. He established the senate of the Areopagus of those who had held the yearly office of archon, and himself became a member of it because he had been archon. But in addition to this, observing that the people were becoming turbulent and unruly, in consequence of their relief from debt, he formed a second senate, consisting of a hundred men selected from each of the four tribes, to deliberate on measures in the first instance, and he permitted no measures to be proposed before the general assembly, which had not been previously discussed in this senate. The upper senate he intended to exercise a general supervision, and to maintain the laws, and he thought that with these two senates as her anchors, the ship of the state would ride more securely, and that the people would be less inclined to disorder. Most writers say that Solon constituted the senate of the Areopagus, as is related above; and this view is supported by the fact that Drakon nowhere mentions or names the Areopagites, but in all cases of murder refers to the Ephetai. However, the eighth law on the thirteenth table of the laws of Solon runs thus:—

"All citizens who were disfranchised before the magistracy of Solon shall resume their rights, except those who have been condemned by the Areopagus, or by the Ephetai, or by the king—archons, in the prytaneum, for murder or manslaughter, or attempts to overthrow the government and who were in exile when this law was made."

This again proves that the senate of the Areopagus existed before the time of Solon; for who could those persons be who were condemned by the court of the Areopagus, if Solon was the first who gave the senate of the Areopagus a criminal jurisdiction; though perhaps some words have been left out, or indistinctly written, and the law means "all those who had been condemned on the charges which now are judged by the court of the Areopagus, the Ephetai, or the Prytanies, when this law was made, must remain disfranchised, though the others become enfranchised?" Of these explanations the reader himself must consider which he prefers.

XX. The strangest of his remaining laws is that which declared disfranchised a citizen who in a party conflict took neither side; apparently his object was to prevent any one regarding home politics in a listless, uninterested fashion, securing his own personal property, and priding himself upon exemption from the misfortunes of his country, and to encourage men boldly to attach themselves to the right party and to share all its dangers, rather than in safety to watch and see which side would be successful. That also is a strange and even ludicrous provision in one of his laws, which permits an heiress, whose husband proves impotent, to avail herself of the services of the next of kin to obtain an heir to her estate. Some, however, say that this law rightly serves men who know themselves to be unfit for marriage, and who nevertheless marry heiresses for their money, and try to make the laws override nature; for, when they see their wife having intercourse with whom she pleases, they will either break off the marriage, or live in constant shame, and so pay the penalty of their avarice and wrong-doing. It is a good provision also, that the heiress may not converse with any one, but only with him whom she may choose from among her husband's relations, so that her offspring may be all in the family. This is pointed at by his ordinance that the bride and bridegroom should be shut in the same room and eat a quince together, and that the husband of an heiress should approach her at least thrice in each month. For even if no children are born, still this is a mark of respect to a good wife, and puts an end to many misunderstandings, preventing their leading to an actual quarrel.

In other marriages he suppressed dowries, and ordered the bride to bring to her husband three dresses and a few articles of furniture of no great value;

for he did not wish marriages to be treated as money bargains or means of gain, but that men and women should enter into marriage for love and happiness and procreation of children. Dionysius, the despot of Syracuse, when his mother wished to be married to a young citizen, told her that he had indeed broken the laws of the state when he seized the throne, but that he could not disregard the laws of nature so far as to countenance such a monstrous union. These disproportioned matches ought not to be permitted in any state, nor should men be allowed to form unequal loveless alliances, which are in no sense true marriages. A magistrate or lawgiver might well address an old man who marries a young girl in the words of Sophokles: "Poor wretch, a hopeful bridegroom you will be;" and if he found a young man fattening like a partridge in the house of a rich old woman, he ought to transfer him to some young maiden who is without a husband. So much for this subject.

XXI. Besides these, Solon's law which forbids men to speak evil of the dead is much praised. It is good to think of the departed as sacred, and it is only just to refrain from attacking the absent, while it is politic, also, to prevent hatred from being eternal. He also forbade people to speak evil of the living in temples, courts of justice, public buildings, or during the national games; and imposed a fine of three drachmas to the person offended, and two to the state. His reason for this was that it shows a violent and uncultivated nature not to be able to restrain one's passion in certain places and at certain times, although it is hard to do so always, and to some persons impossible; and a legislator should frame his laws with a view to what he can reasonably hope to effect, and rather correct a few persons usefully than punish a number to no purpose.

He gained credit also by his law about wills. Before his time these were not permitted at Athens, but the money and lands of a deceased person were inherited by his family in all cases. Solon, however, permitted any one who had no children to leave his property to whom he would, honouring friendship more than nearness of kin, and giving a man absolute power to dispose of his inheritance. Yet, on the other hand, he did not permit legacies to be given without any restrictions, but disallowed all that were obtained by the effects of disease or by administration of drugs to the testator, or by imprisonment and violence, or by the solicitations of his wife, as he rightly considered that to be persuaded by one's wife against one's better judgment is the same as to submit to force. For Solon held that a man's reason was perverted by deceit as much as by violence, and by pleasure no less than by pain.

He regulated, moreover, the journeys of the women, and their mournings and festivals. A woman was not allowed to travel with more than three dresses, nor with more than an obolus' worth of food or drink, nor a basket more than a cubit in length; nor was she to travel at night, except in a waggon with a light carried in front of it. He abolished the habits of tearing themselves at funerals, and of reciting set forms of dirges, and of hiring mourners. He also forbade them to sacrifice an ox for the funeral feast, and to bury more than three garments with the body, and to visit other persons' graves. Most of these things are forbidden by our own laws also; with the addition, that by our laws those who offend thus are fined by the gynaeconomi, or regulators of the women, for giving way to unmanly and womanish sorrow.

XXII. Observing that the city was filled with men who came from all countries to take refuge in Attica, that the country was for the most part poor and unproductive, and that merchants also are unwilling to despatch cargoes to a country which has nothing to export, he encouraged his countrymen to embark in trade, and made a law that a son was not obliged to support his father, if his father had not taught him a trade. As for Lykurgus, whose city was clear of strangers, and whose land was "unstinted, and with room for twice the number," as Euripides says, and who above all had all the Helots, throughout Lacedaemon, who were best kept employed, in order to break their spirit by labour and hardship, it was very well that his citizens should disdain laborious handicrafts and devote their whole attention to the art of war.

But Solon had not the power to change the whole life of his countrymen by his laws, but rather was forced to suit his laws to existing circumstances, and, as he saw that the soil was so poor that it could only suffice for the farmers, and was unable to feed a mass of idle people as well, he gave great honour to trade, and gave powers to the senate of the Areopagus to inquire what each man's source of income might be, and to punish the idle. A harsher measure was that of which we are told by Herakleides of Pontus, his making it unnecessary for illegitimate children to maintain their father. Yet if a man abstains from an honourable marriage, and lives with a woman more for his own pleasure in her society than with a view to producing a family, he is rightly served, and cannot upbraid his children with neglecting him, because he has made their birth their reproach.

XXIII. Altogether Solon's laws concerning women are very strange. He permitted a husband to kill an adulterer taken in the act; but if any one carried off a free woman and forced her, he assessed the penalty at one hundred drachmas. If he obtained her favours by persuasion, he was to pay twenty drachmas, except in the case of those who openly ply for hire, alluding to harlots; for they come to those who offer them money without any concealment. Moreover, he forbade men to sell their sisters and daughters, except in the case of unchastity. Now to punish the same offence at one time with unrelenting severity, and at another in a light and trifling manner, by imposing so slight a fine, is unreasonable, unless the scarcity of specie in the city at that period made fines which were paid in money more valuable than they would now be; indeed, in the valuation of things for sacrifice, a sheep and a drachma were reckoned as each equal to a medimnus of corn. To the victor at the Isthmian games he appointed a reward of a hundred drachmas, and to the victor in the Olympian, five hundred. He gave five drachmas for every wolf that was killed, and one drachma for every wolf's whelp; and we are told by Demetrius of Phalerum that the first of these sums was the price of an ox, and the second that of a sheep. The prices of choice victims, which he settled in his sixteenth tablet of laws, would naturally be higher than those of ordinary beasts, but even thus they are cheap compared with prices at the present day. It was an ancient practice among the Athenians to destroy the wolves, because their country was better fitted for pasture than for growing crops. Some say that the Athenian tribes derive their names, not from the sons of Ion, but from the different professions in which men were then divided: thus the fighting men were named Hoplites, and the tradesmen Ergadeis; the two remaining ones being the Geleontes, or farmers, and the Aigikoreis, or goat-herds and graziers. With regard to water, as the country is not supplied with either rivers or lakes, but the people depend chiefly upon artificial wells, he made a law, that wherever there was a public well within four furlongs, people should use it, but if it were farther off, then they must dig a private well for themselves; but if a man dug a depth of sixty feet on his own estate without finding water, then he was to have the right of filling a six-gallon pitcher twice a day at his neighbour's well; for Solon thought it right to help the distressed, and yet not to encourage laziness. He also made very judicious regulations about planting trees, ordering that they should not be planted within five feet of a neighbour's property, except in the case of olives and fig-trees, which were not to be planted within nine feet; for these trees spread out their roots farther than others, and spoil the growth of any others by taking away their nourishment and by giving off hurtful juices. Trenches and pits he ordered to be dug as far away from another man's property as they were deep; and no hive of bees was to be placed within three hundred feet of those already established by another man.

XXIV. Oil was the only product of the country which he allowed to be exported, everything else being forbidden; and he ordered that if any one broke this law the archon was to solemnly curse him, unless he paid a hundred drachmas into the public treasury. This law is written on the first of his tablets. From this we see that the old story is not altogether incredible, that the export of figs was forbidden, and that the men who informed against those who had done so were therefore called sycophants. He also made laws about damage received from animals, one of which was that a dog who had bitten a man should be delivered up to him tied to a stick three cubits long, an ingenious device for safety.

One is astounded at his law of adopting foreigners into the state, which permits no one to become a full citizen in Athens unless he be either exiled for life from his native city, or transfers himself with his whole family to Athens to practise his trade there. It is said that his object in this was not so much to exclude other classes of people from the city, as to assure these of a safe refuge there; and these he thought would be good and faithful citizens, because the former had been banished from their own country, and the latter had abandoned it of their own freewill. Another peculiarity of Solon's laws was the public dining-table in the prytaneum. Here he did not allow the same person to dine often, while he punished the man who was invited and would not come, because the one seemed gluttonous, and the other contemptuous.

XXV. He ordered that all his laws should remain in force for a hundred years, and he wrote them upon triangular wooden tablets, which revolved upon an axis in oblong recesses, some small remains of which have been preserved in the prytaneum down to the present day. These, we are told by Aristotle, were called Kurbeis. The comic poet Kratinus also says,
"By Solon and by Draco, mighty legislators once, Whose tablets light the fire now to warm a dish of pulse."

Some say that the term Kurbeis is only applied to those on which are written the laws which regulate religious matters.

The senate swore by a collective oath that it would enforce Solon's laws; and each of the Thesmothetae took an oath to the same effect at the altar in the market-place, protesting that, if he transgressed any of the laws, he would offer a golden statue as big as himself to the temple at Delphi.

Observing the irregularity of the months, and that the motions of the moon did not accord either with the rising or setting of the sun, but that frequently she in the same day overtakes and passes by him, he ordered that day to be called "the old and the new," and that the part of it before their conjunction should belong to the old month, while the rest of the day after it belonged to the new one, being, it seems, the first to rightly interpret the verse of Homer—

"The old month ended and the new began."

He called the next day that of the new moon. After the twentieth, he no longer reckoned forwards, but backwards, as the moon decreased, until the thirtieth of the month.

When Solon had passed all his laws, as people came to him every day to praise or blame, or advise him to add or take away from what he had written, while innumerable people wanted to ask questions, and discuss points, and kept bidding him explain what was the object of this or that regulation, he, feeling that he could not do all this, and that, if he did not, his motives would be misunderstood; wishing, moreover, to escape from troubles and the criticism and fault-finding of his countrymen [for, as he himself writes, it is "Hard in great measures every one to please"], made his private commercial business an excuse for leaving the country, and set sail after having obtained from the Athenians leave of absence for ten years. In this time he thought they would become used to his laws.

XXVI. He first went to Egypt, where he spent some time, as he himself says,
    "At Nilus' outlets, by Canopus' strand."

And he also discussed points of philosophy with Psenophis of Heliopolis, and with Sonchis of Sais, the most distinguished of the Egyptian priests. From them he heard the tale of the island Atlantis, as we are told by Plato, and endeavoured to translate it into a poetical form for the enjoyment of his countrymen. He next sailed to Cyprus, where he was warmly received by Philocyprus, one of the local sovereigns, who ruled over a small city founded by Demophon, the son of Theseus, near the river Klarius, in a position which was easily defended, but inconvenient.

As a fair plain lay below, Solon persuaded him to remove the city to a pleasanter and less contracted site, and himself personally superintended the building of the new city, which he arranged so well both for convenience and safety, that many new settlers joined Philocyprus, and he was envied by the neighbouring kings. For this reason, in honour of Solon, he named the new city Soloi, the name of the old one having been Aipeia. Solon himself mentions this event, in one of his elegiac poems, in which he addresses Philocyprus, saying—

"Long may'st thou reign, Ruling thy race from Soloi's throne with glory, But me may Venus of the violet crown Send safe away from Cyprus famed in story. May Heaven to these new walls propitious prove, And bear me safely to the land I love."

XXVII. Some writers argue, on chronological grounds, that Solon's meeting with Croesus must have been an invention. But I cannot think that so famous a story, which is confirmed by so many writers, and, moreover, which so truly exhibits Solon's greatness of mind and wisdom, ought to be given up because of the so-called rules of chronology, which have been discussed by innumerable persons, up to the present day, without their being ever able to make their dates agree. The story goes that Solon at Croesus's desire came to Sardis, and there felt much like a continental when he goes down to the seaside for the first time; for he thinks each river he comes to must be the sea, and so Solon, as he walked through the court and saw many of the courtiers richly attired and each of them swaggering about with a train of attendants and body-guards, thought that each one must be the king, until he was brought before the king himself, who, as far as precious stones, richly dyed clothes, and cunningly worked gold could adorn him, was splendid and admirable, indeed a grand and gorgeous spectacle to behold. When Solon was brought into his presence, he showed none of the feelings and made none of the remarks about the sight, which Croesus expected, but evidently despised such vulgar ostentation. Croesus then ordered his treasures to be exhibited to him, and all the rest of his possessions and valuables; not that Solon needed this, for the sight of Croesus himself was enough to show him what sort of man he was. When, after having seen all this, he was again brought before the king, Croesus asked him whether he knew any man more happy than himself. Solon at once answered that one Tellus, a fellow countryman of his own, was more happy. He explained that Tellus was a good man, and left a family of good sons; that he passed his life beyond the reach of want, and died gloriously in battle for his country. At this, Croesus began to think that Solon must be a cross-grained churlish fellow, if he did not measure happiness by silver and gold, but preferred the life and death of some private man of low degree to such power and empire as his. However, he asked him a second time, whether he knew any one more happy than himself, next to Tellus. Solon answered that he knew two men, Kleobis and Biton, remarkable for their love for each other and for their mother, who, as the oxen that drew their mother travelled slowly, put themselves under the yoke and drew the carriage with her in it to the temple of Here. She was congratulated by all the citizens, and was very proud of them; and they offered sacrifice, drank some wine, and then passed away by a painless death after so much glory.

"Then," asked Croesus angrily, "do you not reckon me at all among happy men?" Solon, who did not wish to flatter him, nor yet to exasperate him farther, answered, "O King of the Lydians, we Greeks have been endowed with moderate gifts, by Heaven, and our wisdom is of a cautious and homely cast, not of a royal and magnificent character; so, being moderate itself, and seeing the manifold chances to which life is exposed, it does not permit us to take a pride in our present possessions, nor to admire the good fortune of any man when it is liable to change. Strange things await every man in the unknown future; and we think that man alone happy whose life has been brought to a fortunate termination. To congratulate a man who is yet alive and exposed to the caprice of fortune is like proclaiming and crowning as victor one who has not yet run his race, for his good fortune is uncertain and liable to reversal." After speaking thus, Solon took his leave, having enraged Croesus, who could not take his good advice.

XXVIII. Aesop, the writer of the fables, who had been sent for to Sardis by Croesus and enjoyed his favour, was vexed at the king's ungracious reception of Solon, and advised him thus: "Solon," said he, "one ought either to say very little to kings or else say what they wish most to hear." "Not so," said Solon; "one should either say very little to them, or else say what is best for them to hear." So at that time Croesus despised Solon; but after he had been defeated by Cyrus, his city taken, and he himself was about to be burned alive upon a pyre erected in the presence of all the Persians and of Cyrus himself, then he thrice cried out, "Solon," as loud as he could. Cyrus, surprised at this, sent to ask what man or god Solon might be, who was invoked by a man in such extremity. Croesus, without any concealment said, "He is one of the wise men of Greece, whom I sent for, not because I wished to listen to him and learn what I was ignorant of, but in order that he might see and tell of my wealth, which I find it is a greater misfortune to lose than it was a blessing to possess. For, while I possessed it, all I enjoyed was opinion and empty talk; whereas, now the loss of it has brought me in very deed into terrible and irreparable misfortunes and sufferings. Now this man, who foresaw what might befall me, bade me look to the end of my life, and not be arrogant on the strength of a fleeting prosperity."

When this was reported to Cyrus, he being a wiser man than Croesus, and finding Solon's words strongly borne out by the example before him, not only released Croesus, but treated him with favour for the rest of his life; so that Solon had the glory of having by the same words saved one king's life and given instruction to another.

XXIX. During Solon's absence the strife of the factions at Athens was renewed; Lykurgus was the chief of the party of the Pediaei, Megakles, the son of Alkmaeon, led the Parali, and Peisistratus, the Diakrii, who were joined by the mass of the poorer classes who hated the rich. Thus the city still obeyed

Solon's laws, but was longing for change, and all men hoped for a new revolution, in which they trusted to get not only their rights, but something more, and to triumph over the opposite faction. In this state of affairs Solon landed at Athens, and was received with respect by all the citizens. Although, on account of his age, he was no longer able to engage in politics as keenly as before, still he met the leaders of the various factions privately and endeavoured to arrange their differences and reconcile them to one another. Peisistratus appeared to pay more attention to him than the others, for he was crafty and pleasant of speech, a protector of the poor, and a man of moderation even in his quarrels. The qualities which he had not, he affected to possess, giving himself out to be a cautious and law-abiding man, who loved even-handed justice and was enraged at any revolutionary proceedings. Thus he deceived the people; but Solon soon saw through him, and detected his plans before any one else. He was not shocked, but endeavoured to turn him from his purpose by advice, saying to him and to others that if his desire to be first and his wish to make himself master could be removed, there would be no more excellent and virtuous citizen than Peisistratus.

At this time Thespis was beginning to introduce the drama, and the novelty of his exhibition attracted many people, although the regular contests were not yet introduced. Solon, who was fond of seeing sights and gaining knowledge, and whose old age was spent in leisure and amusements and good fellowship, went to see Thespis, who acted in his own play, as the ancient custom was. After the play was over, he asked him if he was not ashamed to tell so many lies before so many people. When Thespis answered that there was no harm in saying and doing these things in jest, Solon violently struck the ground with his stick, saying, "If we praise and approve of such jests as these, we shall soon find people jesting with our business."

XXX. When Peisistratus wounded himself and was driven into the market-place in a cart to excite the people, whom he told that he had been so treated by his enemies because he defended the constitution, and while he was surrounded by a noisy crowd of sympathisers, Solon came near him and said, "Son of Hippokrates, you are dishonourably imitating Homer's Ulysses. You are doing this to deceive your fellow citizens, while he mutilated himself to deceive the enemy." Upon this, as the people were willing to take up arms on behalf of Peisistratus, they assembled at the Pnyx, where Ariston proposed that a body-guard of fifty club-bearers should be assigned to Peisistratus. Solon opposed this, urging many arguments, like what we read in his poems:
"You hang upon a crafty speaker's words;"
    and again,

"Each alone a fox in cunning, You grow stupid when you meet."

But as he saw that the poor were eager to serve Peisistratus, while the rich held back from cowardice, he went away, after saying that he was wiser than the one class, and braver than the other; wiser, namely, than those who did not understand what was going on, and braver than those who did understand, but did not dare to oppose the despotism with which they were threatened.

The people carried the proposal, and would not be so mean as to make any stipulation with Peisistratus about the number of his body-guard, but permitted him to keep as many as he pleased until he seized the Acropolis. When this took place, the city was convulsed; Megakles and the other descendants of Alkmaeon fled, but Solon, although he was now very old and had no one to stand by him, nevertheless came into the market-place and addressed the citizens, reproaching them for their folly and remissness, and urging them to make a final effort to retain their freedom. It was then that he made the memorable remark that, in former days it would have been easier for them to have prevented despotism from appearing amongst them, but that now it would be more glorious to cut it down, when it had arrived at its full growth. However, as no one listened to him, because of the general terror, he went home, armed himself, and took his post in the street outside his door, saying, "I have done all I could for my country and her laws." After this he remained quiet, though his friends urged him to leave Athens. He, however, wrote poems reproaching the Athenians—

"Through your own cowardice you suffered wrong, Blame then yourselves and not the gods for this; 'Twas you yourselves that made the tyrant strong, And rightly do you now your freedom miss."

XXXI. At this many of his friends told him that the despot would surely put him to death, and when they asked him what he trusted to, that he performed such mad freaks, he answered, "To my age." But Peisistratus, after he became established as sovereign, showed such marked favour to Solon that he even was advised by him, and received his approval in several cases. For he enforced most of Solon's laws, both observing them himself and obliging his friends to do so. Indeed, when accused of murder before the court of the Areopagus, he appeared in due form to stand his trial, but his accuser let the case fall through. He also made other laws himself, one of which is that those who are maimed in war shall be kept at the public expense. Herakleides says that this was done in imitation of Solon, who had already proposed it in the case of Thersippus. But Theophrastus tells us that it was not Solon, but

Peisistratus, who made the law about idleness, by means of which he rendered the city more quiet, and the country better cultivated.

Solon also attempted to write a great poem about the fable of 'Atlantis,' which he had learned from the chroniclers of Sais particularly concerned the Athenians, but he did not finish it, not, as Plato says, for want of leisure, but rather because of his advanced age, which made him fear that the task was too great for him. His own words tell us that he had abundance of leisure—
"Old I grow, but ever learning,"
    and,
"Venus and Bacchus are all my care, And the Muses, that charm the hearts of men."

Plato eagerly took in hand the scheme of the 'Atlantis,' as though it were a fine site for a palace, which had come to be his by inheritance, still unbuilt on. He placed in the beginning of it such splendid entrance-halls and vestibules as we find in no other tale or legend or poem, but, as he began the work too late, he died before he was able to finish it; so that the more we enjoy what he has written, the more we grieve over what is lost. As the temple of Olympic Zeus among the temples of Athens, so the 'Atlantis' is the only one among Plato's many noble writings that is unfinished.

Solon lived on into the reign of Peisistratus for a long time, according to Herakleides of Pontus, but less than two years, according to Phanias of Eresus. For Peisistratus became despot in the archonship of Komius, and Phanias tells us that Solon died during the archonship of Hegesistratus, Komias' successor. The story that his ashes were scattered round the island of Salamis is legendary and improbable, yet it is confirmed by many trustworthy writers, amongst whom is the philosopher Aristotle.

Life of Poplicola.

I. As a parallel to Solon we shall take Poplicola, who was honoured with this name by the Romans, his original name having been Publius Valerius, a supposed descendant of that Valerius who in ancient times was especially instrumental in making the Romans and Sabines cease to be enemies and become one people; for it was he who persuaded the two kings to meet and make terms of peace. Valerius, a descendant of this hero, was a man of eminence in Rome, which was then ruled by the kings, because of his eloquence and wealth. He always spoke boldly on the side of justice, and assisted the poor and needy with such kindness that it was clear that, in case of a revolution, he would become the first man in the state.

Tarquinius Superbus, the king, had not come to his throne justly, but by wicked and lawless violence, and as he reigned tyrannically and insolently, the people hated him, and seized the opportunity of the death of Lucretia, after her dishonour, to drive him out. Lucius Brutus, who was determined to change the form of government, applied to Valerius first of all, and with his vigorous assistance drove out the king. After these events Valerius kept quiet, as long as it seemed likely that the people would choose a single general to replace their king, because he thought that it was Brutus's right to be elected, as he had been the leader of the revolution. However the people, disgusted with the idea of monarchy, and thinking that they could more easily endure to be ruled by two men, proposed that two consuls should be chosen. Valerius now became a candidate, hoping that he and Brutus would be elected; but he was not chosen. Brutus, instead of Valerius, whom he would have preferred, had as a colleague Tarquinius Collatinus, the husband of Lucretia, who was not a better man than Valerius, but was elected because the men in power at Rome, seeing what intrigues the exiled king was setting on foot to secure his return, wished to have for their general a man who was his sworn personal enemy.

II. Valerius, disgusted at the idea that he was not trusted to fight for his country because he had not suffered any personal wrong at the hands of the king, left the senate, refused to attend public meetings, and ceased to take any part whatever in public affairs, so that people began to fear that in his rage he might go over to the king's party and destroy the tottering edifice of Roman liberty. Brutus suspected some others besides him, and proposed on a certain day to hold a solemn sacrifice and bind the senate by an oath. Valerius, however, came cheerfully into the Forum, and was the first to swear that he would never yield anything to the Tarquins, but would fight for liberty to the death, by which he greatly delighted the senate and encouraged the leading men of the state. His acts too, immediately confirmed his words, for ambassadors came from Tarquin with specious and seductive proposals, such as he thought would win over the people, coming from a king who seemed to have laid aside his insolence and only to wish for his just rights. The consuls thought it right that these proposals should be laid before the people, but Valerius would not permit it, not wishing that the poorer citizens, to whom the war was a greater burden than the monarchy had been, should have any excuse for revolt.

III. After this came other ambassadors, announcing that Tarquin would give up his throne, put an end to the war, and only ask for his own property and that of his relatives and friends, upon which to live in exile. Many were inclined to agree to this, and amongst them Collatinus, when Brutus, an inflexible and harsh-tempered man, rushed into the Forum, calling out that his colleague was a traitor, who wished to furnish the tyrant with the means of continuing the war and recovering his throne, when he ought rather to grudge him food to keep him from starving. The citizens assembled, and Caius Minucius, a private citizen, was the first man who addressed them, encouraging Brutus, and pointing out to the Romans how much better it was that the money should be used to help them than to help their enemies. In spite of this, however, the Romans decided that, as they now possessed the liberty for which they had fought, they would not lose the additional blessing of peace for the sake of this property, but would cast it from them after the tyrant to which it belonged.

Tarquin really cared little for the property, and the demand was merely made in order to sound the people and arrange a plot for the betrayal of the state, which was managed by the ambassadors whom he had nominally sent to look after his property. These men were selling some part of it, keeping some safe, and sending some of it away, and meanwhile intrigued so successfully that they won over two of the best families in Rome, that of the Aquillii, in which were three senators, and that of the Vitellii, among whom were two. All these men were, on the mother's side, nephews of the consul Collatinus, and the Vitellii were also related to Brutus, for he had married their sister, and by her had a large family. The Vitellii, being relatives and intimate friends of the two elder sons of Brutus, induced them to take part in the conspiracy, holding out to them the hope that they might ally themselves to the great house of Tarquin, soon to be restored to the throne, and would rid themselves of their father's stupidity and harshness. By harshness, they alluded to his inexorable punishment of bad men, and the stupidity was that which he himself affected for a long time, in order to conceal his real character from the tyrant, which was made matter of reproach to him afterwards.

IV. So, after they had persuaded these young men, they conferred again with the Aquillii, and determined that all the conspirators should swear a great and terrible oath, in which a man is killed, and each person then pours a libation of his blood, and touches his entrails. The room in which they meant to do this was, as may be supposed, a dark and half-ruined one. Now a servant of the name of Vindicius happened to conceal himself in it; not that he had any designs or any knowledge of what was going on, but chancing to be in the room when the conspirators solemnly entered, he was afraid of being detected there, and so hid himself behind a chest, where he could see what was done and hear what was said by them. They agreed to assassinate both consuls, and wrote a letter to Tarquin acquainting him with their determination, which they gave to the ambassadors, who were lodging in the house of the Aquillii as their guests, and were present at this scene. After this they dispersed, and Vindicius came out from his hiding-place. He was at a loss what use to make of the discovery which Fortune had thrown in his way, for he thought it a shocking thing, as indeed it was, for him to make such a fearful revelation to Brutus about his sons, or to Collatinus about his nephews, and he would not trust any private citizen with a secret of such importance. Tormented by his secret, and unable to remain quiet, he addressed himself to Valerius, chiefly moved to do so by his affable kindly temper; for his house was open all day to those who wished to speak with him, and he never refused an interview or rejected a poor man's petition.

V. When, then, Vindicius came before him and told him all that he knew in the presence only of his wife and his brother Marcus, Valerius was astounded and horrified. He would not let the man go, but locked him up, set his wife to guard the door, and bade his brother to surround the king's quarters, to seize the letter, if possible, keeping a strict watch over all the servants there. He himself, with a large train of clients, friends and servants, went to the house of the Aquillii, who were not within. As no one expected him, he pushed into the house and found the letter lying in the ambassadors' apartments.

While he was thus employed, the Aquillii returned in haste, and assembling a force at the door endeavoured to take away the letter from him. His own party came to his assistance, and with their gowns twisted round their necks with much buffeting made their way to the Forum. The same thing happened at the king's quarters, where Marcus laid hold of another letter which was being taken thither concealed among some baggage, and brought as many of the king's party as he could into the Forum.

VI. When the consuls had put a stop to the confusion, Vindicius, at Valerius's command, was brought out of his prison, and a court was held. The letters were recognised, and the culprits had nothing to say for themselves. All were silent and downcast, and a few, thinking to please Brutus, hinted at banishment as the penalty of their crime. Collatinus by his tears, and Valerius by his silence gave them hopes of mercy. But Brutus, addressing each of his sons by name, said, "Come, Titus, come Tiberius, why do you make no answer to the charges against you?" As, after being asked thrice, they made no answer, he, turning his face to the lictors, said, "I have done my work, do yours." They immediately seized upon the young men, tore off their clothes, tied their hands behind their backs, and scourged them. Although the people had not the heart to look at so dreadful a sight, yet it is said that Brutus never turned away his head, and showed no pity on his stern countenance, but sat savagely looking on at the execution of his sons until at last they were laid on the ground and their heads severed with an axe. Then he handed over the rest of the culprits to be dealt with by his colleague, rose, and left the Forum. His conduct cannot be praised, and yet it is above censure. Either virtue in his mind overpowered every other feeling, or his sorrow was so great as to produce insensibility. In neither case was there anything unworthy, or even human in his conduct, but it was either that of a god or a brute beast. It is better, however, that we should speak in praise of so great a man rather than allow our weakness to distrust his virtue. Indeed the Romans think that even the foundation of the city by Romulus was not so great an event as the confirmation of its constitution by Brutus.

VII. When he left the Forum all men were silent for a long while, shuddering at what had been done. The Aquillii took heart at the mildness of Collatinus, and asked for time to prepare their defence. They also begged that Vindicius might be given up to them, because he was their servant, and ought not to be on the side of their accusers. Collatinus was willing to allow this, but Valerius said that he was not able to give the man up, because he was surrounded by so large a crowd, and called upon the people not to disperse without punishing the traitors. At last he laid his hands upon the two corpses, called for Brutus, and reproached Collatinus for making his colleague act against nature by condemning his own sons to death, and then thinking to please the wives of these traitors and public enemies by saving their lives. The consul, vexed at this, ordered the lictors to seize Vindicius. They forced their way through the crowd, tried to lay hold of him, and struck those who defended him, but the friends of Valerius stood in front of him and beat them off, and the people raised a shout for Brutus. He returned, and when silence was restored said that he had, as a father, full power to condemn his sons to death, but that as for the other culprits, their fate should be decided by the free vote of the citizens, and that any one might come forward and address the people. The people, however, would listen to no speeches, but voted unanimously for their death, and they were all beheaded.

Collatinus, it seems, had been viewed with suspicion before because of his connection with the royal family, and his second name, Tarquinius, was odious to the people. After these events, having utterly failed as consul, he voluntarily laid down that office, and left the city. So now there was another election, and Valerius received the due reward of his patriotism and was gloriously made consul. Thinking that Vindicius ought to receive something for his services, he made him a freedman, the first ever made in Rome, and allowed him to vote in whatever tribe he chose to be enrolled. The other freedmen were not allowed the suffrage till, long after, it was given them by Appius to obtain popularity among them. The whole ceremony is up to the present day called vindicta, after Vindicius, we are told.

VIII. After this they allowed the king's property to be plundered, and destroyed the palace. Tarquinius had obtained the pleasantest part of the Field of Mars, and had consecrated it to that god. This field had just been cut, and the corn lay on the ground, for the people thought that they must not thresh it or make any use of it, because of the ground being consecrated, so they took the sheaves and threw them into the river. In the same way they cut down the trees and threw them in, leaving the whole place for the god, but uncultivated and unfruitful. As there were many things of different sorts all floating together in the river, the current did not carry them far, but when the first masses settled on a shallow place, the rest which were carried down upon them could not get past, but became heaped up there, and the stream compacted them securely by the mud which it deposited upon them, not only increasing the size of the whole mass, but firmly cementing it together. The waves did not shake it, but gently beat it into a solid consistency. Now, from its size, it began to receive additions, as most of what the river brought down settled upon it. It is now a sacred island close by the city, with temples and walks, and in the Latin tongue it has a name which means "between two bridges." Some state that this did not happen when Tarquinia's field was consecrated, but in later times when Tarquinia gave up another field next to that one, for the public use. This Tarquinia was a priestess, one of the Vestal virgins, and she was greatly honoured for having done so, and was allowed to appear as a witness in court, which no other woman could do; she also was permitted to marry, by a decree of the senate, but did not avail herself of it. These are the legends which they tell about this island.

IX. Tarquin now gave up all hopes of recovering his throne by intrigue, and appealed to the Etruscans, who willingly espoused his cause and endeavoured to restore him with a great army. The consuls led out the Romans to fight against them, posting them in holy places one of which is called the Arsian grove, and another the Aesuvian meadow. When they were about to join battle, Aruns, the son of Tarquin, and Brutus, the Roman consul, attacked one another, not by chance, but with fell hatred and rage, the one urging his horse against the tyrant and enemy of his country, the other against the man who drove him into exile. Falling upon one another with more fury than judgment, they made no attempt to defend themselves, but only to strike, and both perished. The struggle, so terribly begun, was continued with equal ferocity on both sides, until the armies, after great losses, were separated by a tempest. Valerius was in great straits, not knowing how the battle had gone, and observing that his soldiers were despondent when they looked at the corpses of their comrades, and elated when they saw those of the enemy, so equal and undecided had been the slaughter. Yet each side, when it viewed its own dead close by, was more inclined to own itself defeated, than to claim the victory because of the supposed losses of the enemy. Night came on, and it was spent as may be imagined by men who had fought so hard. When all was quiet in both camps, we are told that the grove was shaken, and that from it proceeded a loud voice which declared that the Etruscans had lost one man more than the Romans. Apparently it was the voice of a god; for immediately the Romans raised a bold and joyous shout, and the Etruscans, panic-stricken, ran out of their camp and dispersed. The Romans attacked the camp, took prisoners all that were left in it, something less than five thousand, and plundered it. The dead, when counted, proved to be eleven thousand three hundred of the enemy, and of the Romans the same number save one. This battle is said to have been fought on the Calends of March. Valerius triumphed after it in a four-horse chariot, being the first consul that ever did so. And it was a magnificent sight, and did not, as some say, offend the spectators; for, if so, the habit of doing it would not have been so carefully kept up for so many years. The people were also pleased with the honours which Valerius paid to his colleague in arranging a splendid funeral for him; he also pronounced a funeral oration over him, which was so much approved of by the Romans that from that day forth it became the custom for all good and great men at their deaths to have an oration made over them by the leading men of the time. This is said to have been older even than the Greek funeral orations, unless, as Anaximenes tells us, Solon introduced this custom.

X. But the people were vexed and angry, because though Brutus, whom they thought the author of their liberty, would not be consul alone, but had one colleague after another, yet "Valerius," they said, "has got all power into his own hands, and is not so much the heir of the consulship of Brutus as of the tyranny of Tarquin. And what use is it for him to praise Brutus while he imitates Tarquin in his deeds, swaggering down into the Forum with all the rods and axes before him, from a house larger than the king's palace used to be." Indeed, Valerius lived in rather too splendid a house on the Velian Hill, looking down into the Forum, and difficult to climb up to, so that when he walked down from it he did indeed look like a tragedy king leaving his palace. But now he proved how valuable a thing it is for a statesman engaged in important matters to keep his ears open to the truth, and shut against flattery. Hearing from his friends what the people thought of him, he did not argue or grieve at it, but suddenly assembled a number of workmen and during the night destroyed his entire house down to the very foundations, so that on the next day the Romans collected in crowds to see it, admiring the magnanimity of the man, but sorrowing at the destruction of so great and noble a house, which, like many a man, had been put to death undeservedly, and expressing their concern for their consul, who had no house to live in. Valerius, indeed, had to be entertained by his friends, until the people gave him a site and built him a house upon it, of more moderate proportions than the other, in the place where at the present day stands the temple of Vica Pota. Wishing to make not only himself but his office cease to be an object of terror to his countrymen, he removed the axes from the bundles of rods carried by the lictors, and when he entered the assembly of the people he ordered his fasces to be bowed and lowered before them, to show respect to the majesty of the people. This custom the consuls observe to this day. By these acts he did not really humble himself as he appeared to the Romans to be doing, but he so completely destroyed any illwill which had been felt against him that by giving up the semblance of power he really gained the reality, as the people were eager to serve him and obey him. For this reason they surnamed him Poplicola, which means "lover of the people," and this name so took the place of his former one that we shall use it during the remainder of this account of his life.

XI. He permitted any one to become a candidate for the consulship; and while he was sole consul he used his power to effect the greatest of his reforms, because he did not know who his new colleague might be, and whether he would not thwart him through ignorance or illwill. First of all he brought up the senate to its proper number, for many senators had perished, some at Tarquin's hands in former years, and some in the late battle. It is said that he elected no less than a hundred and sixty-four new senators. After this, he enacted laws which greatly added to the power of the people, the first one of which gave accused persons a power of appeal from the decision of the consuls to the people. The second appointed the penalty of death to those who entered upon any public office without the consent of the people. The third was to assist the poor, as it relieved them from taxes and enabled them all to apply themselves with greater assiduity to trade. The law, too, which he enacted about disobedience to the consuls is no less popular in its spirit, and favours the people more than the great nobles. He assessed the fine for disobedience at the price of five oxen and two sheep. Now the value of a sheep was ten obols, and that of an ox a hundred, for at this period the Romans did not make much use of coined money, but possessed abundance of cattle. For this reason at this day they call property peculia, from pecus, a sheep, and on their oldest coins they marked the figure of an ox, a sheep, or a pig. Their children, too, were distinguished by the names of Suillii, Bubulci, Caprarii and Porcii, for capra means a goat, and porcus a pig.

XII. Though Poplicola favoured the people so much in these laws, and showed such great moderation, yet in one instance he appointed a terrible penalty. One of his laws enacted that any citizen was at liberty to put to death anyone who tried to make himself king, without any form of trial. No penalty was to be enforced, if the man could bring forward proofs of the other's intention. His reason for this was that it was impossible for any one to attempt to make himself king, unperceived by some of his countrymen, but quite possible for him, although detected, to become too powerful to be brought to trial. So, before he made his attempt on the crown, any one was at liberty to exact from him that penalty, which he would be unable to do after his success.

His law about the treasury was also much approved. It being necessary that the citizens should contribute taxes to carry on the war, as he did not wish to touch the revenue himself or to allow his friends to do so, and was even unwilling that the public money should be brought into a private man's house, he appointed the Temple of Saturn to be used as a treasury, which it is to this day, and he appointed also two of the younger citizens as quaestors, to manage the accounts. The first quaestors were Publius Venturius and Marcus Minucius, and a large sum of money was collected, for a hundred and thirty thousand persons were taxed, although orphans and widows were exempted.

When he had settled all these matters, he nominated Lucretius, the father of Lucretia, as his colleague, and gave up the fasces to him as a mark of respect, because he was the elder man. This custom, that the elder of the two consuls has the fasces carried before him, remains to this day. As Lucretius died shortly afterwards, a new election took place, and Marcus Horatius was elected, and acted as Poplicola's colleague for the remainder of his year of office.

XIII. As Tarquin was stirring up the Etruscans to a second war with Rome, a great portent is said to have taken place. While he was yet king, and had all but finished the temple of Jupiter Capitolinus, he, either in accordance with some prophecy or otherwise, ordered certain Etruscan workmen at Veii to make an earthenware four-horse chariot to be placed on the top of the temple. Shortly afterwards he was driven from the throne, and the chariot, which had been modelled in clay, was placed in the furnace. Here it did not, as clay generally does, shrink and become smaller in the fire, as the wet dries out of it, but swelled to so great a size, and became so hard and strong that it could only be got out of the furnace by taking off the roof and sides. As this was decided by the prophets to be a sign from Heaven that those who possessed the chariot would be prosperous and fortunate, the Veientines determined not to give it up to the Romans, arguing that it belonged to Tarquin, not to those who had cast him out.

A few days afterwards there were horse-races there; everything proceeded as usual, but as the driver of the winning chariot, after receiving his crown as victor, was driving slowly out of the circus, the horses suddenly became excited for no apparent cause, and, either guided by Heaven or by chance, rushed towards Rome, their driver with them, for he finding it impossible to stop them was forced to let them whirl him along until they reached the Capitol, where they threw him down near what is called the Ratumenan Gate. The Veientines, struck with fear and wonder at this event, permitted the workmen to deliver up the earthenware chariot to the Romans.

XIV. Tarquinius the son of Demaratus, when at war with the Sabines, vowed that he would build the temple of Jupiter Olympius, but it was built by Tarquinius Superbus, the son or grandson of him who made the vow. He had not time to dedicate it, but was dethroned just before its completion. Now when it was finished and thoroughly decorated, Poplicola was eager to have the glory of dedicating it. Many of the nobles, however, grudged him this, and were more incensed at this than at all the glory which he had won as a general and as a legislator; for that, they said, was his vocation, but this was not. They stirred up Horatius to oppose him and urged him to claim the right to dedicate the temple. So when Poplicola was of necessity absent on military service, the senate decreed that Horatius should dedicate it, and brought him up into the Capitol to do so, a thing which they never could have done had Poplicola been present. Some say that the two consuls casts lots, and that the one, sorely against his will, drew the lot to command the army in the field, and the other that to dedicate the temple. But we may conjecture how this was, from the events which took place at the dedication. On the Ides of September, which corresponds with the full moon in our month Metageitnion, all the people assembled in the Capitol, and Horatius, after silence had been enjoined upon all, performed the ceremony of dedication. When, as is customary, he was about to take hold of the doors of the temple and say the prayer of dedication, Marcus, Poplicola's brother, who had long been standing near the doors watching his opportunity, said to him, "Consul, your son has just died of sickness in the camp." All who heard this were grieved, but Horatius, undisturbed, merely said, "Fling his corpse where you please, for I cannot grieve for him," and completed the dedication service. The story was false, invented by Marcus to confuse Horatius. His conduct is a remarkable instance of presence of mind, whether it be that he at once saw through the trick, or believed the story and was not disturbed by it.

XV. The same fortune seems to have attended the second temple also. The first, as we have related, was built by Tarquin, and dedicated by Horatius. This was destroyed by fire in the civil wars. The second was built by Sulla, but the name of Catulus appears as its dedicator, for Sulla died before it was completed. This again was burned during the civil tumults in the time of Vitellius, and Vespasian built a third, which had nearly the same fortune as the others, except that he saw it completed, and did not see it shortly afterwards destroyed, being thus more fortunate than Tarquin in seeing the completion, and than Sulla in seeing the dedication of his work. When Vespasian died the Capitol was burned. The fourth and present temple was built and dedicated by Domitian. It is said that Tarquin spent forty thousand pounds of silver in building the foundations; but there is no private citizen in Rome at the present day who could bear the expense of gilding the existing temple, which cost more than twelve thousand talents. Its columns are of Pentelic marble, exquisitely proportioned, which I myself saw at Athens; but at Rome they were again cut and polished, by which process they did not gain so much in gloss as they lost in symmetry, for they now appear too slender. However, if any one who wonders at the expense of the temple in the Capitol were to see the splendour of any one portico, hall, or chamber in the house of Domitian, he would certainly be led to parody that line of Epicharmus upon an extravagant fellow,

"Not good-natured, but possessed with the disease of giving,"

and would say that Domitian was not pious or admirable, but possessed with the disease of building, and turned everything into bricks and mortar, just as it is said Midas turned things into gold. So much for this.

XVI. Tarquin, after the great battle in which his son was slain by Brutus, took refuge at Clusium and begged Lars Porsena, the most powerful king in Italy, to assist him. He was thought to be an honourable and ambitious man, and promised his aid. First he sent an embassy to Rome, ordering them to receive Tarquin; and when the Romans refused to obey, he declared war against them, and telling them at what place and time he would attack them, marched against them with a great army. At Rome, Poplicola, though absent, was chosen consul for the second time, and with him, Titus Lucretius. He returned to Rome, and by way of putting a slight upon Porsena, went and founded the city of Sigliuria, while his army was close at hand. He built the walls of this place at a vast expense, and sent away seven hundred colonists to it, as if the war with which he was menaced was a very unimportant matter. But, nevertheless, Porsena made a sharp assault upon the walls of Rome, drove away the garrison, and very nearly entered the town. Poplicola forestalled him by sallying from one of the gates, and fought by the banks of the Tiber against overwhelming numbers until he was severely wounded and had to be carried out of the battle. As the same fate befell his colleague Lucretius, the Romans lost heart and endeavoured to save themselves by flight into the town. As the enemy also began to push across the wooden bridge, Rome was in danger of being taken. But Horatius, surnamed Cocles, and with him two of the noblest citizens, named Herminius and Lartius, held the wooden bridge against them. This Horatius was surnamed Cocles because he had lost an eye in the wars, or as some say because of the flatness of his nose, which made his eyes and eyebrows seem to meet, having nothing to separate them, and therefore the people meaning to call him Cyclops, by a mistake of pronunciation, named him Cocles. This man stood at the end of the bridge and kept off the enemy until his friends behind had cut down the bridge. Then he plunged into the river in his armour and swam to the other bank, though wounded by an Etruscan spear in the thigh. Poplicola, in admiration of his valour, at once proposed and passed a decree that every

Roman should give him the price of one day's provisions. Moreover, he gave him as much land as he could plough in one day. And a brazen statue of him was placed in the temple of Vulcan, by which honourable allusion was made to the lameness caused by his wound.

XVII. As Porsena pressed the siege, the Romans suffered from famine, and another separate army of Etruscans invaded their territory. But Poplicola, who was now consul for the third time, though he thought it his chief duty to remain stedfast and hold out the city against Porsena, did nevertheless sally out and attack these men, routing them with a loss of five thousand. Now as to the legend of Mucius, it is told in many different ways, but I will relate it as it seems most probable that it happened. He was a man of great courage, and very daring in war, who, meaning to assassinate Porsena, stole into the camp in an Etruscan dress and speaking the Etruscan language. When he arrived at the raised platform on which the king was sitting, he did not exactly know which was he, and being afraid to ask, he drew his sword and killed the man who of all the party looked most as if he were the king. Hereupon, he was seized and questioned. A fire was burning close by in a brazier which had been brought for Porsena to offer sacrifice. Mucius held his right hand over this, and while the flesh was being consumed looked at Porsena cheerfully and calmly, until he in astonishment acquitted him and restored him his sword, which Mucius took with his left hand. On account of this he is said to have been named Scaevola, which means left-handed. He then said that though he did not fear Porsena, he was conquered by his generosity, and out of kindness would tell him what torture would have failed to extort: "Three hundred young Romans like-minded with myself are at present concealed in your camp. I was chosen by lot to make the first attempt, and am not grieved that I failed to kill a man of honour, who ought to be a friend rather than an enemy to the Romans." Porsena, hearing this, believed it to be true, and became much more inclined to make peace, not, I imagine, so much for fear of the three hundred, as out of admiration for the spirit and valour of the Romans. This Mucius is called Scaevola by all writers, but Athenodorus, the son of Sandon, in his book which is dedicated to Octavia, the sister of Caesar Augustus, says that he was also named Posthumus.

XVIII. Poplicola, who did not think Porsena so terrible as an enemy as he would be valuable as a friend and ally, was willing that he should decide the quarrel between the Romans and Tarquin, and often proposed that he should do so, feeling sure that he would discover him to be a wretch who had been most deservedly dethroned. But Tarquin roughly answered that he would submit his claims to no judge, and least of all to Porsena, who had been his ally and now seemed inclined to desert him. Porsena was angered at this, and, as his son Aruns also pleaded hard for the Romans, put an end to the war upon condition that they should give up the portion of Etruscan territory which they had seized, restore their prisoners, and receive back their deserters. Upon this, ten youths of the noblest families were given as hostages, and as many maidens, among whom was Valeria, the daughter of Poplicola.

XIX. While these negotiations were going on, and Porsena, through his confidence in the good faith of the Romans, had relaxed the discipline of his camp, these Roman maidens came down to bathe in the river at a place where a bank, in the form of a crescent, makes the water smooth and undisturbed. As they saw no guards, nor any one passing except in boats, they determined to swim across, although the stream was strong and deep. Some say that one of them, by name Cloelia, rode on a horse across the river, encouraging the others as they swam. When they had got safe across they went to Poplicola, but he was displeased with them because it made him seem more faithless than Porsena, and he feared lest this daring feat of the maidens might be suspected of being a preconcerted plot of the Romans. For these reasons he sent them back to Porsena. Now Tarquin and his party, foreseeing that this would be done, laid an ambush on the further bank and attacked those who were escorting the girls with superior numbers. Still they made a stout defence, and meanwhile Valeria, the daughter of Poplicola, made her way through the combatants and escaped, and three slaves who also got away took care of her. The others were mixed up with the fight, and were in considerable danger, when Aruns, Porsena's son, came to the rescue, put the enemy to the rout, and saved the Romans. When the girls were brought before Porsena, he asked which it was that had conceived the attempt to escape and encouraged the others. Being told that it was Cloelia, he smiled kindly upon her, and presented her with one of his own horses, splendidly caparisoned. This is relied upon by those who say that it was Cloelia alone who rode on horseback over the river, as proving their case. Others say that it was not because she used a horse, but to honour her manly spirit that the Etruscan king made her this present. A statue of her, on horseback, stands in the Sacred Way as you go up to the Palatine Hill, which by some is said not to be a statue of Cloelia, but of Valeria.

Porsena, after making peace with the Romans, among many other instances of generosity, ordered his army to carry back nothing but their arms when they retired, leaving the entrenched camp full of food and property of every kind for the Romans. For this reason, at the present day, whenever there is a sale of any public property, especially that which is taken in war, proclamation is always made, "Porsena's goods for sale," so that the Romans have never forgotten the kindness which they received from him. A brazen statue of him used to stand near the senate house, of plain and oldfashioned workmanship.

XX. After this the Sabines invaded the country. Marcus Valerius, Poplicola's brother, and Posthumius Tubertus were then consuls, and Marcus, acting by the advice of Poplicola, who was present, won two great battles, in the second of which he slew thirteen thousand of the enemy without the Romans losing a man. He was rewarded for this, in addition to his triumph, by having a house built for him upon the Palatine Hill at the public expense. And whereas all other street doors open inwards, the doors of that house were made to open outwards, as a perpetual memorial of the honour paid him by the people, who thus made way for him. It is said that all the doors in Greece used once to open this way, arguing from the comedies, in which those who are coming out of a house always knock at the door, to warn those who are passing or standing near not to be struck by the leaves of the door, as they open.

XXI. Next year Poplicola was consul for the fourth time. There was an expectation of a war against the Latins and Sabines combined.

Moreover the city seemed to have displeased the gods; for all the pregnant women were delivered prematurely, and of imperfectly formed children. Poplicola, after appeasing the gods below according to the injunctions of the Sibylline books, re-established certain games in accordance with an oracle, brought the city into a more hopeful state of mind, and began to consider what he had to fear from earthly foes, for the enemy's army was large and formidable. There was one Appius Clausus, a Sabine, of great wealth and remarkable personal strength, and a virtuous and eloquent man, who, like all great men, was the object of envy and ill-will to many. He was accused by his enemies of having put an end to the war, because he wished to increase the power of Rome, in order to enable him the more easily to triumph over the liberties of his own country, and make himself king of it. Perceiving that the populace eagerly listened to these tales, and that he was an object of dislike to the war party and the army, he began to fear impeachment: so, having numerous followers, besides his personal friends and relatives, he was able to divide the state into two parties. This caused great delay in the Sabines' preparations for attacking the Romans, and Poplicola, feeling it to be his duty not merely to watch but to assist Clausus, sent envoys, who spoke to him as follows: "Poplicola feels that you are a man of honour, who would be unwilling to take vengeance upon your countrymen, although you have been shamefully treated by them. But if you choose to put yourself in safety by leaving your country and a people that hates you, he will receive you, both in his public and his private capacity, in a manner worthy of your own high character and of the dignity of Rome." After much deliberation, Clausus decided that he could not do better than accept this offer, and assembled all his friends. They in their turn influenced many others, so that he was able to transplant to Rome five thousand of the most peaceful and respectable families of the Sabine nation. Poplicola, who had notice of their arrival, welcomed them kindly and graciously. He made them all citizens of Rome, and gave each of them two acres of land along the river Anio. He gave Clausus twenty-five acres, and enrolled him among the Senators. Clausus afterwards became one of the first men in Rome for wisdom and power, and his descendants, the Claudian family, was one of the most illustrious in history.

XXII. Though the disputes of the Sabines were settled by this migration, yet their popular orators would not let them rest, but vehemently urged that they ought not to let Appius, a deserter and an enemy, prevail upon them to let the Romans go unpunished—a thing which he could not persuade them to do when he was present among them. They proceeded to Fidenae with a great army and encamped there, and laid two thousand men in ambush before Rome, in wooded and broken ground, meaning in the morning to send out a few horsemen to plunder ostentatiously. These men were ordered to ride up close to Rome, and then to retire till their pursuers were drawn into the snare. Poplicola heard of this plan the same day from deserters, and quickly made all necessary arrangements. At evening he sent Postumius Balbus, his son-in-law, with three thousand men to occupy the tops of the hills under which the Sabine ambush was placed. His colleague, Lucretius, was ordered to take the swiftest-footed and noblest youth of the city, and pursue the plundering horsemen, while he himself with the rest of the forces made a circuitous march and outflanked the enemy. It chanced that a thick mist came on about dawn, in the midst of which Postumius charged down from the hills upon the men in ambush with a loud shout, while Lucretius sent his men to attack the cavalry, and Poplicola fell upon the enemy's camp. The Sabines were routed in every quarter, and even when fighting no longer were cut down by the Romans, their rash confidence proving ruinous to them. Each party thought that the others must be safe, and did not care to stay and fight where they were, but those who were in the camp ran to those in the ambush, and those in the ambush towards the camp, each of them meeting those with whom they hoped to take refuge, and finding that those who they had hoped would help them needed help themselves. The Sabines would have been all put to the sword, had not the neighbouring city of Fidenae afforded them a refuge, especially for the men from the camp. Such as could not reach Fidenae were either put to death or taken prisoners.

XXIII. The Romans, accustomed as they are to refer all great success to the intervention of Heaven, thought that the whole glory of this achievement was due to the general. The first thing heard was the victorious soldiers declaring that Poplicola had delivered up the enemy to them blind and lame, and all but in chains, for them to slaughter at their ease. The people were enriched by the plunder and the sale of the prisoners for slaves. Poplicola enjoyed a triumph, and previously delivering over the administration of the city to the two succeeding consuls, died shortly afterwards, having attained to the highest pitch of glory that man can reach. The people, as if they had done nothing during his life to honour him as he deserved, and were now for the first time to show their gratitude, decreed him a public funeral, and moreover that every person should contribute the coin called quadrans, to show him respect. The women also made a common agreement to wear mourning for him for a whole year. He was buried by a decree of the people within the city near the place called Velia, and all his family were given the privilege of burial there. At the present day not one of the family is actually buried there, but the corpse is carried thither, and laid down, while some one places a lighted torch under it for a moment, after which it is carried away. By this ceremony they claim the right, although they forego it, and bury the corpse outside the city.

Comparison of Solon and Poplicola.

I. It is a point peculiar to this comparison, and which does not occur in any of the other Lives which I have written, that in turn one imitates and the other bears witness to his fellow's deeds. Observe, for instance, Solon's definition of happiness before Croesus, how much better it suits Poplicola than Tellus. He says that Tellus was fortunate because of his good luck, his virtue, and his noble children; but yet he makes no mention of him or of his children in his poetry, and he never was a man of any renown, or held any high office.

Now Poplicola's virtues made him the most powerful and glorious of the Romans during his life, and six hundred years after his death the very noblest families of Rome, those named Publicola and Messala and Valerius, are proud to trace their descent from him, even at the present day. Tellus, it is true, died like a brave man fighting in the ranks, but Poplicola slew his enemies, which is much better than being killed oneself, and made his country victorious by skill as a general and a statesman, and, after triumphing and enjoying honours of every kind, died the death which Solon thought so enviable. Besides, Solon, in his answer to Mimnermus about the time of life, has written the verses:

"To me may favouring Heaven send, That all my friends may mourn my end,"

in which he bears witness to the good fortune of Poplicola; for he, when he died, was mourned not only by all his friends and relations but by the whole city, in which thousands wept for him, while all the women wore mourning for him as if he were a son or father of them all that they had lost.

Solon says in his poems,

"I long for wealth, but not procured By means unholy."

Now Poplicola not only possessed wealth honourably acquired, but also was able to spend it, much to his credit, in relieving the needy. Thus if Solon was the wisest, Poplicola was certainly the most fortunate of men; for what Solon prayed for as the greatest blessing, Poplicola possessed and enjoyed to the end of his days.

II. Thus has Solon done honour to Poplicola; and he again honoured Solon by regarding him as the best model a man could follow in establishing a free constitution: for he took away the excessive power and dignity of the consuls and made them inoffensive to the people, and indeed made use of many of Solon's own laws; as he empowered the people to elect their own consuls, and gave defendants a right of appeal to the people from other courts, just as

Solon had done. He did not, like Solon, make two senates, but he increased the existing one to nearly double its number. His grounds for the appointment of quaestors was to give the consul leisure for more important matters, if he was an honest man; and if he was a bad man, to remove the opportunity of fraud which he would have had if he were supreme over the state and the treasury at once. In hatred of tyrants Poplicola exceeded Solon, for he fixed the penalty for a man who might be proved to be attempting to make himself king, whereas the Roman allowed any one to kill him without trial. And while Solon justly prided himself upon his having been offered the opportunity to make himself despot, with the full consent of his fellow-countrymen, and yet having refused it, Poplicola deserves even greater credit for having been placed in an office of almost despotic power, and having made it more popular, not using the privileges with which he was entrusted. Indeed Solon seems to have been the first to perceive that a people

"Obeys its rulers best, When not too free, yet not too much opprest."

III. The relief of debtors was a device peculiar to Solon, which, more than anything else confirmed the liberty of the citizens. For laws to establish equality are of no use if poor men are prevented from enjoying it because of their debts; and in the states which appear to be the most free, men become mere slaves to the rich, and conduct the whole business of the state at their dictation. It should be especially noted that although an abolition of debt would naturally produce a civil war, yet this measure of Solon's, like an unusual but powerful dose of medicine, actually put an end to the existing condition of internal strife; for the well-known probity of Solon's character outweighed the discredit of the means to which he resorted. In fact Solon began his public life with greater glory than Poplicola, for he was the leading spirit, and followed no man, but entirely single handed effected the most important reforms; while Poplicola was more enviable and fortunate at the close of his career.

Solon himself saw his own constitution overthrown, while that of Poplicola preserved order in the city down to the time of the civil wars; and the reason was that Solon, as soon as he had enacted his laws, went on his travels, leaving them written on wooden tablets, defenceless against all assailants; whereas Poplicola remained at home, acted as consul, and by his statesmanship ensured the success and permanence of the new constitution. Moreover, Solon could not stop Peisistratus, although he perceived his designs, but was forced to see a despotism established; while Poplicola destroyed a monarchy which had existed for many years, showing equal virtue with Solon, but greater good fortune and power to enable him to carry out his intentions.

IV. With regard to warlike achievements, Daimachus of Plataea will not even admit that Solon made the campaign against the Megarians, which we have related; but Poplicola both by strategy and personal valour won many great battles. As a statesman, Solon seems to have acted somewhat childishly in pretending that he was mad, in order to make his speech about Salamis, while Poplicola ran the very greatest risks in driving out the tyrant and crushing the conspiracy. He was especially responsible for the chief criminals being put to death, and thus not only drove the Tarquins out of the city, but cut off and destroyed their hopes of return. And while he showed such vigour in enterprises that required spirit and courage, he was equally admirable in peaceful negotiations and the arts of persuasion; for he skilfully won over the formidable Porsena to be the friend instead of the enemy of Rome.

Still we may be reminded that Solon stirred up the Athenians to capture Salamis, which they had given up to the Megarians, while Poplicola withdrew the Romans from a country which they had conquered. We must, however, consider the circumstances under which these events took place. A subtle politician deals with every thing so as to turn it to the greatest advantage, and will often lose a part in order to save the whole, and by sacrificing some small advantage gain another more important one, as did Poplicola on that occasion; for he, by withdrawing from a foreign country, preserved his own, gained the enemy's camp for the Romans, who before were only too glad to save their city from ruin, and at last, by converting his enemy into an arbitrator and winning his cause, obtained all the fruits of victory: for Porsena put an end to the war, and left behind him all his war material to show his respect for the noble character of the consul.

Life of Themistokles.

I. Themistokles came of a family too obscure to entitle him to distinction. His father, Neokles, was a middle-class Athenian citizen, of the township of Phrearri and the tribe Leontis. He was base born on his mother's side, as the epigram tells us:
"My name's Abrotonon from Thrace, I boast not old Athenian race; Yet, humble though my lineage be, Themistokles was born of me."
Phanias, however, says that the mother of Themistokles was a Carian, not a Thracian, and that her name was not Abrotonon but Euterpe. Manthes even tells us that she came from the city of Halikarnassus in Caria. All base-born Athenians were made to assemble at Kynosarges, a gymnasium outside the walls sacred to Herakles, who was regarded as base born among the gods because his mother was a mortal; and Themistokles induced several youths of noble birth to come to Kynosarges with him and join in the wrestling there, an ingenious device for destroying the exclusive privileges of birth. But, for all that, he evidently was of the blood of Lykomedes; for when the barbarians burned down the temple of the Initiation at Phlya, which belonged to the whole race of the descendants of Lykomedes, it was restored by Themistokles, as we are told by Simonides.

II. He is agreed by all to have been a child of vigorous impulses, naturally clever, and inclined to take an interest in important affairs and questions of statesmanship. During his holidays and times of leisure he did not play and trifle as other children do, but was always found arranging some speech by himself and thinking it over. The speech was always an attack on, or a defence of, some one of his playfellows. His schoolmaster was wont to say, "You will be nothing petty, my boy; you will be either a very good or a very bad man."

In his learning, he cared nothing for the exercises intended to form the character, and mere showy accomplishments and graces, but eagerly applied himself to all real knowledge, trusting to his natural gifts to enable him to master what was thought to be too abstruse for his time of life. In consequence of this, when in society he was ridiculed by those who thought themselves well mannered and well educated, he was obliged to make the somewhat vulgar retort that he could not tune a lute or play upon the harp, but he could make a small and obscure state great and glorious.

In spite of all this, Stesimbrotus says that Themistokles was a pupil of Anaxagoras, and attended the lectures of Melissus the physicist; but here he is wrong as to dates. Melissus was the general who was opposed to Perikles, a much younger man than Themistokles, when he was besieging Samos, and Anaxagoras was one of Perikles's friends. One is more inclined to believe those who tell us that Themistokles was a follower and admirer of Mnesiphilus of Phrearri, who was neither an orator nor a natural philosopher, but a man who had deeply studied what went by the name of wisdom, but was really political sharp practice and expedients of statesmanship, which he had, as it were, inherited as a legacy from Solon. Those who in later times mixed up this science with forensic devices, and used it, not to deal with the facts of politics, but the abstract ideas of speculative philosophy, were named Sophists. Themistokles used to converse with this man when he had already begun his political career. In his childhood he was capricious and unsteady, his genius, as yet untempered by reason and experience, showing great capacities both for good and evil, and after breaking out into vice, as he himself used afterwards to admit, saying that the colts which are the hardest to break in usually make the most valuable horses when properly taught. But as for the stories which some have fabricated out of this, about his being disinherited by his father, and about his mother committing suicide through grief at her son's disgrace, they seem to be untrue. On the other hand, some writers tell us that his father, wishing to dissuade him from taking part in politics, pointed out to him the old triremes lying abandoned on the beach, and told him that politicians, when the people had no farther use for them, were cast aside in like manner.

III. Very early in life Themistokles took a vigorous part in public affairs, possessed by vehement ambition. Determined from the very outset that he would become the leading man in the state, he eagerly entered into all the schemes for displacing those who where then at the head of affairs, especially attacking Aristeides, the son of Lysimachus, whose policy he opposed on every occasion. Yet his enmity with this man seems to have had a very boyish commencement; for they both entertained a passion for the beautiful Stesilaus, who, we are told by Ariston the philosopher, was descended from a family residing in the island of Keos. After this difference they espoused different parties in the state, and their different temper and habits widened the breach between them. Aristeides was of a mild and honourable nature, and as a statesman cared nothing for popularity or personal glory, but did what he thought right with great caution and strict rectitude. He was thus often brought into collision with Themistokles, who was trying to engage the people in many new schemes, and to introduce startling reforms, by which he would himself have gained credit, and which Aristeides steadily opposed.

He is said to have been so recklessly ambitious and so frenziedly eager to take part in great events, that though he was very young at the time of the battle of Marathon, when the country rang with the praises of the generalship of Miltiades, he was often to be seen buried in thought, passing sleepless nights and refusing invitations to wine-parties, and that he answered those who asked him the cause of his change of habits, that the trophies of Miltiades would not let him sleep. Other men thought that the victory of Marathon had put an end to the war, but Themistokles saw that it was but the prelude to a greater contest, in which he prepared himself to stand forth as the champion of Greece, and, foreseeing long before what was to come, endeavoured to make the city of Athens ready to meet it.

IV. First of all, he had the courage to propose that the Athenians, instead of dividing amongst themselves the revenues derived from the silver mines at Laurium, should construct ships out of this fund for the war with Aegina. This was then at its height, and the Aeginetans, who had a large navy, were masters of the sea. By this means Themistokles was more easily enabled to carry his point, not trying to terrify the people by alluding to Darius and the Persians, who lived a long way off, and whom few feared would ever come to attack them, but by cleverly appealing to their feelings of patriotism against the Aeginetans, to make them consent to the outlay.

With that money a hundred triremes were built, which were subsequently used to fight against Xerxes. After this he kept gradually turning the thoughts of the Athenians in the direction of the sea, because their land force was unable even to hold its own against the neighbouring states, while with a powerful fleet they could both beat off the barbarians and make themselves masters of the whole of Greece. Thus, as Plato says, instead of stationary soldiers as they were, he made them roving sailors, and gave rise to the contemptuous remark that Themistokles took away from the citizens of Athens the shield and the spear, and reduced them to the oar and the rower's bench. This, we are told by Stesimbrotus, he effected after quelling the opposition of Miltiades, who spoke on the other side. Whether his proceedings at this time were strictly constitutional or no I shall leave to others to determine; but that the only safety of Greece lay in its fleet, and that those triremes were the salvation of the Athenians after their city was taken, can be proved by the testimony, among others, of Xerxes himself; for although his land force was unbroken, he fled after his naval defeat, as though no longer able to contend with the Greeks, and he left Mardonius behind more to prevent pursuit, in my opinion, than with any hopes of conquest.

V. Some writers tell us that he was a keen man of business, and explain that his grand style of living made this necessary; for he made costly sacrifices, and entertained foreigners in a splendid manner, all of which required a large expenditure; but some accuse him of meanness and avarice, and even say that he sold presents which were sent for his table. When Philides the horse-dealer refused to sell him a colt, he threatened that he would soon make a wooden horse of the man's house; meaning that he would stir up lawsuits and claims against him from some of his relations.

In ambition he surpassed every one. When yet a young and unknown man he prevailed upon Epikles of Hermione, the admired performer on the harp, to practise his art in his house, hoping thereby to bring many people to it to listen. And he displeased the Greeks when he went to the Olympian games by vying with Kimon in the luxury of his table, his tents, and his other furniture. It was thought very proper for Kimon, a young man of noble birth, to do so; but for a man who had not yet made himself a reputation, and had not means to support the expense, such extravagance seemed mere vulgar ostentation. In the dramatic contest, which even then excited great interest and rivalry, the play whose expenses he paid for won the prize. He put up a tablet in memory of his success bearing the words: Themistokles of Phrearri was choragus, Phrynichus wrote the play, Adeimantus was archon. Yet he was popular, for he knew every one of the citizens by name, and gave impartial judgment in all cases referred to him as arbitrator. Once, when Simonides of Keos asked him to strain a point in his favour, Themistokles, who was a general at the time, answered that Simonides would be a bad poet if he sang out of tune; and he would be a bad magistrate if he favoured men against the law. At another time he rallied Simonides on his folly in abusing the Corinthians, who inhabited so fine a city, and in having his own statue carved, though he was so ugly. He continued to increase in popularity by judiciously courting the favour of the people, and was at length able to secure the triumph of his own party, and the banishment of his rival Aristeides.

VI. As the Persians were now about to invade Greece, the Athenians deliberated as to who should be their leader. It is said that most men refused the post of General through fear, but that Epikydes, the son of Euphemides, a clever mob-orator, but cowardly and accessible to bribes, desired to be appointed, and seemed very likely to be elected. Themistokles, fearing that the state would be utterly ruined if its affairs fell into such hands, bribed him into forgetting his ambitious designs, and withdrawing his candidature.

He was much admired for his conduct when envoys came from the Persian king to demand earth and water, in token of submission. He seized the interpreter, and by a decree of the people had him put to death, because he had dared to translate the commands of a barbarian into the language of free Greeks. He acted in the same way to Arthmias of Zelea. This man, at the instance of Themistokles, was declared infamous, he and his children and his descendants for ever, because he brought Persian gold among the Greeks. His greatest achievement of all, however, was, that he put an end to all the internal wars in Greece, and reconciled the states with one another, inducing them to defer the settlement of their feuds until after the Persian war. In this he is said to have been greatly assisted by Chileon the Arcadian.

VII. On his appointment as General, he at once endeavoured to prevail upon his countrymen to man their fleet, leave their city, and go to meet the enemy by sea as far from Greece as possible. As this met with great opposition, he, together with the Lacedaemonians, led a large force as far as the Vale of Tempe, which they intended to make their first line of defence, as Thessaly had not at that time declared for the Persians. When, however, the armies were forced to retire from thence, and all Greece, up to Boeotia, declared for the Persians, the Athenians became more willing to listen to Themistokles about fighting by sea, and he was sent with a fleet to guard the straits at Artemisium. Here the Greeks chose the Lacedaemonians, and their general, Eurybiades, to take the command; but the Athenians refused to submit to any other state, because they alone furnished more ships than all the rest. Themistokles, at this crisis perceiving the danger, gave up his claims to Eurybiades, and soothed the wounded pride of the Athenians, telling them that if they proved themselves brave men in the war, they would find that all the other states in Greece would cheerfully recognise their supremacy. On this account he seems more than any one else to deserve the credit of having saved Greece, and to have covered the Athenians with glory by teaching them to surpass their enemies in bravery, and their allies in good sense. When the Persian fleet reached Aphetai, Eurybiades was terrified at the number of ships at the mouth of the Straits, and, learning that two hundred sail more were gone round the outside of Euboea to take him in the rear, he at once wished to retire further into Greece, and support the fleet by the land army in Peloponnesus, for he regarded the Persian king's fleet as utterly irresistible at sea. Upon this the Euboeans, who feared to be deserted by the Greeks, sent one Pelagon with a large sum of money, to make secret proposals to Themistokles. He took the money, Herodotus tells us, and gave it to Eurybiades and his party. One of those who most vehemently opposed him was Architeles, the captain of the Sacred Trireme, who had not sufficient money to pay his crew, and therefore wished to sail back to Athens.

Themistokles stirred up the anger of his men to such a pitch that they rushed upon him and took away his supper. At this, Architeles was much vexed, but Themistokles sent him a basket containing bread and meat, with a talent of silver hidden underneath it, with a message bidding him eat his supper and pay his men the next day, but that, if he did not, Themistokles would denounce him to his countrymen as having received bribes from the enemy. This we are told by Phanias of Lesbos.

VIII. The battles which took place in the Straits with the Persian ships, were indeed indecisive, but the experience gained in them was of the greatest value to the Greeks, as they were taught by their result that multitudes of ships and splendid ensigns, and the boastful war-cries of barbarians, avail nothing against men who dare to fight hand to hand, and that they must disregard all these and boldly grapple with their enemies. Pindar seems to have understood this when he says, about the battle at Artemisium, that there "The sons of Athena laid Their freedom's grand foundation."

for indeed confidence leads to victory. This Artemisium is a promontory of the island of Euboea, stretching northwards beyond Hestiaea; and opposite to it is Olizon, which was once part of the dominions of Philoktetes. There is upon it a small temple of Artemis (Diana), which is called the "Temple towards the East." Round it stand trees and a circle of pillars of white stone. This stone, when rubbed in the hand, has the colour and smell of saffron. On one of these pillars were written the following verses:
"The sons of Athens once o'ercame in fight All Asia's tribes, on yonder sea; They raised these pillars round Diana's shrine, To thank her for their victory."

Even now a place is pointed out on the beach where, under a great heap of sand, there is a deep bed of black ashes where it is thought the wrecks and dead bodies were burned.

IX. But when the news of Thermopylae was brought to the Greeks at Artemisium, that Leonidas had fallen, and Xerxes was in possession of the passes, they retired further into Greece, the Athenians protecting the rear on account of their bravery, and full of pride at their achievements. At all the harbours and landing-places along the coast, Themistokles, as he passed by, cut conspicuous inscriptions on stones, some of which he found on the spot, and others which he himself set up at all the watering-places and convenient stations for ships. In these inscriptions he besought the Ionians, if possible, to come over to the Athenians, who were their fathers, and who were fighting for their liberty; and if they could not do this, to throw the barbarian army into confusion during battle. He hoped that these writings would either bring the Ionians over to the side of the Greeks, or make them suspected of treason by the Persians.

Meanwhile Xerxes invaded Greece through Doris, and came into Phokis, where he burned the city of the Phokaeans. The Greeks made no resistance, although the Athenians begged them to make a stand in Boeotia, and cover Attica, urging that they had fought in defence of the whole of Greece at Artemisium. However, as no one would listen to them, but all the rest of the Greeks determined to defend the Peloponnesus, and were collecting all their forces within it, and building a wall across the Isthmus from sea to sea, the Athenians were enraged at their treachery, and disheartened at being thus abandoned to their fate. They had no thoughts of resisting so enormous an army; and the only thing they could do under the circumstances, to abandon their city and trust to their ships, was distasteful to the people, who saw nothing to be gained by victory, and no advantage in life, if they had to desert the temples of their gods and the monuments of their fathers.

X. At this crisis, Themistokles, despairing of influencing the populace by human reasoning, just as a dramatist has recourse to supernatural machinery, produced signs and wonders and oracles. He argued that it was a portent that the sacred snake during those days deserted his usual haunt. The priests, who found their daily offerings to him of the first fruits of the sacrifices left untouched, told the people, at the instigation of Themistokles, that the goddess Athena (Minerva) had left the city, and was leading them to the sea. He also swayed the popular mind by the oracle, in which he argued that by "wooden walls" ships were alluded to; and that Apollo spoke of Salamis as "divine," not terrible or sad, because Salamis would be the cause of great good fortune to the Greeks. Having thus gained his point, he proposed a decree, that the city be left to the care of the tutelary goddess of the Athenians, that all able-bodied men should embark in the ships of war, and that each man should take the best measures in his power to save the women and children and slaves.

When this decree was passed, most of the Athenians sent their aged folks and women over to Troezen, where they were hospitably received by the Troezenians, who decreed that they should be maintained at the public expense, receiving each two obols a day, that the children should be allowed to pick the fruit from any man's tree, and even that their school expenses should be paid. This decree was proposed by Nikagoras.

The Athenians at this time had no public funds, yet Aristotle tells us that the Senate of the Areopagus, by supplying each fighting man with eight drachmas, did good service in manning the fleet; and Kleidemus tells us that this money was obtained by an artifice of Themistokles. When the Athenians were going down to the Peiraeus, he gave out that the Gorgon's head had been lost from the statue of the goddess. Themistokles, under pretext of seeking for it, searched every man, and found great stores of money hidden in their luggage, which he confiscated, and thus was able to supply the crews of the ships with abundance of necessaries. When the whole city put to sea, the sight affected some to pity, while others admired their courage in sending their families out of the way that they might not be disturbed by weeping and wailing as they went over to Salamis. Yet many of the aged citizens who were left behind at Athens afforded a piteous sight; and even the domestic animals, as they ran howling to the sea-shore, accompanying their masters, touched men's hearts. It is said that the dog of Xanthippus, the father of Perikles, could not endure to be separated from him, and jumping into the sea swam alongside of his trireme, reached Salamis, and then at once died. His tomb is even now to be seen at the place called Kynossema.

XI. Besides these great achievements, Themistokles, perceiving that his countrymen longed to have Aristeides back again, and fearing that he might ally himself with the Persian, and work ruin to Greece out of anger against his own country (for Aristeides had been banished from Athens before the war when Themistokles came into power), proposed a decree, that any citizen who had been banished for a term of years, might return and do his best by word and deed to serve his country together with the other citizens.

Eurybiades, on account of the prestige of Sparta, held the chief command of the fleet, but was unwilling to risk a battle, preferring to weigh anchor and sail to the Isthmus where the land army of the Peloponnesians was assembled. This project was opposed by Themistokles; and it was on this occasion that he made use of the following well-known saying: When Eurybiades said to him, "Themistokles, in the public games they whip those who rise before their turn." "True," said Themistokles, "but they do not crown those who lag behind." And when Eurybiades raised his staff as if he would strike him, Themistokles said, "Strike, but hear me." When Eurybiades, in wonder at his gentle temper, bade him speak, he again urged Eurybiades to remain at Salamis. Some one then said, that a man without a city had no right to tell those who still possessed one to abandon it, but Themistokles turning upon him, answered, "Wretch, we Athenians have indeed abandoned our walls and houses, because we scorn to be slaves for the sake of mere buildings, but we have the greatest city of all Greece, our two hundred ships of war, which now are ready to help you if you choose to be saved by their means; but, if you betray us and leave us, some of the Greeks will soon learn to their cost that the Athenians have obtained a free city and a territory no worse than that which they left behind." When Eurybiades heard Themistokles use this language, he began to fear that the Athenians might really sail away and leave him.

When Eretrieus tried to say something to Themistokles, he answered, "Do you too dare to say anything about war, you, who like a cuttle-fish, have a sword but no heart."

XII. It is said by some writers that while Themistokles was talking about these matters upon the deck of his ship, an owl was seen to fly from the right-hand side of the fleet, and to perch upon his mast; which omen encouraged all the Athenians to fight. But when the Persian host poured down to Phalerum, covering the whole sea-shore, and the king himself was seen with all his forces, coming down to the beach with the infantry, the Greeks forgot the words of Themistokles, and began to cast eager glances towards the Isthmus and to be angry with any one who proposed to do anything else than withdraw. They determined to retire by night, and the steersmen were given orders to prepare for a voyage. Themistokles, enraged at the idea of the Greek fleet dispersing, and losing the advantage of the narrow waters, planned the affair of Sikinnus. This Sikinnus was a Persian who had been taken prisoner, and who was fond of Themistokles and took charge of his children. He sent this man secretly to Xerxes, ordering him to say that Themistokles, the general of the Athenians, has determined to come over to the king of the Persians, and is the first to tell him that the Greeks are about to retreat. He bids him not to allow them to fly, but to attack them while they are disheartened at not being supported by a land force, and destroy their fleet.

Xerxes, who imagined this to be said for his advantage, was delighted, and at once gave orders to the commanders of his ships to make ready for battle at their leisure, all but two hundred, whom he ordered to put to sea at once, surround the whole strait, and close up the passages through the islands, so that no one of the enemy could escape. While this was being done, Aristeides, the son of Lysimachus, who was the first to perceive it, came to the tent of Themistokles, although the latter was his enemy, and had driven him into exile. When Themistokles came to meet him, he told him they were surrounded; knowing the frank and noble character of Aristeides, Themistokles told him the whole plot, and begged him as a man in whom the Greeks could trust, to encourage them to fight a battle in the straits. Aristeides praised Themistokles for what he had done, and went round to the other generals and captains of ships, inciting them to fight. Yet they were inclined to doubt even the word of Aristeides, when a trireme from the island of Tenos, under the command of Panaitios, came in, having deserted from the enemy, and brought the news that the Greeks were really surrounded. Then, in a spirit of anger and despair, they prepared for the struggle.

XIII. At daybreak Xerxes took his seat on a high cliff overlooking all his host, just above the Temple of Herakles, we are told by Phanodemus, where the strait between Salamis and Attica is narrowest, but according to Akestodorus, close to the Megarian frontier, upon the mountains called Horns. Here he sat upon the golden throne, with many scribes standing near, whose duty it was to write down the events of the battle.

While Themistokles was sacrificing on the beach, beside the admiral's ship, three most beautiful captive boys were brought to him, splendidly adorned with gold and fine clothes. They were said to be the children of Sandauke, the sister of Xerxes, and Artäuktes. When Euphrantides the prophet saw them, there shone at once from the victims on the altar a great and brilliant flame, and at the same time some one was heard to sneeze on the right hand, which is a good omen. Euphrantides now besought Themistokles to sacrifice these young men as victims to Dionysus, to whom human beings are sacrificed; so should the Greeks obtain safety and victory. Themistokles was struck with horror at this terrible proposal; but the multitude, who, as is natural with people in great danger, hoped to be saved by miraculous rather than by ordinary means, called upon the God with one voice, and leading the captives up to the altar, compelled him to offer them up as the prophet bade him. This story rests on the authority of Phanias of Lesbos, who was a man of education, and well read in history.

XIV. As for the numbers of the Persian fleet, the poet Aeschylus, as though he knew it clearly, writes as follows in his tragedy of the Persae:
"And well I know a thousand sail That day did Xerxes meet, And seven and two hundred more, The fastest of his fleet."

The Athenian ships, a hundred and eighty in number, had each eighteen men on deck, four of whom were archers, and the rest heavy-armed soldiers. Themistokles now chose the time for the battle as judiciously as he had chosen the place, and would not bring his triremes into line of battle before the fresh wind off the sea, as is usual in the morning, raised a heavy swell in the straits. This did not damage the low flat ships of the Greeks, but it caught the high-sterned Persian ships, over-weighted as they were with lofty decks, and presented their broadsides to the Greeks, who eagerly attacked them, watching Themistokles because he was their best example, and also because Ariamenes, Xerxes's admiral, and the bravest and best of the king's brothers, attacked him in a huge ship, from which, as if from a castle, he poured darts and arrows upon him.

But Ameinias of Dekeleia and Sokles of Pedia, who were both sailing in the same vessel, met him stem to stem. Each ship crashed into the other with its iron beak, and was torn open. Ariamenes attempted to board the Greek ship, but these two men set upon him with their spears, and drove him into the sea. His body was noticed by Queen Artemisia floating amongst the other wreckage, and was by her brought to Xerxes.

XV. At this period of the battle it is said that a great light was seen to shine from Eleusis, and that a great noise was heard upon the Thriasian plain near the sea, as though multitudes of men were escorting the mystic Iacchus in procession. From the place where these sounds were heard a mist seemed to spread over the sea and envelop the ships. Others thought that they saw spirit-forms of armed men come from Aegina, and hold their hands before the ships of the Greeks. These it was supposed were the Aeakid heroes, to whom prayers for help had been offered just before the battle. The first man to capture a ship was Lykomedes, an Athenian captain, who cut off its ensign and dedicated it to Apollo with the laurel crown at the Temple at Phlyae.

In the narrow straits the Persians were unable to bring more than a part of their fleet into action, and their ships got into each other's way, so that the Greeks could meet them on equal terms, and, although they resisted until evening, completely routed them, winning, as Simonides calls it, that "glorious and famous victory," the greatest exploit ever achieved at sea, which owed its success to the bravery of the sailors and the genius of Themistokles.

XVI. After this naval defeat, Xerxes, enraged at his failure, endeavoured to fill up the strait with earth, and so to make a passage for his land forces to Salamis, to attack the Greeks there. Now Themistokles, in order to try the temper of Aristeides, proposed that the fleet should sail to the Hellespont, and break the bridge of boats there, "in order," said he, "that we may conquer Asia in Europe." But Aristeides disapproved of this measure, saying, "Hitherto we have fought against the Persian king, while he has been at his ease; but if we shut him up in Greece, and drive the chief of so large an army to despair, he will no longer sit quietly under a golden umbrella to look on at his battles, but will strain every nerve and superintend every operation in person, and so will easily retrieve his losses and form better plans for the future."

"Instead of breaking down the existing bridge for him, Themistokles," said he, "we ought rather, if possible, at once to build another, and send the man out of Europe as quickly as possible." "Well then," answered Themistokles, "if you think that our interest lies in that direction, we ought all to consider and contrive to send him out of Greece as fast as we can." When this resolution was adopted, Themistokles sent one of the king's eunuchs, whom he had found among the prisoners, bidding him warn Xerxes that "the Greeks had determined after their victory to sail to the Hellespont and break the bridge, but that Themistokles, out of his regard for the king, advises him to proceed as fast as he can to his own sea, and cross over it, while he (Themistokles) gained time for him by delaying the allied fleet." Xerxes, hearing thus, was much alarmed and retired in all haste. And indeed the battle with Mardonius at Plataea shows us which of the two was right; for the Greeks there could scarcely deal with a small part of the Persian army, and what therefore could they have done with the whole?

XVII. Herodotus tells us that, of Greek States, Aegina received the prize of valour, and that, of the generals, it was awarded to Themistokles, though against the will of the voters. When the armies retired to the Isthmus all the generals laid their votes on the altar there, and each man declared himself to deserve the first prize for valour, and Themistokles to deserve the second. However, the Lacedaemonians brought him home with them to Sparta, and gave Eurybiades the first prize for valour, but Themistokles that for wisdom, a crown of olive-leaves. They also gave him the best chariot in their city, and sent three hundred of their young men to escort him out of the country. It is also related that at the next Olympian games, when Themistokles appeared upon the race-course, all the spectators took no further interest in the contests, but passed the whole day in admiring and applauding him, and in pointing him out to such as were strangers; so that he was delighted, and said to his friends that he had now received his reward for all his labours on behalf of Greece.

XVIII. He was by nature excessively fond of admiration, as we may judge from the stories about him which have been preserved. Once, when he was made admiral of the Athenian fleet, he put off all the necessary business of his office until the day appointed for sailing, in order that he might have a great many dealings with various people all at once, and so appear to be a person of great influence and importance. And when he saw the corpses floating in the sea with gold bracelets and necklaces, he himself passed them by, but pointed them out to a friend who was following, saying, "Do you pick them up and keep them; for you are not Themistokles." A beautiful youth, named Antiphates, regarded him coolly at first, but eventually became submissive to him because of his immense reputation. "Young man," said Themistokles, "it has taken some time, but we have at length both regained our right minds."

He used to say that the Athenians neither admired nor respected him, but used him like a plane-tree under which they took shelter in storm, but which in fair weather they lopped and stripped of its leaves. Once when a citizen of Seriphos said to him that he owed his glory, not to himself but to his city, he answered, "Very true; I should not have become a great man if I had been a Seriphian, nor would you if you had been an Athenian." When one of his fellow-generals, who thought that he had done the state good service, was taking a haughty tone, and comparing his exploits with those of Themistokles, he said, "The day after a feast, once upon a time, boasted that it was better than the feast-day itself, because on that day all men are full of anxiety and trouble, while upon the next day every one enjoys what has been prepared at his leisure. But the feast-day answered, 'Very true, only but for me you never would have been at all.' So now," said he, "if I had not come first, where would you all have been now?" His son, who was spoiled by his mother, and by himself to please her, he said was the most powerful person in Greece; for the Athenians ruled the Greeks, he ruled the Athenians, his wife ruled him, and his son ruled his wife. Wishing to be singular in all things, when he put up a plot of ground for sale, he ordered the crier to announce that there were good neighbours next to it. When two men paid their addresses to his daughter, he chose the more agreeable instead of the richer of the two, saying that he preferred a man without money to money without a man. Such was his character, as shown in his talk.

XIX. Immediately after the great war, he began to rebuild and fortify the city. In order to succeed in this, Theopompus says that he bribed the Spartan ephors into laying aside opposition, but most writers say that he outwitted them by proceeding to Sparta nominally on an embassy. Then when the Spartans complained to him that Athens was being fortified, and when Poliarchus came expressly from Aegina to charge him with it, he denied it, and bade them send commissioners to Athens to see whether it was true, wishing both to obtain time for the fortifications to be built, and also to place these commissioners in the hands of the Athenians, as hostages for his own safety. His expectations were realised; for the Lacedaemonians, on discovering the truth, did him no harm, but dissembled their anger and sent him away. After this he built Peiraeus, as he perceived the excellence of its harbours, and was desirous to turn the whole attention of the Athenians to naval pursuits. In this he pursued a policy exactly the opposite to that of the ancient kings of Attica; for they are said to have endeavoured to keep their subjects away from the sea, and to accustom them to till the ground instead of going on board ships, quoting the legend that Athene and Poseidon had a contest for the possession of the land, and that she gained a decision in her favour by the production of the sacred olive. Themistokles, on the other hand, did not so much "stick Peiraeus on to Athens," as Aristophanes the comic poet said, as make the city dependent upon Peiraeus, and the land dependent on the sea. By this means he transferred power from the nobles to the people, because sailors and pilots became the real strength of the State. For this reason the thirty tyrants destroyed the bema, or tribune on the place of public assembly, which was built looking towards the sea, and built another which looked inland, because they thought that the naval supremacy of Athens had been the origin of its democratic constitution, and that an oligarchy had less to fear from men who cultivated the land.

XX. Themistokles had even more extended views than these about making the Athenians supreme at sea. When Xerxes was gone, the whole Greek fleet was drawn up on shore for the winter at Pagasae. Themistokles then publicly told the Athenians that he had a plan which would save and benefit them all, but which must not be divulged. The Athenians bade him tell Aristeides only, and to execute his designs if he approved.

Themistokles then told Aristeides that his design was to burn the whole Greek fleet as they lay on the beach. But Aristeides came forward and told the people that no proposal could be more advantageous or more villainous; so that the Athenians forbade Themistokles to proceed with it. On another occasion the Lacedaemonians proposed, in a meeting of the Amphiktyonic council, that all States that had taken no part in the Persian war should be excluded from that council; Themistokles, fearing that if the Lacedaemonians should exclude Thessaly, Argos, and Thebes, they would have complete control over the votes, and be able to carry what measures they pleased, made representations to the various States, and influenced the votes of their deputies at the meeting, pointing out to them that there were only thirty-one States which took any part in the war, and that most of these were very small ones, so that it would be unreasonable for one or two powerful States to pronounce the rest of Greece outlawed, and be supreme in the council. After this he generally opposed the Lacedaemonians; wherefore they paid special court to Kimon, in order to establish him as a political rival to Themistokles.

XXI. Moreover, he made himself odious to the allies by sailing about the islands and wringing money from them. A case in point is the conversation which Herodotus tells us he held with the people of Andros, when trying to get money from them. He said that he was come, bringing with him two gods, Persuasion and Necessity; but they replied that they also possessed two equally powerful ones, Poverty and Helplessness, by whom they were prevented from supplying him with money. The poet, Timokreon of Rhodes, in one of his songs, writes bitterly of Themistokles, saying that he was prevailed upon by the bribes which he received from exiles to restore them to their native country, but abandoned himself, who was his guest and friend. The song runs as follows:

"Though ye may sing Pausanias or Xanthippus in your lays, Or Leotychides, 'tis Aristeides whom I praise, The best of men as yet produced by holy Athens' State, Since thus upon Themistokles has fall'n Latona's hate: That liar and that traitor base, who for a bribe unclean, Refused to reinstate a man who his own guest had been. His friend too, in his native Ialysus, but who took Three silver talents with him, and his friend forsook. Bad luck go with the fellow, who unjustly some restores From exile, while some others he had banished from our shores, And some he puts to death; and sits among us gorged with pelf. He kept an ample table at the Isthmian games himself, And gave to every guest that came full plenty of cold meat, The which they with a prayer did each and every of them eat, But their prayer was 'Next year be there no Themistokles to meet.'"

And after the exile and condemnation of Themistokles, Timokreon wrote much more abusively about him in a song which begins,

"Muse, far away, Sound this my lay, For it both meet and right is."

It is said that Timokreon was exiled from home for having dealings with the Persians, and that Themistokles confirmed his sentence. When, then, Themistokles was charged with intriguing with the Persians, Timokreon wrote upon him,

"Timokreon is not the only Greek That turned a traitor, Persian gold to seek; I'm not the only fox without a tail, But others put their honour up for sale."

XXII. As the Athenians, through his unpopularity, eagerly listened to any story to his discredit, he was obliged to weary them by constantly repeating the tale of his own exploits to them. In answer to those who were angry with him, he would ask, "Are you weary of always receiving benefits from the same hand?" He also vexed the people by building the Temple of Artemis of Good Counsel, as he called her, hinting that he had taken good counsel for the Greeks. This temple he placed close to his own house in Melite, at the place where at the present day the public executioner casts out the bodies of executed criminals, and the clothes and ropes of men who have hanged themselves. Even in our own times a small statue of Themistokles used to stand in the Temple of Artemis of Good Counsel; and he seems to have been a hero not only in mind, but in appearance. The Athenians made use of ostracism to banish him, in order to reduce his extravagant pretensions, as they always were wont to do in the case of men whom they thought over powerful and unfit for living in the equality of a democracy. For ostracism implied no censure, but was intended as a vent for envious feelings, which were satisfied by seeing the object of their hatred thus humbled.

XXIII. When Themistokles was banished from Athens, he lived in Argos, during which time the proceedings of Pausanias gave a great opportunity to his enemies. He was impeached on a charge of treason by Leobotes, the son of Alkmaeon of Agraulai, and the Spartans joined in the impeachment. Pausanias, indeed, at first concealed his treacherous designs from Themistokles, although he was his friend; but when he saw that Themistokles was banished, and chafing at the treatment he had received, he was encouraged to ask him to share his treason, and showed him the letters which he had received from the Persian king, at the same time inflaming his resentment against the Greeks, whom he spoke of as ungrateful wretches. Themistokles refused utterly to join Pausanias, but nevertheless told no one of his treasonable practices, either because he hoped that he would desist, or that his visionary and impossible projects would be disclosed by other means. And thus it was that when Pausanias was put to death, certain letters and writings on this subject were found, which threw suspicion upon Themistokles. The Lacedaemonians loudly condemned him, and many of his own countrymen, because of the enmity they bore him, brought charges against him. He did not appear in person at first, but answered these attacks by letters. In these he told his accusers that he had always sought to rule, and was not born to obey; so that he never would sell himself and Greece to be a slave to the Persians. But in spite of these arguments, his enemies prevailed upon the Athenians to send men with orders to seize him, and bring him to be tried by Greece.

XXIV. He was apprised of this in time to take refuge in Korkyra, a State which was under obligations to him. For once, when Korkyra was at variance with Corinth, he had been chosen to arbitrate between them, and had reconciled them, giving as his award that the Corinthians were to pay down twenty talents, and each State to have an equal share in the city and island of Leucas, as being a colony from both of them. From thence he fled to Epirus; but, being still pursued by the Athenians and Lacedaemonians, he adopted a desperate resolution. Admetus, the king of the Molossians, had once made some request to the Athenians, which Themistokles, who was then in the height of his power, insultingly refused to grant. Admetus was deeply incensed, and eager for vengeance; but now Themistokles feared the fresh fury of his countrymen more than this old grudge of the king's, put himself at his mercy, and became a suppliant to Admetus in a novel and strange fashion; for he lay down at the hearth of Admetus, holding that prince's infant son, which is considered among the Molossians to be the most solemn manner of becoming a suppliant, and one which cannot be refused. Some say that Phthia, the king's wife, suggested this posture to Themistokles, and placed her infant on the hearth with him; while others say that Admetus, in order to be able to allege religious reasons for his refusal to give up Themistokles to his pursuers, himself arranged the scene with him. After this, Epikrates, of the township of Acharnai, managed to convey his wife and children out of Athens to join him, for which, we are told by Stesimbrotus, Kimon subsequently had him condemned and executed. But, singularly enough, afterwards Stesimbrotus either forgets his wife and children, or makes Themistokles forget them, when he says that he sailed to Sicily and demanded the daughter of the despot Hiero in marriage, promising that he would make all Greece obey him. As Hiero rejected his proposals, he then went to Asia.

XXV. Now it is not probable that this ever took place. Theophrastus, in his treatise on monarchy, relates that when Hiero sent race-horses to Olympia and pitched a costly tent there, Themistokles said to the assembled Greeks that they ought to destroy the despot's tent, and not permit his horses to run. Thucydides too informs us that he crossed to the Aegean sea, and set sail from Pydna, none of his fellow-travellers knowing who he was until the ship was driven by contrary winds to Naxos, which was then being besieged by the Athenians. Then he became alarmed, and told the captain and the pilot who he was, and, partly by entreaties, partly by threats that he would denounce them to the Athenians, and say that they well knew who he was, but were carrying him out of the country for a bribe, he prevailed on them to hold on their course to the coast of Asia.

Of his property, much was concealed by his friends and sent over to him in Asia; but what was confiscated to the public treasury amounted, according to Theopompus, to a hundred talents, and according to Theophrastus to eighty, albeit Themistokles, before his entrance into political life, did not possess property worth three talents.

XXVI. When he sailed to Kyme, he found that many of the inhabitants of the Ionic coast were watching for an opportunity to capture him, especially Ergoteles and Pythodorus (for indeed, to men who cared not how they made their money, he would have been a rich prize, as the Persian king had offered a reward of two hundred talents for him), he fled to Aegae, a little Aeolian city, where he was known by no one except his friend Nikogenes, the richest of all the Aeolians, who was well known to the Persians of the interior. In this man's house he lay concealed for some days. Here, after the feast which followed a sacrifice, Olbius, who took charge of Nikogenes's children, fell into a kind of inspired frenzy, and spoke the following verse:

"Night shall speak and give thee counsel, night shall give thee victory." After this Themistokles dreamed a dream. He thought that a snake was coiling itself upon his belly and crawling up towards his throat. As soon as it reached his throat, it became an eagle and flapped its wings, lifted him up, and carried him a long distance, until he saw a golden herald's staff. The eagle set him down upon this securely, and he felt free from all terror and anxiety. After this he was sent away by Nikogenes, who made use of the following device. Most barbarian nations, and the Persians especially, are violently jealous in their treatment of women. They guard not only their wives, but their purchased slaves and concubines, with the greatest care, not permitting them to be seen by any one out of doors, but when they are at home they lock them up, and when they are on a journey they place them in waggons with curtains all round them. Such a waggon was prepared for Themistokles, and he travelled in it, his escort telling all whom they met that they were conveying a Greek lady from Ionia to one of the king's courtiers.

XXVII. Thucydides and Charon of Lampsakus relate that Xerxes was now dead, and that Themistokles gave himself up to his son; but Ephorus, Deinon, Kleitarchus, Herakleides, and many others, say that it was to Xerxes himself that he came. But the narrative of Thucydides agrees better with the dates, although they are not thoroughly settled.

At this perilous crisis Themistokles first applied to Artabanus, a chiliarch, or officer in command of a regiment of a thousand men, whom he told that he was a Greek, and that he wished to have an interview with the king about matters of the utmost importance, and in which the king was especially interested. He replied, "Stranger, the customs of different races are different, and each has its own standard of right and wrong; yet among all men it is thought right to honour, admire, and to defend one's own customs. Now we are told that you chiefly prize freedom and equality; we on the other hand think it the best of all our laws to honour the king, and to worship him as we should worship the statue of a god that preserves us all. Wherefore if you are come with the intention of adopting our customs, and of prostrating yourself before the king, you may be permitted to see the king, and speak with him; but if not, you must use some other person to communicate with him; for it is not the custom for the king to converse with any one who does not prostrate himself before him." Themistokles, hearing this, said to him, "Artabanus, I am come to increase the glory and power of the king, and will both myself adopt your customs, since the god that has exalted the Persians will have it so, and will also increase the number of those who prostrate themselves before the king. So let this be no impediment to the interview with him which I desire." "Whom of the Greeks," asked Artabanus, "are we to tell him is come? for you do not seem to have the manners of a man of humble station." "No one," answered Themistokles, "must learn my name before the king himself." This is the story which we are told by Phanias. But Eratosthenes, in his treatise on wealth, tells us also that Themistokles was introduced to Artabanus by an Eretrian lady with whom the latter lived.

XXVIII. When he was brought into the king's presence he prostrated himself, and stood silent. The king then told his interpreter to ask him who he was; and when the interpreter had asked this question, he told him to answer, "I am, O King, Themistokles the Athenian, an exile, a man who has wrought much evil to the Persians, but more good than evil, in that I stopped the pursuit when Greece was safe, and I was able to do you a kindness as all was well at home. In my present fallen fortunes I am prepared to be grateful for any mark of favour you may show me, or to deprecate your anger, should you bear a grudge against me. You may see, from the violence of my own countrymen against me, how great were the benefits which I conferred upon the Persians; so now use me rather as a means of proving your magnanimity than of glutting your wrath. Wherefore save me, your suppliant, and do not destroy one who has become the enemy of Greece." Themistokles also introduced a supernatural element into his speech by relating the vision which he saw at the house of Nikogenes, and also a prophecy which he received at the shrine of Jupiter of Dodona, which bade him "go to the namesake of the god," from which he concluded that the god sent him to the king, because they were both great, and called kings. To this speech the Persian king made no answer, although he was astonished at his bold spirit; but in conversation with his friends he spoke as though this were the greatest possible piece of good fortune, and in his prayers begged Arimanios to make his enemies ever continue to banish their ablest men. He is said to have offered a sacrifice to the gods and to have drunk wine at once, and during the night in his soundest sleep he thrice cried out, "I have got Themistokles the Athenian."

XXIX. At daybreak he called together his friends and sent for Themistokles, who augured nothing pleasant from the insults and abuse which he received from the people at the palace gates, when they heard his name. Moreover Roxanes the chiliarch, as Themistokles passed by him in silence into the king's presence, whispered, "Thou subtle serpent of Greece, the king's good genius has led thee hither." But when he was come before the king and had prostrated himself a second time, the king embraced him, and said in a friendly tone that he already owed him two hundred talents: for as he had brought himself he was clearly entitled to the reward which was offered to any one else who would do so. He also promised him much more than this, and encouraged him to speak at length upon the affairs of Greece. To this Themistokles answered, that human speech was like embroidered tapestry, because when spread out it shows all its figures, but when wrapped up it both conceals and spoils them, wherefore he asked for time. The king was pleased with his simile, and bade him take what time he chose. He asked for a year, during which he learned the Persian language sufficiently to talk to the king without an interpreter. This led the people to imagine that he discoursed about the affairs of Greece; but many changes were made at that time in the great officers of the court, and the nobles disliked Themistokles, imagining that he dared to speak about them to the king. Indeed, he was honoured as no other foreigner ever was, and went hunting with the king and lived in his family circle, so that he came into the presence of the king's mother, and became her intimate friend, and at the king's command was instructed in the mysteries of the Magi.

When Demaratus the Spartan was bidden to ask for a boon, he asked to be allowed to drive through Sardis wearing his tiara upright like that of the king. Mithropaustes, the king's cousin, took hold of Demaratus by his tiara, saying, "You have no brains for the king's tiara to cover; do you think you would become Zeus if you were given his thunderbolt to wield?" The king was very angry with Demaratus because of this request, but Themistokles by his entreaties restored him to favour. It is also said that the later Persian kings, whose politics were more mixed up with those of Greece, used to promise any Greek whom they wished to desert to them that they would treat him better than Themistokles. We are told that Themistokles himself, after he became a great man and was courted by many, was seated one day at a magnificent banquet, and said to his children, "My sons, we should have been ruined if it had not been for our ruin." Most writers agree that three cities, Magnesia, Lampsakus, and Myous, were allotted to him for bread, wine, and meat. To these Neanthes of Kyzikus and Phanias add two more, Perkote and Palaiskepsis, which were to supply bedding and clothing respectively.

XXX. On one occasion, when he went down to the seaside on some business connected with Greece, a Persian named Epixyes, Satrap of Upper Phrygia, plotted his assassination. He had long kept some Pisidians who were to kill him when he passed the night in the town of Leontokophalos, which means 'Lion's Head.' It is said that the mother of the gods appeared to him while he was sleeping at noon and said, "Themistokles, be late at Lion's Head, lest you fall in with a lion. As a recompense for this warning, I demand Mnesiptolema for my handmaid." Themistokles, disturbed at this, after praying to the goddess, left the highway and made a circuit by another road, avoiding that place; when it was night he encamped in the open country. As one of the sumpter cattle that carried his tent had fallen into a river, Themistokles's servants hung up the rich hangings, which were dripping with wet, in order to dry them. The Pisidians meanwhile came up to the camp with drawn swords, and, not clearly distinguishing in the moonlight the things hung out to dry, thought that they must be the tent of Themistokles, and that they would find him asleep within it. When they came close to it and raised the hangings, the servants who were on the watch fell upon them and seized them. Having thus escaped from danger, he built a temple to Dindymene at Magnesia to commemorate the appearance of the goddess, and appointed his daughter Mnesiptolema to be its priestess.

XXXI. When he came to Sardis, he leisurely examined the temples and the offerings which they contained, and in the temple of the mother of the gods, he found a bronze female figure called the Water-carrier, about two cubits high, which he himself, when overseer of the water supply of Athens, had made out of the fines imposed upon those who took water illegally.

Either feeling touched at the statue being a captive, or else willing to show the Athenians how much power he possessed in Persia, he proposed to the Satrap of Lydia to send it back to Athens. This man became angry at his demand, and said that he should write to the king, and tell him of it. Themistokles in terror applied himself to the harem of the Satrap, and by bribing the ladies there induced them to pacify him, while he himself took care to be more cautious in future, as he saw that he had to fear the enmity of the native Persians. For this reason, Theopompus tells us, he ceased to wander about Asia, but resided at Magnesia, where, receiving rich presents and honoured equally with the greatest Persian nobles, he lived for a long time in tranquillity; for the king's attention was so entirely directed to the affairs of the provinces of the interior that he had no leisure for operations against Greece. But when Egypt revolted, and the Athenians assisted it, and Greek triremes sailed as far as Cyprus and Cilicia, and Kimon was master of the sea, then the king determined to attack the Greeks, and prevent their development at his expense. Armies were put in motion, generals were appointed, and frequent messages were sent to Themistokles from the king, bidding him attack Greece and fulfil his promises. Themistokles, unmoved by resentment against his countrymen, and uninfluenced by the thought of the splendid position which he might occupy as commander-in-chief, possibly too, thinking that his task was an impossible one, as Greece possessed many great generals, especially Kimon, who had a most brilliant reputation, but chiefly because he would not soil his glory and disgrace the trophies which he had won, determined, as indeed was his best course, to bring his life to a fitting close. He offered sacrifice to the gods, called his friends together, and, having taken leave of them, drank bull's blood, according to the most common tradition, but according to others, some quickly-operating poison, and died at Magnesia in the sixty-fifth year of a life almost entirely spent in great political and military employments.

The King of Persia, when he heard of the manner of his death and his reasons for dying, admired him more than ever, and continued to treat his family and friends with kindness.

XXXII. Themistokles left five children, Neokles, Diokles, Archeptolis, Polyeuktus, Kleophantus, by his first wife Archippe, who was the daughter of Lysander, of the township of Alopekai. Of these Kleophantus is mentioned by Plato the philosopher as being an excellent horseman, but otherwise worthless. Of the elder ones, Neokles was bitten by a horse and died while still a child, and Diokles was adopted by his grandfather Lysander. He also had several daughters by his second wife, of whom Mnesiptolema married Archeptolis, her father's half-brother; Italia married Panthoides of the island of Chios, and Sybaris married Nikomedes, an Athenian. After Themistokles's death, his nephew Phrasikles sailed to Magnesia, and with her brother's consent married Nicomache, and also took charge of the youngest child, who was named Asia.

The people of Magnesia show a splendid tomb of Themistokles in their market-place; but with regard to the fate of his remains we must pay no attention to Andokides, who in his address to his friends, tells us that the Athenians stole them and tore them to pieces, because he would tell any falsehood to excite the hatred of the nobles against the people. Phylarchus, too, writes his history in such dramatic form that he all but resorts to the actual machinery of the stage, bringing forward one Neokles, and Demopolis as the children of Themistokles to make a touching scene, which anyone can see is untrue. Diodorus the topographer, in his treatise 'On Tombs' says, more as a conjecture than as knowing it for a fact, that in the great harbour of Peiraeus a kind of elbow juts out from the promontory of Alkimus, and that when one sails past this, going inwards, where the sea is most sheltered, there is a large foundation, and upon it the tomb of Themistokles, shaped like an altar. It is thought that the comic poet Plato alludes to this in the following verses:

"By the sea's margin, by the watery strand, Thy monument, Themistokles, shall stand; By this directed to thy native shore The merchant shall convey his freighted store; And when our fleets are summoned to the fight, Athens shall conquer with thy tomb in sight."

The descendants of Themistokles are given certain privileges at Magnesia even to the present day, for I know that Themistokles, an Athenian, my friend and fellow-student in the school of Ammonias the philosopher, enjoyed them.

Life of Camillus.

I. The strangest fact in the life of Furius Camillus is that, although he was a most successful general and won great victories, though he was five times appointed dictator, triumphed four times, and was called the second founder of Rome, yet he never once was consul. The reason of this is to be found in the political condition of Rome at that time; for the people, being at variance with the senate, refused to elect consuls, and chose military tribunes instead, who, although they had full consular powers, yet on account of their number were less offensive to the people than consuls. To have affairs managed by six men instead of two appears to have been a consolation to those who had suffered from the arbitrary rule of a few. It was during this period that Camillus reached the height of power and glory, and yet he would not become consul against the will of the people, although several occasions occurred when he might have been elected, but in his various appointments he always contrived, even when he had sole command, to share his power with others, while even when he had colleagues he kept all the glory for himself. His moderation prevented any one from grudging him power, while his successes were due to his genius, in which he confessedly surpassed all his countrymen.

II. The family of the Furii was not a very illustrious one before Camillus gained glory in the great battle with the Aequi and Volsci, where he served under the dictator Postumius Tubertus. Riding out before the rest of the army, he was struck in the thigh by a dart, but tore it out, assailed the bravest of the enemy, and put them to flight. After this, amongst other honours he was appointed censor, an office of great dignity at that time. One admirable measure is recorded of his censorship, that by arguments and threatening them with fines he persuaded the unmarried citizens to marry the widow women, whose number was very great on account of the wars. Another measure to which he was forced was that of taxing orphans, who had hitherto been exempt from taxation. This was rendered necessary by the constant campaigns which were carried on at a great expense, and more especially by the siege of Veii. Some call the inhabitants of this city Veientani. It was the bulwark of Etruria, possessing as many fighting men as Rome itself; the citizens were rich, luxurious, and extravagant in their habits, and fought bravely many times for honour and for power against the Romans. At this period, having been defeated in several great battles, the people of Veii had given up any schemes of conquest, but had built strong and high walls, filled their city with arms and provisions, and all kinds of material of war, and fearlessly endured a siege, which was long, no doubt, but which became no less irksome and difficult to the besiegers. Accustomed as the Romans had been to make short campaigns in summer weather, and to spend their winters at home, they were now for the first time compelled by their tribunes to establish forts and entrench their camp, and pass both summer and winter in the enemy's country for seven years in succession. The generals were complained of, and as they seemed to be carrying on the siege remissly, they were removed, and others appointed, among them Camillus, who was then tribune for the second time. But he effected nothing in the siege at that time, because he was sent to fight the Faliscans and Capenates, who had insulted the Roman territory throughout the war with Veii, when the Roman army was engaged elsewhere, but were now driven by Camillus with great loss to the shelter of their city walls.

III. After this, while the war was at its height, much alarm was caused by the strange phenomenon seen at the Alban lake, which could not be accounted for on ordinary physical principles. The season was autumn, and the summer had not been remarkable for rain or for moist winds, so that many of the streams and marshes in Italy were quite dried up, and others held out with difficulty, while the rivers, as is usual in summer, were very low and deeply sunk in their bed. But the Alban lake, which is self-contained, lying as it does surrounded by fertile hills, began for no reason, except it may be the will of Heaven, to increase in volume and to encroach upon the hillsides near it, until it reached their very tops, rising quietly and without disturbance. At first the portent only amazed the shepherds and herdsmen of the neighbourhood; but when the lake by the weight of its waters broke through the thin isthmus of land which restrained it, and poured down in a mighty stream through the fertile plains below to the sea, then not only the Romans, but all the people of Italy, thought it a portent of the gravest character. Much talk about it took place in the camp before Veii, so that the besieged also learned what was happening at the lake.

IV. As always happens during a long siege, where there are frequent opportunities of intercourse between the two parties, one of the Romans had become intimate with a citizen of Veii, who was learned in legendary lore, and was even thought to have supernatural sources of information. When this man heard of the overflowing of the lake, his Roman friend observed that he was overjoyed, and laughed at the idea of the siege being successful. The Roman told him that these were not the only portents which troubled the Romans at the present time, but that there were others stranger than this, about which he should like to consult him, and, if possible, save himself in the common ruin of his country. The man eagerly attended to his discourse, imagining that he was about to hear some great secrets. The Roman thus decoyed him away farther and farther from the city gate, when he suddenly seized him and lifted him from the ground. Being the stronger man, and being assisted by several soldiers from the camp, he overpowered him, and brought him before the generals. Here the man, seeing that there was no escape, and that no one can resist his destiny, told them of the ancient oracles about his city, how it could not be taken until its enemies drove back the waters of the Alban lake, and prevented its joining the sea. When the senate heard this they were at a loss what to do, and determined to send an embassy to Delphi to enquire of the God. The embassy consisted of men of mark and importance, being Licinius Cossus, Valerius Potitus, and Fabius Ambustus. After a prosperous journey they returned with a response from Apollo, pointing out certain ceremonies which had been neglected in the feast of the Latin games, and bidding them, if possible, force the waters of the Alban lake away from the sea into its ancient course, or, if this could not be done, to divide the stream by canals and watercourses, and so to expend it in the plain. When the answer was brought back, the priests took the necessary steps about the sacrifices, while the people turned their attention to the diversion of the water.

V. In the tenth year of the war, the Senate recalled all the rest of the generals, and made Camillus Dictator. He chose Cornelius Scipio to be his Master of the Knights, and made a vow to the gods, that, if he succeeded in bringing the war to a glorious close, he would celebrate a great festival, and build a shrine to the goddess whom the Romans call Mater Matuta. This goddess, from the rites with which she is worshipped, one would imagine to be the same as the Greek Leukothea. For they bring a slave girl into the temple and beat her, and then drive her out; they take their brothers' children in their arms in preference to their own, and generally their ceremonies seem to allude to the nursing of Bacchus, and to the misfortunes which befell Ino because of her husband's concubine. After this, Camillus invaded the Faliscan territory, and in a great battle overthrew that people, and the Capenates who came to their assistance. Next, he turned his attention to the siege of Veii, and, perceiving that it would be a difficult matter to take the city by assault, he ordered mines to be dug, as the ground near the walls was easily worked, and the mines could be sunk to a sufficient depth to escape the notice of the besieged. As this work succeeded to his wish, he made a demonstration above ground to call the enemy to the walls and distract their attention, while others made their way unperceived through the mine to the Temple of Juno in the citadel, the largest and most sacred edifice in the city. Here, it is said, was the King of the Veientines, engaged in sacrificing. The soothsayer inspected the entrails, and cried with a loud voice, that the goddess would give the victory to whoever offered that victim. The Romans in the mine, hearing these words, quickly tore up the floor, and burst through it with shouts and rattling arms. The enemy fled in terror, and they seized the victims and carried them to Camillus. However, this story sounds rather fabulous.

The city was stormed, and the Romans carried off an enormous mass of plunder. Camillus, who viewed them from the citadel, at first stood weeping, but when, congratulated by the bystanders, raised his hands to heaven and said, "Great Jupiter, and all ye other gods, that see all good and evil deeds alike, ye know that it is not in unrighteous conquest, but in self-defence, that the Romans have taken this city of their lawless enemies. If," he continued, "there awaits us any reverse of fortune to counterbalance this good luck, I pray that it may fall, not upon the city or army of Rome, but, as lightly as may be, upon my own head." After these words he turned round to the right, as is the Roman habit after prayer, and while turning, stumbled and fell. All those present were terrified at the omen, but he recovered himself, saying that, as he had prayed, he had received a slight hurt to temper his great good fortune.

VI. When the city was sacked, he determined to send the statue of Juno to Rome, according to his vow. When workmen were assembled for this purpose, he offered sacrifice, and prayed to the goddess to look kindly on his efforts, and to graciously take up her abode among the gods of Rome. It is said that the statue answered that it wished to do so, and approved of his proceedings. But Livy tells us that Camillus offered his prayers while touching the statue, and that some of the bystanders said, "She consents, and is willing to come." However, those who insist on the supernatural form of the story have one great argument in their favour, in the marvellous fortune of Rome, which never could from such small beginnings have reached, such a pitch of glory and power without many direct manifestations of the favour of Heaven. Moreover, other appearances of the same kind are to be compared with it, such as that statues have often been known to sweat, have been heard to groan, and have even turned away and shut their eyes, as has been related by many historians before our own time. And I have heard of many miraculous occurrences even at the present day, resting on evidence which cannot be lightly impugned. However, the weakness of human nature makes it equally dangerous to put too much faith in such matters or to entirely disbelieve them, as the one leads to superstition and folly, and the other to neglect and contempt of the gods. Our best course is caution, and the "golden mean."

VII. Camillus, either because he was elated by the magnificence of his exploit in having taken a city as large as Rome after a ten years' siege, or else because he had been so flattered by his admirers that his pride overcame his sober judgment, conducted his triumph with great ostentation, especially in driving through Rome in a chariot, drawn by four white horses, which never was done by any general before or since, for this carriage is thought to be sacred to Jupiter, the king and father of the gods. The citizens, unaccustomed to splendour, were displeased with him for this, and their dislike was increased by his opposition to the law for a redistribution of the people. The tribunes proposed that the Senate and people should be divided into two parts, one of which should stay at Rome and the other remove to the captured city, because they would be more powerful if they possessed two great cities, instead of one, and held the land in common, still remaining one nation. The lower classes, which were numerous and poor, eagerly took up the scheme, and continually clamoured round the speakers at the rostra, demanding to have it put to the vote. But the Senate and the nobles thought that it was not a redistribution, but the absolute destruction of Rome which the tribunes were demanding, and in their anger rallied round Camillus. He, fearing to have a contest on the matter, kept putting off the people and inventing reasons for delay, so as to prevent the law being brought forward to be voted upon. This increased his unpopularity; but the greatest and most obvious reason for the dislike which the people bore him arose from his demand for the tenth part of the spoils; very naturally, though perhaps he scarcely deserved it. On his way to Veii it seems he had made a vow, that if he took the city he would dedicate the tenth part of the spoil to Apollo. But when the city was taken and plundered, he either was unwilling to interfere with his countrymen, or else forgot his vow, and allowed them to enrich themselves with the booty. Afterwards, when he had laid down his dictatorship, he brought the matter before the Senate, and the soothsayers declared that the victims for sacrifice showed, when inspected, that the gods were angry and must be propitiated.

VIII. The Senate decreed, not that the plunder should be given up, for that would have been scarcely possible to carry out, but that those who had taken any should be put on their oath, and contribute a tenth part of its value. This measure bore very hardly upon the soldiers, poor hard-working men, who were now compelled to repay so large a proportion of what they had earned and spent. Camillus was clamorously assailed by them, and, having no better excuse to put forward, made the extraordinary statement that he had forgotten his vow when the city was plundered. The people angrily said that he had vowed to offer up a tithe of the enemy's property, but that he really was taking a tithe from the citizens instead. However, all the contributions were made, and it was determined that with them a golden bowl should be made and sent to Apollo at Delphi. There was a scarcity of gold in the city, and while the government were deliberating how it was to be obtained, the matrons held a meeting among themselves, and offered their golden ornaments to make the offering, which came to eight talents' weight of gold. The Senate rewarded them by permitting them to have a funeral oration pronounced over their graves the same as men; for hitherto it had not been customary at Rome to make any speeches at the funerals of women. They also chose three of the noblest citizens to travel with the offering, and sent them in a well-manned ship of war, splendidly equipped. Both storms and calms at sea are said to be dangerous, and they chanced on this occasion to come very near destruction, and miraculously escaped, for in a calm off the Aeolian Islands they were assailed by Liparian triremes, who took them for pirates. At their earnest entreaty these people forbore to run down their vessel, but took it in tow and brought it into their harbour, where they treated it as a piratical craft, and put up the crew and the property on board for sale by public auction. With great difficulty, by the goodness and influence of one man, Timesitheos, a general, they obtained their release, and were allowed to proceed. Timesitheos even launched some ships of his own, with which he escorted them to Delphi, where he also took part in the ceremony of consecration. In return for his services, as was only just, he received special honours at Rome.

IX. The tribunes of the people again began to agitate about the redistribution of land and occupation of Veii, but a war with the Faliscans gave the leading men a seasonable opportunity to elect magistrates after their own hearts for the coming year. Camillus was appointed military tribune, with five others, as it was thought that the State required a general of tried experience. At the decree of the Senate, Camillus raised a force and invaded the Faliscan territory. He now besieged Falerii, a strong city well provided with all munitions of war, which he considered it would be a work of no small time and labour to take; but he was desirous of employing the people in a long siege, to prevent their having leisure for factious proceedings at home. This was ever the policy of the Romans, to work off the elements of internal strife in attacks on their neighbours.

X. The Faliscans thought so little of the siege, from the strength of their defences, that, except when on duty on the walls, they used to walk about their city in their ordinary dress, and their children were sent regularly to

school, and used to be taken by their master to walk and take exercise outside
the walls. For the Faliscans, like the Greeks, had one common school, as they
wished all their children to be brought up together. The schoolmaster
determined to betray these boys to the enemy, and led them outside the walls
for exercise every day, and then led them back again. By this means he
gradually accustomed them to going out as if there was no danger, until
finally he took all the boys and handed them over to the Roman pickets,
bidding them bring him to Camillus. When he was brought before him he said
that he was a schoolmaster, that he preferred the favour of Camillus to his
duty, and that he came to hand over to him the city of Falerii in the persons
of these boys.

Camillus was very much shocked. He said that war is indeed harsh, and is
carried on by savage and unrighteous means, but yet there are laws of war
which are observed by good men, and one ought not so much to strive for
victory, as to forego advantages gained by wicked and villainous means: thus
a truly great general ought to succeed by his own warlike virtues, not by the
baseness of others.

Having spoken thus, he ordered his slaves to tear the schoolmaster's
clothes, tie his hands behind his back, and give the boys sticks and scourges
with which to drive him back to the city. The Faliscans had just discovered
the treachery of their schoolmaster, and, as may be expected, the whole city
was filled with mourning at such a calamity, men and women together
running in confusion to the gates and walls of the city, when the boys drove
in their schoolmaster with blows and insults, calling Camillus their saviour,
their father, and their god. Not only those who were parents, but all the
citizens were struck with admiration at the goodness of Camillus. They at
once assembled, and despatched ambassadors, putting themselves
unreservedly in his hands. These men Camillus sent on to Rome, where they
stated before the Senate, that the Romans, by preferring justice to conquest,
had taught them to prefer submission to freedom, although they did not think
that they fell short of the Romans in strength so much as in virtue. The
Senate referred the ambassadors to Camillus for their first answer; and he,
after receiving a contribution in money, and having made a treaty of alliance
with the Faliscans, drew off his forces.

XI. But the soldiers, who had been looking forward to plundering Falerii,
when they returned to Rome empty handed, abused Camillus to the other
citizens, saying that he was a hater of the people, and grudged poor men a
chance of enriching themselves. When the tribunes reintroduced the proposal
of redistribution of the land, and removing half the city to Veii, Camillus

openly, without caring how unpopular he became, opposed the measure. The people, sorely against their will, gave up the measure, but hated Camillus so fiercely that even his domestic afflictions (for he had just lost one of his two sons by sickness) could not move them to pity. Being of a kind and loving nature, he was dreadfully cast down at this misfortune, and spent all his time within doors mourning with the women of his family, while his enemies were preparing an impeachment against him.

XII. His accuser was Lucius Apuleius, and the charge brought against him was embezzlement of the spoils of Etruria. He was even said to have in his possession some brazen gates which were taken in that country. The people were much excited against him, and it was clear that, whatever the charge against him might be, they would condemn him. Consequently he assembled his friends and comrades, who were a great number in all, and begged them not to permit him to be ruined by false accusations, and made a laughing-stock to his enemies. But when his friends, after consulting together, answered that they did not think that they could prevent his being condemned, but that they would assist him to pay any fine that might be imposed, he, unable to bear such treatment, determined in a rage to leave Rome and go into exile. He embraced his wife and son, and walked from his house silently as far as the gate of the city. There he turned back, and, stretching out his hands towards the Capitol, prayed to the gods that, if he was driven out of Rome unjustly by the insolence and hatred of the people, the Romans might soon repent of their conduct to him, and appear before the world begging him to return, and longing for their Camillus back again.

XIII. Like Achilles, he thus cursed his countrymen and left them. His cause was undefended, and in his absence he was condemned to pay a fine of fifteen thousand ases, which in Greek money is fifteen hundred drachmas, for the as was the Roman coin at that time, and consequently ten copper ases were called a denarius.

Every Roman believes that the prayers of Camillus were quickly heard by Justice, and that a terrible retribution was exacted for his wrongs, which filled all men's mouths at that time; so terrible a fate befell Rome, with such destruction, danger, and disgrace, whether it arose from mere chance, or whether it be the office of some god to punish those who requite virtue with ingratitude.

XIV. The first omen of impending evil was the death of Julius the Censor; for the Romans reverence the office of censor, and account it sacred. Another omen was that, a short time before Camillus went into exile, one Marcus Caedicius, a man of no particular note, and not even a senator, but a thoroughly respectable man, communicated a matter of some importance to the tribunes of the people. He said that the night before he had been walking along what is called the New Road, when some one called him by name. He turned round and could see no one, but heard a voice louder than man's say, "Go, Marcus Caedicius, tell the government early in the morning that in a short time they may expect the Gauls." When the tribunes of the people heard this they laughed him to scorn, and shortly afterwards Camillus left the city.

XV. The Gauls are a people of the Celtic race, and are said to have become too numerous for their own country, and consequently to have left it to search for some other land to dwell in. As they consisted of a large multitude of young warriors, they started in two bodies, one of which, went towards the northern ocean, and, passing the Rhipaean mountains, settled in the most distant part of Europe. The other body established themselves between the Pyrenees and the Alps, and for a long time dwelt near the Senones and Celtorii. At last they tasted wine, which was then for the first time brought thither out of Italy. In an ecstasy of delight at the drink they wildly snatched up their arms, took their families with them, and rushed to the Alps in search of the country which produced such fruits as this, considering all other countries to be savage and uncultivated. The man who first introduced wine among them and encouraged them to proceed to Italy was said to be one Aruns, an Etruscan of some note, who, though a well-meaning man, had met with the following misfortune. He had been left guardian to an orphan named Lucumo, one of the richest and handsomest of his countrymen. This boy lived in the house of Aruns from his childhood, and when he grew up he would not leave it, but pretended to delight in his society. It was long before Aruns discovered that Lucumo had debauched his wife, and that their passion was mutual; but at length they were unable any longer to conceal their intrigue, and the youth openly attempted to carry off the woman from her husband. He went to law, but was unable to contend with the numerous friends and great wealth of Lucumo, and so left the country. Hearing about the Gauls, he went to them and incited them to invade Italy.

XVI. They immediately made themselves masters of the country, which reaches from the Alps down to the sea on both sides of Italy, which in ancient times belonged to the Etruscans, as we see by the names, for the upper sea is called the Adriatic from Adria, an Etruscan city, and the lower is called the Etruscan Sea. It is a thickly wooded country, with plenty of pasturage, and well watered. At that period it contained eighteen fair and large cities, with a thriving commercial population. The Gauls took these cities, drove out their inhabitants, and occupied them themselves. This, however, took place some time previously to our story.

XVII. The Gauls at this time marched against the Etruscan city of Clusium and besieged it. The inhabitants appealed to the Romans to send ambassadors and letters to the barbarians, and they sent three of the Fabian family, men of the first importance in Rome. They were well received, because of the name of Rome, by the Gauls, who desisted from their siege and held a conference with them. The Romans inquired what wrong the Gauls had suffered from the people of Clusium that they should attack their city. To this Brennus, the king of the Gauls, answered with a laugh, "The people of Clusium wrong us by holding a large territory, although they can only inhabit and cultivate a small one, while they will not give a share of it to us, who are numerous and poor. You Romans were wronged in just the same way in old times by the people of Alba, and Fidenae, and Ardea, and at the present day by the Veientines and Capenates, and by many of the Faliscans and Volscians. You make campaigns against these people if they will not share their good things with you, you sell them for slaves and plunder their territory, and destroy their cities; and in this you do nothing wrong, but merely obey the most ancient of all laws, that the property of the weak belongs to the strong, a law which prevails among the gods on the one hand, and even among wild beasts, amongst whom the stronger always encroach upon the weaker ones. So now cease to pity the besieged men of Clusium, for fear you should teach the Gauls to become good-natured and pitiful towards the nations that have been wronged by the Romans."

This speech showed the Romans that Brennus had no thought of coming to terms, and they in consequence went into Clusium and encouraged the inhabitants to attack the barbarians under their guidance, either because they wished to make trial of the valour of the Gauls, or to make a display of their own. The people of Clusium made a sally, and a battle took place near their wall. In this one of the Fabii, Quintus Ambustus by name, was on horseback, and rode to attack a fine powerful Gaul who was riding far in advance of the rest. At first the Roman was not recognised because the fight was sharp, and the flashing of his arms prevented his face being clearly seen. But when he slew his antagonist and jumped down from his horse to strip his body of its spoils, Brennus recognised him, and called the gods to witness his violation of the common law of all nations, in coming to them as an ambassador and fighting against them as an enemy. He immediately put a stop to the battle and took no further heed of the people of Clusium, but directed his army against Rome. However, as he did not wish it to be thought that the bad conduct of the Romans pleased the Gauls, who only wanted a pretext for hostilities, he sent and demanded that Fabius should be delivered up to him to be punished, and at the same time led his army slowly forwards.

XVIII. At Rome the Senate was called together, and many blamed Fabius, while those priests who are called Feciales urged the Senate in the name of religion to throw the whole blame of what had happened upon one guilty head, and, by delivering him up, to clear the rest of the city from sharing his guilt. These Feciales were instituted by the mildest and justest of the kings of Rome, Numa Pompilius, to be guardians of peace, and examiners of the reasons which justify a nation in going to war. However the Senate referred the matter to the people, and when the priests repeated their charges against Fabius before them, the people so despised and slighted religion as to appoint Fabius and his brothers military tribunes. The Gauls, when they heard this, were enraged, and hurried on, disregarding everything but speed. The nations through which they passed, terrified at their glancing arms and their strength and courage, thought that their land was indeed lost and that their cities would at once be taken, but to their wonder and delight the Gauls did them no hurt, and took nothing from their fields, but marched close by their cities, calling out that they were marching against Rome, and were at war with the Romans only, and held all other men to be their friends. To meet this impetuous rush, the military tribunes led out the Romans, who, in numbers indeed were quite a match for the Gauls, for they amounted to no less than forty thousand heavy-armed men, but for the most part untrained and serving for the first time.

Besides this disadvantage, they neglected the duties of religion, for they neither made the usual sacrifices nor consulted the soothsayers. Confusion also was produced by the number of commanders, though frequently before this, in much less important campaigns, they had chosen single generals, whom they called dictators, as they knew that nothing is so important at a dangerous crisis as that all should unanimously and in good order obey the commands of one irresponsible chief. And the unfair treatment which Camillus had received now bore disastrous fruits, for no man dared to use authority except to flatter and gain the favour of the people.

They proceeded about eleven miles from the city, and halted for the night on the banks of the river Allia, which joins the Tiber not far from where their camp was pitched. Here the barbarians appeared, and, after an unskilfully managed battle, the want of discipline of the Romans caused their ruin. The Gauls drove the left wing into the river and destroyed it, but the right of the army, which took refuge in the hills to avoid the enemy's charge on level ground, suffered less, and most of them reached the city safely. The rest, who survived after the enemy were weary of slaughter, took refuge at Veii, imagining that all was over with Rome.

XIX. This battle took place about the summer solstice at the time of full moon, on the very day on which in former times the great disaster befel the Fabii, when three hundred of that race were slain by the Etruscans. But this defeat wiped out the memory of the former one, and the day was always afterwards called that of the Allia, from the river of that name.

It is a vexed question whether we ought to consider some days unlucky, or whether Herakleitus was right in rebuking Hesiod for calling some days good and some bad, because he knew not that the nature of all days is the same. However the mention of a few remarkable instances is germane to the matter of which we are treating. It happened that on the fifth day of the Boeotian month Hippodromios, which the Athenians call Hekatombeion, two signal victories were won by the Boeotians, both of which restored liberty to Greece; one, when they conquered the Spartans at Leuktra, and the other, when, more than two hundred years before this, they conquered the Thessalians under Lattamyas at Kerêssus.

Again, the Persians were beaten by the Greeks on the sixth of Boedromion at Marathon, and on the third they were beaten both at Plataea and at Mykale, and at Arbela on the twenty-fifth of the same month. The Athenians too won their naval victory under Chabrias at Naxos on the full moon of Boedromion, and that of Salamis on the twentieth of that month, as I have explained in my treatise 'On Days.'

The month of Thargelion evidently brings misfortune to the barbarians, for Alexander defeated the Persian king's generals on the Granicus in Thargelion, and the Carthaginians were defeated by Timoleon in Sicily on the twenty-seventh of Thargelion, at which same time Troy is believed to have been taken, according to Ephorus, Kallisthenes, Damastes and Phylarchus.

On the other hand, the month Metageitnion, which the Boeotians call Panemos, is unfavourable to the Greeks, for on the seventh of that month they were defeated by Antipater at Kranon and utterly ruined; and before that, were defeated during that month by Philip at Chaeronea. And on that same day and month and year Archidamus and his troops, who had crossed over into Italy, were cut to pieces by the natives. The twenty-first day of that month is also observed by the Carthaginians as that which has always brought the heaviest misfortunes upon them. And I am well aware that at the time of the celebration of the mysteries Thebes was destroyed for the second time by Alexander, and that after this Athens was garrisoned by Macedonian soldiers on the twentieth of Boedromion, on which day they bring out the mystic Iacchus in procession. And similarly the Romans, under the command of Caepio, on that same day lost their camp to the Gauls, and afterwards, under Lucullus, defeated Tigranes and the Armenians. King Attalus and Pompeius the Great died on their own birthdays. And I could mention many others, who have had both good and evil fortune on the same anniversaries. But the Romans regard that day as especially unlucky, and on account of it, two other days in every month are thought so, as superstitious feeling is increased by misfortune. This subject I have treated at greater length in my treatise on 'Roman Questions.'

XX. If, after the battle, the Gauls had at once followed up the fugitives, nothing could have prevented their taking Rome and destroying every one who was left in it; such terror did the beaten troops produce when they reached home, and such panic fear seized upon every one. However the barbarians scarcely believed in the completeness of their victory, and betook themselves to making merry over their success and to dividing the spoils taken in the Roman camp, so that they afforded those who left the city time to effect their escape, and those who remained in it time to recover their courage and make preparations for standing a siege. They abandoned all but the Capitol to the enemy, and fortified it with additional ramparts and stores of missiles. One of their first acts was to convey most of their holy things into the Capitol, while the Vestal virgins took the sacred fire and their other sacred objects and fled with them from the city. Some indeed say that nothing is entrusted to them except the eternal fire, which King Numa appointed to be worshiped as the origin of all things. For fire has the liveliest motion of anything in nature; and everything is produced by motion or with some kind of motion. All other parts of matter when heat is absent lie useless and apparently dead, requiring the power of fire as the breath of life, to call them into existence and make them capable of action.

Numa therefore, being a learned man and commonly supposed on account of his wisdom to hold communion with the Muses, consecrated fire, and ordered it to be kept unquenched for ever as an emblem of the eternal power that orders all things. Others say that, as among the Greeks, a purificatory fire burns before the temple, but that within are other holy things which no man may see, except only the virgins, who are named Vestals; and a very wide-spread notion is, that the famous Trojan Palladium, which was brought to Italy by Aeneas, is kept there. Others say that the Samothracian gods are there, whom Dardanus brought to Troy after he had founded it, and caused to be worshipped there, which, after the fall of Troy, Aeneas carried off and kept until he settled in Italy. But those who pretend to know most about such matters say that there are two jars of no great size in the temple, one open and empty, and the other full and sealed, and that these may be seen only by the holy virgins. Others think that this is a mistake, arising from the fact that, at the time of which we are treating, the Vestal virgins placed most of their sacred things in two jars and concealed them in the earth under the Temple of Quirinus, which place even to the present day is called the Doliola, or place of the jars.

XXI. However this may be, the Vestals took the most important of their holy things and betook themselves to flight along the Tiber. Here Lucius Albinus, a plebian, was journeying among the fugitives, with his wife and infant children and their few necessaries in a waggon. When he saw the Vestal virgins, without any attendants, journeying on foot and in distress, carrying in their bosoms the sacred images of the gods, he at once removed his wife, children, and property from the waggon and handed it over to them, to escape into one of the Greek cities in Italy. The piety of Albinus and his care for the duties of religion at so terrible a crisis deserve to be recorded.

The rest of the priests and the old men who had been consuls, and been honoured with triumphs, could not bear to leave the city. At the instance of Fabius, the Pontifex Maximus, they put on their sacred vestments and robes of state, and after offering prayer to the gods, as if they were consecrating themselves as victims to be offered on behalf of their country, they sat down in their ivory chairs in the Forum in full senatorial costume, and waited what fortune might befal them.

XXII. On the third day after the battle Brennus appeared, leading his army to attack the city. At first, seeing the gates open and no guards on the walls, he feared some ambuscade, as he could not believe that the Romans had so utterly despaired of themselves. When he discovered the truth, he marched through the Colline Gate, and captured Rome, a little more than three hundred and sixty years after its foundation, if we can believe that any accurate record has been kept of those periods whose confusion has produced such difficulties in the chronology of later times. However, an indistinct rumour of the fall of Rome seems at once to have reached Greece: for Herakleides of Pontus, who lived about that time, speaks in his book 'On the Spirit,' of a rumour from the west that an army had come from the Hyperboreans and had sacked a Greek colony called Rome, which stood somewhere in that direction, near the great ocean. Now, as Herakleides was fond of strange legends, I should not be surprised if he adorned the original true tale of the capture of the city with these accessories of "the

Hyperboreans" and "the great ocean." Aristotle, the philosopher, had evidently heard quite accurately that the city was taken by the Gauls, but he says that it was saved by one Lucius: now Camillus's name was Marcus, not Lucius. All this, however, was pure conjecture.

Brennus, after taking possession of Rome, posted a force to watch the Capitol, and himself went down to the Forum, and wondered at the men who sat there silent, with all their ornaments, how they neither rose from their seats at the approach of the enemy, nor changed colour, but sat leaning on their staffs with fearless confidence, quietly looking at one another. The Gauls were astonished at so strange a sight, and for a long time they forbore to approach and touch them, as if they were superior beings. But when one of them ventured to draw near to Marcus Papirius and gently stroke his long beard, Papirius struck him on the head with his staff, at which the barbarian drew his sword and slew him. Upon this they fell upon the rest and killed them, with any other Romans whom they found, and spent many days in plundering the houses, after which they burned them and pulled them down in their rage at the men in the Capitol, because they would not surrender, but drove them back when they assaulted it. For this reason they wreaked their vengeance on the city, and put to death all their captives, men and women, old and young alike.

XXIII. As the siege was a long one, the Gauls began to want for provisions. They divided themselves into two bodies, one of which remained with the king and carried on the siege, while the others scoured the country, plundering and destroying the villages, not going all together in a body, but scattered in small detachments in various directions, as their elation at their success caused them to have no fear about separating their forces. Their largest and best disciplined body marched towards Ardea, where Camillus, since his banishment, had lived as a private person. All his thoughts, however, were bent not upon avoiding or fleeing from the Gauls, but upon defeating them if possible. And so, seeing that the people of Ardea were sufficient in numbers, but wanting in confidence because of the want of experience and remissness of their leaders, he first began to tell the younger men that they ought not to ascribe the misfortunes of the Romans to the bravery of the Gauls, for the misconduct of the former had given them a triumph which they did not deserve. It would, he urged, be a glorious thing, even at the risk of some danger, to drive away a tribe of savage barbarians, who if they were victorious always exterminated the vanquished: while, if they only showed bravery and confidence, he could, by watching his opportunity, lead them to certain victory. As the younger men eagerly listened to these words, Camillus proceeded to confer with the chief magistrates of the Ardeates. After obtaining their consent also, he armed all those who were capable of service, but kept them within the walls, as he wished to conceal their presence from the enemy who were now close at hand. But when the Gauls after scouring the country returned laden with plunder and carelessly encamped in the plain, and when at night by the influence of wine and sleep all was quiet in their camp, Camillus, who had learned the state of the case from spies, led out the men of Ardea, and marching over the intervening ground in silence, about midnight attacked their entrenched camp with loud shouts and blasts of his trumpet, which threw the Gauls, half-drunk and heavy with sleep as they were, into great confusion. Few recovered their senses so far as to attempt to resist Camillus, and those few fell where they stood; but most of them were slain as they lay helpless with wine and sleep. Such as escaped from the camp and wandered about the fields were despatched by cavalry the next day.

XXIV. The fame of this action, when noised among the neighbouring cities, called many men to arms, especially those Romans who had escaped to Veii after the battle of the Allia. These men lamented their fate, saying, "What a general has Providence removed from Rome in Camillus, whose successes now bring glory to Ardea, while the city that produced and brought up so great a man has utterly perished. And now we, for want of a general to lead us, are sitting still inside the walls of a city not our own, and giving up Italy to the enemy. Come, let us send to the men of Ardea, and beg their general of them, or else ourselves take up our arms and march to him. He is no longer an exile, nor are we any longer his countrymen, for our country is ours no more, but is in the hands of the enemy."

This was agreed, and they sent to beg Camillus to become their general. But he refused, saying that he would not do so without a decree from the citizens in the Capitol; for they as long as they survived, represented the city of Rome, and therefore although he would gladly obey their commands, he would not be so officious as to interfere against their will. The soldiers admired the honourable scruples of Camillus, but there was a great difficulty in representing them to the garrison of the Capitol; indeed, it seemed altogether impossible for a messenger to reach the citadel while the city was in the possession of the enemy.

XXV. One of the younger Romans, Pontius Cominius, of the middle class of citizens, but with an honourable ambition to distinguish himself, undertook the adventure. He would not take any writing to the garrison, for fear that if he were taken the enemy might discover Camillus's plans. He dressed himself in poor clothes, with corks concealed under them, and performed most of the journey fearlessly by daylight, but when he came near the city he went by night. As it was impossible to cross the river by the bridge, which was held by the Gauls, he wrapped what few clothes he had round his head, and trusted to his corks to float him over to the city. After he had landed, he walked round, observing by the lights and the noise where the Gauls were most wakeful, until he reached the Carmentan Gate, where all was quiet. At this place the Capitolian Hill forms a steep and precipitous crag, up which he climbed by a hollow in the cliff, and joined the garrison. After greeting them and making known his name, he proceeded to an interview with the leading men. A meeting of the Senate was called, at which he recounted Camillus's victory, which they had not heard of, and explained the determination of the soldiers. He then begged them to confirm Camillus's appointment as general, because the citizens without the walls would obey no other.

When the Senate heard this, they deliberated, and finally appointed Camillus dictator, and sent back Pontius by the same way that he came, which he was able to accomplish as fortunately as before. He eluded the Gauls, and brought the decree of the senate to the Romans outside the walls.

XXVI. They heard the news with enthusiasm, so that Camillus when he came, found that they already numbered twenty thousand, while he drew many additional troops from the neighbouring friendly cities. Thus was Camillus a second time appointed dictator, and, proceeding to Veii, joined the soldiers there, to whom he added many others from the allies, and prepared to attack the enemy. But meanwhile at Rome, some of the Gauls happening to pass by the place where Pontius climbed up the Capitol, noticed in many places the marks of where he had clutched at the rock with his hands and feet, torn off the plants which grew upon it, and thrown down the mould. They brought the news to the king, who came and viewed the place. He said nothing at the time, but in the evening he called together those Gauls who were lightest and most accustomed to climb mountains, and thus addressed them: "The road up the rock, which we by ourselves could not discover, has been proved by our enemies not to be impassable to men, and it would be disgraceful for us after having begun so well to leave our enterprise incomplete, and to give up the place as impregnable after the enemy themselves have shown us how it may be taken. Where it is easy for one man to climb, it cannot be hard for many to climb one by one, as their numbers will give them confidence and mutual support. Suitable honours and presents will be given to those who distinguish themselves."

XXVII. After this speech of their king, the Gauls eagerly volunteered for the assault, and about midnight many of them climbed silently up the rock, which although rough and precipitous was easier of ascent than they had imagined, so that the first of them reached the top, and were on the point of preparing to attack the rampart and its sleeping garrison, for neither men nor dogs noticed them. But there were sacred geese kept in the temple of Juno, which in other times were fed without stint, but which then, as there was scarcely food enough for the men, were somewhat neglected. These birds are naturally quick of hearing and timid, and now being rendered wakeful and wild by hunger, quickly perceived the Gauls climbing up, and rushing noisily to the place woke the garrison, while the Gauls feeling that they were discovered no longer preserved silence, but violently assaulted the place. The Romans, snatching up whatever arms came first to hand, ran to repulse them: and first of all Manlius, a man of consular rank, strong of body and full of courage, fell in with two of the enemy. As one of them lifted up his battleaxe, Manlius cut off his right hand with his sword, while he dashed his shield into the other's face, and threw him backwards down the cliff. After this he stood upon the wall, and with the help of those who assembled round him, beat off the rest, for not many had reached the top, or effected anything commensurate with the boldness of the attempt. Having thus escaped the danger, the Romans threw their sentinel down the rock; while on Manlius they conferred by vote a reward for his bravery, intended more for honour than advantage; for each man gave him a day's rations, which consisted of half a Roman pound of meal, and the fourth part of a Greek cotyle of wine.

XXVIII. This affair disheartened the Gauls, who were also in want of provisions, for they could not forage as before for fear of Camillus, while disease also crept in among them, encamped as they were in the ruins of Rome among heaps of dead bodies, while the deep layer of ashes became blown by the wind into the air, making it dry and harsh, and the vapours of the conflagrations were injurious to breathe. They were especially distressed by the change from a cloudy country where there are plenty of shady retreats, to the flat burning plains of Rome in autumn, and their siege of the Capitol became wearisome, for they had now beleaguered it for seven months; so that there was much sickness in their camp, and so many died that they no longer buried the dead. Yet for all this the besieged fared no better. Hunger pressed them, and their ignorance of what Camillus was doing disheartened them; for no one could reach them with news, because the city was strictly watched by Gauls. As both parties were in these straits, proposals for a capitulation took place; at first among the outposts on both sides; afterwards the chief men on each side. Brennus, the Gaulish king, and Sulpicius the Roman tribune, met, and it was agreed that the Romans should pay a thousand pounds of gold, and that the Gauls should, on receiving it, at once leave the country. Both parties swore to observe these conditions, but when the gold was being weighed, the Gauls at first tampered with the scales unperceived, and then openly pulled the beam, so that the Romans became angry. But at this Brennus insolently took off his sword and belt, and flung them into the scale; and when Sulpicius asked, "What is this?" "What should it be," replied the Gaul; "but woe to the vanquished!" At this some of the Romans were angry and thought that they ought to take back their gold into the Capitol, and again endure the siege; while others said that they must put up with insults, provided they were not too outrageous, and not think that there was any additional disgrace in paying more than they had agreed, because in paying any ransom at all, they were acting from sheer necessity rather than feelings of honour.

XXIX. While the Romans were thus disputing with the Gauls, and with one another, Camillus with his army was at the gates. Learning what was being done, he ordered the mass of his soldiers to follow him quietly and in good order, and himself pushed on with the picked troops to join the Romans, who all made way for him, and received him as dictator with silence and respect. He then took the gold from the scales and gave it to his victors, and ordered the Gauls to take the scales and the beam, and depart, "for," said he, "it is the custom of the Romans to defend their country not with gold but with iron." At this Brennus became angry, and said that he was being wronged by the treaty being broken; and Camillus answered that the negotiations were illegal, because when they began he was already dictator, and therefore, as no one else had any authority, the treaty had been made by the Gauls with persons who were not authorized to treat. But now, if they wished, they might make fresh proposals, for he was come with full legal powers to pardon such as made their submission, and to punish unrepentant evil-doers. Enraged at this, Brennus began to skirmish, and the two parties, mixed up as they were, in houses and lands where no military formation was possible, did go so far as to draw their swords and push one another about; but Brennus soon recovered his temper, and drew off the Gauls, with but little loss, in their camp.

During the night he got them all under arms, left the city, and, after a march of about eight miles, encamped by the side of the Gabinian Road. But at daybreak, Camillus was upon him, in glittering armour, leading on the Romans who had now recovered their courage. After a long and fiercely contested battle they routed the Gauls and took their camp. Some of the fugitives were at once pursued and slain, but most of them straggled about the country, and were put to death by the people of the neighbouring towns and villages who sallied out upon them.

XXX. Thus was Rome strangely taken, and yet more strangely preserved, after having been for seven months in the possession of the Gauls, for they entered it a few days after the Ides of Quintilis, and left it about the Ides of February. Camillus, as we may easily imagine, entered the city in a triumph, as the saviour of his lost country, and the restorer of Rome to itself; for as he drove into the city he was accompanied by those who had before left it, with their wives and children, while those who had been besieged in the Capitol, and all but starved there, came out to meet him embracing one another, weeping, and scarcely believing in their present happiness. The priests and servants of the gods also appeared with such of the sacred things as they had saved, either by burying them on the spot, or by carrying them away, and now displayed these images, which had not been seen for so long a time, to the citizens, who greeted them with joy, as if the gods themselves were again returning to Rome. Camillus performed a sacrifice to the gods, and purified the city in the manner recommended by experts, and then proceeded to restore all the previously existing temples, while he himself added another to Aius Loquutius, or Rumour, having carefully sought out the place at which the voice in the night miraculously foretold the coming of the Gaulish host to Marcus Caedicius.

XXXI. With great difficulty the sites of the temples were cleared of rubbish by the zeal of Camillus and the labour of the priests; but as the city was utterly destroyed, and required to be entirely rebuilt, the people became disheartened at so great an undertaking. Men who had lost their all were inclined to wait, and indeed required rest after their misfortunes, rather than labours and toils, which neither their bodies nor their purses were able to endure. And thus it came to pass that they turned their thoughts a second time towards Veii, a city which stood quite ready to be inhabited. This gave opportunities to their mob orators to make speeches, as usual, which they knew would be pleasing to the people, in which Camillus was disrespectfully spoken of as depriving them of a city which stood ready to receive them, for his own prviate ambition, and was said to be compelling them to live encamped in the midst of ruins, and re-erect their houses in that vast heap of ashes, all in order that he might be called, not merely the leader and general of Rome, but might usurp the place of Romulus and be called her founder. Fearing disturbances, the Senate would not permit Camillus to lay down his dictatorship for a year, although he wished to do so, and although no dictator before this had ever remained in office for more than six months. In the meantime the senators themselves encouraged and consoled the people by personal appeals, pointing to the tombs and monuments of their ancestors, and recalling to their minds the temples and holy places which Romulus and Numa and the other kings had consecrated and left in charge to them. More especially they dwelt upon the omen of the newly severed head which had been found when the foundations of the Capitol were dug, by which it was proved that that spot was fated to become the head of Italy, and the fire of Vesta which the virgins had relighted after the war, and which it would be a disgrace for them to extinguish, and to abandon the city, whether they were to see it inhabited by foreigners or turned into fields for cattle to feed in. While persistently urging these considerations both in public speeches and in private interviews with the people, they were much affected by the lamentations of the poor over their helpless condition. The people begged that, as they had, like people after a shipwreck, saved their lives and nothing else, they might not, in addition to this misfortune, be compelled to put together the ruins of a city which had been utterly destroyed, while another was standing ready to receive them.

XXXII. Under these circumstances, Camillus determined to debate the question publicly. He himself made a long appeal on behalf of his native place, and many other speeches were delivered. Finally he rose, and bade Lucius Lucretius, whose privilege it was, to vote first, and then after him the rest in order. Silence was enforced, and Lucretius was just on the point of voting when a centurion in command of a detachment of the guard of the day marched by, and in a loud voice called to the standard-bearer: "Pitch the standard here: here it is best for us to stay." When these words were heard so opportunely in the midst of their deliberations about the future, Lucretius reverently said that he accepted the omen, and gave his vote in accordance with it, and his example was followed by all the rest. The people now showed a strange revulsion of feeling, for they encouraged one another to begin the work of rebuilding, not on any regular plan, but just as each man happened to find a convenient place for his work. Consequently they quickly rebuilt the city, for within a year it is said that both the city walls and the private houses were completed; but it was full of intricate, narrow lanes and inconveniently placed houses.

The priests, who had been ordered by Camillus to mark out the boundaries where the temples had stood among the general wreck, when in their circuit of the Palatine Hill they came upon the chapel of Mars, found it, like every other building, destroyed and levelled to the ground by the Gauls, but while thoroughly examining the place they found the augur's staff of Romulus hidden under a deep heap of ashes. This staff is curved at one end, and is

called lituus. They use it to divide the heavens into squares when taking the
auspices, just as Romulus himself did, as he was deeply skilled in divination.
When he vanished from among mankind, the priests kept his staff just like
any other sacred object. That at such a time, when all the other holy things
perished, this should have been preserved, gave them good hopes of Rome,
which that omen seemed to presage would be eternal.

XXXIII. Before they had finished rebuilding the city they became involved
in a war, for the Aequians, Volscians, and Latins combined their forces and
invaded the country, while the Etruscans besieged Sutrium, a city in alliance
with Rome. The tribunes in command of the Roman forces encamped near
the Marcian heights, and were there besieged by the Latins and in danger of
having their camp taken. They sent to Rome for assistance, and the Romans
appointed Camillus dictator for the third time. About this war there are two
different accounts, of which I will mention the legendary one first:—It is said
that the Latins, either merely as a pretext, or really wishing to amalgamate the
two races as before, sent a demand to Rome for free unmarried women to be
delivered up for them to marry. As the Romans were at their wits' ends what
to do, because they feared to go to war, being scarcely recovered from their
late mishap, while they suspected that the women would be used as hostages
if they gave them up, and that the proposal of intermarriage was merely a
feint, a slave girl named Tutula, or, as some say, Philotis, advised the
magistrates to send her and the best-looking of the female slaves, dressed like
brides of noble birth, and that she would manage the rest. The magistrates
approved of her proposal, chose such girls as she thought suitable, and having
dressed them in fine clothes and jewellery, handed them over to the Latins,
who were encamped at no great distance from the city. At night the girls stole
the daggers of the enemies, and Tutula or Philotis climbed up a wild fig-tree,
stretched out her cloak behind her, and raised a torch as a signal, which had
been agreed upon between her and the magistrates, though no other citizen
knew of it. Wherefore, the soldiers rushed out of the gates with a great
clamour and disturbance, calling to one another and scarcely able to keep
their ranks as their chiefs hurried them along. When they reached the
enemy's camp, they found them asleep and not expecting an attack, so that
they took their camp and slew most of them. This took place on the nones of
the month Quintilis, now called July, and the festival which then takes place
is in memory of the events of that day. First they march out of the gates in a
mass, calling out the common names of the country, such as Caius, Marcus,
or Lucius, in imitation of their hurried calling for each other on that
occasion. Next, female slaves splendidly dressed walk round laughing and

romping with all whom they meet. These girls also perform a sort of fight among themselves, like those who on that day took their share in the fight with the Latins: and afterwards they sit down to a feast, under the shade of fig-tree boughs. They call this day the nonae caprotinae, probably from the wild fig-tree from which the slave girl waved the torch; for in Latin a wild fig-tree is called caprificus. Others say that most of these things were said and done when Romulus disappeared, for on this very day he was snatched away, outside the city gates, in a sudden storm and darkness, or as some think during an eclipse of the sun: and they say that the day is called nonae caprotiae from the place, because Romulus was carried off while holding a meeting of the entire people at the place called the Goat's Marsh, as is written in his life.

XXXIV. The other story is approved by most writers, who relate it as follows:—Camillus, after being appointed dictator for the third time, and learning that the army under the command of the military tribunes was being besieged by the Latins and Volscians, was compelled to arm even those citizens who were past the age for service in the field. He marched by a long circuit to the Marcian heights unnoticed by the enemy, and established his army behind them. By lighting fires he announced his arrival to the Romans in the camp, who took courage, and began to meditate sallying out of their camp and attacking the enemy. But the Latins and Volscians kept close within the rampart of their camp, which they fortified with many additional palisades, on all sides, for they now were between two hostile armies, and intended to await succour from home, while they also expected a force from Etruria to come to their aid. Camillus, perceiving this, and fearing that he might be surrounded in his turn, vigorously used his opportunity. The rampart of the allies was formed of wood, and as a strong wind blew down from the mountains at daybreak, he prepared combustibles, and early in the morning got his forces under arms. One division he sent to attack the enemy's camp with darts, and missile weapons, and loud shouts, while he himself, with those who were in charge of the fire, waited for his opportunity on that side towards which the wind usually blew. When the other troops were engaged with the enemy, the sun rose, and a strong wind got up. At this Camillus gave the signal for attack, and at once enveloped the palisades with lighted missiles. As the flames quickly spread in the thick wooden palisades, the Latins, finding their camp girt with flames, were driven into a small compass, and finally obliged to sally out of their entrenchments, outside of which the Romans stood ready to receive them. Few of those who broke out escaped, while all who remained in the camp perished in the flames, until the Romans extinguished them and began to plunder.

XXXV. After this exploit, Camillus left his son Lucius in charge of the camp, to guard the prisoners and the booty, and himself invaded the enemy's country. He took the capital of the Aequi, reduced the Volsci to subjection, and marched at once upon Sutrium to relieve that city, whose inhabitants had not heard of his successes, but were still besieged by the Etruscans. The Sutrians had just surrendered, and had been turned out of their city by the enemy with nothing but the clothes they had on. Camillus met them on the road with their wives and children, weeping over their misfortune. He was greatly moved at so piteous a sight, and, perceiving that the Romans were touched by the despairing entreaties of the people of Sutrium, who clung to them with tears in their eyes, determined that he would at once avenge their wrongs, and march upon Sutrium that very day, arguing that men who were merry with success, having just captured a wealthy city, with no enemy either left within its walls or expected from without, would be found in careless disorder. In this conjecture he was right; for he not only marched through the country, but even obtained possession of the walls and gates unperceived by the enemy, who had posted no guards, but were carousing in the various private houses. Indeed when they learned that the Romans were in possession of the town, they were in such a condition of intoxication that most of them could not even attempt to escape, but shamefully waited in the houses where they were until they were either killed or taken prisoners. Thus was the city of Sutrium twice taken in one day, and thus did the victors lose their prize, and the dispossessed inhabitants regain their homes by Camillus's means.

XXXVI. The triumph which he enjoyed after these campaigns added to his popularity and glory as much as either of the former; for even those who disliked him most, and who had insisted that all his successes were due to good fortune more than to skill, were now forced to admit the brilliancy of his generalship, and to give his genius its due. The chief of his enemies and detractors was Marcus Manlius, he who had been the first man to fling the Gauls down the cliff in the night attack on the Capitol, and who in remembrance of this was surnamed Capitolinus. This man, endeavouring to make himself the first man in Rome, and not being able to surpass the fame of Camillus by fair means, made the accusation against him usual in such cases, that he was intending to make himself king. This falsehood he repeated in his addresses to the people, with whom he was making himself popular, especially with those who were in debt; some of whom he defended, and assisted in coming to terms with their creditors, while others he forcibly rescued from the officers of the law, so that many needy persons were attracted to him, and became the terror of all respectable citizens by their riotous disturbances in the Forum. To put an end to these disorders, Quintus Capitolinus was created dictator, and he put Manlius in prison; but the people upon this went into mourning, a thing only done on the occasion of some great public disaster, and the Senate, terrified at this, ordered Manlius to be acquitted. Manlius was not improved by his captivity, but was more turbulent and disorderly in his conduct than he had been before. Camillus was now again elected military tribune, and Manlius was impeached: but the place in which he was tried told greatly against his accusers. For the very spot on the Capitol on which Manlius fought with the Gauls on that night was visible from the Forum, and the sight of it raised a strong feeling in his favour; while he himself pointed to it, and, with tears in his eyes, reminded them of how he had fought for them, so that his judges were at their wits' end, and often adjourned the trial, for they could not acquit him of a crime which was clearly proved against him, and yet they could not bring themselves to let the law take its course, when the scene before them reminded them constantly of his great exploit. Camillus, perceiving this, removed the court to the Petelian Grove outside the city gates, where, as the Capitol was not visible, the prosecutor was able to press home his charges against Manlius, while the judges were not prevented from punishing him for his recent crimes by their remembrance of what he had done in former times. He was convicted, led to the Capitol, and thrown down the cliff, which thus witnessed both the most glorious deed of his life, and his miserable end. The Romans destroyed his house, on the site of which they built the Temple of Juno Moneta, and decreed that for the future no patrician might dwell upon the Capitol.

XXXVII. Camillus, when appointed military tribune for the sixth time, begged to be excused, as he was growing old, and perhaps feared that such unbroken success and glory would call down upon him the wrath of the gods. His most obvious reason for declining the appointment was the state of his health, for at this time he was sick. However, the people would not permit him to retire, but loudly urged that they did not want him to ride on horseback or fight in the ranks, but merely to advise and superintend. Thus they compelled him to accept the office, and with one of his colleagues, Lucius Furius, at once to lead an army against the enemy. He left the city and encamped near the enemy, where he wished to remain inactive, in order that, if a battle should be necessary, he might recover his health sufficiently to take part in it. But as his colleague Lucius, who longed to distinguish himself, was so eager for action that he could not be restrained, and excited the subordinate officers, Camillus, fearing that it might be supposed that he grudged younger men an opportunity of gaining laurels, agreed, sorely against his will, to allow his colleague to lead out the army and offer battle, while he with a few troops remained behind in the camp. But when he heard that Lucius had rashly engaged and that the Romans were defeated, he could not restrain himself, but leaping from his couch met them with his followers at the gate of the camp. Here he forced his way through the fugitives and attacked the pursuing force, so that those Romans whom he had passed at once turned and followed him, while those who were still outside the camp rallied round him, calling upon one another not to desert their general. The enemy's pursuit was thus checked, and on the following day Camillus marched out with his entire force, entirely defeated them, and entering their camp together with the fugitives, put most of them to the sword. After this, hearing that Satria had been captured by the Etruscans, and all the Roman colonists there put to death, he sent the greater part of his force back to Rome, reserving only the youngest and most vigorous of the soldiers, with whom he assaulted the Etruscans who held the city, and conquered them, killing many, and putting the rest to flight.

XXXVIII. By his return to Rome with great spoils, he proved that those men were right who had not feared that weakness or old age would impair the faculties of a general of daring and experience, but who had chosen him, ill and unwilling to act as he was, rather than men in the prime of life, who were eager to hold military commands. For this reason, when the people of Tusculum were reported to be in insurrection, they bade Camillus take one of the other five tribunes as his colleague, and march against them. Camillus, in spite of all that the rest of the tribunes could urge, for they all wished to be taken, chose Lucius Furius, whom no one could have supposed he would have chosen; for he it was who had been so eager to fight, against the better judgment of Camillus, and so had brought about the defeat in the late war; however, Camillus chose him rather than any other, wishing, it would appear, to conceal his misfortune and wipe out his disgrace.

The people of Tusculum cleverly repaired their fault. When Camillus marched to attack them they filled the country with men working in the fields and tending cattle just as in time of peace; the city gates were open, the boys at school, the lower classes plying various trades, and the richer citizens walking in the market-place in peaceful dress. The magistrates bustled about the city, pointing out where the Romans were to be quartered, as if the thought of treachery had never entered their minds. Camillus, though this conduct did not shake his belief in their guilt, was moved to pity by their repentance. He ordered them to go to Rome and beg the Senate to pardon them; and when they appeared, he himself used his influence to procure their forgiveness, and the admission of Tusculum to the Roman franchise. These were the most remarkable events of his sixth tribuneship.

XXXIX. After this, Licinius Stolo put himself at the head of the plebeians in their great quarrel with the Senate. They demanded that consuls should be re-established, one of whom should always be a plebeian, and that they should never both be patricians. Tribunes of the people were appointed, but the people would not suffer any election of consuls to be held. As this want of chief magistrates seemed likely to lead to still greater disorders, the Senate, much against the will of the people, appointed Camillus dictator for the fourth time. He himself did not wish for the post, for he was loth to oppose men who had been his comrades in many hard-fought campaigns, as indeed he had spent much more of his life in the camp with his soldiers than with the patrician party in political intrigues, by one of which he was now appointed, as that party hoped that if successful he would crush the power of the plebeians, while in case of failure he would be ruined. However, he made an effort to deal with the present difficulty. Knowing the day on which the tribunes intended to bring forward their law, he published a muster-roll of men for military service, and charged the people to leave the Forum and meet him on the Field of Mars, threatening those who disobeyed with a heavy fine. But when the tribunes answered his threats by vowing that they would fine him fifty thousand drachmas unless he ceased his interference with the people's right of voting, he retired to his own house, and after a few days laid down his office on pretence of sickness. This he did, either because he feared a second condemnation and banishment, which would be a disgrace to an old man and one who had done such great deeds, or else because he saw that the people were too strong to be overpowered, and he did not wish to make the attempt.

The Senate appointed another dictator, but he made that very Licinius Stolo, the leader of the popular party, his master of the horse, and thus enabled him to pass a law which was especially distasteful to the patricians, for it forbade any one to possess more than five hundred jugera of land. Stolo, after this success, became an important personage; but, a short time afterwards, he was convicted of possessing more land than his own law permitted, and was punished according to its provisions.

XL. There still remained the difficulty about the consular elections, the most important point at issue between the two parties, and the Senate was greatly disturbed at it, when news arrived that the Gauls, starting from the

Adriatic Sea, were a second time marching in great force upon Rome. At the same time evident traces of their approach could be seen, as the country was being plundered, and such of the inhabitants as could not easily reach Rome were taking refuge in the mountains.

This terrible tidings put an end to all internal disputes. The Senate and people formed themselves into one assembly, and with one voice appointed Camillus dictator for the fifth time. He was now a very old man, being near his eightieth year; but at this pressing crisis he made none of his former excuses, but at once took the chief command and levied an army for the war. As he knew that the chief power of the Gauls lay in their swords, with which they dealt heavy blows on the heads and shoulders of their enemy, without any skill in fence, he prepared for most of his soldiers helmets made entirely of smooth iron, so that the swords would either break or glance off them, while he also had brass rims fitted to their shields, because the wood by itself could not endure a blow. He also instructed the soldiers to use long pikes, and to thrust them forward to receive the sword-cuts of the enemy.

XLI. When the Gauls were encamped on the banks of the Anio, near the city, loaded with masses of plunder, Camillus led out his troops and posted them in a glen from which many valleys branched out, so that the greater part of the force was concealed, and that which was seen appeared to be clinging in terror to the hilly ground. Camillus, wishing to confirm the enemy in this idea, would not move to prevent the country being plundered before his eyes, but palisaded his camp and remained quiet within it, until he saw that the foraging parties of the Gauls straggled in careless disorder, while those in the camp did nothing but eat and drink. Then, sending forward his light troops before daybreak to be ready to harass the Gauls and prevent their forming their ranks properly as they came out of their camp, he marched the heavy-armed men down into the plain at sunrise, a numerous and confident body, and not, as the Gauls fancied, a few disheartened men.

The very fact of his commencing the attack dashed the courage of the Gauls; next, the attacks of the light troops, before they had got into their wonted array and divided themselves into regiments, produced disorder. When at last Camillus led on the heavy-armed troops, the Gauls ran to meet them brandishing their swords, but the Romans with their pikes advanced and met them, receiving their sword-cuts on their armour, which soon made the Gaulish swords bend double, as they were made of soft iron hammered out thin, while the shields of the Gauls were pierced and weighed down by the pikes that stuck in them. They therefore dropped their own arms, and endeavoured to seize the pikes and turn them against their enemies. But the

Romans, seeing them now defenceless, began to use their swords, and slew many of the first ranks, while the rest took to flight all over the flat country; for Camillus had taken care to guard the hills and rough ground, while the Gauls knew that they, in their over-confidence, had been at no pains to fortify their camp, and that the Romans could easily take it.

This battle is said to have been fought thirteen years after the capture of Rome, and in consequence of it the Romans conceived a contempt for these barbarians, whom they had before greatly dreaded, and even believed that their former victories over the Gauls were due to their being weakened by pestilence, and to fortunate circumstances, rather than to their own valour. This raised so great a terror of them, that a law was passed which relieved the priests from military service except in case of a Gaulish invasion.

XLII. This was the last of Camillus's military exploits, though during this campaign he took the city of Velitrae, which yielded to him without a battle. But his greatest political struggle was yet to come, for it was harder to deal with the people now that they were elated with victory. They insisted that the existing constitution should be annulled, and that one of the two consuls should be chosen from among them. They were opposed by the Senate, which would not permit Camillus to lay down his office, as the patricians imagined that with the help of his great power they could more easily defend their privileges. One day, however, as Camillus was sitting publicly doing business in the Forum, a viator or servant sent by the tribunes of the people bade him follow him, and even laid his hand upon him as if to arrest him. At this such a disturbance arose as had never been known before, as Camillus's party endeavoured to push the officer down from the tribunal, while the people clamoured to him to drag the dictator from his seat. Camillus himself, not knowing what to do, would not lay down his office, but called the Senate to meet. Before entering the Senate house, he turned round to the Capitol and prayed that the gods would bring affairs to a happy termination, vowing that when the present disorders were at an end he would build a Temple of Concord. After a violent debate, the Senate agreed to adopt the milder course of yielding to the popular demand, and permitting one of the two consuls to be chosen from the people. When the dictator announced this decision of the Senate to the people, they at once, as was natural, were delighted with the Senate, and escorted Camillus home with applause and shouts. On the next day they met and decreed that the Temple of Concord which Camillus had vowed should be erected on a spot facing the Forum, where these events had taken place; moreover, that the Latin games should continue for four days instead of three, and that all citizens of Rome should at once offer sacrifice and crown themselves with garlands.

In the assembly for the election of consuls, over which Camillus presided there were elected Marcus Aemilius, a patrician, and Lucius Sextius, the first plebeian ever elected consul. This was the result of Camillus's administration.

XLIII. In the following year a pestilence broke out in Rome which destroyed enormous numbers of people, and among them most of the leading men. And in this year died Camillus, at a ripe old age, full of years and honours, more regretted by the Romans than all those who died of the plague.

Life of Perikles.

I. One day in Rome, Caesar, seeing some rich foreigners nursing and petting young lapdogs and monkeys, enquired whether in their parts of the world the women bore no children: a truly imperial reproof to those who waste on animals the affection which they ought to bestow upon mankind. May we not equally blame those who waste the curiosity and love of knowledge which belongs to human nature, by directing it to worthless, not to useful objects? It is indeed unavoidable that external objects, whether good or bad, should produce some effect upon our senses; but every man is able, if he chooses, to concentrate his mind upon any subject he may please. For this reason we ought to seek virtue, not merely in order to contemplate it, but that we may ourselves derive some benefit from so doing. Just as those colours whose blooming and pleasant hues refresh our sight are grateful to the eyes, so we ought by our studies to delight in that which is useful for our own lives; and this is to be found in the acts of good men, which when narrated incite us to imitate them. The effect does not take place in other cases, for we frequently admire what we do not wish to produce; indeed we often are charmed with the work, but despise the workman, as in the case of dyes and perfumery which we take pleasure in, although we regard dyers and perfumers as vulgar artizans. That was a clever saying of Antisthenes, who answered, when he heard that Ismenias was a capital flute-player, "But he must be a worthless man, for if he were not, he would not be such a capital flute-player-!" and King Philip of Macedon, when his son played brilliantly and agreeably on the harp at an entertainment, said to him, "Are you not ashamed, to play so well?"

It is enough for a king, if he sometimes employs his leisure in listening to musicians, and it is quite a sufficient tribute from him to the Muses, if he is present at the performances of other persons.

II. If a man devotes himself to these trifling arts, the time which he wastes upon them proves that he is incapable of higher things. No well nurtured youth, on seeing the statue of Jupiter Olympius at Pisa, wishes that he were a Pheidias, or that he were a Polykleitus on seeing the statue of Juno at Argos, nor yet while he takes pleasure in poetry, does he wish that he were an Anakreon, a Philetas, or an Archilochus; for it does not necessarily follow that we esteem the workman because we are pleased with the work. For this reason men are not benefited by any spectacle which does not encourage them to imitation, and where reflection upon what they have observed does not make them also wish to do likewise; whereas we both admire the deeds to which virtue incites, and long to emulate the doers of them.

We enjoy the good things which we owe to fortune, but we admire virtuous actions; and while we wish to receive the former, we wish ourselves to benefit others by the latter. That which is in itself admirable kindles in us a desire of emulation, whether we see noble deeds presented before us, or read of them in history. It was with this purpose that I have engaged in writing biography, and have arranged this tenth book to contain the lives of Perikles and of Fabius Maximus, who fought against Hannibal, men who especially resembled one another in the gentleness and justice of their disposition, and who were both of the greatest service to their native countries, because they were able to endure with patience the follies of their governments and colleagues. Of my success, the reader of the following pages will be able to judge for themself.

III. Perikles was of the tribe Akamantis, and of the township of Cholargos, and was descended from the noblest families in Athens, on both his father's and mother's side. His father, Xanthippus, defeated the Persian generals at Mykalé, while his mother, Agariste, was a descendant of Kleisthenes, who drove the sons of Peisistratus out of Athens, put an end to their despotic rule, and established a new constitution admirably calculated to reconcile all parties and save the country. She dreamed that she had brought forth a lion, and a few days afterwards was delivered of Perikles. His body was symmetrical, but his head was long out of all proportion; for which reason in nearly all his statues he is represented wearing a helmet, as the sculptors did not wish, I suppose, to reproach him with this blemish. The Attic poets called him squill-head, and the comic poet, Kratinus, in his play 'Cheirones,' says,
"From Kronos old and faction, Is sprung a tyrant dread, And all Olympus calls him, The man-compelling head."

And again in the play of 'Nemesis'
"Come, hospitable Zeus, with lofty head."

Telekleides, too, speaks of him as sitting
"Bowed down With a dreadful frown, Because matters of state have gone wrong, Until at last, From his head so vast, His ideas burst forth in a throng."

And Eupolis, in his play of 'Demoi,' asking questions about each of the great orators as they come up from the other world one after the other, when at last Perikles ascends, says,
"The great headpiece of those below."

IV. Most writers tell us that his tutor in music was Damon, whose name they say should be pronounced with the first syllable short. Aristotle, however, says that he studied under Pythokleides. This Damon, it seems, was a sophist of the highest order, who used the name of music to conceal this accomplishment from the world, but who really trained Perikles for his political contests just as a trainer prepares an athlete for the games. However, Damon's use of music as a pretext did not impose upon the Athenians, who banished him by ostracism, as a busybody and lover of despotism. He was ridiculed by the comic poets; thus Plato represents some one as addressing him,

"Answer me this, I humbly do beseech, For thou, like Cheiron, Perikles did'st teach."

Perikles also attended the lectures of Zeno, of Elea, on natural philosophy, in which that philosopher followed the method of Parmenides. Zeno moreover had made an especial study of how to reduce any man to silence who questioned him, and how to enclose him between the horns of a dilemma, which is alluded to by Timon of Phlius in the following verses:

"Nor weak the strength of him of two-edged tongue, Zeno that carps at all."

But it was Anaxagoras of Klazomenae who had most to do with forming Perikles's style, teaching him an elevation and sublimity of expression beyond that of ordinary popular speakers, and altogether purifying and ennobling his mind. This Anaxagoras was called Nous, or Intelligence, by the men of that day, either because they admired his own intellect, or because he taught that an abstract intelligence is to be traced in all the concrete forms of matter, and that to this, and not to chance, the universe owes its origin.

V. Perikles greatly admired Anaxagoras, and became deeply interested in these grand speculations, which gave him a haughty spirit and a lofty style of oratory far removed from vulgarity and low buffoonery, and also an imperturbable gravity of countenance, and a calmness of demeanour and appearance which no incident could disturb as he was speaking, while the tone of his voice never showed that he heeded any interruption. These advantages greatly impressed the people. Once he sat quietly all day in the market-place despatching some pressing business, reviled in the foulest terms all the while by some low worthless fellow. Towards evening he walked home, the man following him and heaping abuse upon him. When about to enter his own door, as it was dark, he ordered one of his servants to take a torch and light the man home. The poet Ion, however, says that Perikles was overbearing and insolent in conversation, and that his pride had in it a great deal of contempt for others; while he praises Kimon's civil, sensible, and polished address. But we may disregard Ion, as a mere dramatic poet who always sees in great men something upon which to exercise his satiric vein; whereas Zeno used to invite those who called the haughtiness of Perikles a mere courting of popularity and affectation of grandeur, to court popularity themselves in the same fashion, since the acting of such a part might insensibly mould their dispositions until they resembled that of their model.

VI. These were not the only advantages which Perikles gained from his intimacy with Anaxagoras, but he seems to have learned to despise those superstitious fears which the common phenomena of the heavens produce in those who, ignorant of their cause, and knowing nothing about them, refer them all to the immediate action of the gods. Knowledge of physical science, while it puts an end to superstitious terrors, replaces them by a sound basis of piety. It is said that once a ram with one horn was sent from the country as a present to Perikles, and that Lampon the prophet, as soon as he saw this strong horn growing out of the middle of the creature's forehead, said that as there were two parties in the state, that of Thucydides and that of Perikles, he who possessed this mystic animal would unite the two into one. Anaxagoras cut open the beast's skull, and pointed out that its brain did not fill the whole space, but was sunken into the shape of an egg, and all collected at that part from which the horn grew. At the time all men looked with admiration on Anaxagoras, but afterwards, when Thucydides had fallen, and all the state had become united under Perikles, they admired Lampon equally.

There is, I imagine, no reason why both the prophet and the natural philosopher should not have been right, the one discovering the cause, and the other the meaning. The one considered why the horn grew so, and for what reason; the other declared what it meant by growing so, and for what end it took place. Those who say that when the cause of a portent is found out the portent is explained away, do not reflect that the same reasoning which explains away heavenly portents would also put an end to the meaning of the conventional signals used by mankind. The ringing of bells, the blaze of beacon fires, and the shadows on a dial are all of them produced by natural causes, but have a further meaning. But perhaps all this belongs to another subject.

VII. Perikles when young greatly feared the people. He had a certain personal likeness to the despot Peisistratus; and as his own voice was sweet, and he was ready and fluent in speech, old men who had known Peisistratus were struck by his resemblance to him. He was also rich, of noble birth, and had powerful friends, so that he feared he might be banished by ostracism, and consequently held aloof from politics, but proved himself a brave and daring soldier in the wars. But when Aristeides was dead, Themistokles banished, and Kimon generally absent on distant campaigns, Perikles engaged in public affairs, taking the popular side, that of the poor and many against that of the rich and few, quite contrary to his own feelings, which were entirely aristocratic. He feared, it seems, that he might be suspected of a design to make himself despot, and seeing that Kimon took the side of the nobility, and was much beloved by them, he betook himself to the people, as a means of obtaining safety for himself, and a strong party to combat that of Kimon. He immediately altered his mode of life; was never seen in any street except that which led to the market-place and the national assembly, and declined all invitations to dinner and such like social gatherings, so utterly that during the whole of his long political life he never dined with one of his friends, except when his first cousin, Euryptolemus, was married. On this occasion he sat at table till the libations were poured, upon which he at once got up and went away. For solemnity is wont to unbend at festive gatherings, and a majestic demeanour is hard to keep up when one is in familiar intercourse with others. True virtue, indeed, appears more glorious the more it is seen, and a really good man's life is never so much admired by the outside world as by his own intimate friends. But Perikles feared to make himself too common even with the people, and only addressed them after long intervals—not speaking upon every subject, and, not constantly addressing them, but, as Kritolaus says, keeping himself like the Salaminian trireme for great crises, and allowing his friends and the other orators to manage matters of less moment. One of these friends is said to have been Ephialtes, who destroyed the power of the Council of the Areopagus, "pouring out," as Plato, the comic poet, said, "a full and unmixed draught of liberty for the citizens," under the influence of which the poets of the time said that the Athenian people

"Nibbled at Euboea, like a horse that spurns the rein, And wantonly would leap upon the islands in the main."

VIII. Wishing to adopt a style of speaking consonant with his haughty manner and lofty spirit, Perikles made free use of the instrument which Anaxagoras as it were put into his hand, and often tinged his oratory with natural philosophy. He far surpassed all others by using this "lofty intelligence and power of universal consummation," as the divine Plato calls it; in addition to his natural advantages, adorning his oratory with apt illustrations drawn from physical science.

For this reason some think that he was nicknamed the Olympian; though some refer this to his improvement of the city by new and beautiful buildings, and others from his power both as a politician and a general. It is not by any means unlikely that these causes all combined to produce the name. Yet the comedies of that time, when they allude to him, either in jest or earnest, always appear to think that this name was given him because of his manner of speaking, as they speak of him as "thundering and lightening," and "rolling fateful thunders from his tongue." A saying of Thucydides, the son of Melesias, has been preserved, which jestingly testifies to the power of Perikles's eloquence. Thucydides was the leader of the conservative party, and for a long time struggled to hold his own against Perikles in debate. One day Archidamus, the King of Sparta, asked him whether he or Perikles was the best wrestler. "When I throw him in wrestling," Thucydides answered, "he beats me by proving that he never was down, and making the spectators believe him." For all this Perikles was very cautious about his words, and whenever he ascended the tribune to speak, used first to pray to the gods that nothing unfitted for the present occasion might fall from his lips. He left no writings, except the measures which he brought forward, and very few of his sayings are recorded. One of these was, that he called Aegina "the eyesore of the Peiraeus," and that "he saw war coming upon Athens from Peloponnesus." Stesimbrotus tells us that when he was pronouncing a public funeral oration over those who fell in Samos, he said that they had become immortal, even as the gods: for we do not see the gods, but we conceive them to be immortal by the respect which we pay them, and the blessings which we receive from them; and the same is the case with those who die for their country.

IX. Thucydides represents the constitution under Perikles as a democracy in name, but really an aristocracy, because the government was all in the hands of one leading citizen. But as many other writers tell us that during his administration the people received grants of land abroad, and were indulged with dramatic entertainments, and payments for their services, in consequence of which they fell into bad habits, and became extravagant and licentious, instead of sober hard-working people as they had been before, let us consider the history of this change, viewing it by the light of the facts themselves. First of all, as we have already said, Perikles had to measure himself with Kimon, and to transfer the affections of the people from Kimon to himself. As he was not so rich a man as Kimon, who used from his own ample means to give a dinner daily to any poor Athenian who required it, clothe aged persons, and take away the fences round his property, so that any one might gather the fruit, Perikles, unable to vie with him in this, turned his attention to a distribution of the public funds among the people, at the suggestion, we are told by Aristotle, of Damonides of Oia. By the money paid for public spectacles, for citizens acting as jurymen and other paid offices, and largesses, he soon won over the people to his side, so that he was able to use them in his attack upon the Senate of the Areopagus, of which he himself was not a member, never having been chosen Archon, or Thesmothete, or King Archon, or Polemarch. These offices had from ancient times been obtained by lot, and it was only through them that those who had approved themselves in the discharge of them were advanced to the Areopagus. For this reason it was that Perikles, when he gained strength with the populace, destroyed this Senate, making Ephialtes bring forward a bill which restricted its judicial powers, while he himself succeeded in getting Kimon banished by ostracism, as a friend of Sparta and a hater of the people, although he was second to no Athenian in birth or fortune, had won most brilliant victories over the Persians, and had filled Athens with plunder and spoils of war, as will be found related in his life. So great was the power of Perikles with the common people.

X. One of the provisions of ostracism was that the person banished should remain in exile for ten years. But during this period the Lacedaemonians with a great force invaded the territory of Tanagra, and, as the Athenians at once marched out to attack them, Kimon came back from exile, took his place in full armour among the ranks of his own tribe, and hoped by distinguishing himself in the battle amongst his fellow citizens to prove the falsehood of the Laconian sympathies with which he had been charged. However, the friends of Perikles drove him away, as an exile. On the other hand, Perikles fought more bravely in that battle than he had ever fought before, and surpassed every one in reckless daring. The friends of Kimon also, whom Perikles had accused of Laconian leanings, fell, all together, in their ranks; and the Athenians felt great sorrow for their treatment of Kimon, and a great longing for his restoration, now that they had lost a great battle on the frontier, and expected to be hard pressed during the summer by the Lacedaemonians. Perikles, perceiving this, lost no time in gratifying the popular wish, but himself proposed the decree for his recall; and Kimon on his return reconciled the two States, for he was on familiar terms with the Spartans, who were hated by Perikles and the other leaders of the common people. Some say that, before Kimon's recall by Perikles, a secret compact was made with him by Elpinike, Kimon's sister, that Kimon was to proceed on foreign service against the Persians with a fleet of two hundred ships, while Perikles was to retain his power in the city. It is also said that, when Kimon was being tried for his life, Elpinike softened the resentment of Perikles, who was one of those appointed to impeach him. When Elpinike came to beg her brother's life of him, he answered with a smile, "Elpinike, you are too old to meddle in affairs of this sort." But, for all that, he spoke only once, for form's sake, and pressed Kimon less than any of his other prosecutors. How, then, can one put any faith in Idomeneus, when he accuses Perikles of procuring the assassination of his friend and colleague Ephialtes, because he was jealous of his reputation? This seems an ignoble calumny, which Idomeneus has drawn from some obscure source to fling at a man who, no doubt, was not faultless, but of a generous spirit and noble mind, incapable of entertaining so savage and brutal a design. Ephialtes was disliked and feared by the nobles, and was inexorable in punishing those who wronged the people; wherefore his enemies had him assassinated by means of Aristodikus of Tanagra. This we are told by Aristotle. Kimon died in Cyprus, while in command of the Athenian forces.

XI. The nobles now perceived that Perikles was the most important man in the State, and far more powerful than any other citizen; wherefore, as they still hoped to check his authority, and not allow him to be omnipotent, they set up Thucydides, of the township of Alopekae, as his rival, a man of good sense, and a relative of Kimon, but less of a warrior and more of a politician, who, by watching his opportunities, and opposing Perikles in debate, soon brought about a balance of power. He did not allow the nobles to mix themselves up with the people in the public assembly, as they had been wont to do, so that their dignity was lost among the masses; but he collected them into a separate body, and by thus concentrating their strength was able to use it to counterbalance that of the other party. From the beginning these two factions had been but imperfectly welded together, because their tendencies were different; but now the struggle for power between Perikles and Thucydides drew a sharp line of demarcation between them, and one was called the party of the Many, the other that of the Few. Perikles now courted the people in every way, constantly arranging public spectacles, festivals, and processions in the city, by which he educated the Athenians to take pleasure in refined amusements; and also he sent out sixty triremes to cruise every year, in which many of the people served for hire for eight months, learning and practising seamanship. Besides this he sent a thousand settlers to the Chersonese, five hundred to Naxos, half as many to Andros, a thousand to dwell among the Thracian tribe of the Bisaltae, and others to the new colony in Italy founded by the city of Sybaris, which was named Thurii. By this means he relieved the state of numerous idle agitators, assisted the necessitous, and overawed the allies of Athens by placing his colonists near them to watch their behaviour.

XII. The building of the temples, by which Athens was adorned, the people delighted, and the rest of the world astonished, and which now alone prove that the tales of the ancient power and glory of Greece are no fables, was what particularly excited the spleen of the opposite faction, who inveighed against him in the public assembly, declaring that the Athenians had disgraced themselves by transferring the common treasury of the Greeks from the island of Delos to their own custody. "Perikles himself," they urged, "has taken away the only possible excuse for such an act—the fear that it might be exposed to the attacks of the Persians when at Delos, whereas it would be safe at Athens. Greece has been outraged, and feels itself openly tyrannised over, when it sees us using the funds which we extorted from it for the war against the Persians, for gilding and beautifying our city, as if it were a vain woman, and adorning it with precious marbles, and statues, and temples, worth a thousand talents." To this Perikles replied, that the allies had no right to consider how their money was spent, so long as Athens defended them from the Persians; while they supplied neither horses, ships, nor men, but merely money, which the Athenians had a right to spend as they pleased, provided they afforded them that security which it purchased. It was right, he argued, that, after the city had provided all that was necessary for war, it should devote its surplus money to the erection of buildings which would be a glory to it for all ages, while these works would create plenty by leaving no man unemployed, and encouraging all sorts of handicraft, so that nearly the whole city would earn wages, and thus derive both its beauty and its profit from itself. For those who were in the flower of their age, military service offered a means of earning money from the common stock; while, as he did not wish the mechanics and lower classes to be without their share, nor yet to see them receive it without doing work for it, he had laid the foundations of great edifices which would require industries of every kind to complete them; and he had done this in the interests of the lower classes, who thus, although they remained at home, would have just as good a claim to their share of the public funds as those who were serving at sea, in garrison, or in the field. The different materials used, such as stone, brass, ivory, gold, ebony, cypress-wood, and so forth, would require special artizans for each, such as carpenters, modellers, smiths, stone masons, dyers, melters and moulders of gold, and ivory painters, embroiderers, workers in relief; and also men to bring them to the city, such as sailors and captains of ships and pilots for such as came by sea; and, for those who came by land, carriage builders, horse breeders, drivers, rope makers, linen manufacturers, shoemakers, road menders, and miners. Each trade, moreover, employed a number of unskilled labourers, so that, in a word, there would be work for persons of every age and every class, and general prosperity would be the result.

XIII. These buildings were of immense size, and unequalled in beauty and grace, as the workmen endeavoured to make the execution surpass the design in beauty; but what was most remarkable was the speed with which they were built. All these edifices, each of which one would have thought, it would have taken many generations to complete, were all finished during the most brilliant period of one man's administration. We are told that Zeuxis, hearing Agatharchus, the painter, boasting how easily and rapidly he could produce a picture, said, "I paint very slowly." Ease, and speed of execution, seldom produces work of any permanent value or delicacy. It is the time which is spent in laborious production for which we are repaid by the durable character of the result. And this makes Perikles's work all the more wonderful, because it was built in a short time, and yet has lasted for ages. In beauty each of them at once appeared venerable as soon as it was built; but even at the present day the work looks as fresh as ever, for they bloom with an eternal freshness which defies time, and seems to make the work instinct with an unfading spirit of youth.

The overseer and manager of the whole was Pheidias, although there were other excellent architects and workmen, such as Kallikrates and Iktinus, who built the Parthenon on the site of the old Hekatompedon, which had been destroyed by the Persians, and Koroebus, who began to build the Temple of Initiation at Eleusis, but who only lived to see the columns erected and the architraves placed upon them. On his death, Metagenes, of Xypete, added the frieze and the upper row of columns, and Xenokles, of Cholargos, crowned it with the domed roof over the shrine. As to the long wall, about which Sokrates says that he heard Perikles bring forward a motion, Kallikrates undertook to build it. Kratinus satirises the work for being slowly accomplished, saying

"He builds in speeches, but he does no work."

The Odeum, which internally consisted of many rows of seats and many columns, and externally of a roof sloping on all sides from a central point, was said to have been built in imitation of the king of Persia's tent, and was built under Perikles's direction. For this reason Kratinus alludes to him in his play of the 'Thracian Woman'—

"Our Jove with lofty skull appears; The Odeum on his head he bears, Because he fears the oyster-shell no more."

Perikles at that period used his influence to pass a decree for establishing a musical competition at the Panathenaic festival; and, being himself chosen judge, he laid down rules as to how the candidates were to sing, and play the flute or the harp. At that period, and ever afterwards, all musical contests took place in the Odeum.

The Propylaea, before the Acropolis, were finished in five years, by Mnesikles the architect; and a miraculous incident during the work seemed to show that the goddess did not disapprove, but rather encouraged and assisted the building. The most energetic and active of the workmen fell from a great height, and lay in a dangerous condition, given over by his doctors. Perikles grieved much for him; but the goddess appeared to him in a dream, and suggested a course of treatment by which Perikles quickly healed the workman. In consequence of this, he set up the brazen statue of Athene the Healer, near the old altar in the Acropolis. The golden statue of the goddess was made by Pheidias, and his name appears upon the basement in the inscription. Almost everything was in his hands, and he gave his orders to all the workmen—as we have said before—because of his friendship with Perikles. This led to their both being envied and belied; for it was said that Perikles, with the connivance of Pheidias, carried on intrigues with Athenian ladies, who came ostensibly to see the works. This accusation was taken up by the comic poets, who charged him with great profligacy, hinting that he had an improper passion for the wife of Menippus, his friend, and a lieutenant-general in the army. Even the bird-fancying of Pyrilampes, because he was a friend of Perikles, was misrepresented, and he was said to give peacocks to the ladies who granted their favours to Perikles. But, indeed, how can we wonder at satirists bringing foul accusations against their betters, and offering them up as victims to the spite of the populace, when we find Stesimbrotus, of Thasos, actually inventing that unnatural and abominable falsehood of Perikles's intrigue with his own daughter-in-law. So hard is it to discover the truth, because the history of past ages is rendered difficult by the lapse of time; while in contemporary history the truth is always obscured, either by private spite and hatred, or by a desire to curry favour with the chief men of the time.

XIV. When the speakers of Thucydides's party complained that Perikles had wasted the public money, and destroyed the revenue, he asked the people in the assembly whether they thought he had spent much. When they answered "Very much indeed," he said in reply, "Do not, then, put it down to the public account, but to mine; and I will inscribe my name upon all the public buildings." When Perikles said this, the people, either in admiration of his magnificence of manner, or being eager to bear their share in the glory of the new buildings, shouted to him with one accord to take what money he pleased from the treasury, and spend it as he pleased, without stint. And finally, he underwent the trial of ostracism with Thucydides, and not only succeeded in driving him into exile, but broke up his party.

XV. As now there was no opposition to encounter in the city, and all parties had been blended into one, Perikles undertook the sole administration of the home and foreign affairs of Athens, dealing with the public revenue, the army, the navy, the islands and maritime affairs, and the great sources of strength which Athens derived from her alliances, as well with Greek as with foreign princes and states. Henceforth he became quite a different man: he no longer gave way to the people, and ceased to watch the breath of popular favour; but he changed the loose and licentious democracy, which had hitherto existed, into a stricter aristocratic, or rather monarchical, form of government. This he used honourably and unswervingly for the public benefit, finding the people, as a rule, willing to second the measures which he explained to them to be necessary, and to which he asked their consent, but occasionally having to use violence, and to force them, much against their will, to do what was expedient; like a physician dealing with some complicated disorder, who at one time allows his patient innocent recreation, and at another inflicts upon him sharp pains and bitter, though salutary, draughts. Every possible kind of disorder was to be found among a people possessing so great an empire as the Athenians; and he alone was able to bring them into harmony, by playing alternately upon their hopes and fears, checking them when over-confident, and raising their spirits when they were cast down and disheartened. Thus, as Plato says, he was able to prove that oratory is the art of influencing men's minds, and to use it in its highest application, when it deals with men's passions and characters, which, like certain strings of a musical instrument, require a skilful and delicate touch. The secret of his power is to be found, however, as Thucydides says, not so much in his mere oratory, as in his pure and blameless life, because he was so well known to be incorruptible, and indifferent to money; for though he made the city, which was a great one, into the greatest and richest city of Greece, and though he himself became more powerful than many independent sovereigns, who were able to leave their kingdoms to their sons, yet Perikles did not increase by one single drachma the estate which he received from his father.

XVI. This is the clear account of his power which is given by Thucydides the historian; though the comic poets misrepresent him atrociously, calling his immediate followers the New Peisistratidae, and calling upon him to swear that he never would make himself despot, as though his pre-eminence was not to be borne in a free state. And Telekleides says, that the Athenians delivered up into his hands

"The tribute from the towns, the towns themselves, The city walls, to build or to destroy, The right of making either peace or war, And all the wealth and produce of the land."

And all this was not on any special occasion, or when his administration was especially popular, but for forty years he held the first place among such men as Ephialtes, Leokrates, Myronides, Kimon, Tolmides, and Thucydides; and, after the fall and banishment of Thucydides by ostracism, he united in himself for five-and-twenty years all the various offices of state, which were supposed to last only for one year; and yet during the whole of that period proved himself incorruptible by bribes. As to his paternal estate, he was loth to lose it, and still more to be troubled with the management of it; consequently, he adopted what seemed to him the simplest and most exact method of dealing with it. Every year's produce was sold all together, and with the money thus obtained, he would buy what was necessary for his household in the market, and thus regulate his expenditure. This did not make him popular with his sons when they grew up; nor yet did the women of his family think him a liberal manager, but blamed his exact regulation of his daily expenses, which allowed none of the superfluities common in great and wealthy households, but which made the debit and credit exactly balance each other. One servant, Euangelos, kept all his accounts, as no one else had either capacity or education enough to be able to do so. These proceedings differed greatly from those of Anaxagoras the philosopher, who left his house, and let his estate go to ruin, while he pursued his lofty speculations. I conceive, however, that the life of a philosopher and that of a practical politician are not the same, as the one directs his thoughts to abstract ideas, while the other devotes his genius to supplying the real wants of mankind, and in some cases finds wealth not only necessary, but most valuable to him, as indeed it was to Perikles, who assisted many of the poorer citizens. It is said that, as Perikles was engaged in public affairs, Anaxagoras, who was now an old man and in want, covered his head with his robe, and determined to starve himself to death; but when Perikles heard of this, he at once ran to him, and besought him to live, lamenting, not Anaxagoras's fate, but his own, if he should lose so valuable a political adviser. Then Anaxagoras uncovered his head, and said to him, "Perikles, those who want to use a lamp supply it with oil."

XVII. As the Lacedaemonians began to be jealous of the prosperity of the Athenians, Perikles, wishing to raise the spirit of the people and to make them feel capable of immense operations, passed a decree, inviting all the Greeks, whether inhabiting Europe or Asia, whether living in large cities or small ones, to send representatives to a meeting at Athens to deliberate about the restoration of the Greek temples which had been burned by the barbarians, about the sacrifices which were due in consequence of the vows which they had made to the gods on behalf of Greece before joining battle, and about the sea, that all men might be able to sail upon it in peace and without fear. To carry out this decree twenty men, selected from the citizens over fifty years of age, were sent out, five of whom invited the Ionian and Dorian Greeks in Asia and the islands as far as Lesbos and Rhodes, five went to the inhabitants of the Hellespont and Thrace as far as Byzantium, and five more proceeded to Boeotia, Phokis, and Peloponnesus, passing from thence through Lokris to the neighbouring continent as far as Akarnania and Ambrakia; while the remainder journeyed through Euboea to the Oetaeans and the Malian gulf, and to the Achaeans of Phthia and the Thessalians, urging them to join the assembly and take part in the deliberations concerning the peace and well-being of Greece. However, nothing was effected, and the cities never assembled, in consequence it is said of the covert hostility of the Lacedaemonians, and because the attempt was first made in Peloponnesus and failed there: yet I have inserted an account of it in order to show the lofty spirit and the magnificent designs of Perikles.

XVIII. In his campaigns he was chiefly remarkable for caution, for he would not, if he could help it, begin a battle of which the issue was doubtful; nor did he wish to emulate those generals who have won themselves a great reputation by running risks, and trusting to good luck. But he ever used to say to his countrymen, that none of them should come by their deaths through any act of his. Observing that Tolmides, the son of Tolmaeus, elated by previous successes and by the credit which he had gained as a general, was about to invade Boeotia in a reckless manner, and had persuaded a thousand young men to follow him without any support whatever, he endeavoured to stop him, and made that memorable saying in the public assembly, that if Tolmides would not take the advice of Perikles, he would at any rate do well to consult that best of advisers, Time. This speech had but little success at the time; but when, a few days afterwards, the news came that Tolmides had fallen in action at Koronea, and many noble citizens with him, Perikles was greatly respected and admired as a wise and patriotic man.

XIX. His most successful campaign was that in the Chersonesus, which proved the salvation of the Greeks residing there: for he not only settled a thousand colonists there, and thus increased the available force of the cities, but built a continuous line of fortifications reaching across the isthmus from one sea to the other, by which he shut off the Thracians, who had previously ravaged the peninsula, and put an end to a constant and harassing border warfare to which the settlers were exposed, as they had for neighbours tribes of wild plundering barbarians.

But that by which he obtained most glory and renown was when he started from Pegae, in the Megarian territory, and sailed round the Peloponnesus with a fleet of a hundred triremes; for he not only laid waste much of the country near the coast, as Tolmides had previously done, but he proceeded far inland, away from his ships, leading the troops who were on board, and terrified the inhabitants so much that they shut themselves up in their strongholds. The men of Sikyon alone ventured to meet him at Nemea, and them he overthrew in a pitched battle, and erected a trophy. Next he took on board troops from the friendly district of Achaia, and, crossing over to the opposite side of the Corinthian Gulf, coasted along past the mouth of the river Achelous, overran Akarnania, drove the people of Oeneadae to the shelter of their city walls, and after ravaging the country returned home, having made himself a terror to his enemies, and done good service to Athens; for not the least casualty, even by accident, befel the troops under his command.

XX. When he sailed into the Black Sea with a great and splendidly equipped fleet, he assisted the Greek cities there, and treated them with consideration; and showed the neighbouring savage tribes and their chiefs the greatness of his force, and his confidence in his power, by sailing where he pleased, and taking complete control over that sea. He left at Sinope thirteen ships, and a land force under the command of Lamachus, to act against Timesileon, who had made himself despot of that city. When he and his party were driven out, Perikles passed a decree that six hundred Athenian volunteers should sail to Sinope, and become citizens there, receiving the houses and lands which had formerly been in the possession of the despot and his party. But in other cases he would not agree to the impulsive proposals of the Athenians, and he opposed them when, elated by their power and good fortune, they talked of recovering Egypt and attacking the seaboard of the Persian empire. Many, too, were inflamed with that ill-starred notion of an attempt on Sicily, which was afterwards blown into a flame by Alkibiades and other orators. Some even dreamed of the conquest of Etruria and Carthage, in consequence of the greatness which the Athenian empire had already reached, and the full tide of success which seemed to attend it.

XXI. Perikles, however, restrained these outbursts, and would not allow the people to meddle with foreign states, but used the power of Athens chiefly to preserve and guard her already existing empire, thinking it to be of paramount importance to oppose the Lacedaemonians, a task to which he bent all his energies, as is proved by many of his acts, especially in connection with the Sacred War. In this war the Lacedaemonians sent a force to Delphi, and made the Phokaeans, who held it, give it up to the people of Delphi: but as soon as they were gone Perikles made an expedition into the country, and restored the temple to the Phokaeans; and as the Lacedaemonians had scratched the oracle which the Delphians had given them, on the forehead of the brazen wolf there, Perikles got a response from the oracle for the Athenians, and carved it on the right side of the same wolf.

XXII. Events proved that Perikles was right in confining the Athenian empire to Greece. First of all Euboea revolted, and he was obliged to lead an army to subdue that island. Shortly after this, news came that the Megarians had become hostile, and that an army, under the command of Pleistoanax, king of the Lacedaemonians, was menacing the frontier of Attica. Perikles now in all haste withdrew his troops from Euboea, to meet the invader. He did not venture on an engagement with the numerous and warlike forces of the enemy, although repeatedly invited by them to fight: but, observing that Pleistoanax was a very young man, and entirely under the influence of Kleandrides, whom the Ephors had sent to act as his tutor and counsellor because of his tender years, he opened secret negotiations with the latter, who at once, for a bribe, agreed to withdraw the Peloponnesians from Attica. When their army returned and dispersed, the Lacedaemonians were so incensed that they imposed a fine on their king, and condemned Kleandrides, who fled the country, to be put to death. This Kleandrides was the father of Gylippus, who caused the ruin of the Athenian expedition in Sicily. Avarice seems to have been hereditary in the family, for Gylippus himself, after brilliant exploits in war, was convicted of taking bribes, and banished from Sparta in disgrace. This is more fully set forth in the Life of Lysander.

XXIII. When Perikles submitted the accounts of the campaign to the people, there was an item of ten talents, "for a necessary purpose," which the people passed without any questioning, or any curiosity to learn the secret. Some historians, amongst whom is Theophrastus the philosopher, say that Perikles sent ten talents annually to Sparta, by means of which he bribed the chief magistrates to defer the war, thus not buying peace, but time to make preparations for a better defence. He immediately turned his attention to the insurgents in Euboea, and proceeding thither with a fleet of fifty sail, and five thousand heavy armed troops, he reduced their cities to submission. He banished from Chalkis the "equestrian order," as it was called, consisting of men of wealth and station; and he drove all the inhabitants of Hestiaea out of their country, replacing them by Athenian settlers.

He treated these people with this pitiless severity, because they had captured an Athenian ship, and put its crew to the sword.

XXIV. After this, as the Athenians and Lacedaemonians made a truce for thirty years, Perikles decreed the expedition against Samos, on the pretext that they had disregarded the commands of the Athenians, to cease from their war with the Milesians. It was thought that he began this war with the Samians to please Aspasia, and this is, therefore, a good opportunity to discuss that person's character, and how she possessed so great influence and ability that the leading politicians of the day were at her feet, while philosophers discussed and admired her discourse. It is agreed that she was of Milesian origin, and that her father's name was Axiochus; and she is said to have reserved her favours for the most powerful personages in Greece, in imitation of Thargelia, an Ionian lady of ancient times, of great beauty, ability, and attractions, who had many lovers among the Greeks, and brought them all over to the Persian interest, by which means the seeds of the Persian faction were sown in many cities of Greece, as they were all men of great influence and position.

Now some writers say that Perikles valued Aspasia only for her wisdom and political ability. Indeed Sokrates and his friends used to frequent her society; and those who listened to her discourse used to bring their wives with them, that they too might profit by it, although her profession was far from being honourable or decent, for she kept courtesans in her house. Aeschines says that Lysikles, the sheep dealer, a low-born and low-minded man, became one of the first men in Athens, because he lived with Aspasia after Perikles's death. In Plato's dialogue too, called 'Menexenus,' though the first part is written in a humorous style, yet there is in it thus much of serious truth, that she was thought to discuss questions of rhetoric with many Athenians. But Perikles seems to have been more enamoured of Aspasia's person than her intellect. He was married to a woman who was nearly related to him, who had previously been the wife of Hipponikus, by whom she became the mother of Kallias the rich. By her Perikles had two sons, Xanthippus and Paralus; but afterwards, as they could not live comfortably together, he, at his wife's wish, handed her over to another husband, and himself lived with Aspasia, of whom he was passionately fond. It is said that he never went in or out of his house during the day without kissing her. In the comedies of the time, she is

spoken of as the new Omphale and as Deianeira, and sometimes as Hera (Juno). Kratinus plainly speaks of her as a harlot in the following lines:
"To him Vice bore a Juno new, Aspasia, shameless harlot."

He is thought to have had a bastard son by her, who is mentioned by Eupolis in his play of 'The Townships,' where Perikles is introduced, asking, "Lives then my son?" to which Myronides answers:
"He lives, and long had claimed a manly name, But that he feared his harlot mother's shame."

It is said that Aspasia became so illustrious and well known that the Cyrus who fought with his brother for the empire of Persia, called his favourite concubine Aspasia, though she had before been named Milto. She was a Phokaean by birth, the daughter of Hermotimus. After the death of Cyrus in battle, she was taken into the king's harem, and acquired great influence with him. These particulars about Aspasia occurred to my memory, and I thought that perhaps I might please my readers by relating them.

XXV. Perikles is accused of going to war with Samos to save the Milesians, at the request of Aspasia. These States were at war about the possession of the city of Priéne, and the Samians, who were victorious, would not lay down their arms and allow the Athenians to settle the matter by arbitration, as they ordered them to do. For this reason Perikles proceeded to Samos, put an end to the oligarchical form of government there, and sent fifty hostages and as many children to Lemnos, to ensure the good behaviour of the leading men. It is said that each of these hostages offered him a talent for his own freedom, and that much more was offered by that party which was loth to see a democracy established in the city. Besides all this, Pissuthnes the Persian, who had a liking for the Samians, sent and offered him ten thousand pieces of gold if he would spare the city. Perikles, however, took none of these bribes, but dealt with Samos as he had previously determined, and returned to Athens. The Samians now at once revolted, as Pissuthnes managed to get them back their hostages, and furnished them with the means of carrying on the war. Perikles now made a second expedition against them, and found them in no mind to submit quietly, but determined to dispute the empire of the seas with the Athenians. Perikles gained a signal victory over them in a sea-fight off the Goats' Island, beating a fleet of seventy ships with only forty-four, twenty of which were transports.

XXVI. Simultaneously with his victory and the flight of the enemy he obtained command of the harbour of Samos, and besieged the Samians in their city. They, in spite of their defeat, still possessed courage enough to sally out and fight a battle under the walls; but soon a larger force arrived from Athens, and the Samians were completely blockaded.

Perikles now with sixty ships sailed out of the Archipelago into the Mediterranean, according to the most current report intending to meet the Phoenician fleet which was coming to help the Samians, but, according to Stesimbrotus, with the intention of attacking Cyprus, which seems improbable. Whatever his intention may have been, his expedition was a failure, for Melissus, the son of Ithagenes, a man of culture, who was then in command of the Samian forces, conceiving a contempt for the small force of the Athenians and the want of experience of their leaders after Perikles's departure, persuaded his countrymen to attack them. In the battle the Samians proved victorious, taking many Athenians prisoners, and destroying many of their ships. By this victory they obtained command of the sea, and were able to supply themselves with more warlike stores than they had possessed before. Aristotle even says that Perikles himself was before this beaten by Melissus in a sea-fight. The Samians branded the figure of an owl on the foreheads of their Athenian prisoners, to revenge themselves for the branding of their own prisoners by the Athenians with the figure of a samaina. This is a ship having a beak turned up like a swine's snout, but with a roomy hull, so as both to carry a large cargo and sail fast. This class of vessel is called samaina because it was first built at Samos by Polykrates, the despot of that island. It is said that the verse of Aristophanes,
"The Samians are a deeply lettered race,"
alludes to this branding.

XXVII. When Perikles heard of the disaster which had befallen his army, he returned in all haste to assist them. He beat Melissus, who came out to meet him, and, after putting the enemy to rout, at once built a wall round their city, preferring to reduce it by blockade to risking the lives of his countrymen in an assault. As time went on the Athenians became impatient and eager to fight, and it was hard to restrain their ardour. Perikles divided the whole force into eight divisions, and made them all draw lots. The division which drew the white bean he permitted to feast and take their ease, while the rest did their duty. For this reason those who are enjoying themselves call it a "white day," in allusion to the white bean. Ephorus tells us that Perikles made use of battering engines in this siege, being attracted by their novelty, and that Artemon the mechanician was present, who was surnamed Periphoretus because he was lame, and carried in a litter to see such of the works as required his superintendence. This story is proved to be false by Herakleides of Pontus, he quoting Anakreon's poems, in which

Artemon Periphoretus is mentioned many generations before the revolt and siege of Samos. He tells us that Artemon was an effeminate coward who spent most of his time indoors, with two slaves holding a brazen shield over his head for fear that anything should fall upon it, and if he was obliged to go out, used to be carried in a hammock slung so low as almost to touch the ground, from which he received the name of Periphoretus.

XXVIII. In the ninth month of the siege the Samians surrendered. Perikles demolished their walls, confiscated their fleet, and imposed a heavy fine upon them, some part of which was paid at once by the Samians, who gave hostages for the payment of the remainder at fixed periods. Douris, of Samos, makes a lamentable story of this, accusing Perikles and the Athenians of great cruelty, no mention of which is to be found in Thucydides, Ephorus, or Aristotle. He obviously does not tell the truth when he says that Perikles took the captains and marine soldiers of each ship to the market-place at Miletus, bound them to planks, and after they had been so for ten days and were in a miserable state, knocked them on the head with clubs and cast out their bodies without burial. But Douris, even in cases where he has no personal bias, prefers writing an exciting story to keeping to the exact truth, and in this instance probably exaggerated the sufferings of his countrymen in order to gratify his dislike of the Athenians.

Perikles, after the reduction of Samos, returned to Athens, where he buried those who had fallen in the war in a magnificent manner, and was much admired for the funeral oration which, as is customary, was spoken by him over the graves of his countrymen. When he descended from the rostrum the women greeted him, crowning him with garlands and ribbons like a victorious athlete, and Elpinike drawing near to him said, "A fine exploit, truly, Perikles, and well worthy of a crown, to lose many of our brave fellow-citizens, not fighting with Persians or Phoenicians, as my brother Kimon did, but in ruining a city of men of our own blood and our own allies." At these words of Elpinike, Perikles merely smiled and repeated the verse of Archilochus—"Too old thou art for rich perfumes."

Ion says that his victory over the Samians wonderfully flattered his vanity. Agamemnon, he was wont to say, took ten years to take a barbarian city, but he in nine months had made himself master of the first and most powerful city in Ionia. And the comparison was not an unjust one, for truly the war was a very great undertaking, and its issue quite uncertain, since, as Thucydides tells us, the Samians came very near to wresting the empire of the sea from the Athenians.

XXIX. After these events, as the clouds were gathering for the Peloponnesian war, Perikles persuaded the Athenians to send assistance to the people of Korkyra, who were at war with the Corinthians, and thus to attach to their own side an island with a powerful naval force, at a moment when the Peloponnesians had all but declared war against them.

When the people passed this decree, Perikles sent only ten ships under the command of Lacedaemonius, the son of Kimon, as if he designed a deliberate insult; for the house of Kimon was on peculiarly friendly terms with the Lacedaemonians. His design in sending Lacedaemonius out, against his will, and with so few ships, was that if he performed nothing brilliant he might be accused, even more than he was already, of leaning to the side of the Spartans. Indeed, by all means in his power, he always threw obstacles in the way of the advancement of Kimon's family, representing that by their very names they were aliens, one son being named Lacedaemonius, another Thessalus, another Eleius. Moreover, the mother of all three was an Arcadian.

Now Perikles was much reproached for sending these ten ships, which were of little value to the Korkyreans, and gave a great handle to his enemies to use against him, and in consequence sent a larger force after them to Korkyra, which arrived there after the battle. The Corinthians, enraged at this, complained in the congress of Sparta of the conduct of the Athenians, as did also the Megarians, who said that they were excluded from every market and every harbour which was in Athenian hands, contrary to the ancient rights and common privileges of the Hellenic race. The people of Aegina also considered themselves to be oppressed and ill-treated, and secretly bemoaned their grievances in the ears of the Spartans, for they dared not openly bring any charges against the Athenians. At this time, too, Potidaea, a city subject to Athens, but a colony of Corinth, revolted, and its siege materially hastened the outbreak of the war. Archidamus, indeed, the king of the Lacedaemonians, sent ambassadors to Athens, was willing to submit all disputed points to arbitration, and endeavoured to moderate the excitement of his allies, so that war probably would not have broken out if the Athenians could have been persuaded to rescind their decree of exclusion against the Megarians, and to come to terms with them. And, for this reason, Perikles, who was particularly opposed to this, and urged the people not to give way to the Megarians, alone bore the blame of having begun the war.

XXX. It is said, that when an embassy arrived at Athens from Lacedaemon to treat upon these matters, Perikles argued that there was a law which forbade the tablet, on which the decree against the Megarians was written, to be taken down. "Then," said Polyalkes, one of the ambassadors, "do not take it down, but turn it with its face to the wall; for there is no law against that!"

Clever as this retort was, it had no effect on Perikles. He had, it seems, some private spite at the Megarians, though the ground of quarrel which he put publicly forward was that the Megarians had applied to their own use some of the sacred ground; and he passed a decree for a herald to be sent to the Megarians, and then to go on to the Lacedaemonians to complain of their conduct. This decree of Perikles is worded in a candid and reasonable manner; but the herald, Anthemokritus, was thought to have met his death at the hands of the Megarians, and Charinus passed a decree to the effect that Athens should wage war against them to the death, without truce or armistice; that any Megarian found in Attica should be punished with death, and that the generals, when taking the usual oath for each year, should swear in addition that they would invade the Megarian territory twice every year; and that Anthemokritus should be buried near the city gate leading into the Thriasian plain, which is now called the Double Gate.

Now, the Megarians say that they were not to blame for the murder of Anthemokritus, and lay it upon Perikles and Aspasia, quoting the hackneyed rhymes from the 'Acharnians,' of Aristophanes:
"Some young Athenians in their drunken play, From Megara Simaetha stole away, The men of Megara next, with angered soul, Two of Aspasia's choicest harlots stole."

XXXI. How the dispute originated it is hard to say, but all writers agree in throwing on Perikles the blame of refusing to reverse the decree. Some attribute his firmness to a wise calculation, saying that the demand was merely made in order to try him, and that any concessions would have been regarded as a sign of weakness; while others say that he treated the Lacedaemonians so cavalierly through pride and a desire to show his own strength. But the worst motive of all, and that to which most men attribute his conduct, was as follows: Pheidias, the sculptor, was, as we have related, entrusted with the task of producing the statue of the tutelary goddess of Athens. His intimacy with Perikles, with whom he had great influence, gained for him many enemies, who, wishing to experiment on the temper of the people towards Perikles himself, bribed Menon, one of Pheidias's fellow-workmen, to seat himself in the market-place as a suppliant who begged that he might receive protection while he denounced and prosecuted Pheidias. The people took this man under its protection, and Pheidias was prosecuted before the Senate. The alleged charges of theft were not proved, for Pheidias, by the advice of Perikles, had originally fashioned the golden part of the statue in such a manner that it could all be taken off and weighed, and this Perikles bade the prosecutor do on this occasion. But the glory which Pheidias obtained by the reality of his work made him an object of envy and hatred, especially when in his sculpture of the battle with the Amazons on the shield of the goddess he introduced his own portrait as a bald-headed old man lifting a great stone with both hands, and also a very fine representation of Perikles, fighting with an Amazon. The position of the hand, which was holding a spear before the face of Perikles, was ingeniously devised as if to conceal the portrait, which, nevertheless, could plainly be seen on either side of it. For this, Pheidias was imprisoned, and there fell sick and died, though some say that his enemies poisoned him in order to cast suspicion upon Perikles. At the instance of Glykon, the people voted to Menon, the informer, an immunity from public burdens, and ordered the generals of the State to provide for the wretch's safety.

XXXII. About the same time Aspasia was prosecuted for impiety, at the suit of Hermippus, the comic playwright, who moreover accused her of harbouring free-born Athenian ladies, with whom Perikles carried on intrigues. Also Diopeithes proposed a decree, that prosecutions should be instituted against all persons who disbelieved in religion, and held theories of their own about heavenly phenomena. This was aimed at Perikles through the philosopher Anaxagoras. As the people adopted this decree, and eagerly listened to these slanderous accusations, another decree was carried by Drakontides, that Perikles should lay the accounts of his dealings with the public revenue before the Prytanes, and that the judges should carry their suffrage from the altar in the Acropolis, and go and determine the cause in the city. At the motion of Hagnon this part of the decree was reversed, but he succeeded in having the action conducted before fifteen hundred judges, in a form of trial which one might call either one for theft, or taking of bribes, or for public wrong-doing. Aspasia was acquitted, quite contrary to justice, according to Aeschines, because Perikles shed tears and made a personal appeal to the judges on her behalf. He feared that Anaxagoras would be convicted, and sent him out of the city before his trial commenced. And now, as he had become unpopular by means of Pheidias, he at once blew the war into a flame, hoping to put an end to these prosecutions, and to restore his own personal ascendancy by involving the State in important and dangerous crises, in which it would have to rely for guidance upon himself alone.

These are the causes which are assigned for his refusal to permit the Athenians to make any concession to the Lacedaemonians, but the real history of the transaction will never be known.

XXXIII. Now, as the Lacedaemonians knew that if he could be removed from power they would find the Athenians much more easy to deal with, they bade them, "drive forth the accursed thing," alluding to Perikles's descent from the Alkmaeonidae by his mother's side, as we are told by Thucydides the historian. But this attempt had just the contrary effect to that which they intended; for, instead of suspicion and dislike, Perikles met with much greater honour and respect from his countrymen than before, because they saw that he was an object of especial dislike to the enemy. For this reason, before the Peloponnesians, under Archidamus, invaded Attica, he warned the Athenians that if Archidamus, when he laid waste everything else, spared his own private estate because of the friendly private relations existing between them, or in order to give his personal enemies a ground for impeaching him, that he should give both the land and the farm buildings upon it to the State.

The Lacedaemonians invaded Attica with a great host of their own troops and those of their allies, led by Archidamus, their king. They proceeded, ravaging the country as they went, as far as Acharnae (close to Athens), where they encamped, imagining that the Athenians would never endure to see them there, but would be driven by pride and shame to come out and fight them. However, Perikles thought that it would be a very serious matter to fight for the very existence of Athens against sixty thousand Peloponnesian and Boeotian heavy-armed troops, and so he pacified those who were dissatisfied at his inactivity by pointing out that trees when cut down quickly grow again, but that when the men of a State are lost, it is hard to raise up others to take their place. He would not call an assembly of the people, because he feared that they would force him to act against his better judgment, but, just as the captain of a ship, when a storm comes on at sea, places everything in the best trim to meet it, and trusting to his own skill and seamanship, disregarding the tears and entreaties of the sea-sick and terrified passengers; so did Perikles shut the gates of Athens, place sufficient forces to ensure the safety of the city at all points, and calmly carry out his own policy, taking little heed of the noisy grumblings of the discontented. Many of his friends besought him to attack, many of his enemies threatened him and abused him, and many songs and offensive jests were written about him, speaking of him as a coward, and one who was betraying the city to its enemies. Kleon too attacked him, using the anger which the citizens felt against him to advance his own personal popularity, as we see from the following lines of Hermippus:

"King of Satyrs, wherefore fear you Spear to wield, and only dare to Talk in swelling phrase, while yet you Cower, Teles like, And when goaded on, past bearing, By our Kleon's tongue so daring, Only gnash your teeth despairing, Still afraid to strike."

XXXIV. Perikles was unmoved by any of these attacks, but quietly endured all this storm of obloquy. He sent a fleet of a hundred ships to attack Peloponnesus, but did not sail with it himself, remaining at home to keep a tight hand over Athens until the Peloponnesians drew off their forces. He regained his popularity with the common people, who suffered much from the war, by giving them allowances of money from the public revenue, and grants of land; for he drove out the entire population of the island of Aegina, and divided the land by lot among the Athenians. A certain amount of relief also was experienced by reflecting upon the injuries which they were inflicting on the enemy; for the fleet as it sailed round Peloponnesus destroyed many small villages and cities, and ravaged a great extent of country, while Perikles himself led an expedition into the territory of Megara and laid it all waste. By this it is clear that the allies, although they did much damage to the Athenians, yet suffered equally themselves, and never could have protracted the war for such a length of time as it really lasted, but, as Perikles foretold, must soon have desisted had not Providence interfered and confounded human counsels. For now the pestilence fell among the Athenians, and cut off the flower of their youth. Suffering both in body and mind they raved against Perikles, just as people when delirious with disease attack their fathers or their physicians. They endeavoured to ruin him, urged on by his personal enemies, who assured them that he was the author of the plague, because he had brought all the country people into the city, where they were compelled to live during the heat of summer, crowded together in small rooms and stifling tents, living an idle life too, and breathing foul air instead of the pure country breezes to which they were accustomed. The cause of this, they said, was the man who, when the war began, admitted the masses of the country people into the city, and then made no use of them, but allowed them to be penned up together like cattle, and transmit the contagion from one to another, without devising any remedy or alleviation of their sufferings.

XXXV. Hoping to relieve them somewhat, and also to annoy the enemy, Perikles manned a hundred and fifty ships, placed on board, besides the sailors, many brave infantry and cavalry soldiers, and was about to put to sea. The Athenians conceived great hopes, and the enemy no less terror from so large an armament. When all was ready, and Perikles himself had just embarked in his own trireme, an eclipse of the sun took place, producing total darkness, and all men were terrified at so great a portent. Perikles, observing that his helmsman was alarmed and knew not what to do, held his cloak over the man's eyes and asked him if he thought that a terrible portent. As he answered that he did not, Perikles said: "What is the difference, then, between it and an eclipse of the sun, except that the eclipse is caused by something larger than my cloak?" This subject is discussed by the philosophers in their schools.

Perikles sailed with the fleet, but did nothing worthy of so great a force. He besieged the sacred city of Epidaurus, but, although he had great hopes of taking it, he failed on account of the plague, which destroyed not only his own men, but every one who came in contact with them. After this he again endeavoured to encourage the Athenians, to whom he had become an object of dislike. However, he did not succeed in pacifying them, but they condemned him by a public vote to be general no more, and to pay a fine which is stated at the lowest estimate to have been fifteen talents, and at the highest fifty. This was carried, according to Idomeneus, by Kleon, but according to Theophrastus by Simmias; whilst Herakleides of Pontus says that it was effected by Lakrateides.

XXXVI. He soon regained his public position, for the people's outburst of anger was quenched by the blow they had dealt him, just as a bee leaves its sting in the wound; but his private affairs were in great distress and disorder, as he had lost many of his relatives during the plague, while others were estranged from him on political grounds. Xanthippus too, the eldest of his legitimate sons, who was a spendthrift by nature and married to a woman of expensive habits, a daughter of Tisander, the son of Epilykus, could not bear with his father's stingy ways and the small amount of money which he allowed him. He consequently sent to one of his friends and borrowed money from him as if Perikles had authorised him to do so. When the friend asked for his money back again, Perikles prosecuted him, at which proceeding young Xanthippus was enraged and abused his father, sneering at his way of life and his discussions with the sophists. When some athlete accidentally killed Epitimus of Pharsalus with a javelin, he said that Perikles spent the whole day arguing with Protagoras whether in strict accuracy the javelin, or the man who threw it, or the stewards of the games, ought to be considered the authors of the mishap. And, besides this, Stesimbrotus tells us that Xanthippus put about that scandal about his father and his own wife, so that the father and son remained irreconcilable enemies until Xanthippus's death, which happened during the plague, by an attack of that disorder. At the same time Perikles lost his sister and most of his relations, especially those who supported his policy. Yet he would not yield, nor abate his firmness and constancy of spirit because of these afflictions, but was not observed to weep or mourn, or attend the funeral of any of his relations, until he lost Paralus, the last of his legitimate offspring. Crushed by this blow, he tried in vain to keep up his grand air of indifference, and when carrying a garland to lay upon the corpse he was overpowered by his feelings, so as to burst into a passion of tears and sobs, which he had never done before in his whole life.

XXXVII. Athens made trial of her other generals and public men to conduct her affairs, but none appeared to be of sufficient weight or reputation to have such a charge entrusted to him. The city longed for Perikles, and invited him again to lead its counsels and direct its armies; and he, although dejected in spirits and living in seclusion in his own house, was yet persuaded by Alkibiades and his other friends to resume the direction of affairs. The people apologised for their ungrateful treatment of him, and when he was again in office and elected as general, he begged of them to be released from the operations of the law of bastardy, which he himself had originally introduced, in order that his name and race might not altogether become extinct for want of an heir. The provisions of the law were as follows:—Perikles many years before, when he was at the height of his power and had children born to him, as we have related, of legitimate birth, proposed a law that only those born of an Athenian father and mother should be reckoned Athenian citizens. But when the king of Egypt sent a present of forty thousand medimni of wheat to be divided among the citizens, many lawsuits arose about the citizenship of men whose birth had never been questioned before that law came into force, and many vexatious informations were laid. Nearly five thousand men were convicted of illegitimacy of birth and sold for slaves, while those who retained their citizenship and proved themselves to be genuine Athenians amounted to fourteen thousand and forty. It was indeed an unreasonable request that a law which had been enforced in so many instances should now be broken in the person of its own author, but Perikles's domestic misfortunes, in which he seemed to have paid the penalty for his former haughtiness and pride, touched the hearts of the Athenians so much that they thought his sorrows deserving of their pity, and his request such as he was entitled to make and they to grant in common charity, and they consented to his illegitimate son being enrolled in his own tribe and bearing his own name. This man was subsequently put to death by the people, together with all his colleagues, for their conduct after the sea-fight at Arginusae.

XXXVIII. After this it appears that Perikles was attacked by the plague, not acutely or continuously, as in most cases, but in a slow wasting fashion, exhibiting many varieties of symptoms, and gradually undermining his strength. Theophrastus, in his treatise on Ethics, discusses whether a man's character can be changed by disease, and whether virtue depends upon bodily health. As an example, he quotes a story that Perikles, when one of his friends came to visit him during his sickness, showed him a charm hung round his neck, as a proof that he must be indeed ill to submit to such a piece of folly. As he was now on his deathbed, the most distinguished of the citizens and his surviving friends collected round him and spoke admiringly of his nobleness and immense power, enumerating also the number of his exploits, and the trophies which he had set up for victories gained; for while in chief command he had won no less than nine victories for Athens. They were talking thus to one another in his presence, imagining that he could no longer understand them, but had lost his power of attending to them. He, however, was following all that they said, and suddenly broke silence, saying that he was surprised at their remembering and praising him for the exploits which depended entirely upon fortune for their success, and which many other generals had done as well as himself, while they did not mention his greatest and most glorious title to fame. "No Athenian," said he, "ever wore black because of me."

XXXIX. Perikles was to be admired, not only for his gentleness and mildness of spirit, which he preserved through the most violent political crises and outbreaks of personal hatred to himself, but also for his lofty disposition. He himself accounted it his greatest virtue that he never gave way to feelings of envy or hatred, but from his own exalted pinnacle of greatness never regarded any man as so much his enemy that he could never be his friend. This alone, in my opinion, justifies that outrageous nickname of his, and gives it a certain propriety; for so serene and impartial a man, utterly uncorrupt though possessed of great power, might naturally be called Olympian. Thus it is that we believe that the gods, who are the authors of all good and of no evil to men, rule over us and over all created things, not as the poets describe them in their bewildering fashion, which their own poems prove to be untrue. The poets describe the abode of the gods as a safe and untroubled place where no wind or clouds are, always enjoying a mild air and clear light, thinking such a place to be fittest for a life of immortal blessedness; while they represent the gods themselves as full of disorder and anger and spite and other passions, which are not becoming even to mortal men of common sense. Those reflections, however, perhaps belong to another subject.

Events soon made the loss of Perikles felt and regretted by the Athenians. Those who during his lifetime had complained that his power completely threw them into the shade, when after his death they had made trial of other orators and statesmen, were obliged to confess that with all his arrogance no man ever was really more moderate, and that his real mildness in dealing with men was as remarkable as his apparent pride and assumption. His power, which had been so grudged and envied, and called monarchy and despotism, now was proved to have been the saving of the State; such an amount of corrupt dealing and wickedness suddenly broke out in public affairs, which he before had crushed and forced to hide itself, and so prevented its becoming incurable through impunity and licence.

Life of Fabius Maximus.

I. Such a man did Perikles show himself to be in his most memorable acts, as far as they are extant.

Let us now turn our attention to Fabius.

The first of the family is said to descend from one of the nymphs, according to some writers, according to others from an Italian lady who became the mother of Fabius by Hercules near the river Tiber. From him descended the family of the Fabii, one of the largest and most renowned in Rome. Some say that the men of this race were the first to use pitfalls in hunting, and were anciently named Fodii in consequence; for up to the present day ditches are called fossae, and to dig is called fodere in Latin: and thus in time the two sounds became confused, and they obtained the name of Fabii. The family produced many distinguished men, the greatest of whom was Rullus, who was for that reason named Maximus by the Romans. From him Fabius Maximus, of whom I am now writing, was fourth in descent. His own personal nickname was Verrucosus, because he had a little wart growing on his upper lip. The name of Ovicula, signifying sheep, was also given him while yet a child, because of his slow and gentle disposition. He was quiet and silent, very cautious in taking part in children's games, and learned his lessons slowly and with difficulty, which, combined with his easy obliging ways with his comrades, made those who did not know him think that he was dull and stupid. Few there were who could discern, hidden in the depths of his soul, his glorious and lion-like character. Soon, however, as time went on, and he began to take part in public affairs, he proved that his apparent want of energy was really due to serenity of intellect, that he was cautious because he weighed matters well beforehand, and that while he was never eager or easily moved, yet he was always steady and trustworthy. Observing the immense extent of the empire, and the numerous wars in which it was engaged, he exercised his body in warlike exercises, regarding it as his natural means of defence, while he also studied oratory as the means by which to influence the people, in a style suited to his own life and character. In his speeches there were no flowery passages, no empty graces of style, but there was a plain common sense peculiar to himself, and a depth of sententious maxims which is said to have resembled Thucydides. One of his speeches is extant, a funeral oration which he made in public over his son who died after he had been consul.

II. He was consul five times, and in his first consulship obtained a triumph over the Ligurians. They were defeated by him and driven with great loss to take refuge in the Alps, and thus were prevented from ravaging the neighbouring parts of Italy as they had been wont to do. When Hannibal invaded Italy, won his first battle at the Trebia, and marched through Etruria, laying everything waste as he went, the Romans were terribly disheartened and cast down, and terrible prodigies took place, some of the usual kind, that is, by lightning, and others of an entirely new and strange character. It was said that shields of their own accord became drenched with blood: that at Antium standing corn bled when it was cut by the reapers; that red-hot stones fell from heaven, and that the sky above Falerii was seen to open and tablets to fall, on one of which was written the words "Mars is shaking his arms."

None of these omens had any effect upon Caius Flaminius, the consul, for, besides his naturally spirited and ambitious nature, he was excited by the successes which he had previously won, contrary to all reasonable probability. Once, against the express command of the Senate, and in spite of the opposition of his colleague, he engaged with the Gauls and won a victory over them. Fabius also was but little disturbed by the omens, because of their strange and unintelligible character, though many were alarmed at them. Knowing how few the enemy were in numbers, and their great want of money and supplies, he advised the Romans not to offer battle to a man who had at his disposal an army trained by many previous encounters to a rare pitch of perfection, but rather to send reinforcements to their allies, keep a tight hand over their subject cities, and allow Hannibal's brilliant little force to die away like a lamp which flares up brightly with but little oil to sustain it.

III. This reasoning had no effect upon Flaminius, who said that he would not endure to see an enemy marching upon Rome, and would not, like Camillus of old, fight in the streets of Rome herself. He ordered the military tribunes to put the army in motion, and himself leaped upon his horse's back. The horse for no visible reason shied in violent terror, and Flaminius was thrown headlong to the ground. He did not, however, alter his determination, but marched to meet Hannibal, and drew up his forces for battle near the lake Thrasymenus, in Etruria. When the armies met, an earthquake took place which destroyed cities, changed the courses of rivers, and cast down the crests of precipices; but in spite of its violence, no one of the combatants perceived it. Flaminius himself, after many feats of strength and courage, fell dead, and around him lay the bravest Romans. The rest fled, and the slaughter was so great that fifteen thousand were killed, and as many more taken prisoners.

Hannibal generously desired to bury the body of Flaminius with military honours, to show his esteem for the consul's bravery; but it could not be found among the slain, and no one knew how it disappeared.

The defeat at the Trebia had not been clearly explained either by the general who wrote the despatch, or by the messenger who carried it, as they falsely represented it to have been a drawn battle; but as soon as the praetor Pomponius heard the news of this second misfortune, he assembled the people in the Forum, and said, without any roundabout apologies whatever, "Romans, we have lost a great battle, the army is destroyed, and the consul Flaminius has fallen. Now, therefore, take counsel for your own safety." These words produced the same impression on the people that a gust of wind does upon the sea. No one could calmly reflect after such a sudden downfall of their hopes. All, however, agreed that the State required one irresponsible ruler, which the Romans call a dictatorship, and a man who would fulfil this office with fearless energy. Such a man, they felt, was Fabius Maximus, who was sufficiently qualified for the office by his abilities and the respect which his countrymen bore him, and was moreover at that time of life when the strength of the body is fully capable of carrying out the ideas of the mind, but when courage is somewhat tempered by discretion.

IV. As soon as the people had passed their decree, Fabius was appointed dictator, and appointed Marcus Minucius his master of the horse. First, however, he begged of the Senate to allow him the use of a horse during his campaigns. There was an ancient law forbidding this practice, either because the main strength of the army was thought to lie in the columns of infantry, and for that reason the dictator ought to remain always with them, or else because, while in all other respects the dictator's power is equal to that of a king, it was thought well that in this one point he should have to ask leave of the people. Next, however, Fabius, wishing at once to show the greatness and splendour of his office, and so make the citizens more ready to obey him, appeared in public with all his twenty-four lictors at once; and when the surviving consul met him, he sent an officer to bid him dismiss his lictors, lay aside his insignia of office, and come before him as a mere private citizen. After this he began in the best possible way, that is, by a religious ceremony, and assured the people that it was in consequence of the impiety and carelessness of their late general, not by any fault of the army, that they had been defeated. Thus he encouraged them not to fear their enemies, but to respect the gods and render them propitious, not that he implanted any superstitious observances among them, but he confirmed their valour by piety, and took away from them all fear of the enemy by the hopes which he held out to them of divine protection. At this time many of the holy and mysterious books, which contain secrets of great value to the State, were inspected. These are called the Sibylline books. One of the sentences preserved in these was said to have an evident bearing on contemporary events; what it was can only be guessed at by what was done. The dictator appeared before the people and publicly vowed to the gods a ver sacrum, that is, all the young which the next spring should produce, from the goats, the sheep, and the kine on every mountain, and plain, and river, and pasture within the bounds of Italy. All these he swore that he would sacrifice, and moreover that he would exhibit musical and dramatic shows, and expend upon them the sum of three hundred and thirty-three sestertia, and three hundred and thirty-three denarii, and one-third of a denarius. The sum total of this in our Greek money is eighty-three thousand five hundred and eighty-three drachmas and two obols. What the particular virtue of this exact number may be it is hard to determine, unless it be on account of the value of the number three, which is by nature perfect, and the first of odd numbers, the first also of plurals, and containing within itself all the elements of the qualities of number.

V. Fabius, by teaching the people to rest their hopes on religion, made them view the future with a more cheerful heart. For his own part, he trusted entirely to himself to win the victory, believing that Heaven grants men success according to the valour and conduct which they display. He marched against Hannibal, not with any design of fighting him, but of wearing out his army by long delays, until he could, by his superior numbers and resources, deal with him easily. With this object in view he always took care to secure himself from Hannibal's cavalry, by occupying the mountains overhanging the Carthaginian camp, where he remained quiet as long as the enemy did, but when they moved he used to accompany them, showing himself at intervals upon the heights at such a distance as not to be forced to fight against his will, and yet, from the very slowness of his movements, making the enemy fear that at every moment he was about to attack. By these dilatory manoeuvres he incurred general contempt, and was looked upon with disgust by his own soldiers, while the enemy, with the exception of one man, thought him utterly without warlike enterprise. That man was Hannibal himself. He alone perceived Fabius's true generalship and thorough comprehension of the war, and saw that either he must by some means be brought to fight a battle, or else the Carthaginians were lost, if they could not make use of their superiority in arms, but were to be worn away and reduced in number and resources, in which they were already deficient. He put in force every conceivable military stratagem and device, like a skilful wrestler when he tries to lay hold of his antagonist, and kept attacking Fabius, skirmishing round him, and drawing him from place to place, in his endeavours to make him quit his policy of caution. But Fabius was convinced that he was right, and steadily declined battle. His master of the horse, Minucius, who longed for action, gave him much trouble. This man made unseemly boasts, and harangued the army, filling it with wild excitement and self-confidence. The soldiers in derision used to call Fabius Hannibal's lacquey, because he followed him wherever he went, and thought Minucius a really great general, and worthy of the name of Roman. Minucius, encouraged in his arrogant vauntings, began to ridicule the habit of encamping on the mountain-tops, saying that the dictator always took care to provide them with good seats from which to behold the spectacle of the burning and plundering of Italy, and used to ask the friends of Fabius whether he took his army up so near the sky because he had ceased to take any interest in what went on on the earth below, or whether it was in order to conceal it from the enemy among the clouds and mists. When Fabius was informed of these insults by his friends, who begged him to wipe away this disgrace by risking a battle, he answered, "If I did so, I should be more cowardly than I am now thought to be, in abandoning the policy which I have determined on because of men's slanders and sneers. It is no shame to fear for one's country, but to regard the opinions and spiteful criticisms of the people would be unworthy of the high office which I hold, and would show me the slave of those whom I ought to govern and restrain when they would fain do wrong."

VI. After this, Hannibal made a blunder. Wishing to move his army further from that of Fabius, and to gain an open part of the country where he could obtain forage, he ordered his guides one night after supper to lead the way at once to Casinatum. They, misunderstanding him because of his foreign pronunciation, led his forces to the borders of Campania, near the city of Casilinum, through the midst of which flows the river Lothronus, which the Romans call Vulturnus. This country is full of mountains, except one valley that runs towards the sea-coast, where the river at the end of its course overflows into extensive marshes, with deep beds of sand. The beach itself is rough and impracticable for shipping.

When Hannibal was marching down this valley, Fabius, by his superior knowledge of the country, came up with him, placed four thousand men to guard the narrow outlet, established the main body in a safe position in the mountains, and with the light-armed troops fell upon and harassed the rear of Hannibal's army, throwing it all into disorder, and killing about eight hundred men. Upon this, Hannibal determined to retrace his steps. Perceiving the mistake which he had made, and the danger he was in, he crucified his guides, but still could not tell how to force his way out through the Roman army which was in possession of the mountain passes. While all were terrified and disheartened, believing themselves to be beset on all sides by dangers from which there was no escape, Hannibal decided on extricating himself by stratagem. Taking about two thousand captured oxen, he ordered his soldiers to bind a torch or faggot of dry wood to their horns, and at night at a given signal to set them on fire, and drive the animals towards the narrow outlet near the enemy's camp. While this was being done, he got the remainder of the troops under arms and led them slowly forward. The cattle, while the flame was moderate, and burned only the wood, walked steadily forward towards the mountain side, astonishing the shepherds on the mountain, who thought that it must be an army, marching in one great column, carrying torches. But when their horns were burned to the quick, causing them considerable pain, the beasts, now scorched by the fire from one another as they shook their heads, set off in wild career over the mountains, with their foreheads and tails blazing, setting fire to a great part of the wood through which they passed. The Romans watching the pass were terribly scared at the sight; for the flames looked like torches carried by men running, and they fell into great confusion and alarm, thinking that they were surrounded, and about to be attacked on all sides by the enemy. They dared not remain at their post, but abandoned the pass, and made for the main body. At that moment Hannibal's light troops took possession of the heights commanding the outlet, and the main army marched safely through, loaded with plunder.

VII. It happened that while it was yet night Fabius perceived the trick; for some of the oxen in their flight had fallen into the hands of the Romans; but, fearing to fall into an ambuscade in the darkness, he kept his men quiet under arms. When day broke he pursued and attacked the rearguard, which led to many confused skirmishes in the rough ground, and produced great confusion, till Hannibal sent back his practised Spanish mountaineers from the head of his column. These men, being light and active, attacked the heavily-armed Roman infantry and beat off Fabius' attack with very considerable loss. Now Fabius's unpopularity reached its highest pitch, and he was regarded with scorn and contempt. He had, they said, determined to refrain from a pitched battle, meaning to overcome Hannibal by superior generalship, and he had been defeated in that too. And Hannibal himself, wishing to increase the dislike which the Romans felt for him, though he

burned and ravaged every other part of Italy, forbade his men to touch
Fabius's own estates, and even placed a guard to see that no damage was done
to them. This was reported at Rome, greatly to his discredit; and the tribunes
of the people brought all kinds of false accusations against him in public
harangues, instigated chiefly by Metilius, who was not Fabius's personal
enemy, but being a relative of Minucius, the Master of the Horse, thought
that he was pressing the interests of the latter by giving currency to all these
scandalous reports about Fabius. He was also disliked by the Senate because
of the terms which he had arranged with Hannibal about the exchange of
prisoners. The two commanders agreed that the prisoners should be
exchanged man for man, and that if either party had more than the other, he
should redeem for two hundred and fifty drachmas per man. When, then, this
exchange took place, two hundred and forty Romans were found remaining
in Hannibal's hands. The Senate determined not to send these men's ransom,
and blamed Fabius for having acted improperly and against the interests of
the State in taking back men whose cowardice had made them fall into the
hands of the enemy. Fabius, on hearing this, was not moved at the discontent
of the citizens, but having no money, as he could not bear to deceive
Hannibal and give up his countrymen, sent his son to Rome with orders to
sell part of his estate, and bring him the money at once to the camp. The
young man soon sold the land, and quickly returned. Fabius now sent the
ransom to Hannibal and recovered the prisoners, many of whom afterwards
offered to repay him; but he would take nothing, and forgave their debt to
them all.

VIII. After this the priests recalled him to Rome to perform certain
sacrifices. He now transferred the command to Minucius, and not merely
ordered him as dictator not to fight or entangle himself with the enemy, but
even gave him much advice and besought him not to do so, all of which
Minucius set at nought, and at once attacked the enemy. Once he observed
that Hannibal had sent the greater part of his army out to forage for
provisions, and, attacking the remaining troops, he drove them into their
intrenched camp, slew many, and terrified the rest, who feared that he might
carry the camp by assault. When Hannibal's forces collected again, Minucius
effected his retreat with safety, having excited both himself and the army with
his success, and filled them with a spirit of reckless daring. Soon an inflated
report of the action reached Rome. Fabius, when he heard of it, said that with
Minucius he feared success more than failure; but the populace were
delighted, and joyfully collected in the Forum, where Metilius the tribune
ascended the rostra, and made a speech glorifying Minucius, and accusing

Fabius not merely of remissness or cowardice, but of actual treachery, accusing also the other leading men of the city of having brought on the war from the very beginning in order to destroy the constitution; and he also charged them with having placed the city in the hands of one man as dictator, who by his dilatory proceedings would give Hannibal time to establish himself firmly and to obtain reinforcements from Africa to enable him to conquer Italy.

IX. When Fabius addressed the people, he did not deign to make any defence against the accusations of the tribune, but said that he should accomplish his sacrifices and sacred duties as quickly as possible, in order to return to the army and punish Minucius for having fought a battle against his orders. At this a great clamour was raised by the people, who feared for their favourite Minucius, for a dictator has power to imprison any man, and even to put him to death; and they thought that Fabius, a mild-tempered man now at last stirred up to wrath, would be harsh and inexorable. All refrained from speaking, but Metilius, having nothing to fear because of the privileges of his office of tribune (for that is the only office which does not lose its prerogatives on the election of a dictator, but remains untouched though all the rest are annulled), made a violent appeal to the people, begging them not to give up Minucius, nor allow him to be treated as Manlius Torquatus treated his son, who had him beheaded, although he had fought most bravely and gained a crown of laurel for his victory. He asked them to remove Fabius from his dictatorship, and to bestow it upon one who was able and willing to save the country. Excited as they were by these words, they yet did not venture upon removing Fabius from his post, in spite of their feeling against him, but they decreed that Minucius should conduct the war, having equal powers with the dictator, a thing never before done in Rome, but which occurred shortly afterwards, after the disaster at Cannae, when Marcus Junius was dictator in the camp, and, as many members of the Senate had perished in the battle, they chose another dictator, Fabius Buteo. However, he, after enrolling the new senators, on the same day dismissed his lictors, got rid of the crowd which escorted him, and mixed with the people in the Forum, transacting some business of his own as a private man.

X. Now the people, by placing Minucius on the same footing with the dictator, thought to humble Fabius, but they formed a very false estimate of his character. He did not reckon their ignorance to be his misfortune, but as Diogenes the philosopher, when some one said "They are deriding you," answered "But I am not derided," thinking that those alone are derided who are affected and disturbed by it, so Fabius quietly and unconcernedly endured all that was done, hereby affording an example of the truth of that philosophic maxim that a good and honest man can suffer no disgrace. Yet he grieved over the folly of the people on public grounds, because they had given a man of reckless ambition an opportunity for indulging his desire for battle; and, fearing that Minucius would be altogether beside himself with pride and vain glory, and would soon do some irreparable mischief, he left Rome unperceived by any one. On reaching the camp, he found Minucius no longer endurable, but insolent and overbearing, and demanding to have the sole command every other day. To this Fabius would not agree, but divided his forces with him, thinking it better to command a part than partly to command the whole of the army. He took the first and fourth legion, and left the second and third to Minucius, dividing the auxiliary troops equally with him.

As Minucius gave himself great airs, and was gratified at the thought that the greatest officer in the State had been humbled and brought low by his means, Fabius reminded him that if he judged aright, he would regard Hannibal, not Fabius, as his enemy; but that if he persisted in his rivalry with his colleagues, he must beware lest he, the honoured victor, should appear more careless of the safety and success of his countrymen, than he who had been overcome and ill-treated by them.

XI. Minucius thought all this to be merely the expression of the old man's jealousy. He took his allotted troops, and encamped apart from him. Hannibal was not ignorant of what was passing, and watched all their movements narrowly.

There was a hill between the two armies, which it was not difficult to take, which when taken would afford an army a safe position, and one well supplied with necessaries. The plain by which it was surrounded appeared to be perfectly smooth, but was nevertheless intersected with ditches and other hollow depressions. On this account Hannibal would not take the hill, although he could easily have done so, but preferred to leave it untouched, in order to draw the enemy into fighting for its possession. But as soon as he saw Fabius separated from Minucius, he placed during the night some troops in the depressions and hollows which we have mentioned, and at daybreak sent a few men to take the hill, in order to draw Minucius into fighting for it, in which he succeeded. Minucius first sent out his light troops, then his cavalry, and finally, seeing that Hannibal was reinforcing the troops on the hill, he came down with his entire force. He fought stoutly, and held his own against the soldiers on the hill, who shot their missiles at him; when Hannibal, seeing him thoroughly deceived, and offering an unprotected flank to the troops in the ambush, gave them the signal to charge. Upon this they attacked the Romans from all sides, rushing upon them with loud shouts, cutting off the rearmost men, and throwing the whole army into confusion and panic. Minucius himself lost heart and kept glancing first at one and then at another of his officers, none of whom ventured to stand their ground, but betook themselves in a confused mass to running away, a proceeding which brought them no safety, for the Numidian horsemen, as the day was now theirs, scoured the plain, encompassing the fugitives, and cut off all stragglers.

XII. Fabius had carefully watched the Romans, and saw in what danger they were. Conscious, it would seem, of what was going to happen, he had kept his troops under arms, and gained his information of what was going on, not from the reports of scouts, but from his own eyesight, from a convenient height outside of his camp. As soon as he saw the army surrounded and panic-stricken, and heard the cries of the Romans, who no longer fought, but were overcome by terror, and betaking themselves to flight, he smote his thigh and with a deep sigh, said to his friends, "By Hercules, now Minucius has ruined himself, quicker than I expected, and yet slower than his manoeuvres warranted." Having given orders to carry out the standards as quickly as possible, and for the whole army to follow, he said aloud, "My men, hurry on your march: think of Marcus Minucius; he is a brave man and loves his country. If he has made any mistake in his haste to drive out the enemy, we will blame him for that at another time." The appearance of Fabius scared and drove back the Numidians, who were slaughtering the fugitives in the plain; next he bore against those who were attacking the Roman rear, slaying all he met, though most of them, before they were cut off and treated as they had treated the Romans, betook themselves to flight. Hannibal seeing that the fortune of the battle was changed, and how Fabius himself, with a strength beyond his years, was forcing his way through the thickest battle up the hill to reach Minucius, withdrew his troops, and, sounding a retreat, led them back into his entrenched camp, affording a most seasonable relief to the Romans. It is said that Hannibal as he retired, spoke jokingly about Fabius to his friends in the words, "Did I not often warn you that the dark cloud which has so long brooded on the mountain tops, would at last break upon us with blasts of hail and storm?"

XIII. After the battle Fabius collected the spoils of such of the enemy as were slain, and drew off his forces without letting fall a single boastful or offensive expression about his colleague. But Minucius assembled his own troops, and thus addressed them, "My fellow-soldiers, it is beyond human skill to make no mistakes in matters of importance, but it is the part of a man of courage and sense to use his mistakes as warnings for the future. I myself confess that I have little fault to find with Fortune, and great reason to thank her; for in the space of one day I have learned what I never knew in all my previous life: that is, that I am not able to command others, but myself require a commander, and I have no ambition to conquer a man by whom it is more glorious to be defeated. The dictator is your leader in everything except in this, that I will lead you to express your thankfulness to him, by being the first to offer myself to him as an example of obedience and willingness to carry out his orders." After these words he ordered the eagles to be raised aloft and all the soldiers to follow them to the camp of Fabius. On entering it, he proceeded to the General's tent, to the surprise and wonderment of all. When Fabius was come out, he placed his standards in the ground before him, and himself addressed him as father in a loud voice, while his soldiers greeted those of Fabius by the name of their Patrons, which is the name by which freed men address those who have set them free. Silence being enforced, Minucius said: "Dictator, you have won two victories to-day, for you have conquered Hannibal by your bravery, and your colleague by your kindness and your generalship. By the one you have saved our lives, and by the other you have taught us our duty, for we have been disgracefully defeated by Hannibal, but beneficially and honourably by you. I call you my excellent father, having no more honourable appellation to bestow, since I owe a greater debt of gratitude to you than to him who begot me. To him I merely owe my single life, but to you I owe not only that but the lives of all my men." After these words he embraced Fabius, and the soldiers followed his example, embracing and kissing one another, so that the camp was full of joy and of most blessed tears.

XIV. After this, Fabius laid down his office, and consuls were again elected. Those who were first elected followed the defensive policy of Fabius, avoiding pitched battles with Hannibal, but reinforcing the allies and preventing defections. But when Terentius Varro was made consul, a man of low birth, but notorious for his rash temper and his popularity with the people, he made no secret, in his inexperience and self-confidence, of his intention of risking everything on one cast. He was always reiterating in his public speeches that under such generals as Fabius the war made no progress, whereas he would conquer the enemy the first day he saw him. By means of these boastful speeches he enrolled as soldiers such a multitude as the Romans had never before had at their disposal in any war, for there collected for the battle eighty-eight thousand men. This caused great disquietude to Fabius and other sensible Romans, who feared that if so many of the youth of Rome were cut off, the city would never recover from the blow. They addressed themselves therefore to the other consul, Paulus Aemilius, a man of great experience in war, but disagreeable to the people and afraid of them because he had once been fined by them. Fabius encouraged him to attempt to hold the other consul's rashness in check, pointing out that he would have to fight for his country's safety with Terentius Varro no less than with Hannibal. Varro, he said, will hasten to engage because he does not know his own strength, and Hannibal will do so because he knows his own weakness. "I myself, Paulus," said he, "am more to be believed than Varro as to the condition of Hannibal's affairs, and I am sure that if no battle takes place with him for a year, he will either perish in this country or be compelled to quit it; because even now, when he seems to be victorious and carrying all before him, not one of his enemies have come over to his side, while scarcely a third of the force which he brought from home is now surviving." It is said that Paulus answered as follows: "For my own part, Fabius, it is better for me to fall by the spears of the enemy than be again condemned by the votes of my own countrymen; but if public affairs are indeed in this critical situation, I will endeavour rather to approve myself a good general to you than to all those who are urging me to the opposite course." With this determination Paulus began the campaign.

XV. Varro induced his colleague to adopt the system of each consul holding the chief command on alternate days. He proceeded to encamp near Hannibal on the banks of the river Aufidus, close to the village of Cannae. At daybreak he showed the signal of battle (a red tunic displayed over the General's tent), so that the Carthaginians were at first disheartened at the daring of the consul and the great number of his troops, more than twice that of their own army. Hannibal ordered his soldiers to get under arms, and himself rode with a few others to a rising ground, from which he viewed the enemy, who were already forming their ranks. When one Gisco, a man of his own rank, said to him that the numbers of the enemy were wonderful, Hannibal with a serious air replied, "Another circumstance much more wonderful than this has escaped your notice, Gisco." When Gisco asked what it might be, Hannibal answered, "It is, that among all those men before you there is not one named Gisco." At this unexpected answer they all began to laugh, and as they came down the hill they kept telling this joke to all whom they met, so that the laugh became universal, and Hannibal's staff was quite overpowered with merriment. The Carthaginian soldiers seeing this took courage, thinking that their General must be in a position to despise his enemy if he could thus laugh and jest in the presence of danger.

XVI. In the battle Hannibal employed several stratagems: first, in securing the advantage of position, by getting the wind at his back, for it blew a hurricane, raising a harsh dust from the sandy plains, which rose over the Carthaginians and blew in the faces of the Romans, throwing them into confusion. Secondly, in his disposition of his forces he showed great skill. The best troops were placed on the wings, and the centre, which was composed of the worst, was made to project far beyond the rest of the line. The troops on each wing were told that when the Romans had driven in this part of the line and were so become partly enclosed, that each wing must turn inwards, and attack them in the flank and rear and endeavour to surround them. This was the cause of the greatest slaughter; for when the centre gave way, and made room for the pursuing Romans, Hannibal's line assumed a crescent form, and the commanders of the select battalions charging from the right and left of the Romans attacked them in flank, destroying every man except such as escaped being surrounded. It is related that a similar disaster befel the Roman cavalry. The horse of Paulus was wounded, and threw its rider, upon which man after man of his staff dismounted and came to help the consul on foot. The cavalry, seeing this, took it for a general order to dismount, and at once attacked the enemy on foot. Hannibal, seeing this, said, "I am better pleased at this than if he had handed them over to me bound hand and foot." This anecdote is found in those writers who have described the incidents of the battle in detail. Of the consuls, Varro escaped with a few followers to Venusia. Paulus, in the whirling eddies of the rout, covered with darts which still stuck in his wounds, and overwhelmed with sorrow at the defeat, sat down on a stone to await his death at the hands of the enemy. The blood with which his face and head were covered made it hard for any one to recognise him; but even his own friends and servants passed him by, taking no heed of him. Only Cornelius Lentulus, a young patrician, saw and recognised him. Dismounting from his horse and leading it up to him he begged him to take it and preserve his life, at a time when the State especially needed a wise ruler. But he refused, and forced the youth, in spite of his tears, to remount his horse. He then took him by the hand, saying, "Lentulus, tell Fabius Maximus, and bear witness yourself, that Paulus Aemilius followed his instructions to the last, and departed from nothing of what was agreed upon between us; but he was vanquished first by Varro, and secondly by Hannibal." Having given Lentulus these instructions he sent him away, and flinging himself on to the enemy's swords perished. In that battle it is reckoned that fifty thousand Romans fell, and four thousand were taken prisoners, besides not less than ten thousand who were taken after the battle in the camps of the two consuls.

XVII. After this immense success, Hannibal was urged by his friends to follow up his victory and enter Rome with the fugitives, promising that five days thereafter he should sup in the Capitol. It is not easy to say what reasons could have deterred him from doing so, and it seems rather as if some divinity prevented his march, and inspired him with the dilatory and timid policy which he followed. It is said that the Carthaginian, Barca, said to him, "You know how to win a victory, but do not know how to use one." Yet so great a change was effected by this victory that he, who before it had not possessed a single city, market, or harbour in Italy, and had to obtain his provisions with the utmost difficulty by plunder, having no regular base of operations, but merely wandering about with his army as though carrying on brigandage on a large scale, now saw nearly the whole of Italy at his feet. Some of the largest and most powerful States came over to him of their own accord, and he attacked and took Capua, the most important city next to Rome itself.

It would appear that the saying of Euripides, that "adversity tries our friends," applies also to good generals. That which before this battle was called Fabius's cowardice and remissness, was now regarded as more than human sagacity, and a foresight so wonderful as to be beyond belief. Rome at once centred her last hopes upon Fabius, taking refuge in his wisdom as men take sanctuary at an altar, believing his discretion to be the chief cause of her surviving this present crisis, even as in the old Gaulish troubles. For though he had been so cautious and backward at a time when there seemed to be no imminent danger, yet now when every one was giving way to useless grief and lamentation, he alone walked through the streets at a calm pace, with a composed countenance and kindly voice, stopped all womanish wailings and assemblies in public to lament their losses, persuaded the Senate to meet, and gave fresh courage to the magistrates, being really himself the moving spirit and strength of the State, which looked to him alone to command it.

XVIII. He placed guards at the gates to prevent the mob from quitting the city, and regulated the period of mourning, bidding every man mourn for thirty days in his own house, after which all signs of mourning were to be put away. As the feast of Ceres fell during those days, it was thought better to omit both the sacrifices and the processions than to have them marred by the consciousness of their misfortune, which would be painfully evident in the small number of worshippers and their downcast looks. However, everything that the soothsayers commanded to appease the anger of the gods and to expiate prodigies was carried out. Fabius Pictor, a relative of the great Fabius, was sent to Delphi, and of two of the Vestal virgins who were found to have been seduced, one was buried alive, as is the usual custom, while the other died by her own hand. Especially admirable was the spirit and the calm composure of the city when the consul Varro returned after his flight. He came humbled to the dust, as a man would who had been the cause of a terrible disaster, but at the gate the Senate and all the people went out to greet him. The chief men and the magistrates, amongst whom was Fabius, having obtained silence, spoke in praise of him "because he had not despaired of the State after such a calamity, but had come back to undertake the conduct of affairs and do what he could for his countrymen as one who thought they might yet be saved."

XIX. When they learned that Hannibal after the battle had turned away from Rome to other parts of Italy, the Romans again took courage and sent out armies and generals. Of those the most remarkable were Fabius Maximus and Claudius Marcellus, both equally admirable, but from an entirely different point of view. Marcellus, as has been related in his Life, was a man of activity and high spirit, rejoicing in a hand-to-hand fight, and just like the lordly warriors of Homer. With a truly venturesome audacity, he in his first battles outdid in boldness even the bold Hannibal himself; while Fabius, on the other hand, was convinced that his former reasoning was true, and believed that without any one fighting or even meddling with Hannibal, his army would wear itself out and consume away, just as the body of an athlete when overstrained and exerted soon loses its fine condition. For this reason Poseidonius calls Fabius the shield, and Marcellus the sword of Rome, because the steadiness of Fabius, combined with the warlike ardour of Marcellus, proved the saving of the state. Hannibal, frequently meeting Marcellus, who was like a raging torrent, had his forces shaken and weakened; while Fabius, like a deep quiet river kept constantly undermining them and wasting them away unperceived. Hannibal was at length reduced to such extremities that he was weary of fighting Marcellus, and feared Fabius even though he did not fight: for these were the persons whom he generally had to deal with, as praetors, consuls, or pro-consuls, for each of them was five times consul. He drew Marcellus, when consul for the fifth time, into an ambuscade; but although he tried every art and stratagem upon Fabius he could effect nothing, except once, when he very nearly succeeded in ruining him. He forged letters from the leading citizens of Metapontum, and then sent them to Fabius. These letters were to the effect that the city would surrender if he appeared before it, and that the conspirators were only waiting for his approach. Fabius was so much moved by these letters as to take a part of his army and commence a night march thither; but meeting with unfavourable omens on the way he turned back, and soon afterwards learned that the letters were a stratagem of Hannibal's, who was waiting for him under the city walls. This escape one may attribute to the favour of Heaven.

XX. In the case of revolts and insurrections among the subject cities and allies, Fabius thought it best to restrain them and discountenance their proceedings in a gentle manner, not treating every suspected person with harshness, or inquiring too strictly into every case of suspected disloyalty. It is said that a Marsian soldier, one of the chief men of the allies for bravery and nobility of birth, was discovered by Fabius to be engaged in organizing a revolt. Fabius showed no sign of anger, but admitted that he had not been treated with the distinction he deserved, and said that in the present instance he should blame his officers for distributing rewards more by favour than by merit; but that in future he should be vexed with him if he did not apply directly to himself when he had any request to make. Saying this, he presented him with a war horse and other marks of honour, so that thenceforth the man always served him with the utmost zeal and fidelity. He thought it a shame that trainers of horses and dogs should be able to tame the savage spirit of those animals by careful attention and education rather than by whips and clogs, and yet that a commander of men should not rely chiefly on mild and conciliatory measures, but treat them more harshly than gardeners treat the wild fig-trees, wild pears, and wild olives, which they by careful cultivation turn into trees bearing good fruit. His captains informed him that a certain soldier, a Lucanian by birth, was irregular and often absent from his duty. He made inquiries as to what his general conduct was. All agreed that it would be difficult to find a better soldier, and related some of his exploits. Fabius at length discovered that the cause of his absence was that he was in love with a certain girl, and that he continually ran the risk of making long journeys from the camp to meet her. Without the knowledge of the soldier, he sent and apprehended this girl, whom he concealed in his own tent. Then he invited the Lucanian to a private interview, and addressed him as follows:—"You have been observed frequently to pass the night outside of the camp, contrary to the ancient practice and discipline of the Roman army: but also, you have been observed to be a brave man. Your crime is atoned for by your valiant deeds, but for the future I shall commit you to the custody of another person." Then, to the astonishment of the soldier, he led the girl forward, joined their hands, and said: "This lady pledges her word that you will remain in the camp with us. You must prove by your conduct that it was not from any unworthy motive, for which she was the pretext, but solely through love for her that you used to desert your post." This is the story which is related about him.

XXI. Fabius obtained possession of Tarentum by treachery in the following manner. In his army was a young man of Tarentum whose sister was devotedly attached to him. Her lover was a Bruttian, and one of the officers of Hannibal's garrison there. This gave the Tarentine hopes of effecting his purpose, and with the consent of Fabius he went into the city, being commonly supposed to have run away to see his sister. For the first few days the Bruttian remained in his quarters, as she wished her amour with him not to be known to her brother. He then, however, said: "There was a rumour in the army that you were intimate with one of the chiefs of the garrison. Who is he? for if he is as they say, a man of courage and distinction—war, which throws everything into confusion, will care little what countryman he may be. Nothing is disgraceful which we cannot avoid; but it is a blessing, at a time when justice has no power, that we should yield to a not disagreeable necessity." Upon this the lady sent for her Bruttian admirer and introduced him to her brother. He, by encouraging the stranger in his passion, and assuring him that he would induce his sister to look favourably on it, had no difficulty in inducing the man, who was a mercenary soldier, to break his faith in expectation of the great rewards which he was promised by Fabius. This is the account given of the transaction by most writers, though some say that the lady by whose means the Bruttian was seduced from his allegiance was not a Tarentine, but a Bruttian by race, who was on intimate terms with Fabius; and that as soon as she discovered that a fellow-countryman and acquaintance of hers was in command of the Bruttian garrison, told Fabius of it, and by interviews which she had with the officer outside the walls gradually won him over to the Roman interests.

XXII. While these negotiations were in progress, Fabius, wishing to contrive something to draw Hannibal away, sent orders to the troops at Rhegium to ravage the Bruttian country and take Caulonia by storm. The troops at Rhegium were a body of eight thousand men, mostly deserters: and the most worthless of those disgraced soldiers whom Marcellus brought from Sicily, so that their loss would not cause any sorrow or harm to Rome; while he hoped that by throwing them out as a bait to Hannibal he might draw him away from Tarentum, as indeed he did. Hannibal at once started with his army to attack them, and meanwhile, on the sixth day after Fabius arrived before Tarentum, the young man having previously concerted measures with the Bruttian and his sister, came to him by night and told him that all was ready; knowing accurately and having well inspected the place where the Bruttian would be ready to open the gate and let in the besiegers. Fabius would not depend entirely upon the chance of treachery; but though he himself went quietly to the appointed place, the rest of the army attacked the town both by sea and land, with great clamour and disturbance, until, when most of the Tarentines had run to repel the assault, the Bruttian gave the word to Fabius, and, mounting his scaling ladders, he took the place. On this occasion Fabius seems to have acted unworthily of his reputation, for he ordered the chief Bruttian officers to be put to the sword, that it might not be said that he gained the place by treachery. However, he did not obtain this glory, and gained a reputation for faithlessness and cruelty. Many of the Tarentines were put to death, thirty thousand were sold for slaves, and the city was sacked by the soldiers. Three thousand talents were brought into the public treasury.

While everything else was being carried off, it is said that the clerk who was taking the inventory asked Fabius what his pleasure was with regard to the gods, meaning the statues and pictures. Fabius replied, "Let us leave the Tarentines their angry gods." However, he took the statue of Hercules from Tarentum and placed it in the Capitol, and near to it he placed a brazen statue of himself on horseback, acting in this respect much worse than Marcellus, or rather proving that Marcellus was a man of extraordinary mildness and generosity of temper, as is shown in his Life.

XXIII. Hannibal is said to have been hastening to relieve Tarentum, and to have been within five miles of it when it was taken. He said aloud: "So then, the Romans also have a Hannibal; we have lost Tarentum just as we gained it." Moreover in private he acknowledged to his friends that he had long seen that it was very difficult, and now thought it impossible for them to conquer Italy under existing circumstances.

Fabius enjoyed a second triumph for this success, which was more glorious than his first. He had contended with Hannibal and easily baffled all his attempts just as a good wrestler disengages himself with ease from the clutches of an antagonist whose strength is beginning to fail him; for Hannibal's army was no longer what it had been, being partly corrupted by luxury and plunder, and partly also worn out by unremitting toils and battles.

One Marcus Livius had been in command of Tarentum when Hannibal obtained possession of it. In spite of this, he held the citadel, from which he could not be dislodged, until Tarentum was recaptured by the Romans. This man was vexed at the honours paid to Fabius, and once, in a transport of envy and vain glory, he said before the Senate that he, not Fabius, was the real author of the recapture of the town. Fabius with a smile answered: "Very true; for if you had not lost the place, I could never have recaptured it."

XXIV. The Romans, among many other marks of respect for Fabius, elected his son consul. When he had entered on this office and was making some arrangements for the conduct of the war, his father, either because of his age and infirmities or else intending to try his son, mounted on horseback and rode towards him through the crowd of bystanders. The young man seeing him at a distance would not endure this slight, but sent a lictor to bid his father dismount and come on foot, if he wanted anything of the consul. Those present were vexed at this order, and looked on Fabius in silence, as if they thought that he was unworthily treated, considering his great reputation: but he himself instantly alighted, ran to his son, and embracing him, said: "You both think and act rightly, my son; for you know whom you command, and how great an office you hold. Thus it was that we and our ancestors made Rome great, by thinking less of our parents and of our children than of the glory of our country." It is even said to be true that the great grandfather of Fabius, although he had been consul five times, had finished several campaigns with splendid triumphs, and was one of the most illustrious men in Rome, yet acted as lieutenant to his son when consul in the field, and that in the subsequent triumph the son drove into Rome in a chariot and four, while he with the other officers followed him on horseback, glorying in the fact that although he was his son's master, and although he was and was accounted the first citizen in Rome, yet he submitted himself to the laws and the chief magistrate. Nor did he deserve admiration for this alone.

Fabius had the misfortune to lose his son, and this he bore with fortitude, as became a man of sense and an excellent parent. He himself pronounced the funeral oration which is always spoken by some relative on the deaths of illustrious men, and afterwards he wrote a copy of his speech and distributed it to his friends.

XXV. Cornelius Scipio meanwhile had been sent to Spain, where he had defeated the Carthaginians in many battles and driven them out of the country, and had also overcome many tribes, taken many cities, and done glorious deeds for Rome. On his return he was received with great honour and respect, and, feeling that the people expected some extraordinary exploit from him, he decided that it was too tame a proceeding to fight Hannibal in Italy, and determined to pour troops into Africa, attack Carthage, and transfer the theatre of war from Italy to that country. He bent all his energies to persuade the people to approve of this project, but was violently opposed by Fabius, who spread great alarm through the city, pointing out that it was being exposed to great danger by a reckless young man, and endeavouring by every means in his power to prevent the Romans from adopting Scipio's plan.

He carried his point with the Senate, but the people believed that he was envious of Scipio's prosperity and desired to check him, because he feared that if he did gain some signal success, and either put an end to the war altogether or remove it from Italy, he himself might be thought a feeble and dilatory general for not having finished the war in so many campaigns.

It appears that at first Fabius opposed him on grounds of prudence and caution, really fearing the dangers of his project, but that the contest gradually became a personal one, and he was moved by feelings of jealousy to hinder the rise of Scipio; for he tried to induce Crassus, Scipio's colleague, not to give up the province of Africa to Scipio, but if the expedition were determined on, to go thither himself, and he prevented his being supplied with funds for the campaign. Scipio being thus compelled to raise funds himself, obtained them from the cities in Etruria which were devoted to his interests. Crassus likewise was not inclined to quarrel with him, and was also obliged to remain in Italy by his office of Pontifex Maximus.

XXVI. Fabius now tried another method to oppose Scipio. He dissuaded the youth of the city from taking service with him by continually vociferating in all public meetings that Scipio not only was himself running away from Hannibal, but also was about to take all the remaining forces of Italy out of the country with him, deluding the young men with vain hopes, and so persuading them to leave their parents and wives, and their city too, while a victorious and invincible enemy was at its very gates. By these representations he alarmed the Romans, who decreed that Scipio should only use the troops in Sicily, and three hundred of the best men of his Spanish army. In this transaction Fabius seems to have acted according to the dictates of his own cautious disposition.

However, when Scipio crossed over into Africa, news came to Rome at once of great and glorious exploits performed and great battles won. As substantial proof of these there came many trophies of war, and the king of Numidia as a captive. Two camps were burned and destroyed, with great slaughter of men, and loss of horses and war material in the flames. Embassies also were sent to Hannibal from Carthage, begging him in piteous terms to abandon his fruitless hopes in Italy and come home to help them, while in Rome the name of Scipio was in every man's mouth because of his successes. At this period Fabius proposed that a successor to Scipio should be sent out, without having any reason to allege for it except the old proverb that it is dangerous to entrust such important operations to the luck of one man, because it is hard for the same man always to be lucky. This proposal of his offended most of his countrymen, who thought him a peevish and malignant old man, or else that he was timid and spiritless from old age, and excessively terrified at Hannibal; for, even when Hannibal quitted Italy and withdrew his forces, Fabius would not permit the joy of his countrymen to be unmixed with alarm, as he informed them that now the fortunes of Rome were in a more critical situation than ever, because Hannibal would be much more to be dreaded in Africa under the walls of Carthage itself, where he would lead an army, yet reeking with the blood of many Roman dictators, consuls and generals, to attack Scipio. By these words the city was again filled with terror, and although the war had been removed to Africa yet its alarms seemed to have come nearer to Rome.

XXVII. However Scipio, after no long time, defeated Hannibal in a pitched battle and crushed the pride of Carthage under foot. He gave the Romans the enjoyment of a success beyond their hopes, and truly
"Restored the city, shaken by the storm."

Fabius Maximus did not survive till the end of the war, nor did he live to hear of Hannibal's defeat, or see the glorious and lasting prosperity of his country, for about the time when Hannibal left Italy he fell sick and died.

The Thebans, we are told, buried Epameinondas at the public expense, because he died so poor that they say nothing was found in his house except an iron spit. Fabius was not honoured by the Romans with a funeral at the public expense, yet every citizen contributed the smallest Roman coin towards the expenses, not that he needed the money, but because they buried him as the father of the people, so that in his death he received the honourable respect which he had deserved in his life.

Comparison of Perikles and Fabius Maximus.

I. Such is the story of these men's lives. As they both gave many proofs of ability in war and politics, let us first turn our attention to their warlike exploits. And here we must notice that Perikles found the Athenian people at the height of their power and prosperity, so that from the flourishing condition of the State it could scarcely meet with any great disaster, whereas Fabius performed his great services to Rome when it was in the last extremity of danger, and did not merely, like Perikles, confirm the prosperity of his country, but greatly improved it, having found it in a lamentable condition. Moreover, the successes of Kimon, the victories of Myronides and Leokrates, and the many achievements of Tolmides rather gave Perikles when in chief command an occasion for public rejoicing and festivity, than any opportunity for either conquests abroad or defensive wars at home. Fabius, on the other hand, had before his eyes the spectacle of many defeats and routs of Roman armies, of many consuls and generals fallen in battle, of lakes, plains and forests filled with the bodies of the slain, and of rivers running with blood. Yet with his mature and unbending intellect he undertook to extricate Rome from these dangers, and as it were by his own strength alone supported the State, so that it was not utterly overwhelmed by these terrible disasters. Nevertheless it would appear not to be so hard a task to manage a State in adversity, when it is humble and is compelled by its misfortunes to obey wise counsellors, as it is to check and bridle a people excited and arrogant with good fortune, which was especially the case with Perikles and the Athenians. On the other hand, considering the terrible nature of the blows which had fallen on the Romans, Fabius must have been a great and strong-minded man not to be disconcerted by them, but still to be able to carry out the policy upon which he had determined.

II. We may set the capture of Samos by Perikles against the retaking of Tarentum by Fabius, and also the conquest of Euboea by the one against that of the Campanian cities by the other, though Capua itself was recovered by the consuls, Fulvius and Appius. Fabius seems never to have fought a pitched battle, except that one which gained him his first triumph, while Perikles set up nine trophies for victories by sea and land. But again, there is no action of Perikles which can be compared to that of Fabius when he snatched away Minucius from the grasp of Hannibal, and saved an entire Roman army from destruction. That was an exploit glorious for the courage, generalship, and kindness of heart displayed by Fabius; but, on the other hand Perikles, made no such blunder as did Fabius, when out-generalled by Hannibal with the cattle. Here, although Fabius caught his enemy in a defile which he had entered by chance, yet he let him escape by night, and next day found his tardy movements outstripped, and himself defeated by the man whom he had just before so completely cut off. If it be the part of a good general, not merely to deal with the present, but to make conjectures about the future, we may remark that the Peloponnesian war ended just as Perikles had foretold, for the Athenians frittered away their strength; whereas the Romans, contrary to the expectation of Fabius, by sending Scipio to attack Carthage gained a complete victory, not by chance, but by the skill of their general and the courage of their troops, who overthrew the enemy in a pitched battle. Thus the one was proved to be right by the misfortunes of his country, and the other proved to be wrong by its success, indeed it is just as much a fault in a general to receive a check from want of foresight as to let slip an opportunity through diffidence; and both these failings, excess of confidence and want of confidence, are common to all except the most consummate generals. Thus much for their military talents.

III. In political matters, the Peloponnesian war is a great blot upon the fame of Perikles; for it is said to have been caused by his refusal to yield the least point to the Lacedaemonians. I do not imagine, however, that Fabius Maximus would have yielded anything to the Carthaginians, but would have bravely risked any danger in defence of the Roman Empire. The kind treatment of Minucius by Fabius and his mildness of character contrast very favourably with the bitter party feud of Perikles with Kimon and Thucydides, who were men of good birth, and belonging to the conservative party, and whom Perikles drove into exile by the ostracism. Then, too, the power of Perikles was much greater than that of Fabius. Perikles would not permit the State to suffer disaster because of the bad management of her generals. One of them alone, Tolmides, succeeded in having his own way, against the wishes of Perikles, and perished in an attack on the Boeotians, while all the rest, because of his immense influence and power, submitted themselves to his authority and regulated their proceedings by his ideas. Whereas Fabius, although he could avoid any error in managing his own army, was thwarted by his being powerless to control the movements of other generals.

For the Romans would not have suffered so many defeats if Fabius had enjoyed the same power that Perikles did in Athens. As to their generosity with regard to money, the one was remarkable for never receiving bribes, while the other spent much on ransoming prisoners at his own expense; although this was not much above six talents, while it is hard for any one to tell the amount of money which Perikles might have taken from foreign princes and Greek allied states, all of which he refused and kept his hands clean. As to the great public works, the construction of the temples, and of the public buildings with which Perikles adorned Athens, the whole of the edifices in Rome together, before the time of the emperors, are not worthy to be compared to them, for they far surpassed them both in largeness of scale and in beauty of design.

Life of Alkibiades.

I. The pedigree of Alkibiades is said to begin with Eurysakes the son of Ajax, while on the mother's side he descended from Alkmaeon, being the son of Deinomache, the daughter of Megakles. His father Kleinias fought bravely at Artemisium in a trireme fitted out at his own expense, and subsequently fell fighting the Boeotians, in the battle of Koronea. Alkibiades after this was entrusted to Perikles and Ariphron, the two sons of Xanthippus, who acted as his guardians because they were the next of kin. It has been well remarked that the friendship of Sokrates for him did not a little to increase his fame, seeing that Nikias, Demosthenes, Lamakus, Phormio, Thrasybulus, and Theramenes, were all men of mark in his lifetime, and yet we do not know the name of the mother of any one of them, while we know the name even of the nurse of Alkibiades, who was a Laconian, named Amykla, and that of Zopyrus, his paedagogus, one of which pieces of information we owe to Antisthenes, and the other to Plato. As to the beauty of Alkibiades, it is not necessary to say anything except that it was equally fascinating when he was a boy, a youth, and a man. The saying of Euripides, that all beauties have a beautiful autumn of their charms, is not universally true, but it was so in the case of Alkibiades and of a few other persons because of the symmetry and vigour of their frames. Even his lisp is said to have added a charm to his speech, and to have made his talk more persuasive. His lisp is mentioned by Aristophanes in the verses in which he satirises Theorus, in which Alkibiades calls him Theolus, for he pronounced the letter r like l. Archippus also gives a sneering account of the son of Alkibiades, who, he said, swaggered in his walk, trailing his cloak, that he might look as like his father as possible, and

"Bends his affected neck, and lisping speaks."

II. His character, in the course of his varied and brilliant career, developed many strange inconsistencies and contradictions. Emulation and love of distinction were the most prominent of his many violent passions, as is clear from the anecdotes of his childhood. Once when hard pressed in wrestling, rather than fall, he began to bite his opponent's hands. The other let go his hold, and said, "You bite, Alkibiades, like a woman." "No," said he, "like a lion." While yet a child, he was playing at knucklebones with other boys in a narrow street, and when his turn came to throw, a loaded waggon was passing. He at first ordered the driver to stop his team because his throw was to take place directly in the path of the waggon. Then as the boor who was driving would not stop, the other children made way; but Alkibiades flung himself down on his face directly in front of the horses, and bade him drive on at his peril. The man, in alarm, now stopped his horses, and the others were terrified and ran up to him.

In learning he was fairly obedient to all his teachers, except in playing the flute, which he refused to do, declaring that it was unfit for a gentleman. He said that playing on the harp or lyre did not disfigure the face, but that when a man was blowing at a flute, his own friends could scarcely recognise him. Besides, the lyre accompanies the voice of the performer, while the flute takes all the breath of the player and prevents him even from speaking. "Let the children of the Thebans," he used to say, "learn to play the flute, for they know not how to speak; but we Athenians according to tradition have the goddess Athene (Minerva) for our patroness, and Apollo for our tutelary divinity; and of these the first threw away the flute in disgust, and the other actually flayed the flute player Marsyas." With such talk as this, between jest and earnest, Alkibiades gave up flute-playing himself, and induced his friends to do so, for all the youth of Athens soon heard and approved of Alkibiades's derision of the flute and those who learned it. In consequence of this the flute went entirely out of fashion, and was regarded with contempt.

III. In Antiphon's scandalous chronicle, we read that Alkibiades once ran away from home to the house of one of his admirers.

Ariphron, his other guardian, proposed to have him cried; but Perikles forbade it, saying that, if he was dead, he would only be found one day sooner because of it, while if he was safe, he would be disgraced for life. Antiphon also tells us that he killed one of his servants by striking him with a club, at the gymnasium of Sibyrtus. But perhaps we ought not to believe these stories, which were written by an enemy with the avowed purpose of defaming his character.

IV. His youthful beauty soon caused him to be surrounded with noble admirers, but the regard of Sokrates for him is a great proof of his natural goodness of disposition, which that philosopher could discern in him, but which he feared would wither away like a faded flower before the temptations of wealth and position, and the mass of sycophants by whom he was soon beset. For no one ever was so enclosed and enveloped in the good things of this life as Alkibiades, so that no breath of criticism or free speech could ever reach him. Yet, with all these flatterers about him, trying to prevent his ever hearing a word of wholesome advice or reproof, he was led by his own goodness of heart to pay special attention to Sokrates, to whom he attached himself in preference to all his rich and fashionable admirers.

He soon became intimate with Sokrates, and when he discovered that this man did not wish to caress and admire him, but to expose his ignorance, search out his faults, and bring down his vain unreasoning conceit, he then

     "Let fall his feathers like a craven cock."

He considered that the conversation of Sokrates was really a divine instrument for the discipline and education of youth; and thus learning to despise himself, and to admire his friend, charmed with his good nature, and full of reverence for his virtues, he became insensibly in love with him, though not as the world loveth; so that all men were astonished to see him dining with Sokrates, wrestling with him, and sharing his tent, while he treated all his other admirers with harshness and some even with insolence, as in the case of Anytus the son of Anthemion. This man, who was an admirer of Alkibiades, was entertaining a party of friends, and asked him to come. Alkibiades refused the invitation, but got drunk that night at a riotous party at his own house, in which state he proceeded in a disorderly procession to Anytus. Here he looked into the room where the guests were, and seeing the tables covered with gold and silver drinking-cups, ordered his slaves to carry away half of them, and then, without deigning to enter the room, went home again. Anytus' guests were vexed at this, and complained of his being so arrogantly and outrageously treated. "Say rather, considerately," answered Anytus, "for although he might have taken them all, yet he has left us the half of them."

V. In this same way he used to treat his other admirers, with the exception, it is said, of one of the resident aliens, a man of small means who sold all that he had and carried the money, amounting to about a hundred staters, to Alkibiades, begging him to accept it. Alkibiades laughed at him, and invited him to dinner. After dinner he gave him back his money, and ordered him next day to go and overbid those who were about to bid for the office of farmer of the taxes. The poor man begged to be excused, because the price was several talents, but Alkibiades threatened to have him beaten if he did not do so, for he had some private grudge of his own against the farmers of the taxes. Accordingly the alien went next morning early into the market-place and bid a talent. The tax farmers now clustered round him angrily, bidding him name some one as security, imagining that he would not be able to find one. The poor man was now in great trouble and was about to steal away, when Alkibiades, who was at some distance, called out to the presiding magistrates, "Write down my name. I am his friend, and I will be surety for him." On hearing this, the tax farmers were greatly embarrassed, for their habit was to pay the rent of each year with the proceeds of the next, and they saw no way of doing so in this instance. Consequently they begged the man to desist from bidding, and offered him money. Alkibiades would not permit him to take less than a talent, and when this was given him he let him go. This was the way in which he did him a kindness.

VI. The love of Sokrates, though he had many rivals, yet overpowered them all, for his words touched the heart of Alkibiades and moved him to tears. Sometimes his flatterers would bribe him by the offer of some pleasure, to which he would yield and slip away from Sokrates, but he was then pursued like a fugitive slave by the latter, of whom he stood in awe, though he treated every one else with insolence and contempt. Kleanthes used to say that Sokrates's only hold upon him was through his ears, while he scorned to meddle with the rest of his body. And indeed Alkibiades was very prone to pleasure, as one would gather from what Thucydides says on the subject. Those too who played on his vanity and love of distinction induced him to embark on vast projects before he was ripe for them, assuring him that as soon as he began to take a leading part in politics, he would not only eclipse all the rest of the generals and orators, but would even surpass Perikles in power and renown. But just as iron which has been softened in the fire is again hardened by cold, and under its influence contracts its expanded particles, so did Sokrates, when he found Alkibiades puffed up by vain and empty conceit, bring him down to his proper level by his conversation, rendering him humble minded by pointing out to him his many deficiencies.

VII. After he had finished his education, he went into a school, and asked the master for a volume of Homer. When the master said that he possessed none of Homer's writings, he struck him with his fist, and left him. Another schoolmaster told him that he had a copy of Homer corrected by himself. "Do you," asked he, "you who are able to correct Homer, teach boys to read! One would think that you could instruct men."

One day he wished to speak to Perikles, and came to his house. Hearing that he was not at leisure, but was engaged in considering how he was to give in his accounts to the Athenians, Alkibiades, as he went away, said, "It would be better if he considered how to avoid giving in any accounts at all to the Athenians."

While yet a lad he served in the campaign of Potidaea, where he shared the tent of Sokrates, and took his place next him in the ranks. In an obstinate engagement they both showed great courage, and when Alkibiades was wounded and fell to the ground, Sokrates stood in front of him, defending him, and so saved his life and arms from the enemy. Properly, therefore, the prize for valour belonged to Sokrates; but when the generals appeared anxious to bestow it upon Alkibiades because of his great reputation, Sokrates, who wished to encourage his love for glory, was the first to give his testimony in his favour, and to call upon them to crown him as victor and to give him the suit of armour which was the prize. And also at the battle of Delium, when the Athenians were routed, Alkibiades, who was on horseback, when he saw Sokrates retreating on foot with a few others, would not ride on, but stayed by him and defended him, though the enemy were pressing them and cutting off many of them. These things, however, happened afterwards.

VIII. He once struck Hipponikus, the father of Kallias, a man of great wealth and noble birth, a blow with his fist, not being moved to it by anger, or any dispute, but having agreed previously with his friends to do so for a joke. When every one in the city cried out at his indecent and arrogant conduct, Alkibiades next morning at daybreak came to the house of Hipponikus, knocked, and came to him. Here he threw off his cloak, and offered him his body, bidding him flog him and punish him for what he had done. Hipponikus, however, pardoned him, and they became friends, so much so that Hipponikus chose him for the husband of his daughter Hipparete. Some writers say that not Hipponikus but Kallias his son gave Hipparete to Alkibiades to wife, with a dowry of ten talents, and that when her first child was born Alkibiades demanded and received ten more talents, as if he had made a previous agreement to that effect. Upon this Kallias, fearing that Alkibiades might plot against his life, gave public notice in the assembly that if he died childless, he would leave his house and all his property to the State.

Hipparete was a quiet and loving wife, but was so constantly insulted by her husband's amours with foreign and Athenian courtesans, that she at length left his house and went to her brother's. Alkibiades took no heed of this, but continued in his debauchery.

It was necessary for her to deliver her petition for separation to the magistrate with her own hand, and when she came to do so, Alkibiades laid hold of her, and took her home with him through the market-place, no one daring to oppose him and take her from him. She lived with him until her death, which took place not long after Alkibiades sailed for Ephesus. In this instance his violence does not seem to have been altogether lawless or without excuse, for the object of the law in making a wife appear in person in public seems to be that she may have an opportunity of meeting her husband and making up her quarrel with him.

IX. He had a dog of remarkable size and beauty, for which he had paid seventy minae. It had a very fine tail, which he cut off. When his friends blamed him, and said that every one was sorry for the dog and angry with him for what he had done, he laughed and said, "Then I have succeeded; for I wish the Athenians to gossip about this, for fear they should say something worse about me."

X. It is said that his first public act was on the occasion of a voluntary subscription for the State. He did not intend doing anything of the sort, but as he was passing he heard a great noise, and finding that voluntary subscriptions were being made, went and subscribed. The people cheered and applauded him, at which he was so much delighted as to forget a quail which he had in his cloak. When it escaped and ran about bewildered, the Athenians applauded all the more, and many rose and chased it. It was caught by the pilot Antiochus, who restored it, and became one of Alkibiades's greatest friends. Starting with great advantages from his noble birth, his wealth, his recognised bravery in battle, and his many friends and relatives, he relied upon nothing so much as on his eloquence for making himself popular and influential. His rhetorical powers are borne witness to by the comic dramatists; and the greatest of orators, Demosthenes, in his speech against Meidias, speaks of Alkibiades as being most eloquent, besides his other charms. If we are to believe Theophrastus, who has inquired more diligently into these various tales than any one else, Alkibiades excelled all men of his time in readiness of invention and resource. However, as he wished not merely to speak to the purpose, but also to clothe his thoughts in the most appropriate language, he did not always succeed in combining the two, and often hesitated and stopped, seeking for the right word, and not continuing his speech until it occurred to him.

XI. He was renowned for his stud, and for the number of his racing chariots. No other person, king or commoner, ever entered seven four-horse chariots for the race at Olympia except Alkibiades. His winning the first, second, and fourth prizes with these, as Thucydides tells us, though Euripides says that he won the third also, excels in glory any other successes by other persons in these races. The poem of Euripides runs as follows:
"Son of Kleinias, thee I sing, In truth it is a noble thing, First, second, and third place To win in chariot race, To hear the herald thrice thy name proclaim, And thrice to bear away the olive crown of fame."

XII. His success was rendered all the more conspicuous by the manner in which the various States vied with one another in showing him honour. Ephesus pitched a magnificent tent for his accommodation, Chios furnished his horses with provender, and himself with animals for sacrifice; and Lesbos supplied him with wine, and every thing else necessary for giving great entertainments. Yet even at this brilliant period of his life he incurred discredit, either by his own fault or through the spite of his enemies. The story is that an Athenian named Diomedes, a respectable man and a friend of Alkibiades, was desirous of winning a victory at Olympia. Hearing that there was a chariot and four which belonged to the city of Argos, and knowing that Alkibiades had great influence and many friends in that place, he persuaded him to buy the chariot for him. Alkibiades, however, bought the chariot and entered it for the race as his own, leaving Diomedes to call upon heaven and earth to witness his ill-treatment. It appears that a trial took place about this matter, and Isokrates wrote a speech about this chariot in defence of the son of Alkibiades, in which Tisias, not Diomedes, is mentioned as the prosecutor.

XIII. When, as a mere boy, Alkibiades plunged into political life, he at once surpassed most of the statesmen of the age. His chief rivals were Phaeax, the son of Erasistratus, and Nikias, the son of Nikeratus, the latter a man advanced in life, and bearing the reputation of being an excellent general, while the former, like Alkibiades himself, was a young man of good family, just rising into notice, but inferior to him in many respects, particularly in oratory. Though affable and persuasive in private circles, he could not speak equally well in public, for he was, as Eupolis says,

"At conversation best of men, at public speaking worst."

In a certain attack on Alkibiades and Phaeax, we find, among other charges, Alkibiades accused of using the gold and silver plate of the city of Athens as his own for his daily use.

There was at Athens one Hyperbolus, of the township of Peirithois, whom Thucydides mentions as a worthless man, and one who was constantly ridiculed by the comic dramatists. From his utter disregard of what was said of him, and his carelessness for his honour, which, though it was mere shameless impudence and apathy, was thought by some to show firmness and true courage, he was pleasing to no party, but frequently made use of by the people when they wished to have a scurrilous attack made upon those in power. At this time he was about to resort to the proceeding called ostracism, by which from time to time the Athenians force into exile those citizens who are remarkable for influence and power, rather because they envy them than because they fear them.

But as it was clear that one of the three, Nikias, Phaeax, and Alkibiades, would be ostracised, Alkibiades combined their several parties, arranged matters with Nikias, and turned the ostracism against Hyperbolus himself. Some say that it was not Nikias but Phaeax with whom Alkibiades joined interest, and that with the assistance of his political party he managed to expel Hyperbolus, who never expected any such treatment; for before that time this punishment had never been extended to low persons of no reputation, as Plato, the comic dramatist, says in the lines where he mentions Hyperbolus:

"Full worthy to be punished though he be, Yet ostracism's not for such as he."

We have elsewhere given a fuller account of this affair.

XIV. Alkibiades was dissatisfied at the respect shown for Nikias, both by enemies of the State and by the citizens of Athens. Alkibiades was the proxenus of the Lacedaemonians at Athens, and paid especial court to those Spartans who had been captured at Pylos; yet, when the Lacedaemonians discovered that it was chiefly by Nikias's means that they obtained peace, and recovered their prisoners, they were lavish of their attentions to him. The common phrase among the Greeks of that time was that Perikles had begun the war, and Nikias had finished it; and the peace was usually called the peace of Nikias. Alkibiades, irritated beyond measure at his rival's success, began to meditate how he could destroy the existing treaty. He perceived that the Argives, hating and fearing Sparta, wished to break off from it, and he encouraged them by secret assurances of an Athenian alliance, and also both by his agents and in person he urged the leading men not to give way to the Lacedaemonians, or yield any points to them, but to turn to Athens, and await their co-operation, for the Athenians, he said, already began to regret that they had made peace at all, and would soon break it.

When the Lacedaemonians made an alliance with the Boeotians, and delivered up Panaktus to the Athenians in a dismantled condition, not with its walls standing, as they ought to have done, Alkibiades exasperated the rage of the Athenians by his speeches, and raised a clamour against Nikias by the plausible accusation that he, when general, had hung back from capturing the enemy's forces which were cut off in the island of Sphakteria, and that when they had been captured by another, he had released them and restored them to their homes, in order to gain the favour of the Lacedaemonians. And for all that, although he was such a friend of the Lacedaemonians, he had not dissuaded them from forming alliances with Corinth and with the Boeotians, while he prevented the Athenians from becoming allies of any Greek State which might wish it, if the step did not happen to please the Lacedaemonians.

Upon this, while Nikias was smarting under these accusations, ambassadors arrived from Lacedaemon with instructions to propose reasonable terms, and announcing that they came with full powers to conclude the negotiations for peace on an equitable basis. The Senate received them willingly, and next day they were to appear before the people. Fearing that they would succeed, Alkibiades contrived to obtain a private interview with them, in which he addressed them as follows: "What is this that you do, men of Sparta! Do you not know that the Senate always treats those who appear before it in a kindly and reasonable manner, but the people are always full of pride and ambition? If you say that you have plenary powers, they will bewilder you by their violence and force great concessions from you. So come, cease this folly, if you wish to negotiate with the Athenians in a moderate way, and not to be forced into conceding points against your will. Discuss all the points at issue, but do not say that you have full power to decide them. I will do my best to assist you, as a friend to Lacedaemon." After these words he confirmed his promise by an oath, and thus completely detached them from Nikias and left them trusting him only, and admiring him as a man of remarkable sense and intelligence. On the following day the people assembled, and the ambassadors appeared before them. When they were politely asked by Alkibiades in what capacity they came, they said that they were not plenipotentiaries. Immediately upon this Alkibiades assailed them with furious invective, as though they, not he, were in the wrong, calling them faithless equivocators, who had not come either to speak or to do anything honest. The Senate was vexed at its treatment, and the people were excessively enraged, while Nikias, who knew nothing of the trick, was astounded and covered with confusion at the conduct of the ambassadors.

XV. The Lacedaemonian alliance being put an end to by this means, Alkibiades, who was now elected one of the generals of Athens, at once formed an alliance with Argos, Elis and Mantinea. No one approved of the way in which he effected this, but still the result was very important, as it agitated all the States in Peloponnesus, and set them against one another, brought so many men into line to fight the Lacedaemonians at the battle of Mantinea, and removed the scene of conflict so far from Athens, that the Lacedaemonians could gain no great advantage by victory, whereas if they failed, they would have to struggle for their very existence. After this battle the select regiment at Argos, called the "Thousand," endeavoured to overthrow the government and establish themselves as masters of the city; and with the assistance of the Lacedaemonians they destroyed the constitution. But the people took up arms again, and defeated the usurpers; and Alkibiades coming to their aid, made the victory of the popular side more complete. He persuaded the citizens to build long walls down to the sea, and to trust entirely to the Athenian naval forces for support. He even sent them carpenters and stonemasons from Athens, and showed great zeal on their behalf, which tended to increase his personal interest and power no less than that of his country. He advised the people of Patrae also to join their city to the sea by long walls; and when some one said to the people of Patrae, that the Athenians would swallow them up, he answered, "Perhaps they may, but it will be by degrees and beginning with the feet, whereas the Lacedaemonians will seize them by the head and do it at once."

However, Alkibiades ever pressed the Athenians to establish their empire by land as well as by sea, reminding them of the oath which the young men take in the Temple of Agraulos, and which it was their duty to confirm by their deeds. This oath is, that they will regard wheat, barley, vines and olives as the boundaries of Attica, by which it is hinted that they ought to make all cultivated and fruitful lands their own.

XVI. In the midst of all this display of political ability, eloquence, and statesmanlike prudence, he lived a life of great luxury, debauchery, and profuse expenditure, swaggering through the market-place with his long effeminate mantle trailing on the ground. He had the deck of his trireme cut away, that he might sleep more comfortably, having his bed slung on girths instead of resting on the planks; and he carried a shield not emblazoned with the ancestral bearings of his family, but with a Cupid wielding a thunderbolt. The leading men of Athens viewed his conduct with disgust and apprehension, fearing his scornful and overbearing manner, as being nearly allied to the demeanour of a despot, while Aristophanes has expressed the feeling of the people towards him in the line,

"They love, they hate, they cannot live without him."

And again he alludes to him in a bitterer spirit in the verse:
"A lion's cub 'tis best you should not rear, For if you do, your master he'll appear."

His voluntary contributions of money to the State, his public exhibitions and services, and displays of munificence, which could not be equalled in splendour, his noble birth, his persuasive speech, his strength, beauty, and bravery, and all his other shining qualities, combined to make the Athenians endure him, and always give his errors the mildest names, calling them youthful escapades and honourable emulation. For example, he locked up Agatharchus the painter, and when he had painted his house let him go with a present. He boxed Taurea's ears because he was exhibiting shows in rivalry with him, and contending with him for the prize. And he even took one of the captive Melian women for his mistress, and brought up a child which he had by her. This was thought to show his good nature; but this term cannot be applied to the slaughter of all the males above puberty in the island of Melos, which was done in accordance with a decree promoted by Alkibiades.

When Aristophon painted the courtesan Nemea embracing Alkibiades, all men eagerly crowded to see it; but older men were vexed at these things too, thinking them only fit for despots, and considering them to be open violations of the laws. Indeed Archestratus spoke very much to the purpose when he said that Greece could not bear more than one Alkibiades. Once, when Alkibiades had made a successful speech in the public assembly, and was being conducted home in triumph by his friends, Timon the misanthrope met him, and did not get out of his way, as he did to every one else, but came up to him and took him by the hand, saying, "Go on, my boy, increase in glory; for your increase will bring ruin to all this crowd." Some laughed, some cursed him, but others took his words to heart. So various were the opinions formed about Alkibiades, because of the inconsistency of his character.

XVII. Even during the lifetime of Perikles, the Athenians had a hankering after Sicily, and after his death they endeavoured to obtain possession of it, by sending troops to the assistance of those cities which were oppressed by the Syracusans, and thus paving the way for a greater armament. It was, however, Alkibiades who fanned their desires into a flame, and who persuaded them to abandon these half-hearted attempts, to proceed with a great force to the island, and to endeavour to subdue it. He raised great expectations among the people, but his own aspirations were far more entensive; for he regarded the conquest of Sicily not merely as an end, but as a stepping-stone to greater things. While Nikias was dissuading the people from the attempt, on the ground that it would be a difficult matter to capture the city of Syracuse, Alkibiades was dreaming of Carthage and Libya; and after these were gained, he meditated the conquest of Italy and of Peloponnesus, regarding Sicily as little more than a convenient magazine and place of arms. He greatly excited the younger Athenians by his vast designs, and they listened eagerly to the marvellous stories of the old who had served in that country; so that many of them would spend their time sitting in the gymnasia and public seats, drawing sketches of the shape of the island of Sicily, and of the position of Libya and Carthage. It is said that Sokrates the philosopher, and Meton the astronomer, did not expect that the state would gain any advantage from this expedition; the former probably receiving a presentiment of disaster, as was his wont, from his familiar spirit. Meton either made calculations which led him to fear what was about to happen, or else gathered it from the art of prophecy. He feigned madness, and seizing a torch, attempted to set his house on fire. Some say that Meton made no pretence of madness, but that he burned down his house one night, and next morning came and besought the Athenians, after such a misfortune, to exempt his son from serving with the expedition. Thus he deceived his fellow citizens and carried his point.

XVIII. Nikias, much against his will, was chosen to lead the expedition. His unwillingness was in a great measure due to the fact that Alkibiades was to act as his colleague; for the Athenians thought that the war would be conducted better if the rashness of Alkibiades was tempered by the prudence of Nikias, because the third general, Lamachus, although advanced in years, yet had the reputation of being no less daring and reckless a soldier than Alkibiades himself.

When the public assembly were debating about the number of the troops and the preparation for the armament, Nikias made another attempt to oppose the whole measure and to put a stop to the war. Alkibiades, however, took the other side and carried all before him. The orator Demostratus moved, that the generals should be empowered to demand whatever stores and war material they pleased, and have absolute power to carry on the war at their own discretion. This was agreed to by the people, and all was ready for setting sail, when unlucky omens occurred. The festival of Adonis took place at that very time, and during it the women carry about in many parts of the city figures dressed like corpses going to be buried, and imitate the ceremony of a funeral by tearing their hair and singing dirges. And besides this, the mutilation of the Hermae in one night, when all of them had their faces disfigured, disturbed many even of those who, as a rule, despised such things. A story was put about that the Corinthians, of whom the Syracusans were a colony, had done it, hoping that such an evil omen might make the Athenians either postpone or give up their expedition. But the people paid no heed to this insinuation, and still less to those who argued that there was no omen in the matter at all, but that it was the work of extravagant young men after their wine. They regarded the incident with feelings of rage and fear, imagining that it proved the existence of an organised plot aimed at greater matters. Both the Senate and the General Assembly met several times during the next few days, and inquired sharply into every thing that could throw any light upon it.

XIX. During this time, Androkles, a popular speaker, brought forward several slaves and resident aliens, who charged Alkibiades and his friends with mutilating certain other statues, and with parodying the ceremonies of initiation to the sacred mysteries when in their cups. They said that the part of the Herald was taken by Theodorus, that of the Torch-bearer by Polytion, and that of Hierophant by Alkibiades himself, while the rest of the company were present and were initiated, and were addressed by them as Mysts, which means persons who have been initiated into the mysteries. These are the charges which we find specified in the indictment drawn against Alkibiades by Thessalus the son of Kimon, in which he accuses Alkibiades of sacrilege against the two goddesses, Demeter (Ceres) and Proserpine. The people now became very much enraged with Alkibiades, and were still more exasperated by his personal enemy Androkles. Alkibiades was at first alarmed, but soon perceived that all the sailors of the fleet about to sail to Sicily were on his side, as were also the soldiers. A body of a thousand Argives and Mantineans also were heard to say that they were going to cross the seas and fight in a distant land all for the sake of Alkibiades, and that if he did not meet with fair play, they would at once desert. Encouraged by this, he appeared at the appointed time to defend himself, which disconcerted and disheartened his enemies, who feared that the people might deal leniently with him because they required his services. Matters being in this posture, they prevailed upon some of the orators who were not known to be enemies to Alkibiades, but who hated him nevertheless, to move before the people that it was an absurd proceeding for the irresponsible general of so great a force of Athenians and their allies to waste his time while the court was drawing lots for the jury, and filling water-clocks with water. "Let him sail, and may good luck attend him, and when the war is finished let him return and speak in his defence, for the laws will be the same then as now." Alkibiades saw clearly their malicious object in postponing his trial, and said publicly that it was very hard to leave such accusations and slanders behind him, and to be sent out in command of a great expedition with such a terrible fate hanging over him. If he could not prove his innocence, he ought to be put to death; and if he could clear himself of these charges, it was only just that he should be enabled to attack the enemy with a light heart, without having to fear false accusers at home.

XX. He did not, however, succeed in this, but was ordered to sail, and put to sea with his colleagues, having under their orders a fleet of nearly one hundred and forty triremes, five thousand one hundred heavy-armed troops, archers, slingers, and light-armed troops to the number of about thirteen hundred, and all other stores and provisions in proportion. After reaching Italy and capturing Rhegium, he gave his opinion as to the manner in which the war ought to be conducted; but as Nikias opposed him and was joined by Lamachus, he sailed over to Sicily and induced the city of Catana to join them, but did nothing further, because he was sent for at once to return and stand his trial at Athens. At first, as we have stated, Alkibiades was only vaguely suspected, and only the testimony of slaves and resident aliens could be obtained against him; but afterwards, during his absence, his enemies had worked hard to get up a case against him, and connected his sacrilegious conduct about the mysteries with the mutilation of the Hermae, which they argued were all the work of one body of conspirators, bent upon revolution and the destruction of the existing form of government. All those who were in any degree implicated were cast into prison without a trial, and they were much vexed they had not immediately brought Alkibiades to trial and obtained judgment against him on such grave charges as these. Any of his friends, relations, or acquaintances who fell into their hands received very harsh treatment.

Thucydides has omitted the names of those who impeached him, but others give their names as Diokleides and Teukrus, among whom is Phrynichus the comic dramatist, who writes as follows:—

"And, dearest Hermes, do not fall And break your head; and, worst of all, To some new Diokleides show the way, By slander base to swear men's lives away."

And again Hermes says:

"I will not fall. I will not for my pains Let Teukrus fatten on informers' gains."

Though really the informers brought no decided evidence forward for any important charge, one of them, when asked how he recognised the faces of the statue-breakers, answered that he saw them by the light of the moon: a signal falsehood, because it was done on the night of the new moon. This answer made the more thoughtful citizens unwilling to press the charge, but had no effect whatever on the people, who were as eager as ever, and continued to cast into prison any man who might be informed against.

XXI. One of those who was imprisoned was the orator Andokides, whom Hellanikus, the historian, reckons as a descendant of Odysseus (Ulysses). Andokides was thought to be a man of aristocratic and antipopular sentiments, and what made him particularly suspected of having taken part in the statue-breaking, was that the large statue of Hermes, near his house, the gift of the tribe Aegeis, was one of the very few which remained unbroken. Wherefore even at the present day it is called the Hermes of Andokides, and everyone speaks of it by that name in spite of the inscription on it.

It happened that Andokides, while in custody, formed an acquaintance and friendship for one of the other persons who were imprisoned on the same charge, a man of the name of Timaeus, of inferior birth and position to himself, but much cleverer and more courageous. This man persuaded Andokides to inform against himself and some few others, because, by a decree of the people, any one who acted as informer was to be given a free pardon, whereas no one could count upon the results of a trial, which the more prominent citizens had especial reasons for dreading. He pointed out that it was better to save his life by a lie than to be put to death with infamy as if he was really guilty; moreover, looking at the whole affair, it was best to sacrifice a few persons of doubtful character to the fury of the people, and thereby to save many good men from becoming its victims. Andokides was convinced by these arguments of Timaeus, and by informing against himself and some others obtained a pardon for himself, while all those whose names he mentioned were put to death, except such as had fled the country.

To procure greater credit to his information, Andokides even accused his own servants. However, the people did not abate their rage, but, ceasing to take any further interest in the statue-breakers, they turned savagely against Alkibiades. Finally, they despatched the Salaminian trireme after him, ingeniously ordering its officers not to use any personal violence, but to speak him fair and bid him return to stand his trial and set himself right with the people.

They were afraid of an outbreak, or even of a mutiny in the army in Sicily, which Alkibiades could have raised with the greatest ease, if he had wished to do so. Indeed, the soldiers became disheartened when he left them, and looked forward to long delays and periods of dull inaction under Nikias's command, now that he who used to spur matters on was gone. Lamachus, indeed, was a brave and skilful soldier, but his poverty prevented his opinions from carrying their due weight.

XXII. Alkibiades the moment he sailed away lost Messina for the Athenians. There was a party in that city ready to deliver it up, which he knew well, and by disclosing their intentions to the Syracusan party he effectually ruined the plot. At Thurii he landed, and concealed himself so that he could not be found. When one of his friends said to him, "Alkibiades, do you not trust your native country?" He answered, "Yes, in other matters; but when my life is at stake I would not trust my own mother, for fear that she might mistake a black bean for a white one." Afterwards hearing that the Athenians had condemned him to death, he said, "I will show them that I am still alive."

The indictment against him is framed thus:

"Thessalus, the son of Kimon, of the township of Lakia, accuses Alkibiades, the son of Kleinias, of the township of the Skambonidae, of sacrilege against the two goddesses, Demeter and Kora, by parodying the sacred mysteries and giving a representation of them in his own house, wearing himself such a robe as the Hierophant does when he shows the holy things, and calling himself the Hierophant, Poulytion, the Torch-bearer, Theodorus, of the township of

Phegaea, the Herald, and addressing the rest of the company as Mysts and Epopts (Initiates and Novices), contrary to the rules and ceremonies established by the Eumolpidae, and Kerykes, and the priests of Eleusis." As he did not appear, they condemned him, forfeited his goods, and even caused all the priests and priestesses to curse him publicly. It is said that Theano, the daughter of Menon, the priestess of the temple of Agraulos, was the only one who refused to carry out this decree, alleging that it was to pray and not to curse that she had become a priestess.

XXIII. While these terrible decrees and sentences were being passed against Alkibiades, he was living at Argos; for as soon as he left Thurii, he fled to the Peloponnesus, where, terrified at the violence of his enemies, he determined to abandon his country, and sent to Sparta demanding a safe asylum, on the strength of a promise that he would do the Spartans more good than he had in time past done them harm. The Spartans agreed to his request, and invited him to come. On his arrival, he at once effected one important matter, by stirring up the dilatory Spartans to send Gylippus at once to Syracuse with reinforcements for that city, to destroy the Athenian army in Sicily. Next, he brought them to declare war against the Athenians themselves; while his third and most terrible blow to Athens was his causing the Lacedaemonians to seize and fortify Dekeleia, which did more to ruin Athens than any other measure throughout the war. With his great public reputation, Alkibiades was no less popular in private life, and he deluded the people by pretending to adopt the Laconian habits. When they saw him closely shaved, bathing in cold water, eating dry bread and black broth, they wondered, and began to doubt whether this man ever had kept a professed cook, used perfumes, or endured to wear a Milesian mantle. For Alkibiades, among his other extraordinary qualities, had this especial art of captivating men by assimilating his own manners and habits to theirs, being able to change, more quickly than the chameleon, from one mode of life to another. The chameleon, indeed, cannot turn itself white; but Alkibiades never found anything, good or bad, which he could not imitate to the life. Thus at Sparta he was fond of exercise, frugal and severe; in Ionia, luxurious, frivolous, and lazy; in Thrace, he drank deep; in Thessaly he proved himself a good horseman; while, when he was consorting with the satrap Tissaphernes, he outdid even the Persian splendour and pomp. It was not his real character that he so often and so easily changed, but as he knew that if he appeared in his true colours, he would be universally disliked, he concealed his real self under an apparent adoption of the ways and fashions of whatever place he was in. In Lacedaemon you would say, looking at his appearance,

"'Tis not Achilles' son, 'tis he himself."

He was just such a man as Lykurgus himself would have trained; but if you examined his habits and actions more closely, you would say:

"'Tis the same woman still."

For while King Agis was away in the wars, Alkibiades seduced his wife Timaea, so that she became pregnant by him, and did not even deny the fact. When her child was born it was called Leotychides in public, but in her own house she whispered to her friends and attendants that his name was Alkibiades, so greatly was she enamoured of him. He himself used to say in jest that he had not acted thus out of wanton passion, but in order that his race might one day rule in Lacedaemon. King Agis heard of all this from many informants, but was most convinced of its truth by a computation of the time before the birth of the child. Terrified at an earthquake, he had once quitted his wife's chamber, and for ten months afterwards had never conversed with her. As it was at the end of this period that Leotychides was born, he declared that the child was not his; and for this reason he never succeeded to the throne.

XXIV. After the Athenian disaster in Sicily, ambassadors came to Sparta from Chios, Lesbos, and Kyzikus. The claims of the Lesbians were favoured by the Boeotians, and those of the people of Kyzikus by Pharnabazus; but, at the recommendation of Alkibiades, the Lacedaemonians decided to give the preference to the Chians. He himself sailed to that island, caused nearly the whole of the cities of Ionia to revolt from Athens, and injured the Athenian cause much by constantly assisting the Lacedaemonian generals. King Agis, however, was already his personal enemy, because of Alkibiades's intrigue with his wife, and now was enraged at his successes; for it was said that scarcely anything was done without Alkibiades. The other leading men in Sparta also hated Alkibiades, because he had thrown them into the shade; and they had sufficient influence with the home government to obtain an order for his execution, to be sent to the generals in Ionia.

Alkibiades received warning of this in good time. Alarmed at the news, he still continued to co-operate with the Lacedaemonians, but utterly refused to trust his person among them. To ensure his safety, he betook himself to Tissaphernes, the satrap or viceroy for the king of Persia in that province, and at once became the most important personage amongst his followers. The barbarian being himself a lover of deceit and of crooked ways, admired his cleverness and versatility; while no man's nature could resist the fascinations and charms of the society of Alkibiades, which Tissaphernes now enjoyed daily. Although he hated the Greeks as much as any Persian, yet he was so overpowered by the flatteries of Alkibiades, that he in his turn repaid him with compliments even more excessive. He decreed that the pleasantest of his parks, a place charmingly wooded and watered, with delightful walks and summer-houses, should be called "the Alkibiades;" and all men from that time forth spoke of it by that name.

XXV. Now that Alkibiades had determined that the Spartans were not to be trusted, and that he was in fear of Agis, their king, he began to speak evil of them to Tissaphernes, withholding him from assisting them thoroughly, and enabling them to conquer the Athenians, but advising him rather to starve the Lacedaemonians forces by insufficient supplies, so as to play one side off against the other, and thus encourage them to wear each other out, in order that in the end both might be so weakened as to fall an easy prey to the Persians.

Tissaphernes at once adopted this policy, and made no secret of his regard and admiration for Alkibiades, who was now looked up to by the Greeks on both sides, while the Athenians repented of their decrees against him. He also began to fear that if their city were to be utterly destroyed he would necessarily fall into the hands of his enemies, the Lacedaemonians.

The most important post in the Athenian empire at this time was the island of Samos. Here lay the greater part of their fleet, and it was from this headquarters that they sent out expeditions to recover the revolted cities of Ionia, and guarded those which they still retained, as, in spite of their great losses, they still possessed a fleet capable of holding its own against the Lacedaemonians. They were in great fear of Tissaphernes and the Phoenician fleet of a hundred and fifty sail of triremes, which was said to be on the point of arriving, because if it really came all would be over with Athens. Alkibiades, knowing this, sent a secret message to the Athenian leaders at Samos, holding out hopes of bringing Tissaphernes over to the Athenian side. He would not, he said, do this to please the populace of Athens, because he could not trust them, but he would effect it if the nobility would, like brave gentlemen, put an end to the insolent behaviour of the lower orders, and would themselves undertake to save the city and empire of Athens.

All were eager to adopt the proposal of Alkibiades, except Phrynichus of the demos or township of Deirades, who suspected the real truth, that Alkibiades cared nothing about the form of government which might be established at Athens, but was seeking for some excuse for being restored to his native country, and thought, by his harsh language about the people, to ingratiate himself with the nobles. He was, however, overruled; and, being now clearly marked as the personal enemy of Alkibiades, sent a secret message to Astyochus, the admiral of the Lacedaemonian fleet, bidding him beware of Alkibiades, who was playing a double game. However, he met his match in perfidy. Astyochus, desirous of gaining the favour of Tissaphernes, and seeing that Alkibiades had great influence with him, betrayed Phrynichus's letter to them. Alkibiades upon this at once sent persons to Samos to charge Phrynichus with this act of treason, and he, seeing that all men were shocked at what he had done, and were indignant with him, and being at his wit's end, endeavoured to heal one mischief by another. He sent a second letter to Astyochus, reproaching him for his betrayal of confidence, and promising that he would enable him to capture the fleet and camp of the Athenians. However, the treachery of Phrynichus did no harm to the Athenians, because of the counter treachery of Astyochus, who communicated this letter also to Alkibiades. Now Phrynichus, expecting a second charge of treason from Alkibiades, was beforehand with him, in announcing to the Athenians that the enemy were about to attack them, and advising them to keep near their ships, and to fortify their camp. This they proceeded to do, when there came a second letter from Alkibiades, warning them against Phrynichus, who meditated betraying the harbour to the enemy. This letter was not believed at the time, for men imagined that Alkibiades, who knew perfectly well all the movements and intentions of the enemy, was making use of that knowledge to destroy his personal enemy Phrynichus, by exciting an undeserved suspicion against him. Yet, when afterwards Hermon, one of the Athenian horse-patrol, stabbed Phrynichus with his dagger in the market-place, the Athenians, after trying the case, decided that the deceased was guilty of treason, and crowned Hermon and his comrades with garlands.

XXVI. The friends of Alkibiades being in a majority at Samos, now despatched Peisander to Athens to attempt the subversion of the republic, and to encourage the nobles to seize the government, and put an end to the democratic constitution. If this was done, they conceived that Alkibiades would make Tissaphernes their friend and ally, and this was the pretext and excuse put forward by those who established the oligarchy. When, however, the so-called Five Thousand, who really were the Four Hundred, were at the head of affairs, they paid but little attention to Alkibiades, and were very remiss in carrying on the war, partly because they distrusted the citizens, who were not yet accustomed to the new constitution, and partly because they thought that the Lacedaemonians, who were always favourable to oligarchical governments, would deal more tenderly with them on that account. The Athenian populace remained quiet, though sorely against its will, because of the terror inspired by the oligarchs, for no small number of citizens who had opposed the Four Hundred had been put to death; but the men of Samos, as soon as they heard the news, were indignant, and wished at once to sail to Peiraeus. They sent at once for Alkibiades, elected him their general, and bade him lead them on to crush this new despotism. Alkibiades on this occasion acted like a really great commander, and not at all as one would expect of a man who had suddenly been raised to power by popular favour.

He refused to curry favour with the soldiery by carrying out their wishes, regardless of their having found him a homeless exile, and having made him the commander of so many ships and so many men; but he resisted their impulse, and by preventing their committing so great an error, without doubt saved the Athenian empire. For if the fleet had left Samos, the enemy could without a battle have made themselves masters of the whole of Ionia, the Hellespont, and the islands in the Aegean while Athenians would have fought with Athenians in their own city. All this was prevented by Alkibiades alone, who not only persuaded the populace, and pointed out the folly of such proceedings in public speeches, but even entreated and commanded each individual man to remain at Samos. He was assisted in this by Thrasybulus, of the township of Steiria, who was present, and spoke in his loud voice, which was said to be the loudest of any Athenian of his time. This was a noble achievement of Alkibiades, and so, too, was his undertaking that the Phoenician fleet, which the Lacedaemonians expected would be sent by the Persian king to help them, should either be won over to the Athenian side, or at any rate prevented from joining the Lacedaemonians. In order to effect this, he sailed away in great haste, and, although the Phoenician fleet was at Aspendus, yet Tissaphernes brought it no further, and deceived the Lacedaemonians. Both parties gave Alkibiades the credit of having detained it, and more especially the Lacedaemonians, who imagined that he was teaching the Persians to allow the Greeks to destroy one another, for it was perfectly clear that such a force, if added to either of the contending parties, must have made them complete masters of the sea.

XXVII. After this the government of the Four Hundred was dissolved, as the friends of Alkibiades eagerly took the side of the popular party. Although the Athenians now wished and even commanded Alkibiades to return to his native city, yet he felt that he ought not to come home emptyhanded, and owing his restoration to the good nature of the people, but rather to return after some glorious achievement. With this intention he at first left Samos with a few ships and cruised in the seas near Knidus and Kôs; then, hearing that Mindarus, the Spartan admiral, had gone to the Hellespont with all his fleet, and that the Athenian fleet had followed him, he hurried to the assistance of the Athenian commanders.

Sailing northwards with eighteen triremes he chanced to arrive towards evening, at the end of a sea-fight off Abydos, in which neither party had won any decided advantage. The appearance of his squadron caused very different feelings among the combatants, for the Athenians were alarmed, and the enemy encouraged. However, he soon hoisted an Athenian flag, and bore down upon that part of the Peloponnesian fleet which had been hitherto victorious. He put them to flight, compelled them to run their ships ashore, and then attacking them, disabled their ships, and broke them to pieces, forcing the crews to swim ashore, where Pharnabazus the satrap led a force to the water's edge to fight for the preservation of the vessels. In the end the Athenians took thirty ships, recovered those of their own which had been captured, and erected a trophy, as victors.

Alkibiades gained great glory by this splendid piece of good fortune, and at once went off with rich presents and a gorgeous military retinue, to display his fresh laurels to Tissaphernes. He met, however, with a very different reception to that which he expected, for Tissaphernes, whose mind had been poisoned against him by the Lacedaemonians, and who feared that the king might be displeased with his own dealings with Alkibiades, considered that he had arrived at a very opportune moment, and at once seized him and imprisoned him at Sardis; thinking that this arbitrary act would prove to the world that the other suspicions of an understanding between them were unfounded.

XXVIII. Thirty days afterwards, Alkibiades by some means obtained a horse, eluded his guards, and fled for refuge to Klazomenae. He gave out that he had been privately released by Tissaphernes himself, in order to disgrace that satrap, and at once sailed to the Athenian fleet in the Hellespont. Learning that Mindarus and Pharnabazus were both in the city of Kyzikus, he encouraged his soldiers by a speech, in which he told them that they would have to fight at sea, on land, and against the town walls too, for that if they were not completely victorious they could get no pay. He manned his ships and proceeded to Prokonessus, ordering all small vessels which they met to be seized and detained in the interior of the fleet, in order that the enemy might not learn his movements. It happened also that a heavy thunderstorm with rain and darkness assisted his design, as he not only was unseen by the enemy, but was never suspected of any intention of attack by the Athenians themselves, who had given up any idea of going to sea when he ordered them on board. Little by little the clouds cleared away, and disclosed the

Peloponnesian fleet cruising off the harbour of Kyzikus. Alkibiades, fearing that if the enemy saw how numerous his own fleet was, they would take refuge on shore, ordered the other commanders to remain behind under easy sail, and himself with forty ships went on ahead to entice them to an engagement. The Peloponnesians, deceived by this manoeuvre, at once attacked these few ships, despising their small numbers. But the little squadron engaged them until the rest came up, when they fled ashore in terror. Alkibiades with twenty of the fastest sailing ships broke through the enemy's line, ran his ships ashore, landed their crews, and attacked the fugitives from the enemy's fleet with terrible slaughter. Mindarus and Pharnabazus now came to the rescue, but they were beaten back; Mindarus died fighting bravely, and Pharnabazus only saved himself by flight. By this battle the Athenians obtained possession of many dead bodies of their enemies, many stand of arms, the whole of the hostile fleet, and the town of Kyzikus, which they took by storm, putting its Peloponnesian garrison to the sword, as soon as Pharnabazus withdrew his troops. They now not merely obtained a firm hold on the Hellespont, but were able to drive the Lacedaemonians from the sea in all quarters. A despatch was captured, written in the Laconian fashion, informing the Ephors of the disaster. "Our ships are gone; Mindarus is slain; the men are starving; we know not what to do."

XXIX. The men who had served under Alkibiades were so elated by this victory that they disdained to mix with the rest of the army, alleging that the others had often been defeated, and that they were invincible. Indeed, not long before, Thrasyllus had received a defeat near Ephesus, upon which the Ephesians erected the brazen trophy to the disgrace of the Athenians; so that the soldiers of Alkibiades reproached those of Thrasyllus with this, glorifying themselves and their commander, and refusing to allow the others to make use of their places of exercise or their quarters in camp. However, when Pharnabazus with a large force of infantry and calvary attacked them while they were invading the territory of Abydos, Alkibiades led them out to fight him, defeated him, and, together with Thrasyllus, pursued him till nightfall. After this the soldiers fraternised with each other and returned to their camp rejoicing together. On the following day Alkibiades erected a trophy and ravaged the country of Pharnabazus, no one daring to oppose him. He even took priests and priestesses prisoners, but released them without ransom.

The city of Chalkedon had revolted from Athens, and received a Lacedaemonian harmost and garrison. Alkibiades was eager to attack them, but, hearing that they had collected all the property in their country and placed it in the hands of the Bithynians, a friendly tribe, he led his whole army to the Bithynian frontier and sent a herald to that people reproaching them for what they had done. In terror, the Bithynians gave up the property to him, and entered into an alliance with him.

XXX. He now completely invested Chalkedon, by building a wall reaching from sea to sea. Pharnabazus came down to raise the siege, and Hippokrates, the harmost of the city, led out his forces and attacked the Athenians at the same time. Alkibiades arranged his army so as to be able to fight them both at once, forced Pharnabazus to retreat with disgrace, killed Hippokrates, and put his force to flight with severe loss. He now took a cruise round the Hellespont, to raise contributions from the towns on the coast, during which he took Selymbria, where he, very unnecessarily, was exposed to great personal risk. The party who intended to betray the city had arranged to show a torch as a signal at midnight, but were compelled to do so before the appointed time, fearing one of the conspirators, who suddenly changed his mind. When then the torch was raised, the army was not ready for the assault, but Alkibiades, taking some thirty men with him, ran at full speed up to the walls, giving orders to the rest to follow. The city gate was opened for him, and, twenty peltasts having joined his thirty soldiers, he entered, when he perceived the men of Selymbria under arms marching down the street to meet him. To await their onset would have been ruin, while pride forbade a hitherto invincible general to retire. Ordering his trumpet to sound, he bade one of those present proclaim aloud that the Selymbrians ought not to appear in arms against the Athenians. This speech made some of the townspeople less eager to fight, as they imagined that their enemies were all within the walls, while it encouraged others who hoped to arrange matters peaceably. While they were standing opposite to one another and parleying, Alkibiades's army came up, and he, truly conjecturing that the Selymbrians were really disposed to be friendly, began to fear that his Thracian troops might sack the city; for many of these barbarians were serving in his army as volunteers, from a particular attachment they had to his person. He therefore sent them all out of the city, and did not permit the terrified people of Selymbria to suffer any violence, but, having exacted a contribution of money and placed a garrison in the town, he sailed away.

XXXI. Meanwhile the generals who were besieging Chalkedon made an agreement with Pharnabazus, on these conditions. They were to receive a sum of money; the people of Chalkedon were to become subjects of Athens as before; Pharnabazus was not to lay waste the province; and he was to provide an escort and a safe-conduct for an Athenian embassy to the Persian king.

On the return of Alkibiades, Pharnabazus desired him to swear to observe these conditions, but Alkibiades refused to do so unless Pharnabazus swore first. After this capitulation he proceeded to Byzantium, which had revolted from Athens, and built a wall round that city. Anaxilaus and Lykurgus, with some others, now offered to betray the city if the lives and property of the inhabitants were spared. Upon this Alkibiades put about a report that his presence was urgently required on the Ionian coast, and sailed away by daylight with all his fleet. The same night he landed with all his soldiers, and marched up to the walls in silence, while the fleet, with a great clamour and disturbance, forced its way into the harbour. The suddenness of this assault, entirely unexpected as it was, terrified the people of Byzantium, and gave those of them who inclined to the Athenian side an opportunity of admitting Alkibiades quietly, while the attention of every one was directed to the ships in the harbour. The town did not, however, surrender altogether without fighting; for the Peloponnesians, Megarians, and Boeotians who were in it drove the Athenians back into their ships with loss, and when they heard that the land forces had entered the town they formed in line and engaged them. A severe battle took place, but Alkibiades on the right wing, and Theramenes on the left, were at length victorious, and took prisoners the survivors, some three hundred in number. After this battle no citizen of Byzantium was either put to death or banished, those being the terms on which the conspirators had delivered up the city, namely, that they should suffer no loss of life or property.

Anaxilaus was afterwards tried at Sparta for having betrayed the city, and justified what he had done, saying that he was not a Lacedaemonian, but a Byzantine, and that he saw Byzantium, not Sparta, in danger, as the city was surrounded by the enemy's siege works, no provisions being brought in to it, and what there was in it being consumed by the Peloponnesians and Boeotians, while the people of Byzantium with their wives and children were starving. He did not, he said, betray the city to the enemy, but relieved it from the miseries of war, imitating therein the noblest Lacedaemonians, whose only idea of what was noble and just was what would serve their own country. The Lacedaemonians, on hearing this speech, were ashamed to press the charge, and acquitted him.

XXXII. Now, at length, Alkibiades began to wish to see his native country again, and still more to be seen and admired by his countrymen after his splendid series of victories. He proceeded home with the Athenian fleet, which was magnificently adorned with shields and trophies, and had many prizes in tow, and the flags of many more which he had captured and destroyed—all of them together amounting to not less than two hundred. But we cannot believe the additions which Douris the Samian, who says that he is a descendant of Alkibiades, makes to this story, to the effect that Chrysogonus, the victor at the Pythian games, played on the flute to mark the time for the rowers, while Kallipides the tragedian, attired in his buskins, purple robe, and other theatrical properties, gave them orders, and that the admiral's ship came into harbour with purple sails, as if returning from a party of pleasure. Neither Theopompus, nor Ephorus, nor Xenophon mentions these circumstances, nor was it likely that he should present himself before the Athenians in such a swaggering fashion, when he was returning home from exile, after having suffered such a variety of misfortunes. The truth is, he sailed to Athens with considerable misgivings, and on his arrival would not leave his ship until from her deck he saw Euryptolemus his cousin, with many of his friends and relatives, assembled to welcome him.

When he landed, the people seemed to have no eyes for the other generals, but all rushed towards him, and escorted him on his way, cheering him, embracing him, and crowning him with flowers. Those who could not get near him gazed upon him from a distance, and the older men pointed him out to the younger ones. Yet the joy of the citizens was mingled with tears in the midst of their rejoicings, when they thought of their past disasters, for they reflected that they would not have failed in Sicily, or met with any of their other terrible disappointments, if they had not parted with Alkibiades when in the full tide of prosperity. He had found Athens barely able to hold her own at sea, by land mistress of little more than the ground on which the city stood, and torn by internal strife; from which miserable and forlorn condition he had restored her so completely, that she was again not only omnipotent at sea, but also victorious everywhere on land.

XXXIII. Before his return a decree had been passed authorising him to do so, at the instance of Kritias, the son of Kallaeschrus, who himself alludes to it in his poems, mentioning the service which he performed for Alkibiades in the following verse:

"I moved your restoration by decree, And that you're home again you owe to me."

Immediately on the return of Alkibiades, the people assembled in the Pnyx, where he addressed them. He spoke with tears of his misfortunes, for which he partly reproached his countrymen, though he attributed them chiefly to his own unlucky fortune, and he greatly raised their hopes by speaking encouragingly about their probable successes in the future. He was honoured with golden crowns, and elected sole general with absolute power both by sea and land. A decree was also passed by which his property was restored to him, and the Eumolpidae and Kerykes were ordered to retract the curses which they had invoked upon him at the instance of the people. When all the rest obeyed, Theodorus the hierophant excused himself, saying, If he has done the State no wrong, I never cursed him.

XXXIV. While Alkibiades was in this glorious career of prosperity, some persons in spite of his success foreboded evil from the day which he had chosen for his return home; for on the day on which he sailed into the harbour the statue of Athene on the Acropolis is stripped of its garments and ornaments, which are cleaned, while it in the meanwhile is covered up to conceal it from human eyes. This ceremony takes place on the 25th of the month Thargelion, which day is considered by the Athenians to be the unluckiest of all. Moreover, the goddess did not appear to receive Alkibiades with a kindly welcome, but to turn away her face from him and drive him from her presence. Be this as it may, all went well and just as Alkibiades wished. A fleet of a hundred triremes was manned, and placed at his disposal, but he with creditable pride refused to set sail until after the celebration of the Eleusinian mysteries. Since the permanent occupation of Dekeleia and of the passes commanding the road to Eleusis by the enemy, the procession had been necessarily shorn of many of its distinctive features, as it had to be sent by sea. All the customary sacrifices, dances, and other rites which used to be practised on the road, when Iacchus is carried along in solemn procession, were of necessity omitted. It seemed therefore to Alkibiades that it would both honour the gods and increase his own reputation among men, if he restored the ancient form of this ceremony, escorting the procession with his troops and protecting it from the enemy; for he argued that Agis would lose prestige if he did not attack, but allowed the procession to pass unmolested, whereas if he did attack, Alkibiades would be able to fight in a holy cause, in defence of the most sacred institutions of his country, with all his countrymen present as witnesses of his own valour. When he determined to do this, after concerting measures with the Eumolpidae and Kerykes, he placed vedettes on the mountains and sent an advanced guard off at day-break, following with the priests, novices, and initiators marching in the midst of his army, in great good order and perfect silence. It was an august and solemn procession, and all who did not envy him said that he had performed the office of a high priest in addition of that of a general. The enemy made no attack, and he led his troops safely back to Athens, full of pride himself, and making his army proud to think itself invincible while under his command. He had so won the affections of the poor and the lower orders, that they were strangely desirous of living under his rule. Many even besought him to put down the malignity of his personal enemies, sweep away laws, decrees, and other pernicious nonsense, and carry on the government without fear of a factious opposition.

XXXV. What his own views about making himself despot of Athens may have been we cannot tell; but the leading citizens took alarm at this, and hurried him away as quickly as possible to sea, voting whatever measures he pleased, and allowing him to choose his own colleagues. He set sail with his hundred ships, reached Andros, and defeated the inhabitants of that island, and the Lacedaemonian garrison there. He did not, however, capture the city, and this afterwards became one of the points urged against him by his enemies. Indeed, if there ever was a man destroyed by his reputation, it was Alkibiades. Being supposed to be such a prodigy of daring and subtlety, his failures were regarded with suspicion, as if he could have succeeded had he been in earnest; for his countrymen would not believe that he could really fail in anything which he seriously attempted. They expected to hear of the capture of Chios, and of the whole Ionian coast, and were vexed at not at once receiving the news of a complete success. They did not take into account the want of money which Alkibiades felt, while warring against men who had the king of Persia for their paymaster, and which made frequent absences from his camp necessary to provide subsistence for his troops. It was one of these expeditions, indeed, which exposed him to the last and most important of the many charges brought against him. Lysander had been sent by the Lacedaemonians to take the command of their fleet. On his arrival, by means of the money paid by Cyrus, he raised the pay of his sailors from three obols a day to four. Alkibiades, who could with difficulty pay his men even three obols, went to Caria to levy contributions, leaving in command of the fleet one Antiochus, a good seaman, but a thoughtless and silly man. He had distinct orders from Alkibiades not to fight even if the enemy attacked him, but such was his insolent disregard of these instructions that he manned his own trireme and one other, sailed to Ephesus, and there passed along the line of the enemy's ships, as they lay on the beach, using the most scurrilous and insulting language and gestures. At first Lysander put to sea with a few ships to pursue him, but as the Athenians came out to assist him, the action became general. The entire fleets engaged and Lysander was victorious. He killed Antiochus, captured many ships and men, and set up a trophy. When Alkibiades on his return to Samos heard of this, he put to sea with all his ships, and offered battle to Lysander; but he was satisfied with his previous victory, and refused the offer.

XXXVI. Thrasybulus, the son of Thrason, a bitter personal enemy of Alkibiades, now set sail for Athens to accuse him, and to exasperate his enemies in the city against him. He made a speech to the people, representing that Alkibiades had ruined their affairs and lost their ships by insolently abusing his authority and entrusting the command, during his own absence, to men who owed their influence with him to deep drinking and cracking seamen's jokes, and that he securely traversed the provinces to raise money, indulging in drunken debauches with Ionian courtezans, while the enemy's fleet was riding close to his own. He was also blamed for the construction of certain forts in Thrace, near Bisanthe, which he destined as a place of refuge for himself, as if he could not or would not live in his native city.

The Athenians were so wrought upon by these charges against Alkibiades, that they elected other generals to supersede him, thus showing their anger and dislike for him. Alkibiades, on learning this, left the Athenian camp altogether, got together a force of foreign troops, and made war on the irregular Thracian tribes on his own account, thus obtaining much plunder and freeing the neighbouring Greek cities from the dread of the barbarians. Now when the generals Tydeus, Menander, and Adeimantus came with the entire Athenian fleet to Aegospotamoi, they used early every morning to go to Lampsakus to challenge the fleet of Lysander, which lay there, to a sea-fight. After this ceremony they would return and spend the whole day in careless indolence, as if despising their enemy. Alkibiades, who lived close by, did not disregard their danger, but even rode over on horseback and pointed out to the generals that they were very badly quartered in a place where there was no harbour and no city, having to obtain all their provisions from Sestos, and, when the ships were once hauled up on shore, allowing the men to leave them unguarded and straggle where they pleased, although they were in the presence of a fleet which was trained to act in silence and good order at the command of one man.

XXXVII. Though Alkibiades gave this advice, and urged the generals to remove to Sestos, they would not listen to him. Tydeus indeed rudely bade him begone, for they, not he, were now generals. Alkibiades, too, suspected that there was some treachery in the case, and retired, telling his personal friends, who escorted him out of the camp, that if he had not been so outrageously insulted by the generals, he could in a few days have compelled the Lacedaemonians either to fight a battle at sea against their will, or abandon their ships. To some this seemed mere boasting, while others thought that he could very possibly effect it by bringing many Thracian light-armed troops and cavalry to assault the camp on the land side. However, the result soon proved that he had rightly seen the fault of the Athenian position. Lysander suddenly and unexpectedly assailed it, and except eight triremes which escaped under Konon, took all the rest, nearly two hundred in number. Lysander also put three thousand prisoners to the sword. He shortly afterwards captured Athens, burned her ships, and pulled down her Long Walls. Alkibiades, terrified at seeing the Lacedaemonians omnipotent by sea and land, shifted his quarters to Bithynia, sending thither a great amount of treasure, and taking much with him, but leaving much more in his Thracian fortresses. In Bithynia, however, he suffered much loss at the hands of the natives, and determined to proceed to the court of Artaxerxes, thinking that the Persian king, if he would make trial of him, would find that he was not inferior to Themistokles in ability, while he sought him in a much more honourable way; for it was not to revenge himself on his fellow-citizens, as Themistokles did, but to assist his own country against its enemy that he meant to solicit the king's aid. Imagining that Pharnabazus would be able to grant him a safe passage to the Persian court, he went into Phrygia to meet him, and remained there for some time, paying his court to the satrap, and receiving from him marks of respect.

XXXVIII. The Athenians were terribly cast down at the loss of their empire; but when Lysander robbed them of their liberty as well, by establishing the government of the Thirty Tyrants, they began to entertain thoughts which never had occurred to them before, while it was yet possible that the State might be saved from ruin. They bewailed their past blunders and mistakes, and of these they considered their second fit of passion with Alkibiades to have been the greatest. They had cast him off for no fault of his own, but merely because they were angry with his follower for having lost a few ships disgracefully; they had much more disgraced themselves by losing the services of the ablest and bravest general whom they possessed. Even in their present abasement a vague hope prevailed among them that Athens could not be utterly lost while Alkibiades was alive; for he had not during his former exile been satisfied with a quiet life, and surely now, however prosperous his private circumstances might be, he would not endure to see the triumph of the Lacedaemonians, and the arrogant tyranny of the Thirty. Indeed this was proved to be no vain dream by the care which the Thirty took to watch all the motions of Alkibiades. At last, Kritias informed Lysander, that while Athens was governed by a democracy, the Lacedaemonian empire in Greece could never be safe; and if the Athenians were ever so much inclined to an oligarchical form of government, Alkibiades, if he lived, would not long suffer them to submit to it. However, Lysander was not prevailed upon by these arguments until a despatch came from Sparta bidding him make away with Alkibiades, either because the home government feared his ability and enterprise, or because they wished to please his enemy, King Agis.

XXXIX. Lysander now sent orders for his death to Pharnabazus, who entrusted their execution to his brother Magaeus and his uncle Susamithres. Alkibiades was at this time dwelling in a village in Phrygia, with Timandra the courtezan, and one night he dreamed that he was dressed in his mistress's clothes, and that she, holding his head in her arms, was painting his face and adorning him like a woman. Others say that he saw Magaeus in his dream cutting off his head, and his body all in flames. All, however, agree that the dream took place shortly before his death. His murderers did not dare to enter the house, but stood round it in a circle and set it on fire. Alkibiades, on discovering them, flung most of the bedding and clothes on to the fire, wrapped his cloak round his left arm, and with his dagger in his right dashed through the flames unhurt, not giving his clothes time to catch fire. None of the barbarians dared to await his onset, but as soon as they saw him they scattered, and from a distance shot at him with darts and arrows. After he had fallen and the barbarians were gone, Timandra took up his corpse, covered it with her own clothes, and, as far as was in her power, showed it every mark of honour and respect.

This Timandra is said to have been the mother of Lais, commonly called the Corinthian, who really was brought as a captive from Hykkara, a small town in Sicily. Some writers, although they agree in their account of the manner of his death, differ as to its cause, alleging that it was neither due to Pharnabazus nor to Lysander nor the Lacedaemonians, but that Alkibiades had debauched a girl of noble birth and was living with her, and that her relatives, enraged at this insult, during the night set fire to the house in which Alkibiades was living, and, as has been related, shot him as he leaped out through the flames.

Life of Caius Marcius Coriolanus.

I. The patrician family of the Marcii at Rome produced many illustrious men, amongst whom was Ancus Marcius, the grandson of Numa, who became king after the death of Tullus Hostilius. To this family also belonged Publius and Quintus Marcius, who supplied Rome with abundance of excellent water, and Censorinus, twice appointed censor by the Roman people, who afterwards passed a law that no one should hold that office twice.

Caius Marcius, the subject of this memoir, was an orphan, and brought up by a widowed mother. He proved that, hard though the lot of an orphan may be, yet it does not prevent a man's becoming great and distinguished, and that the bad alone allege it as an excuse for an intemperate life. He also proves to us that a naturally noble nature, if it be not properly disciplined, will produce many good and bad qualities together, just as a rich field, if not properly tilled, will produce both weeds and good fruit. The immense energy and courage of his mind used to urge him to attempt and to perform great exploits, but his harsh and ambitious temper made it difficult for him to live on friendly terms with his companions. They used to admire his indifference to pleasure and pain, and his contempt for bribes, but in politics they were angered by his morose and haughty manner, too proud for a citizen of a republic. Indeed there is no advantage to be gained from a liberal education so great as that of softening and disciplining the natural ferocity of our disposition, by teaching it moderation, and how to avoid all extremes. However, at that period warlike virtues were valued above all others at Rome, which is proved by the Romans possessing only one word for virtue and for bravery, so that virtue, a general term, is applied by them to the particular form, courage.

II. Marcius, having an especial passion for war, was familiar from childhood with the use of arms. Reflecting that artificial weapons are of little use without a body capable of wielding them, he so trained himself for all possible emergencies that he was both able to run swiftly and also to grapple with his foe so strongly that few could escape from him. Those who entered into any contest with him, when beaten, used to ascribe their defeat to his immense bodily strength, which no exertions could tire out.

III. He served his first campaign while yet a youth, when Tarquin, the exiled King of Rome, after many battles and defeats, staked all upon one last throw, and assembled an army to attack Rome. His force consisted chiefly of Latins, but many other Italian states took his part in the war, not from any attachment to his person, but through fear and dislike of the growing power of Rome. In the battle which ensued, in which various turns of fortune took place, Marcius, while fighting bravely under the eye of the dictator himself, saw a Roman fallen and helpless near him. He at once made for this man, stood in front of him, and killed his assailant. After the victory, Marcius was among the first who received the oak-leaf crown. This crown is given to him who has saved the life of a citizen in battle, and is composed of oak-leaves, either out of compliment to the Arcadians, whom the oracle calls 'acorn eaters,' or because in any campaign in any country it is easy to obtain oak-boughs, or it may be that the oak, sacred to Jupiter the protector of cities, forms a suitable crown for one who has saved the life of a citizen. The oak is the most beautiful of all wild trees, and the strongest of those which are artificially cultivated. It afforded men in early times both food and drink, by its acorns and the honey found in it, while by the bird-lime which it produces, it enables them to catch most kinds of birds and other creatures, as additional dainties.

This was the battle in which they say that the Dioscuri, Castor and Pollux, appeared, and immediately after the battle were soon in the Forum at Rome announcing the victory, with their horses dripping with sweat, at the spot where now there is a temple built in their honour beside the fountain. In memory of this, the day of the victory, the 15th of July, is kept sacred to the Dioscuri.

IV. To win distinction early in life is said to quench and satisfy the eagerness of some men whose desire for glory is not keen; but for those with whom it is the ruling passion of their lives, the gaining of honours only urges them on, as a ship is urged by a gale, to fresh achievements. They do not regard themselves as having received a reward, but as having given a pledge for the future, and they feel it their duty not to disgrace the reputation which they have acquired, but to eclipse their former fame by some new deed of prowess. Marcius, feeling this, was ever trying to surpass himself in valour, and gained such prizes and trophies that the later generals under whom he served were always striving to outdo the former ones in their expressions of esteem for him, and their testimony to his merits. Many as were the wars in which Rome was then engaged, Marcius never returned from any without a prize for valour or some especial mark of distinction. Other men were brave in order to win glory, but Marcius won glory in order to please his mother. That she should hear him praised, see him crowned, and embrace him weeping for joy, was the greatest honour and happiness of his life. Epameinondas is said to have had the same feelings, and to have considered it to be his greatest good-fortune that his father and mother were both alive to witness his triumphant success at the battle of Leuktra. He, however, enjoyed the sympathy and applause of both parents, but Marcius, being fatherless, lavished on his mother all that affection which should have belonged to his father, besides her own share. So boundless was his love for Volumnia that at her earnest desire he even married a wife, but still continued to live in the house of his mother.

V. At this time, when his reputation and influence were very considerable because of his prowess, there was a party-quarrel going on in Rome between the patricians, who wished to defend the privileges of men of property, and the people, who were suffering terrible ill-treatment at the hands of their creditors. Those who possessed a small property were forced either to pledge or to sell it, while those who were absolutely destitute were carried off and imprisoned, though they might be scarred and enfeebled from the wars in which they had served in defence of their country. The last campaign was that against the Sabines, after which their rich creditors promised to treat them with less harshness. In pursuance of a decree of the Senate, Marcus Valerius the consul was the guarantee of this promise. But when, after serving manfully in this campaign and conquering the enemy, they met with no better treatment from their creditors, and the Senate seemed unmindful of its engagements, allowing them to be imprisoned and distresses to be levied upon their property as before, there were violent outbreaks and riots in the city. This disturbed condition of the commonwealth was taken advantage of by the enemy, who invaded the country and plundered it. When the consuls called all men of military age to arms, no one obeyed, and then at last the patricians hesitated. Some thought that they ought to yield to the lower classes, and make some concessions instead of enforcing the strict letter of the law against them; while others, among whom was Marcius, opposed this idea, not because he thought the money of great consequence, but because he considered this to be the beginning of an outburst of democratic insolence which a wise government would take timely measures to suppress before it gathered strength.

VI. As the Senate, although it frequently met, came to no decision on this matter, the plebeians suddenly assembled in a body, left the city, and established themselves on what was afterwards called the Mons Sacer, or Sacred Hill, near the river Anio. They abstained from all factious proceedings, and merely stated that they had been driven from the city by the wealthy classes. Air and water and a place in which to be buried, they said, could be obtained anywhere in Italy, and they could get nothing more than this in Rome, except the privilege of being wounded or slain in fighting battles on behalf of the rich. At this demonstration, the Senate became alarmed, and sent the most moderate and popular of its members to treat with the people. The spokesman of this embassy was Menenius Agrippa, who, after begging the plebeians to come to terms, and pleading the cause of the Senate with them, wound up his speech by the following fable: Once upon a time, said he, all the members revolted against the belly, reproaching it with lying idle in the body, and making all the other members work in order to provide it with food; but the belly laughed them to scorn, saying that it was quite true that it took all the food which the body obtained, but that it afterwards distributed it among all the members. "This," he said, "is the part played by the Senate in the body politic. It digests and arranges all the affairs of the State, and provides all of you with wholesome and useful measures."

VII. Upon this they came to terms, after stipulating that five men should be chosen to defend the cause of the people, who are now known as tribunes of the people. They chose for the first tribunes the leaders of the revolt, the chief of whom were Junius Brutus and Sicinius Vellutus. As soon as the State was one again, the people assembled under arms, and zealously offered their services for war to their rulers. Marcius, though but little pleased with these concessions which the plebeians had wrung from the patricians, yet, noticing that many patricians were of his mind, called upon them not to be outdone in patriotism by the plebeians, but to prove themselves their superiors in valour rather than in political strength.

VIII. Corioli was the most important city of the Volscian nation, with which Rome then was at war. The consul Cominius was besieging it, and the Volscians, fearing it might be taken, gathered from all quarters, meaning to fight a battle under the city walls, and so place the Romans between two fires. Cominius divided his army, and led one part of it to fight the relieving force, leaving Titus Lartius, a man of the noblest birth in Rome, to continue the siege with the rest of his troops. The garrison of Corioli, despising the small numbers of their besiegers, attacked them and forced them to take shelter within their camp. But there Marcius with a few followers checked their onset, slew the foremost, and with a loud voice called on the Romans to rally. He was, as Cato said a soldier should be, not merely able to deal weighty blows, but struck terror into his enemies by the loud tones of his voice and his martial appearance, so that few dared to stand their ground before him. Many soldiers rallied round him and forced the enemy to retreat; but he, not satisfied with this, followed them close and drove them in headlong flight back to the city. On arriving there, although he saw that the Romans were slackening their pursuit as many missiles were aimed at them from the city walls, and none of them thought of daring to enter together with the fugitives into a city full of armed men, yet he stood and cheered them on, loudly telling them that fortune had opened the city gates as much to the pursuers as to the pursued. Few cared to follow him, but he, forcing his way through the crowd of fugitives, entered the city with them, none daring at first to withstand him. Soon, when the enemy saw how few of the Romans were within the gates, they rallied and attacked them. Marcius, in the confused mass of friends and foes, fought with incredible strength, swiftness, and courage, overthrowing all whom he attacked, driving some to the further parts of the town, and forcing others to lay down their arms, so that Lartius was able to march the rest of the Roman army into the gates unmolested.

IX. When the city was taken, the greater part of the soldiers fell to plundering it, which greatly vexed Marcius. He loudly exclaimed that it was a disgraceful thing, when the consul was on the point of engaging with the enemy, that they should be plundering, or, on the pretext of plunder, keeping themselves safe out of harm's way. Few paid any attention to him, but with those few he marched on the track of the main body, frequently encouraging his followers to greater speed, and not to give way to fatigue, and frequently praying to Heaven that he might not come too late for the battle, but arrive in time to share the labours and perils of his countrymen. There was at that time a custom among the Romans, when they were drawn up in order of battle, ready to take their shields in their hands, and to gird themselves with the trabea, to make their will verbally, naming their heir in the presence of three or four witnesses. The Roman army was found by Marcius in the act of performing this ceremony. At first some were alarmed at seeing him appear with only a few followers, covered with blood and sweat; but when he ran joyously up to the consul and told him that Corioli was taken, Cominius embraced him, and all the ranks took fresh courage, some because they heard, and others because they guessed the glorious news. They eagerly demanded to be led to battle. Marcius now enquired of Cominius how the enemy's line of battle was arranged, and where it was strongest. When the consul answered that he believed that the men of Antium, the proudest and bravest troops of the Volscians, were posted in the centre, he answered, "I beg of you, place us opposite to those men." The consul, filled with admiration for his spirit, placed him there. As soon as the armies met, Marcius charged before the rest, and the Volscians gave way before his onset. The centre, where he attacked, was quite broken, but the ranks on either side wheeled round and surrounded him, so that the consul feared for his safety, and despatched the choicest of his own troops to his aid. They found a hot battle raging round Marcius, and many slain, but by the shock of their charge they drove off the enemy in confusion. As they began to pursue them, they begged Marcius, now weary with toil and wounds, to retire to the camp, but he, saying that "it was not for victors to be weary," joined in the pursuit. The rest of the Volscian army was defeated, many were slain, and many taken.

X. On the next day Lartius and the rest joined the consul. He ascended a rostrum, and after returning suitable thanks to Heaven for such unexampled successes, turned to Marcius. First he praised his conduct in the highest terms, having himself witnessed some part of it, and having learned the rest from Lartius. Next, as there were many prisoners, horses, and other spoil, he bade him, before it was divided, choose a tenth part for himself. He also presented him with a horse and trappings, as a reward for his bravery. As all the Romans murmured their approval, Marcius coming forward said that he gladly accepted the horse, and was thankful for the praise which he had received from the consul. As for the rest, he considered that to be mere pay, not a prize, and refused it, preferring to take his share with the rest. "One especial favour," said he, "I do beg of you. I had a friend among the Volscians, who now is a captive, and from having been a rich and free man has fallen to the condition of a slave. I wish to relieve him from one of his many misfortunes—that of losing his liberty and being sold for a slave." After these words, Marcius was cheered more than he had been before, and men admired his disinterestedness more than they had admired his bravery. Even those who grudged him his extraordinary honours now thought that by his unselfishness he had shown himself worthy of them, and admired his courage in refusing such presents more than the courage by which he had won the right to them. Indeed, the right use of riches is more glorious than that of arms, but not to desire them at all is better even than using them well.

XI. When the cheering caused by Marcius's speech had subsided, Cominius said: "Fellow soldiers, we cannot force a man against his will to receive these presents; but, unless his achievements have already won it for him, let us give him the title of Coriolanus, which he cannot refuse, seeing for what it is bestowed, and let us confirm it by a general vote."

Hence he obtained the third name of Coriolanus. From this we may clearly see that his own personal name was Caius, and that Marcius was the common name of his family, while the third name was added afterwards to mark some particular exploit, peculiarity, or virtue in the bearer. So also did the Greeks in former ages give men names derived from their actions, such as Kallinikus (the Victor), or Soter (the Preserver); or from their appearance, as Fusco (the Fat), or Gripus (the Hook-nosed); or from their virtues, as Euergetes (the

Benefactor), or Philadelphus (the Lover of his Brethren), which were names of the Ptolemies: or from their success, as Eudaemon (the Fortunate), a name given to the second king of the race of Battus. Some princes have even had names given them in jest, as Antigonus was called Doson (the Promiser), and Ptolemy Lathyrus (the Vetch).

The Romans used this sort of name much more commonly, as for instance they named one of the Metelli Diadematus, or wearer of the diadem, because he walked about for a long time with his head bound up because of a wound in the forehead.

Another of the same family was named Celer (the Swift), because of the wonderful quickness with which he provided a show of gladiators on the occasion of his father's funeral. Some even to the present day derive their names from the circumstances of their birth, as for instance a child is named Proculus if his father be abroad when he is born, and Postumus if he be dead. If one of twins survive, he is named Vopiscus. Of names taken from bodily peculiarities they use not only Sulla (the Pimply), Niger (the Swarthy), Rufus (the Red-haired), but even such as Caecus (the Blind), and Claudus (the Lame), wisely endeavouring to accustom men to consider neither blindness nor any other bodily defect to be any disgrace or matter of reproach, but to answer to these names as if they were their own. However, this belongs to a different branch of study.

XII. When the war was over, the popular orators renewed the party-quarrels, not that they had any new cause of complaint or any just grievance to proceed upon; but the evil result which had necessarily been produced by their former riotous contests were now made the ground of attacks on the patricians. A great part of the country was left unsown and untilled, while the war gave no opportunities for importation from other countries. The demagogues, therefore, seeing that there was no corn in the market, and that even if there had been any, the people were not able to buy it, spread malicious accusations against the rich, saying that they had purposely produced this famine in order to pay off an old grudge against the people. At this juncture ambassadors arrived from the town of Velitrae, who delivered up their city to the Romans, desiring that they would send some new inhabitants to people it, as a pestilence had made such havoc among the citizens that there was scarcely a tenth part of them remaining alive.

The wiser Romans thought that this demand of the people of Velitrae would confer a most seasonable relief on themselves, and would put an end to their domestic troubles, if they could only transfer the more violent partizans of the popular party thither, and so purge the State of its more disorderly elements. The consuls accordingly chose out all these men and sent them to colonize Velitrae, and enrolled the rest for a campaign against the Volsci, that they might not have leisure for revolutionary plottings, but that when they were all gathered together, rich and poor, patrician and plebeian alike, to share in the common dangers of a camp, they might learn to regard one another with less hatred and illwill.

XIII. But Sicinnius and Brutus, the tribunes of the people, now interposed, crying aloud that the consuls were veiling a most barbarous action under the specious name of sending out colonists. They were despatching many poor men to certain destruction by transporting them to a city whose air was full of pestilence and the stench from unburied corpses, where they were to dwell under the auspices of a god who was not only not their own, but angry with them. And after that, as if it was not sufficient for them that some of the citizens should be starved, and others be exposed to the plague, they must needs plunge wantonly into war, in order that the city might suffer every conceivable misery at once, because it had refused any longer to remain in slavery to the rich. Excited by these speeches, the people would not enrol themselves as soldiers for the war, and looked with suspicion on the proposal for the new colony. The Senate was greatly perplexed, but Marcius, now a person of great importance and very highly thought of in the State, began to place himself in direct opposition to the popular leaders, and to support the patrician cause. In spite of the efforts of the demagogues, a colony was sent out to Velitrae, those whose names were drawn by lot being compelled by heavy penalties to go thither; but as the people utterly refused to serve in the campaign against the Volscians, Marcius made up a troop of his own clients, with which and what others he could persuade to join him he made an inroad into the territory of Antium. Here he found much corn, and captured many prisoners and much cattle. He kept none of it for himself, but returned to Rome with his troops loaded with plunder. This caused the others to repent of their determination, when they saw the wealth which these men had obtained, but it embittered their hatred of Marcius, whom they regarded as gaining glory for himself at the expense of the people.

XIV. Shortly after this, however, Marcius stood for the consulship, and then the people relented and felt ashamed to affront such a man, first in arms as in place, and the author of so many benefits to the State. It was the custom at Rome for those who were candidates for any office to address and ingratiate themselves with the people, going about the Forum in a toga without any tunic underneath it, either in order to show their humility by such a dress, or else in order to display the wounds which they had received, in token of their valour. At that early period there could be no suspicion of bribery, and it was not for that reason that the citizens wished their candidates to come down among them ungirt and without a tunic. It was not till long afterwards that votes were bought and sold, and that a candidature became an affair of money. This habit of receiving bribes, when once introduced, spread to the courts of justice and to the armies of the commonwealth, and finally brought the city under the despotic rule of the emperors, as the power of arms was not equal to that of money. For it was well said that he who first introduced the habit of feasting and bribing voters ruined the constitution. This plague crept secretly and silently into Rome, and was for a long time undiscovered. We cannot tell who was the first to bribe the people or the courts of law at Rome. At Athens it is said that the first man who gave money to the judges for his acquittal was Anytus the son of Anthemion, when he was tried for treachery at Pylos towards the end of the Peloponnesian War, a period when men of uncorrupted simplicity and virtue were still to be found in the Forum at Rome.

XV. Marcius displayed many scars, gained in the numerous battles in which for seventeen years in succession he had always taken a prominent part. The people were abashed at these evidences of his valour, and agreed among themselves that they would return him as consul. But when, on the day of election, he appeared in the Forum, escorted by a splendid procession of the entire Senate, and all the patricians were seen collected round him evidently intent upon obtaining his election, many of the people lost their feeling of goodwill towards him, and regarded him with indignation and envy; which passions were assisted by their fear lest, if a man of such aristocratic tendencies and such influence with the patricians should obtain power, he might altogether destroy the liberties of the people. For these reasons they did not elect Marcius. When two persons had been elected consuls, the Senate was much irritated, considering that it, rather than its candidate Marcius, had been insulted, while he was much enraged, and could not bear his disgrace with any temper or patience, being accustomed always to yield to the more violent and ferocious emotions as being the more spirited course, without any mixture of gravity and self-restraint, virtues so necessary for political life. He had never learned how essential it is for one who undertakes to deal with men, and engage in public business, to avoid above all things that self-will which, as Plato says, is of the family of solitude, and to become longsuffering and patient, qualities which some foolish people hold very cheap. Marcius, plain and straightforward, thinking it to be the duty of a brave man to bear down all opposition, and not reflecting that it is rather a sign of weakness and feebleness of mind to be unable to restrain one's passion, flung away in a rage, bitterly irritated against the people. The young aristocracy of Rome, who had ever been his fast friends, now did him an ill service by encouraging and exasperating his anger by their expressions of sympathy; for he was their favourite leader and a most kind instructor in the art of war when on a campaign, as he taught them to delight in deeds of prowess without envying and grudging one another their proper meed of praise.

XVI. While this was the state of affairs at Rome, a large amount of corn arrived there, some of which had been bought in Italy, but most of it sent as a present from Sicily by Gelon the despot; which gave most men hopes that the famine would come to an end, and that the quarrel between the patricians and plebeians would, under these improved circumstances, be made up. The Senate at once assembled, and the people eagerly waited outside the doors of the senate house, expecting and hoping that prices would be lowered, and that the present of corn would be distributed gratis among them; and indeed some of the senators advised the adoption of that course. Marcius, however, rose and bitterly inveighed against those who favoured the people, calling them demagogues and betrayers of their own order, alleging that by such gratification they did but cherish that spirit of boldness and arrogance which had been spread among the people against the patricians, which they would have done well to crush upon its first appearance, and not suffer the plebeians to grow so strong by giving so much power to the tribunes of the people. Now, he urged, they had become formidable because every demand they made had been agreed to, and nothing done against their wishes; they contemned the authority of the consuls, and lived in defiance of the constitution, governed only by their own seditious ringleaders, to whom they gave the title of tribunes. For the Senate to sit and decree largesses of corn to the populace, as is done in the most democratic States in Greece, would merely be to pay them for their disobedience, to the common ruin of all classes. "They cannot," he went on to say, "consider this largess of corn to be a reward for the campaign in which they have refused to serve, or for the secession by which they betrayed their country, or the scandals which they have been so willing to believe against the Senate. As they cannot be said to deserve this bounty, they will imagine that it has been bestowed upon them by you because you fear them, and wish to pay your court to them. In this case there will be no bounds to their insubordination, and they never will cease from riots and disorders. To give it them is clearly an insane proceeding; nay, we ought rather, if we are wise, to take away from them this privilege of the tribuneship, which is a distinct subversion of the consulate, and a cause of dissension in the city, which now is no longer one, as before, but is rent asunder in such a manner that there is no prospect of our ever being reunited, and ceasing to be divided into two hostile factions."

XVII. With much talk to this effect Marcius excited the young men, with whom he was influential, and nearly all the richer classes, who loudly declared that he was the only man in the State who was insensible both to force and to flattery. Some of the elders, however, opposed him, foreseeing what would be the result of his policy. Indeed, no good resulted from it. The tribunes of the people, as soon as they heard that Marcius had carried his point, rushed down into the forum and called loudly upon the people to assemble and stand by them. A disorderly assembly took place, and on a report being made of Marcius's speech, the fury of the people was so great that it was proposed to break into the senate house; but the tribunes turned all the blame upon Marcius alone, and sent for him to come and speak in his own defence. As this demand was insolently refused, the tribunes themselves, together with the aediles, went to bring him by force, and actually laid hands upon him. However, the patricians rallied round him, thrust away the tribunes of the people, and even beat the aediles, their assistants in this quarrel. Night put an end to the conflict, but at daybreak the consuls, seeing the people terribly excited, and gathering in the forum from all quarters, began to fear the consequences of their fury. They assembled the senators and bade them endeavour, by mild language and healing measures, to pacify the multitude, as it was no season for pride or for standing upon their dignity, but if they were wise they would perceive that so dangerous and critical a posture of affairs required a temperate and popular policy. The majority of the senators yielded, and the consuls proceeded to soothe the people in the best way they could, answering gently such charges as had been brought against them, even speaking with the utmost caution when blaming the people for their late outrageous conduct, and declaring that there should be no difference of opinion between them about the way in which corn should be supplied, and about the price of provisions.

XVIII. As the people now for the most part had cooled down, and from their attentive and orderly demeanour were evidently much wrought upon by the words of the consuls, the tribunes came forward and addressed them. They said that now that the Senate had come to a better frame of mind, the people would willingly make concessions in their turn; but they insisted that Marcius should apologise for his conduct, or deny if he could that he had excited the Senate to destroy the constitution, that when summoned to appear he had disobeyed, and that finally he had, by beating and insulting the aediles in the market-place, done all that lay in his power to raise a civil war and make the citizens shed one another's blood. Their object in saying this was either to humble Marcius, by making him entreat the clemency of the people, which was much against his haughty temper, or else expecting that he would yield to his fiery nature and make the breach between himself and the people incurable. The latter was what they hoped for from their knowledge of his character.

Marcius came forward to speak in his defence, and the people stood listening in dead silence. But when, instead of the apologetic speech which they expected, he began to speak with a freedom which seemed more like accusing them than defending himself, while the tones of his voice and the expression of his countenance showed a fearless contempt for his audience, the people became angry, and plainly showed their disapprobation of what he said. Upon this, Sicinnius, the boldest of the tribunes, after a short consultation with his colleagues, came forward and said that the tribunes had condemned Marcius to suffer the penalty of death, and ordered the aediles to lead him at once to the Capitol, and cast him down the Tarpeian rock. When the aediles laid hold of him, many of the people themselves seemed struck with horror and remorse, and the patricians in the wildest excitement, called upon one another to rescue him, and by main force tore him from his assailants and placed him in the midst of themselves. Some of them held out their hands and besought the populace by signs, as no voice could be heard in such an uproar. At last the friends and relations of the tribunes, seeing that it was impossible to carry out their sentence on Marcius without much bloodshed, persuaded them to alter the cruel and unprecedented part of the sentence, and not to put him to death by violence, or without a trial, but to refer the matter to the people, to be voted upon by them. Upon this Sicinnius, turning to the patricians, demanded what they meant by rescuing Marcius from the people when they intended to punish him. They at once retorted, "Nay, what do you mean by dragging one of the bravest and best men in Rome to a cruel and illegal death?" "You shall not," answered Sicinnius, "make that a ground of quarrel with the people, for we allow you what you demand, that this man be put on his trial. You, Marcius, we summon to appear in the forum on the third market-day ensuing, and prove your innocence if you can, as the votes of your countrymen will be then taken about your conduct."

XIX. The patricians were glad enough to terminate the affair in this way, and retired rejoicing, bearing Marcius with them. During the time which was to elapse before the third market-day (which the Romans hold on every ninth day, and therefore call them nundinae), they had some hope that a campaign against the people of Antium would enable them to put off the trial until the people's anger had abated through length of time and warlike occupations; afterwards, as they came to terms at once with the Antiates, the patricians held frequent meetings, in which they expressed their fear of the people, and considered by what means they could avoid delivering Marcius up to them, and prevent their mob orators from exciting them. Appius Claudius, who had the reputation of being the bitterest enemy of the people in Rome, gave it as his opinion that the Senate would destroy itself and ruin the State utterly if it permitted the people to assume the power of trying patricians and voting on their trials; while the older men, and those who were more inclined to the popular side, thought that this power would render the people gentle and temperate, and not savage and cruel. The people, they said, did not despise the Senate, but imagined that they were despised by it, so that this privilege of holding the trial would agreeably salve their wounded vanity, and, as they exercised their franchise, they would lay aside their anger.

XX. Marcius, perceiving that the Senate, divided between their regard for himself and their fear of the people, knew not what to do, himself asked the tribunes of the people what it was that he was charged with, and what indictment they intended to bring against him at his trial. When they answered that the charge against him was one of treason, because he had attempted to make himself absolute despot in Rome, and that they would prove it, he at once rose, saying that he would at once defend himself before the people on that score, and that if he were convicted, he would not refuse to undergo any punishment whatever; "Only," said he, "do not bring forward some other charge against me, and deceive the Senate." When they had agreed upon these conditions, the trial took place.

The tribunes, however, when the people assembled, made them vote by tribes, and not by centuries; by which device the votes of rich respectable men who had served the State in the wars would be swamped by those of the needy rabble who cared nothing for truth or honour. In the next place, they passed by the charge of treason, as being impossible to prove, and repeated what Marcius had originally said before the Senate, when he dissuaded them from lowering the price of corn, and advised the abolition of the office of tribune. A new count in the indictment was that he had not paid over the money raised by the sale of the plunder after his expedition against Antium, but had divided it among his own followers. This last accusation is said to have disturbed Marcius more than all the rest, as he had never expected it, and was not prepared with any answer that would satisfy the people, so that the praises which he bestowed on those who had made that campaign with him only angered the far greater number who had not done so. At last the people voted. Marcius was condemned by a majority of the tribes, and was sentenced to perpetual banishment. After sentence was passed, the people displayed greater joy than if they had won a pitched battle, while the Senate was downcast and filled with regret at not having run any risks rather than allow the people to obtain so much power, and use it so insolently. Nor was there any need for distinctions of dress or anything else to distinguish the two parties, because a plebeian might be told at once by his delight, a patrician by his sorrow.

XXI. Marcius himself, however, remained unmoved. Proud and haughty as ever, he appeared not to be sorry for himself, and to be the only one of the patricians who was not. This calmness, however, was not due to any evenness of temper or any intention of bearing his wrongs meekly. It arose from concentrated rage and fury, which many do not know to be an expression of great grief. When the mind is inflamed with this passion, it casts out all ideas of submission or of quiet. Hence an angry man is courageous, just as a fever patient is hot, because of the inflamed throbbing excitement of his mind. And Marcius soon showed that this was his own condition. He went home, embraced his weeping wife and mother, bade them bear this calamity with patience, and at once proceeded to the city gates, escorted by the patricians in a body. Thence, taking nothing with him, and asking no man for any thing, he went off, accompanied by three or four of his clients. He remained for a few days at some farms near the city, agitated deeply by conflicting passions. His anger suggested no scheme by which he might benefit himself, but only how to revenge himself on the Romans. At length he decided that he would raise up a cruel war against them, and proceeded at once to make application to the neighbouring nation of the Volscians, whom he knew to be rich and powerful, and only to have suffered sufficiently by their late defeats to make them desirous of renewing their quarrel with Rome.

XXII. There was a certain citizen of Antium named Tullus Aufidius, who, from his wealth, courage, and noble birth, was regarded as the most important man in the whole Volscian nation. Marcius knew that this man hated him more than any other Roman; for in battle they had often met, and by challenging and defying one another, as young warriors are wont to do, they had, in addition to their national antipathy, gained a violent personal hatred for one another. In spite of this, however, knowing the generous nature of Tullus, and longing more than any Volscian to requite the Romans for their treatment, he justified the verses,

"'Tis hard to strive with rage, which aye, Though life's the forfeit, gains its way."

He disguised himself as completely as he could, and, like Ulysses,

"Into the city of his foes he came."

XXIII. It was evening when he entered Antium, and although many met him, no one recognised him. He went to Tullus's house, and entering, sat down by the hearth in silence, with his head wrapped in his cloak. The domestics, astonished at his behaviour, did not dare to disturb him, as there was a certain dignity about his appearance and his silence, but went and told Tullus, who was at supper, of this strange incident. Tullus rose, went to him, and inquired who he was and what he wanted. Then at length Marcius uncovered his face, and, after a short pause, said, "If you do not recognise me, Tullus, or if you do not believe your eyes, I must myself tell you who I am. I am Caius Marcius, who has wrought you and the Volscians more mischief than any one else, and who, lest I should deny this, have received the additional title of Coriolanus. This I cannot lose: every thing else has been taken from me by the envious spite of the people, and the treacherous remissness of the upper classes. I am an exile, and I now sit as a suppliant on your hearth, begging you, not for safety or protection, for should I have come hither if I feared to die, but for vengeance against those who drove me forth, which I am already beginning to receive by putting myself in your hands. If then, my brave Tullus, you wish to attack your foes, make use of my misfortunes, and let my disgrace be the common happiness of all the Volscians. I shall fight for you much better than I have fought against you, because I have the advantage of knowing exactly the strength and weakness of the enemy. If, however, you are tired of war, I have no wish for life, nor is it to your credit to save the life of one who once was your personal enemy, and who now is worn out and useless." Tullus was greatly delighted with this speech, and giving him his right hand, answered, "Rise, Marcius, and be of good courage. You have brought us a noble present, yourself; rest assured that the Volscians will not be ungrateful." He then feasted Marcius with great hospitality, and for some days they conferred together as to the best method of carrying on the war.

XXIV. Rome meanwhile was disturbed by the anger of the patricians towards the plebeians, especially on account of the banishment of Marcius, and by many portents which were observed both by the priests and by private persons, one of which was as follows. There was one Titus Latinus, a man of no great note, but a respectable citizen and by no means addicted to superstition. He dreamed that he saw Jupiter face to face, and that the god bade him tell the Senate that "they had sent a bad dancer before his procession, and one who was very displeasing to him."

On first seeing this vision he said that he disregarded it; but after it had occurred a second and a third time he had the unhappiness to see his son sicken and die, while he himself suddenly lost the use of his limbs.

He told this story in the senate house, to which he had been carried on a litter; and as soon as he had told it, he found his bodily strength return, rose, and walked home.

The senators, greatly astonished, inquired into the matter. It was found that a slave, convicted of some crime, had been ordered by his master to be flogged through the market-place, and then put to death. While this was being done, and the wretch was twisting his body in every kind of contortion as he writhed under the blows, the procession by chance was following after him. Many of those who walked in it were shocked at the unseemliness of the spectacle, and disgusted at its inhumanity, but no one did anything more than reproach and execrate a man who treated his slaves with so much cruelty.

At that period men treated their slaves with great kindness, because the master himself worked and ate in their company, and so could sympathise more with them. The great punishment for a slave who had done wrong was to make him carry round the neighbourhood the piece of wood on which the pole of a waggon is rested. The slave who has done this and been seen by the neighbours and friends, lost his credit, and was called furcifer, for the Romans call that piece of timber furca, "a fork," which the Greeks call hypostates, "a supporter."

XXV. So when Latinus related his dream to the senators, and they were wondering who the bad and unacceptable dancer could be who had led the procession, some of them remembered the slave who had been flogged through the market-place and there put to death. At the instance of the priests, the master of the slave was punished for his cruelty, and the procession and ceremonies were performed anew in honour of the gods. Hence we may see how wisely Numa arranged this, among other matters of ceremonial. Whenever the magistrates or priests were engaged in any religious rite, a herald walked before them crying in a loud voice "Hoc age." The meaning of the phrase is, "Do this," meaning to tell the people to apply their minds entirely to the religious ceremony, and not to allow any thought of worldly things to distract their attention, because men as a rule only attend to such matters by putting a certain constraint on their thoughts.

It is the custom in Rome to begin a sacrifice, a procession, or a spectacle, over again, not only when anything of this kind happens, but for any trifling reason. Thus, if one of the horses drawing the sacred car called Thensa stumbles, or the charioteer takes the reins in his left hand, they have decreed that the procession must begin again. In later times they have been known to perform one sacrifice thirty times, because every time some slight omission or mistake took place.

XXVI. Meanwhile Marcius and Tullus in Antium held private conferences with the chief men of the Volscians, and advised them to begin the war while Rome was divided by its domestic quarrels. They discountenanced this proposal, because a truce and cessation of hostilities for two years had been agreed upon: but the Romans themselves gave them a pretext for breaking the truce, by a proclamation which was made at the public games, that all Volscians should quit the city before sunset. Some say this was effected by a stratagem of Marcius, who sent a false accusation against the Volscians to the magistrates at Rome, saying that during the public games they meant to attack the Romans and burn the city. This proclamation made them yet bitterer enemies to the Romans than before; and Tullus, wishing to bring the business to a climax, induced his countrymen to send ambassadors to Rome to demand back the cities and territory which the Romans had taken from the Volscians in the late war. The Romans were very indignant when they heard these demands, and made answer, that the Volscians might be the first to take up arms, but that the Romans would be the last to lay them down. Upon this, Tullus convoked a general assembly, in which, after determining upon war, he advised them to summon Marcius to their aid, not owing him any grudge for what they had suffered at his hands, but believing that he would be more valuable to them as a friend than he had been dangerous as an enemy.

XXVII. Marcius was called before the assembly, and having addressed the people, was thought by them to know how to speak as well as how to fight, and was considered to be a man of great ability and courage. He, together with Tullus, was nominated general with unlimited powers. As he feared the Volscians would take a long time to prepare for the war, and that meanwhile the opportunity for attack might pass away, he ordered the leading men in the city to make all necessary preparations, and himself taking the boldest and most forward as volunteers, without levying any troops by compulsory conscription, made a sudden and unexpected inroad into the Roman territory. Here he obtained so much plunder that the Volscians were wearied with carrying it off and consuming it in their camp. However, his least object was to obtain plunder and lay waste the country; his main desire was to render the patricians suspected by the people. While all else was ravaged and destroyed, he carefully protected their farms, and would not allow any damage to be done or anything to be carried off from them. This increased the disorders at Rome, the patricians reproaching the people for having unjustly banished so able a man, while the plebeians accused them of having invited Marcius to attack in order to obtain their revenge, and said that, while others fought, they sat as idle spectators, having in the war itself a sure safeguard of their wealth and estates. Having produced this new quarrel among the Romans, and, besides loading the Volscians with plunder, having taught them to despise their enemy, Marcius led his troops back in safety.

XXVIII. By great and zealous exertions the entire Volscian nation was soon assembled under arms. The force thus raised was very large; part was left to garrison the cities, as a measure of precaution, while the rest was to be used in the campaign against Rome. Marcius now left Tullus to determine which corps he would command. Tullus, in answer, said that as Marcius, he knew, was as brave a man as himself, and had always enjoyed better fortune in all his battles, he had better command the army in the field. He himself, he added, would remain behind, watch over the safety of the Volscian cities, and supply the troops with necessaries. Marcius, strengthened by this division of the command, marched to the town of Circeii, a Roman colony. As it surrendered, he did it no harm, but laid waste the country of Latium, where he expected the Romans would fight a battle in defence of their allies the Latins, who frequently sent to entreat their protection. But at Rome the people were unwilling to fight, and the consuls were just at the expiry of their term of office, so that they did not care to run any risks, and therefore rejected the appeals of the Latins. Marcius now led his troops against the Latian cities, Tolerium, Labici, Pedum, and Bola, all of which he took by storm, sold the inhabitants for slaves, and plundered the houses. Those cities, however, which voluntarily came to his side he treated with the utmost consideration, even pitching his camp at a distance, for fear they might be injured by the soldiery against his will, and never plundering their territory.

XXIX. When at last he took Bollae, a town not more than twelve miles from Rome, obtaining immense booty and putting nearly all the adult inhabitants to the sword, then not even those Volscians who had been appointed to garrison the cities would any longer remain at their posts, but seized their arms and joined the army of Marcius, declaring that he was their only general, and that they would recognise no other leader. His renown and glory spread throughout all Italy, and all men were astonished that one man by changing sides should have produced so great a change. The affairs of Rome were in the last disorder, the people refusing to fight, while internal quarrels and seditious speeches took place daily, until news came that

Lavinium was being invested by the enemy. This town contains the most ancient images and sacred things of the tutelary deities of Rome, and is the origin of the Roman people, being the first town founded by Aeneas.

Upon this a very singular change of opinions befel both the people and the Senate. The people were eager to annul their sentence against Marcius, and to beg him to return, but the Senate, after meeting and considering this proposal, finally rejected it, either out of a mere spirit of opposition to anything proposed by the people, or because they did not wish him to return by favour of the people; or it may be because they themselves were now angry with him for having shown himself the enemy of all classes alike, although he had only been injured by one, and for having become the avowed enemy of his country, in which he knew that the best and noblest all sympathised with him, and had suffered along with him. When this resolution was made known to the people, they were unable to proceed to vote or to pass any bill on the subject, without a previous decree of the Senate.

XXX. Marcius when he heard of this was more exasperated than ever. He raised his siege of Lavinium, marched straight upon Rome, and pitched his camp five miles from the city, at the place called Fossae Cluiliae. The appearance of his army caused much terror and disturbance, but nevertheless put an end to sedition, for no magistrate or patrician dared any longer oppose the people's desire to recall him. When they beheld the women running distractedly through the city, the old men weeping and praying at the altars, and no one able to take courage and form any plan of defence, it was agreed that the people had been right in wishing to come to terms with Marcius, and that the Senate had committed a fatal error in inflicting a new outrage upon him, just at the time when all unkindness might have been buried. It was determined, therefore, by the whole city that an embassy should be despatched to Marcius, to offer him restoration to his own country, and to beg of him to make peace. Those of the Senate who were sent were relations of Marcius, and expected to be warmly welcomed by a man who was their near relation and personal friend. Nothing of the kind, however, happened. They were conducted through the enemy's camp, and found him seated, and displaying insufferable pride and arrogance, with the chiefs of the Volscians standing round him. He bade the ambassadors deliver their message; and after they had, in a supplicatory fashion, pronounced a conciliatory oration, he answered them, dwelling with bitterness on his own unjust treatment; and then in his capacity of general-in-chief of the Volscians, he bade them restore the cities and territory which they had conquered in the late war, and to grant the franchise to the Volscians on the same terms as enjoyed by the Latins.

These, he said, were the only conditions on which a just and lasting peace could be made. He allowed them a space of thirty days for deliberation, and on the departure of the ambassadors immediately drew off his forces.

XXXI. This affair gave an opportunity to several of the Volscians, who had long envied and disliked his reputation, and the influence which he had with the people. Among these was Tullus himself, who had not been personally wronged by Marcius, but who, as it is natural he should, felt vexed at being totally eclipsed and thrown into the shade, for the Volscians now thought Marcius the greatest man in their whole nation, and considered that any one else ought to be thankful for any measure of authority that he might think fit to bestow. Hence secret hints were exchanged, and private meetings held, in which his enemies expressed their dissatisfaction, calling the retreat from Rome an act of treason, not indeed that he had betrayed any cities or armies to the enemy, but he had granted them time, by which all other things are won and lost. He had given the enemy a breathing time, they said, of thirty days, being no less than they required to put themselves in a posture of defence.

Marcius during this time was not idle, for he attacked and defeated the allies of the Romans, and captured seven large and populous towns. The Romans did not venture to come to help their allies, but hung back from taking the field, and seemed as if paralysed and benumbed. When the term had expired, Marcius presented himself a second time before Rome, with his entire army. The Romans now sent a second embassy, begging him to lay aside his anger, withdraw the Volscians from the country, and then to make such terms as would be for the advantage of both nations. The Romans, they said, would yield nothing to fear; but if he thought that special concessions ought to be made to the Volscians, they would be duly considered if they laid down their arms. To this Marcius answered that, as general of the Volscians, he could give them no answer; but that as one who was still a citizen of Rome he would advise them to adopt a humbler frame of mind, and come to him in three days with a ratification of his proposals. If they should come to any other determination, he warned them that it would not be safe for them to come to his camp again with empty words.

XXXII. When the ambassadors returned, and the Senate heard their report, they determined in this dreadful extremity to let go their sheet anchor. They ordered all the priests, ministers, and guardians of the sacred mysteries, and all the hereditary prophets who watched the omens given by the flight of birds, to go in procession to Marcius, dressed in their sacred vestments, and beseech him to desist from the war, and then to negotiate conditions of peace between his countrymen and the Volscians. Marcius received the priests in his camp, but relaxed nothing of his former harshness, bidding the Romans either accept his proposals or continue the war.

When the priests returned, the Romans resolved in future to remain within the city, repulse any assault which might be made on the walls, and trust to time and fortune, as it was evident that they could not be saved by anything that they could do. The city was full of confusion, excitement, and panic terror, until there happened something like what is mentioned in Homer, but which men as a rule are unwilling to believe. He observes that on great and important occasions

"Athene placed a thought within his mind;"
and again—
"But some one of th' immortals changed my mind,
And made me think of what the folk would say;"
and—
"Because he thought it, or because the god
Commanded him to do so."

Men despise the poet, as if, in order to carry out his absurd mythological scheme, he denied each man his liberty of will. Now Homer does nothing of this kind, for whatever is reasonable and likely he ascribes to the exercise of our own powers, as we see in the common phrase—

"But I reflected in my mighty soul;"
and—
"Thus spoke he, but the son of Peleus raged,
Divided was his soul within his breast;"
and again—
"But she persuaded not The wise Bellerophon, of noble mind."

But in strange and unlikely actions, where the actors must have been under the influence of some supernatural impulse, he does speak of the god not as destroying, but as directing the human will; nor does the god directly produce any decision, but suggests ideas which influence that decision. Thus the act is not an involuntary one, but opportunity is given for a voluntary act, with confidence and good hope superadded. For either we must admit that the gods have no dealings and influence at all with men, or else it must be in this way that they act when they assist and strengthen us, not of course by moving our hands and feet, but by filling our minds with thoughts and ideas which either encourage us to do what is right, or restrain us from what is wrong.

XXXIII. At Rome at this time the women were praying in all the temples, especially in that of Jupiter in the Capitol, where the noblest ladies in Rome were assembled. Among them was Valeria, the sister of the great Poplicola, who had done such great services to the State both in peace and war. Poplicola died some time before, as has been related in his Life, but his sister was held in great honour and esteem in Rome, as her life did credit to her noble birth. She now experienced one of the divine impulses of which I have spoken, and, inspired by Heaven to do what was best for her country, rose and called on the other ladies to accompany her to the house of Volumnia, the mother of Marcius. On entering, and finding her sitting with her daughter-in-law, nursing the children of Marcius, Valeria placed her companions in a circle round them, and spoke as follows: "Volumnia, and you, Virgilia, we have come to you, as women to women, without any decree of the Senate or instructions from a magistrate; but Heaven, it would appear, has heard our prayers, and has inspired us with the idea of coming hither to beg of you to save our countrymen, and to gain for yourselves greater glory than that of the Sabine women when they reconciled their husbands and their fathers. Come with us to Marcius, join us in supplicating him for mercy, and bear an honourable testimony to your country, that it never has thought of hurting you, however terribly it has been injured by Marcius, but that it restores you to him uninjured, although possibly it will gain no better terms by so doing." When Valeria had spoken thus, the other women applauded, and Volumnia answered in the following words: "My friends, besides those sufferings which all are now undergoing, we are especially to be pitied. We have lost the glory and goodness of our Marcius, and now see him more imprisoned in than protected by the army of the enemy. But the greatest misfortune of all is that our country should have become so weak as to be obliged to rest its hopes of safety on us. I cannot tell if he will pay any attention to us, seeing that he has treated his native country with scorn, although he used to love it better than his mother, his wife, and his children. However, take us, and make what use of us you can. Lead us into his presence, and there, if we can do nothing else, we can die at his feet supplicating for Rome."

XXXIV. Having spoken thus, she took Virgilia and her children, and proceeded, in company with the other women, to the Volscian camp. Their piteous appearance produced, even in their enemies, a silent respect. Marcius himself was seated on his tribunal with the chief officers; and when he saw the procession of women was at first filled with amazement; but when he recognised his mother walking first, although he tried to support his usual stern composure, he was overcome by his emotion. He could not bear to receive her sitting, but descended and ran to meet her. He embraced his mother first, and longest of all; and then his wife and children, no longer restraining his tears and caresses, but completely carried away by his feelings.

XXXV. When he had taken his fill of embraces, perceiving that his mother desired to address him, he called the chiefs of the Volscians together, and listened to Volumnia, who addressed him as follows:

"You may judge, my son, by our dress and appearance, even though we keep silence, to what a miserable condition your exile has reduced us at home. Think now, how unhappy we must be, beyond all other women, when fortune has made the sight which ought to be most pleasing to us, most terrible, when I see my son, and your wife here sees her husband, besieging his native city. Even that which consoles people under all other misfortunes, prayer to the gods, has become impossible for us. We cannot beg of heaven to give us the victory and to save you, but our prayers for you must always resemble the imprecations of our enemies against Rome. Your wife and children are in such a position, that they must either lose you or lose their native country. For my own part, I cannot bear to live until fortune decides the event of this war. If I cannot now persuade you to make a lasting peace, and so become the benefactor instead of the scourge of the two nations, be well assured that you shall never assail Rome without first passing over the corpse of your mother. I cannot wait for that day on which I shall either see my countrymen triumphing over my son, or my son triumphing over his country. If indeed I were to ask you to betray the Volscians and save your country, this would be a hard request for you to grant; for though it is base to destroy one's own fellow citizens, it is equally wrong to betray those who have trusted you. But we merely ask for a respite from our sufferings, which will save both nations alike from ruin, and which will be all the more glorious for the Volscians because their superiority in the field has put them in a position to grant us the greatest of blessings, peace and concord, in which they also will share alike with us. You will be chiefly to be thanked for these blessings, if we obtain them, and chiefly to be blamed if we do not. For though the issue of war is always doubtful, this much is evident, that if you succeed, you will become your country's evil genius, and if you fail, you will have inflicted the greatest miseries on men who are your friends and benefactors, merely in order to gratify your own private spite."

XXXVI. While Volumnia spoke thus, Marcius listened to her in silence. After she had ceased, he stood for a long while without speaking, until she again addressed him. "Why art thou silent, my son? Is it honourable to make everything give way to your rancorous hatred, and is it a disgrace to yield to your mother, when she pleads for such important matters? Does it become a great man to remember that he has been ill treated, and does it not rather become him to recollect the debt which children owe to their parents. And yet no one ought to be more grateful than you yourself, who punish ingratitude so bitterly: in spite of which, though you have already taken a deep revenge on your country for its ill treatment of you, you have not made your mother any return for her kindness. It would have been right for me to gain my point without any pressure, when pleading in such a just and honourable cause; but if I cannot prevail by words, this resource alone is left me." Saying this, she fell at his feet, together with his wife and children. Marcius, crying out, "What have you done to me, mother?" raised her from the ground, and pressing her hand violently, exclaimed, "You have conquered; your victory is a blessed one for Rome, but ruinous to me, for I shall retreat conquered by you alone." After speaking thus, and conferring for a short time in private with his mother and his wife, he at their own request sent them back to Rome, and the following night led away the Volscian army. Various opinions were current among the Volscians about what had taken place. Some blamed him severely, while others approved, because they wished for peace. Others again, though they disliked what he had done, yet did not regard him as a traitor, but as a soft-hearted man who had yielded to overwhelming pressure. However, no one disobeyed him, but all followed him in his retreat, though more out of regard for his noble character than for his authority.

XXXVII. The Roman people, when the war was at an end, showed even more plainly than before what terror and despair they had been in. As soon as they saw the Volscians retreating from their walls, all the temples were opened, and filled with worshippers crowned with garlands and sacrificing as if for a victory. The joy of the senate and people was most conspicuously shown in their gratitude to the women, whom they spoke of as having beyond all doubt saved Rome. The senate decreed that the magistrates should grant to the women any mark of respect and esteem which they themselves might choose. The women decided on the building of the temple of Female Fortune, the expenses of which they themselves offered to subscribe, only asking the state to undertake the maintenance of the services in it. The senate praised their public spirit, but ordered the temple and shrine to be built at the public expense. Nevertheless, the women with their own money provided a second image of the goddess, which the Romans say, when it was placed in the temple was heard to say,

"A pleasing gift have women placed me here."

XXXVIII. The legend says that this voice was twice heard, which seems impossible and hard for us to believe. It is not impossible for statues to sweat, to shed tears, or to be covered with spots of blood, because wood and stone often when mouldering or decaying, collect moisture within them, and not only send it forth with many colours derived from their own substance, but also receive other colours from the air; and there is nothing that forbids us to believe that by such appearances as these heaven may foreshadow the future. It is also possible that statues should make sounds like moaning or sighing, by the tearing asunder of the particles of which they are composed; but that articulate human speech should come from inanimate things is altogether impossible, for neither the human soul, nor even a god can utter words without a body fitted with the organs of speech. Whenever therefore we find many credible witnesses who force us to believe something of this kind, we must suppose that the imagination was influenced by some sensation which appeared to resemble a real one, just as in dreams we seem to hear when we hear not, and to see when we see not. Those persons, however, who are full of religious fervour and love of the gods, and who refuse to disbelieve or reject anything of this kind, find in its miraculous character, and in the fact that the ways of God are not as our ways, a great support to their faith. For He resembles mankind in nothing, neither in nature, nor movement, nor learning, nor power, and so it is not to be wondered at if He does what seems to us impossible. Nay, though He differs from us in every respect, it is in his works that He is most unlike us. But, as Herakleitus says, our knowledge of things divine mostly fails for want of faith.

XXXIX. When Marcius returned to Antium, Tullus, who had long hated him and envied his superiority, determined to put him to death, thinking that if he let slip the present opportunity he should not obtain another. Having suborned many to bear witness against him, he called upon him publicly to render an account to the Volscians of what he had done as their general. Marcius, fearing to be reduced to a private station while his enemy Tullus, who had great influence with his countrymen, was general, answered that he had been given his office of commander-in-chief by the Volscian nation, and to them alone would he surrender it, but that as to an account of what he had done, he was ready at that moment, if they chose, to render it to the people of Antium. Accordingly the people assembled, and the popular orators endeavoured by their speeches to excite the lower classes against Marcius. When, however, he rose to speak, the mob were awed to silence, while the nobility, and those who had gained by the peace, made no secret of their good will towards him, and of their intention to vote in his favour. Under these circumstances, Tullus was unwilling to let him speak, for he was a brilliant orator, and his former services far outweighed his last offence. Indeed, the whole indictment was a proof of how much they owed him, for they never could have thought themselves wronged by not taking Rome, if Marcius had not brought them so near to taking it. Tullus, therefore, thought that it would not do to wait, or to trust to the mob, but he and the boldest of his accomplices, crying out that the Volscians could not listen to the traitor, nor endure him to play the despot over them by not laying down his command, rushed upon him in a body and killed him, without any of the bystanders interfering in his behalf. However, the most part of the nation was displeased at this act, as was soon proved by the numbers who came from every city to see his dead body, by the splendid funeral with which he was honoured, and by the arms and trophies which were hung over his tomb, as that of a brave man and a consummate general.

The Romans, when they heard of his death, made no sign of either honour or anger towards him, except that they gave permission to the women, at their request, to wear mourning for him for ten months, as if they were each mourning for her father, her brother, or her son. This was the extreme limit of the period of mourning, which was fixed by Numa Pompilius, as has been related in his Life.

The loss of Marcius was at once felt by the Volscians. First of all, they quarrelled with the Aequi, their friends and allies, and even came to blows with them; next, they were defeated by the Romans in a battle in which Tullus was slain, and the flower of the Volscian army perished. After this disaster they were glad to surrender at discretion, and become the subjects of Rome.

Comparison of Alkibiades and Coriolanus.

I. As all the most memorable achievements of both Alkibiades and Coriolanus are now before us, we may begin our comparison by observing that as to military exploits, the balance is nearly even; for both alike gave proofs of great personal bravery and great skill in generalship, unless it be thought that Alkibiades proved himself the more perfect general because of his many victories both by sea and land. Both alike obtained great success for their native countries while they remained in command of their countrymen, and both succeeded even more remarkably when fighting against them. As to their respective policy, that of Alkibiades was disliked by the more respectable citizens, because of his personal arrogance, and the arts to which he stooped to gain the favour of the lower classes; while the proud ungracious haughtiness of Coriolanus caused him to be hated by the people of Rome. In this respect neither of them can be praised; yet he who tries to gain the favour of the people is less to blame than he who insults them for fear he should be thought to court them. Although it is wrong to flatter the people in order to gain power, yet to owe one's power only to terror, and to ill treat and keep down the masses is disgraceful as well as wrong.

II. It is not difficult to see why Marcius is considered to have been a simple-minded and straightforward character, while Alkibiades has the reputation of a false and tricky politician. The latter has been especially blamed for the manner in which he deceived and outwitted the Lacedaemonian ambassadors, by which, as we learn from Thucydides, he brought the truce between the two nations to an end. Yet that stroke of policy, though it again involved Athens in war, rendered her strong and formidable, through the alliance with Argos and Mantinea, which she owed to Alkibiades. Marcius also, we are told by Dionysius, produced a quarrel between the Romans and the Volscians by bringing a false accusation against those Volscians who came to see the festival at Rome; and in this case the wickedness of his object increased his guilt, because he did not act from a desire of personal aggrandisement, or from political rivalry, as did Alkibiades, but merely yielding to what Dion calls the unprofitable passion of anger, he threw a large part of Italy into confusion, and in his rage against his native country destroyed many innocent cities. On the other hand, the anger of Alkibiades caused great misfortune to his countrymen; yet as soon as he found that they had relented towards him he returned cheerfully to his allegiance, and after being banished for the second time, did not take any delight in seeing their generals defeated, and could not sit still and let them make mistakes and uselessly expose themselves to danger. He did just what Aristeides is so much praised for doing to Themistokles; he went to the generals, although they were not his friends, and pointed out to them what ought to be done.

Marcius, again, is to be blamed for having made the whole of Rome suffer for what only a part of it had done, while the best and most important class of citizens had been wronged equally with himself, and warmly sympathised with him. Afterwards, although his countrymen sent him many embassies, beseeching his forgiveness for their one act of ignorance and passion, he would not listen to them, but showed that it was with the intention of utterly destroying Rome, not of obtaining his own restoration to it, that he had begun that terrible and savage war against it. This, then, may be noted as the difference between their respective positions: Alkibiades went back to the Athenian side when the Spartans began to plot against him, because he both feared them and hated them; but Marcius, who was in every respect well treated by the Volscians, could not honourably desert their cause. He had been elected their commander-in-chief, and besides this great power enjoyed their entire confidence; while Alkibiades, though his assistance was found useful by the Lacedaemonians, was never trusted by them, but remained without any recognised position, first in Sparta and then in the camp in Asia Minor, till he finally threw himself into the arms of Tissaphernes, unless, indeed, he took this step to save Athens, hoping some day to be restored to her.

III. As to money, Alkibiades has been blamed for receiving it discreditably in bribes, and for spending it in luxurious extravagance; while the generals who offered Marcius money as an honourable reward for his valour could not prevail upon him to accept it. This, however, made him especially unpopular in the debates about freeing the people from debt, because it was said that he pressed so hardly on the poor, not because he wished to make money by them, but purely through arrogance and pride. Antipater, in a letter to a friend on the death of Aristotle the philosopher, observes, "Besides his other abilities, the man had the art of persuasion." Now Marcius had not this art; and its absence made all his exploits and all his virtues unpleasant even to those who benefited by them, as they could not endure his pride and haughtiness, which brooked no compeer. Alkibiades, on the other hand, knew how to deal on friendly terms with every one, and we need not therefore be surprised at the pleasure which men took in his successes, while even some of his failures had a charm of their own for his friends. Hence it was that Alkibiades, even after inflicting many grievous losses upon his countrymen, was chosen by them as commander-in-chief, whereas Marcius, when after a splendid display of courage and conduct he tried for the consulship which he deserved, failed to obtain it. The one could not be hated by his countrymen, even when they were ill treated by him; while the other, though admired by all, was loved by none.

IV. Marcius, indeed, effected nothing great when in command of his own countrymen, but only when fighting against them, whereas the Athenians frequently benefited by the successes of Alkibiades, when he was acting as their commander-in-chief. Alkibiades when present easily triumphed over his enemies, whereas Marcius, although present, was condemned by the Romans, and put to death by the Volscians. Moreover, though he was wrongfully slain, yet he himself furnished his enemies with a pretext for his murder, by refusing the public offer of peace made by the Romans, and then yielding to the private entreaties of his mother and wife, so that he did not put an end to the enmity between the two nations, but left them at war, and yet lost a favourable opportunity for the Volscians.

If he was influenced by a feeling of duty towards the Volscians, he ought to have obtained their consent before withdrawing their forces from before Rome; but if he cared nothing for them, or for anything except the gratification of his own passion, and with this feeling made war upon his country, and only paused in the moment of victory, it was not creditable to him to spare his country for his mother's sake, but rather he should have spared his country and his mother with it; for his mother and his wife were but a part of Rome, which he was besieging. That he should have treated the public supplications of ambassadors and the prayers of priests with contempt, and afterwards have drawn off his forces to please his mother, is not so much a credit to her as a disgrace to his country, which was saved by the tears and entreaties of one woman, as though it did not deserve to survive on its own merits. The mercy which he showed the Romans was so harshly and offensively granted that it pleased neither party; he withdrew his forces without having either having come to an understanding with his friends or his foes. All this must be attributed to his haughty, unbending temper, which is in all cases odious, but which in an ambitious man renders him savage and inexorable. Such men will not seek for popularity, thinking themselves already sufficiently distinguished, and then are angry at finding themselves unpopular.

Indeed, neither Metellus, nor Aristeides, nor Epameinondas would stoop to court the favour of the people, and had a thorough contempt for all that the people can either give or take away; yet although they were often ostracised, convicted, and condemned to pay fines, they were not angry with their fellow countrymen for their folly, but came back and became reconciled to them as soon as they repented. The man who will not court the people, ought least of all to bear malice against them, reflecting that anger at not being elected to an office in the state, must spring from an excessive desire to obtain it.

V. Alkibiades made no secret of his delight in being honoured and his vexation when slighted, and in consequence endeavoured to make himself acceptable to all with whom he had to do. Marcius was prevented by his pride from courting those who could have bestowed honour and advancement upon him, while his ambition tortured him if these were withheld.

These are the points which we find to blame in his character, which in all other respects was a noble one. With regard to temperance, and contempt for money, he may be compared with the greatest and purest men of Greece, not merely with Alkibiades, who cared only too little for such things, and paid no regard to his reputation.

Life of Timoleon.

It was for the sake of others that I first undertook to write biographies, but I soon began to dwell upon and delight in them for myself, endeavouring to the best of my ability to regulate my own life, and to make it like that of those who were reflected in their history as it were in a mirror before me. By the study of their biographies, we receive each man as a guest into our minds, and we seem to understand their character as the result of a personal acquaintance, because we have obtained from their acts the best and most important means of forming an opinion about them. "What greater pleasure could'st thou gain than this?" What more valuable for the elevation of our own character? Demokritus says, that we ought to pray that we may meet with propitious phantasms, and that from the infinite space which surrounds us good and congenial phantasms, rather than base and sinister ones, may be brought into contact with us. He degrades philosophy by foisting into it a theory which is untrue, and which leads to unbounded superstition; whereas we, by our familiarity with history, and habit of writing it, so train ourselves by constantly receiving into our minds the memorials of the great and good, that should anything base or vicious be placed in our way by the society into which we are necessarily thrown, we reject it and expel it from our thoughts, by fixing them calmly and severely on some of these great examples. Of these, I have chosen for you in this present instance, the life of Timoleon the Corinthian, and that of Aemilius Paulus, men who both laid their plans with skill, and carried them out with good fortune, so as to raise a question whether it was more by good luck or by good sense that they succeeded in their most important achievements.

I. The state of affairs at Syracuse, before the mission of Timoleon to Sicily, was this. Dion had driven out the despot Dionysius, but was immediately afterwards slain by treachery, and those who, under Dion, had freed the Syracusans, quarrelled amongst themselves. The city, which received a constant succession of despots, was almost forsaken because of its many troubles. Of the rest of Sicily, one part was rendered quite ruined and uninhabited by the wars, and most of the cities were held by barbarians of various nations, and soldiers who were under no paymaster. As these men willingly lent their aid to effect changes of dynasty, Dionysius, in the twelfth year of his exile, collected a body of foreign troops, drove out Nysaeus, the then ruler of Syracuse, again restored his empire, and was re-established as despot. He had strangely lost the greatest known empire at the hands of a few men, and more strangely still became again the lord of those who had driven him out, after having been an exile and a beggar. Those then of the Syracusans who remained in the city were the subjects of a despot not naturally humane, and whose heart now had been embittered by misfortune: but the better class of citizens and the men of note fled to Hiketes, the ruler of Leontini, swore allegiance to him, and chose him as their general for the war. This man was nowise better than the avowed despots, but they had no other resource, and they trusted him because he was a Syracusan by birth, and had a force capable of encountering that of their own despot.

II. Meanwhile the Carthaginians came to Sicily with a great fleet, and were hovering off the island watching their opportunity. The Sicilians in terror wished to send an embassy to Greece, and ask for help from the Corinthians, not merely on account of their kinship with them, and of the many kindnesses which they had received from them, but also because they saw that the whole city loved freedom, and hated despots, and that it had waged its greatest and most important wars, not for supremacy and greed of power, but on behalf of the liberty of Greece. But Hiketes who had obtained his post of commander-in-chief with a view, not to the liberation of Syracuse, but the establishment of himself as despot there, had already had secret negotiations with the Carthaginians, though in public he commended the Syracusans, and sent ambassadors of his own with the rest to Peloponnesus: not that he wished that any assistance should come thence, but, in case the Corinthians, as was probable, should refuse their help because of the disturbed state of Greece, he hoped that he should more easily be able to bring matters round to suit the Carthaginian interest, and to use them as allies either against the Syracusan citizens, or against their despot. Of this treacherous design he was shortly afterwards convicted.

III. When the ambassadors arrived, the Corinthians, who had always been in the habit of watching over the interests of their colonies, especially Syracuse, and who were not at war with any of the Greek States at that time, but living in peace and leisure, eagerly voted to help them. A General was now sought for, and while the government was nominating and proposing those who were eager for an opportunity of distinguishing themselves, a man of the people stood up and named Timoleon, the son of Timodemus, one who no longer took any part in politics, and who had no hope or thought of obtaining the post: but some god, it seems, put it into the man's mind to name him, such a kind fortune was at once shown at his election, and such success attended his actions, illustrating his noble character. He was of a good family, both his father Timodemus, and his mother Demariste being of rank in the city. He was a lover of his country, and of a mild temper, except only that he had a violent hatred for despotism and all that is base. His nature was so happily constituted, that in his campaigns he showed much judgment when young, and no less daring when old. He had an elder brother, Timophanes, who was in no respect like him, but rash, and inflamed with a passion for monarchy by worthless friends and foreign soldiers, with whom he spent all his time: he was reckless in a campaign, and loved danger for its own sake, and by this he won the hearts of his fellow-citizens, and was given commands, as being a man of courage and of action. Timoleon assisted him in obtaining these commands, by concealing his faults or making them appear small, and by magnifying the clever things which he did.

IV. Now in the battle which the Corinthians fought against the Argives and Kleoneans, Timoleon was ranked among the hoplites, and his brother Timophanes, who was in command of the cavalry, fell into great danger. His horse received a wound, and threw him off among the enemy. Of his companions, some at once dispersed in panic, while those who remained by him, being a few against many, with difficulty held their own. When Timoleon saw what had happened, he ran to the rescue, and held his shield in front of Timophanes as he lay, and, after receiving many blows, both from missiles and in hand-to-hand fight, on his arms and body, with difficulty drove back the enemy and saved his brother.

When the Corinthians, fearing lest they might again suffer what they did once before when their own allies took their city, decreed that they would keep four hundred mercenary soldiers, they made Timophanes their commander.

But he, disdaining truth and honour, immediately took measures to get the city into his own power, and showed his tyrannical disposition by putting to death many of the leading citizens without a trial. Timoleon was grieved at this, and, treating the other's crime as his own misfortune, endeavoured to argue with him, and begged him to abandon his foolish and wicked design, and to seek for some means of making amends to his fellow-citizens. However, as he rejected his brother's advice, and treated him with contempt, Timoleon took Aeschylus, his kinsman, brother of the wife of Timophanes, and his friend the seer, whom Theopompus calls Satyrus, but Ephorus and Timaeus call Orthagoras, and, after an interval of a few days, again went to his brother. The three men now stood round him, and besought him even now to listen to reason, and repent of his ambition; but as Timophanes at first laughed at them, and then became angry and indignant, Timoleon stepped a little aside, and covering his face, stood weeping, while the other two drew their swords and quickly despatched him.

V. When this deed was noised abroad, the more generous of the Corinthians praised Timoleon for his abhorrence of wickedness and his greatness of soul, because, though of a kindly disposition, and fond of his own family, he had nevertheless preferred his country to his family, and truth and justice to his own advantage. He had distinguished himself in his country's cause both by saving his brother's life, and by putting him to death when he plotted to reduce her to slavery. However, those who could not endure to live in a democracy, and who were accustomed to look up to those in power, pretended to rejoice in the death of the tyrant, but by their abuse of Timoleon for having done an unholy and impious deed, reduced him to a state of great melancholy. Hearing that his mother took it greatly to heart, and that she used harsh words and invoked terrible curses upon him, he went to her to try to bring her to another state of mind, but she would not endure the sight of him, but shut the door against him. Then indeed he became very dejected, and disordered in his mind, so as to form an intention of destroying himself by starvation; but this his friends would not permit, but prevailed on him by force and entreaty so that he determined to live, but alone by himself. He gave up all interest in public affairs, and at first did not even enter the city, but passed his time wandering in the wildest part of the country in an agony of mind.

VI. Thus our judgments, if they do not borrow from reason and philosophy a fixity and steadiness of purpose in their acts, are easily swayed and influenced by the praise or blame of others, which make us distrust our own opinions.

For not only, it seems, must the deed itself be noble and just, but also the principle from which we do it must be stable and unchangeable, so that we may make up our minds and then act from conviction. If we do not, then like those epicures who most eagerly seize upon the daintiest food and soonest become satiated and nauseate it, so we become filled with sorrow and remorse when the deed is done, because the splendid ideas of virtue and honour which led us to do it fade away in our minds on account of our own moral weakness. A remorseful change of mind renders even a noble action base, whereas the determination which is grounded on knowledge and reason cannot change even if its actions fail. Wherefore Phokion the Athenian, who opposed the measures of Leosthenes, when Leosthenes seemed to have succeeded, and he saw the Athenians sacrificing and priding themselves on their victory, said that he should have wished that he had himself done what had been done, but he should wish to have given the same counsel that he did give. Aristeides the Lokrian, one of the companions of Plato, put this even more strongly when Dionysius the elder asked for one of his daughters in marriage. "I had rather," he said, "see the girl a corpse, than the consort of a despot." A short time afterwards when Dionysius put his sons to death and insultingly asked him whether he were still of the same mind about the disposal of his daughter, he answered, that he was grieved at what had happened, but had not changed his mind about what he had said. And these words perhaps show a greater and more perfect virtue than Phokion's.

VII. Now Timoleon's misery, after the deed was done, whether it was caused by pity for the dead or filial reverence for his mother, so broke down and humbled his spirit that for nearly twenty years he took no part in any important public affair. So when he was nominated as General, and when the people gladly received his name and elected him, Telekleides, who at that time was the first man in the city for power and reputation, stood up and spoke encouragingly to Timoleon, bidding him prove himself brave and noble in the campaign. "If," said he, "you fight well, we shall think that we slew a tyrant, but if badly, that we murdered your brother."

While Timoleon was preparing for his voyage and collecting his soldiers, letters were brought to the Corinthians from Hiketes plainly showing that he had changed sides and betrayed them.

For as soon as he had sent off his ambassadors to Corinth, he openly joined the Carthaginians, and in concert with them attempted to drive out Dionysius and establish himself as despot of Syracuse.

Fearing that the opportunity would escape him if an army and general came from Corinth before he had succeeded, he sent a letter to the Corinthians to say that they need not incur the trouble and expense of sending an expedition to Sicily and risking their lives, especially as the Carthaginians would dispute their passage, and were now watching for their expedition with a numerous fleet; and that, as they had been so slow, he should be obliged to make these Carthaginians his allies to attack the despot.

When these letters were read, even if any of the Corinthians had been lukewarm about the expedition, now their anger against Hiketes stirred them up to co-operate vigorously with Timoleon and assist him in equipping his force.

VIII. When the ships were ready, and everything had been provided for the soldiers, the priestesses of Proserpine had a dream that the two goddesses appeared dressed for a journey, and said that they were going to accompany Timoleon on his voyage to Sicily.

Hereupon the Corinthians equipped a sacred trireme, and named it after the two goddesses. Timoleon himself proceeded to Delphi and sacrificed to the god, and when he came into the place where oracles were delivered, a portent occurred to him. From among the various offerings suspended there, a victor's wreath, embroidered with crowns and symbols of victory slipped down and was carried by the air so as to alight upon the head of Timoleon; so that it appeared that the god sent him forth to his campaign already crowned with success. He started with only seven ships from Corinth, two from Korkyra, and one from Leukadia; and as he put to sea at night and was sailing with a fair wind, he suddenly saw the heavens open above his ship and pour down a flood of brilliant light. After this a torch like that used at the mysteries rose up before them, and, proceeding on the same course, alighted on that part of Italy for which the pilots were steering. The seers explained that this appearance corroborated the dream of the priestesses, and that the light from heaven showed that the two goddesses were joining the expedition; for Sicily is sacred to Proserpine, as the myth tells us that she was carried off there, and that the island itself was given her as a wedding present.

The fleet, encouraged by these proofs of divine favour, crossed the open sea, and proceeded along the Italian coast. But the news from Sicily gave Timoleon much concern, and dispirited his soldiers. For Hiketes had conquered Dionysius, and taken the greater part of Syracuse; he had driven him into the citadel and what is called the island, and was besieging and blockading him there, and urging the Carthaginians to take measures to prevent Timoleon from landing in Sicily, in order that, when the Greeks were driven off, he and his new allies might partition the island between themselves.

IX. The Carthaginians sent twenty triremes to Rhegium, having on board ambassadors from Hiketes to Timoleon charged with instructions as bad as his deeds. For their proposals were plausible, though their plan was base, being that Timoleon, if he chose, should come as an adviser to Hiketes and partake of his conquests; but that he should send his ships and soldiers back to Corinth, as the war was within a little of being finished, and as the Carthaginians were determined to oppose his passage by force if he attempted it. So the Corinthians, when they reached Rhegium, found these ambassadors, and saw the Carthaginian fleet cruising to intercept them. They were enraged at this treatment, and all were filled with anger against Hiketes, and with fear for the people of Sicily, who, they clearly saw, were to be the prize of the treachery of Hiketes and the ambition of the Carthaginians. Yet it seemed impossible that they should overcome both the fleet of the barbarians which was riding there, double their own in number, and also the forces under Hiketes at Syracuse, of which they had expected to be put in command.

X. Nevertheless Timoleon met the ambassadors and the Carthaginian admirals, and mildly informed them that "he would accede to their proposals, for what could he do if he refused them? but that he wished, before they parted, to listen to them, and to answer them publicly before the people of Rhegium, a city of Greek origin and friendly to both parties; as this would conduce to his own safety, and they also would be the more bound to stand by their proposal about the Syracusans if they took the people of Rhegium as their witnesses." He made this overture to help a plot which he had of stealing a march upon them, and the leading men of the Rhegines assisted him in it, as they wished the Corinthian influence to prevail in Sicily, and feared to have the barbarians for neighbours. Accordingly they called together an assembly and shut the city gates, that the citizens might not attend to anything else, and then, coming forward, they made speeches of great length, one man treating the subject after another without coming to any conclusion, but merely wasting the time, until the Corinthian triremes had put to sea. The Carthaginians were kept at the assembly without suspecting anything, because Timoleon himself was present and gave them to understand that he was just upon the point of rising and making them a speech. But when news was secretly conveyed to him that the fleet was under way, and that his ship alone was left behind waiting for him, he slipped through the crowd, the Rhegines who stood round the bema helping to conceal him, and, gaining the seashore, sailed off with all haste.

They reached Tauromenium in Sicily, where they were hospitably received by Andromachus, the ruler and lord of that city, who had long before invited them thither. This Andromachus was the father of Timaeus, the historian, and being as he was by far the most powerful of the legitimate princes of Sicily, ruled his subjects according to law and justice, and never concealed his dislike and hatred of the despots. For this reason he permitted Timoleon to make his city his headquarters, and prevailed on the citizens to cast in their lot with the Syracusans and free their native land.

XI. At Rhegium meanwhile, the Carthaginians, when the assembly broke up and Timoleon was gone, were infuriated at being outwitted, and became a standing joke to the people of Rhegium, because they, although they were Phoenicians, yet did not seem to enjoy a piece of deceit when it was at their own expense. They then sent an ambassador in a trireme to Tauromenium, who made a long speech to Andromachus, threatening him in a bombastic and barbarian style with their vengeance if he did not at once turn the

Corinthians out of his city. At last he pointed to his outstretched hand, and turning it over threatened that he would so deal with the city. Andromachus laughed, and made no other answer than to hold out his own hand in the same way, now with one side up, and now with the other, and bade him sail away unless he wished to have his ship so dealt with.

Hiketes, when he heard of Timoleon's arrival, in his terror sent for many of the Carthaginian ships of war; and now the Syracusans began utterly to despair of their safety, seeing the Carthaginians in possession of the harbour, Hiketes holding the city, and Dionysius still master of the promontory, while Timoleon was as it were hanging on the outskirts of Sicily in that little fortress of Tauromenium, with but little hope and a weak force, for he had no more than one thousand soldiers and the necessary supplies for them. Nor had the cities of Sicily any trust in him, as they were in great distress, and greatly exasperated against those who pretended to lead armies to their succour, on account of the treachery of Kallippus and Pharax; who, one an Athenian and the other a Lacedaemonian, but both giving out that they were come to fight for freedom and to put down despotism, did so tyrannise themselves, that the reign of the despots in Sicily seemed to have been a golden age, and those who died in slavery were thought more happy than those who lived to see liberty.

XII. So thinking that the Corinthian would be no better than these men, and that the same plausible and specious baits would be held out to lure them with hopes and pleasant promises under the yoke of a new master, they all viewed the proposals of the Corinthians with suspicion and shrank back from them except the Adranites. These were the inhabitants of a small city, sacred to Adranus, a god whose worship extends especially throughout Sicily. They were at feud with one another, as one party invited Hiketes and the Carthaginians, while the other sent for Timoleon to help them. And by some chance it happened that as each party strove to get there first, they both arrived at the same time; Hiketes with five thousand soldiers, whereas Timoleon altogether had no more than twelve hundred.

Starting with these men from Tauromenium, which is forty-two miles from Adranum, he made but a short march on the first day, and then encamped. On the next day he marched steadily forward, passed some difficult country, and late in the day heard that Hiketas had just reached the little fortress and was encamping before it. On this the officers halted the van of the army, thinking that the men would be fresher after taking food and rest; but Timoleon went to them and begged them not to do so, but to lead them on as fast as they could, and fall upon the enemy while they were in disorder, as it was probable they would be, having just come off their march, and being busy about pitching their tents, and cooking their supper. Saying this he seized his shield, and led the way himself as to an assured victory; and the rest, reassured, followed him confidently. They were distant only about thirty furlongs. These were soon passed, and they fell headlong upon the enemy, who were in confusion, and fled as soon as they discovered their attack. For this reason no more than three hundred of them were slain, but twice as many were taken prisoners, and their camp was captured. The people of Adranum now opened their gates, and made their submission to Timoleon, relating with awe and wonder how, at the outset of the battle, the sacred doors of the temple flew open of their own accord, and the spear of the god was seen to quiver at the point, while his face was covered with a thick sweat.

XIII. These portents, it seems, did not merely presage the victory, but also the subsequent events, of which this was the prosperous beginning. Immediately several cities sent ambassadors and joined Timoleon, as did also Mamercus the despot of Katana, a man of warlike tastes and great wealth, who made an alliance with him. But the most important thing of all was that Dionysius himself, who had now lost all hope of success, and was on the point of being starved out, despising Hiketes for being so shamefully beaten, but admiring Timoleon, sent to him and offered to deliver up both himself and the citadel to the Corinthians.

Timoleon, accepting this unexpected piece of good fortune, sent Eukleides and Telemachus, Corinthian officers, into the citadel, and four hundred men besides, not all together nor openly, for that was impossible in the face of the enemy, who were blockading it, but by stealth, and in small bodies. So these soldiers took possession of the citadel, and the palace with all its furniture, and all the military stores. There were a good many horses, and every species of artillery and missile weapon. Also there were arms and armour for seventy thousand men, which had been stored up there for a long time, and Dionysius also had two thousand soldiers, all of whom he handed over to Timoleon with the rest of the fortress, and then, with his money and a few of his friends, he put to sea, and passed unnoticed through Hiketes's cruisers. He proceeded to the camp of Timoleon, appearing for the first time as a private person in great humility, and was sent to Corinth in one ship, and with a small allowance of money. He had been born and bred in the most splendid and greatest of empires, and had reigned over it for ten years, but for twelve more, since the time that Dion attacked him, he had constantly been in troubles and wars, during which all the cruelties which he had exercised on others, were more than avenged upon himself, by the miserable death of his wife and family, which are more particularly dwelt upon in the life of Dion.

XIV. Now when Dionysius reached Corinth, there was no one in Greece who did not wish to see him and speak to him. Some, who rejoiced in his misfortunes, came to see him out of hatred, in order to trample on him now that he was down, while others sympathised with him in his change of fortune, reflecting on the inscrutable ways of the gods, and the uncertainty of human affairs. For that age produced nothing in nature or art so remarkable as that change of fortune which showed the man, who not long before had been supreme ruler of Sicily, now dining at Corinth at the cook's shop, lounging at the perfumer's, drinking at the taverns, instructing female singers, and carefully arguing with them about their songs in the theatre, and about the laws of music. Some thought that Dionysius acted thus from folly, and indolent love of pleasure, but others considered that it was in order that he might be looked down upon, and not be an object of terror or suspicion to the Corinthians, as he would have been if they thought that he ill brooked his reverse of fortune, and still nourished ambitious designs, and that his foolish and licentious mode of life was thus to be accounted for.

XV. But for all that, certain of his sayings are remembered, which sufficiently prove that he showed real greatness of mind in adapting himself to his altered circumstances. When he arrived at Leukas, which, like Syracuse, was a Corinthian colony, he said that he was like a young man who has got into disgrace. They associate gaily with their brothers, but are ashamed to meet their fathers, and avoid them: and so he was ashamed to go to the parent city, but would gladly live there with them. Another time in Corinth, when some stranger coarsely jeered at the philosophic studies in which he used to delight when in power, and at last asked him what good he had obtained from the wisdom of Plato, "Do you think," answered he, "that I have gained nothing from Plato, when I bear my reverse of fortune as I do." When Aristoxenus, the musician, and some others asked him what fault he had found with Plato, and why, he answered that absolute power, amongst its many evils, was especially unfortunate in this, that none of a despot's so-called friends dare to speak their mind openly. And he himself, he said, had been by such men deprived of the friendship of Plato. A man, who thought himself witty, once tried to make a joke of Dionysius by shaking out his cloak, when he came into his presence, as is the custom before despots, to show that one has no concealed weapons; but he repaid the jest by begging him to do it when he left him, that he might be sure that he had not stolen any of his property.

Philip of Macedon once, when they were drinking together, made some sneering remark about the poetry and tragedies which Dionysius the elder had written, pretending to be at a loss to know how he found time for such pursuits; but Dionysius cleverly answered, "He wrote them during the time which you and I, and all who are thought such lucky fellows, spend over our wine."

Plato never saw Dionysius at Corinth, for he was dead at that time; but Diogenes of Sinope, when he first met him, said, "How unworthily you live, Dionysius." Dionysius answered him, "Thank you, Diogenes, for sympathising with my misfortunes." "Why," said Diogenes; "do you suppose that I sympathise with you, and am not rather grieved that a slave like you, a man fit, like your father, to grow old and die on a miserable throne, should be living in luxury and enjoyment amongst us?" So, when I compare with these sayings of his the lamentations which Philistius pours forth over the daughters of Leptines, that they had fallen from the glories of sovereign power into a humble station, they seem to me like the complainings of a woman who has lost her perfumes, her purple dresses, or her jewels.

These details, I think, for readers who are at leisure, are not foreign to the design of biography, and not without value.

XVI. If the fall of Dionysius seems strange, the good fortune of Timoleon was no less wonderful. Within fifty days of his landing in Sicily, he was master of the citadel of Syracuse, and sent back Dionysius to Peloponnesus. Encouraged by his success, the Corinthians sent him a reinforcement of two thousand hoplites and two hundred horse. These men reached Thurii, but there found it impossible to cross over into Sicily, as the Carthaginians held the sea with a great fleet. As it was necessary for them to remain there for a time, they made use of their leisure to perform a most excellent action. For the Thurians made an expedition against the Bruttii, and meanwhile these men took charge of their city, and guarded it carefully and trustily as if it had been their own.

Hiketes meanwhile was besieging the citadel of Syracuse, and preventing corn from being brought by sea to the Corinthians. He also obtained two strangers, whom he sent to assassinate Timoleon, who, trusting in the favour shown him by the gods, was living carelessly and unsuspectingly among the people of Adranum. These men, hearing that he was about to offer sacrifice, came into the temple with daggers under their cloaks, and mingling with the crowd round the altar, kept edging towards him. They were just on the point of arranging their attack, when a man struck one of them on the head with his sword, and he fell. Neither the assailant nor the accomplice of the fallen man stood his ground, but the one with his sword still in his hand ran and took refuge on a high rock, while the other laid hold of the altar, and begged for pardon at Timoleon's hands if he revealed the whole plot. When assured of his safety he confessed that he and the man who had been killed had been sent thither to assassinate Timoleon. Meanwhile others brought back the man from the rock, who loudly declared that he had done no wrong, but had justly slain him in vengeance for his father, whom this wretch had killed at Leontini. Several of those present bore witness to the truth of his story, and they marvelled much at the ways of Fortune, how she makes the most incongruous elements work together to accomplish her purposes. The Corinthians honoured the man with a present of ten minae, because he had co-operated with the guardian angel of Timoleon, and had put off the satisfaction of his private wrong until a time when it saved the life of the general. This good fortune excited men's feelings so that they guarded and reverenced Timoleon as a sacred person sent by heaven to restore the liberties of Sicily.

XVII. When Hiketes failed in this attempt on Timoleon, and saw that many were joining him, he began to blame himself for only using the great Carthaginian force that was present by stealth, and as if he was ashamed of it, concealing his alliance and using them clandestinely, and he sent for Mago, their General, to come with all the force at his disposal. He sailed in with a formidable fleet of a hundred and fifty ships, and took possession of the harbour, disembarked sixty thousand troops, and encamped with them in the city of Syracuse, so that all men thought that the long-talked-of and expected subjugation of Sicily to the barbarian was imminent. For the Carthaginians during their endless wars in Sicily had never before taken Syracuse, but now, by the invitation of the traitor Hiketes, the city was turned into a barbarian camp. The Corinthians in the citadel were in a position of great danger and difficulty, as they no longer had sufficient provisions, because the harbours were blockaded, and they perpetually had to divide their forces for skirmishes and battles at the walls, and to repel every device and method of attack known in sieges.

XVIII. Timoleon, however, relieved them by sending corn from Katana in small fishing-smacks and boats, which, chiefly in stormy weather, stole in through the triremes of the barbarians when they were scattered by the roughness of the sea. Mago and Hiketes, perceiving this, determined to take Katana, from which place the besieged drew their supplies, and they sailed from Syracuse with the best of their troops. The Corinthian Neon, the General in command of the besieged force, observing from the citadel that those of the enemy who were left behind kept careless guard, suddenly fell upon them, and, slaying some and routing the rest he made himself master of Achradina, which is the strongest and least assailable part of the city of Syracuse, which, as it were, consists of several towns.

Being now in possession of abundance of provisions and money, he did not leave the place, and go back to the citadel on the promontory, but fortified the circuit of Achradina and held it conjointly with the Acropolis, with which he connected its fortifications. A horseman from Syracuse brought the news of the capture of Achradina to Mago and Hiketes when they were close to Katana. Alarmed at the news they returned with all speed, having neither taken the city they went to take, nor kept the one which they had taken.

XIX. It may be doubted whether these actions owe more to fortune than to courage and conduct; but the next event can only be ascribed to fortune. The Corinthian troops at Thurii were in fear of the Carthaginian triremes under Hanno which were watching them, and as the sea had for many days been excessively rough, in consequence of a gale, determined to march on foot through the Bruttii. Partly by persuasion and partly by force they made their way to Rhegium, while the sea was still very stormy. The Carthaginian Admiral, who no longer expected the Corinthians, and thought that he was waiting there to no purpose, persuaded himself that he had invented a masterpiece of deceit. He ordered his sailors to crown themselves with garlands, decked out his triremes with Greek shields and wreaths of palm, and set out for Syracuse. As he passed the citadel they cheered loudly, and with uproarious merriment called out to the garrison that they had come back after a complete victory over the Corinthians, hoping by this means to dispirit the besieged. But while he was playing these silly tricks the Corinthians had reached Rhegium, and as no one disputed their passage, and the cessation of the gale had made the straits singularly smooth and calm, they embarked in the passage boats and what fishing-smacks were to be found, and crossed over into Sicily, so easily and in such calm weather that they were able to make their horses swim alongside of the vessels and tow them by their halters.

XX. As soon as they had crossed, Timoleon met them, and at once obtained possession of Messina, and, after reviewing them, marched on Syracuse at once, confiding more in his good fortune and his former successes than in the number of his troops, which amounted to no more than four thousand. When Mago heard of this march, he was much disquieted, and his suspicions of his allies were increased by the following circumstance. In the marshes round the city, into which runs much fresh water from springs and rivers which find their way into the sea, there was a great quantity of eels, which afforded plenty of sport for those who cared to fish for them; and the mercenary soldiers on both sides used to meet and fish whenever there was a cessation of hostilities. As they were all Greeks, and had no private grounds for hatred, they would cheerfully risk their lives in battle against each other, but during times of truce they conversed freely. So then, while engaged in fishing, they talked to one another, and admired the beauty of the sea, and the fine situation of the city. Then one of the Corinthian garrison said, "Can it be that you, Greeks as you are, should be endeavouring to betray to the barbarian so great and beautiful a city as this, and that you should be trying to establish these base and cruel Carthaginians nearer to our country? Rather ought you to wish that there were more Sicilies to act as bulwarks of Greece. Do you suppose that these men have gathered together their host from the pillars of Herakles and the Atlantic coast, and risked their lives at sea, merely to support the dynasty of Hiketes? He, if he had the spirit of a real prince, never would have turned out his brethren, and invited the enemy into his native land, but would have made terms with Timoleon and the Corinthians, and been honoured accordingly." These words were noised abroad in the camp by the mercenaries, and gave Mago the pretext which he had long been waiting for, to abandon their cause on the plea of suspecting their fidelity. Wherefore, although Hiketes begged him to remain, and pointed out how far superior he was to the enemy, yet he, thinking that Timoleon's army surpassed his in courage and good fortune as much as his did in numbers, weighed anchor at once and sailed to Africa, letting Sicily slip through his fingers, to his great disgrace, for no assignable reason.

XXI. On the next day appeared Timoleon with his troops in battle array. As soon as they learned their departure, and saw the harbour, they proceeded to mock at the cowardice of Mago, and they sent a crier round the city offering a reward to any one who would tell them to what place the Carthaginian force had run away. Nevertheless, Hiketes still showed a bold front, and did not relax his hold on the city, and, as the part which was in his possession was strong and hard of access, Timoleon divided his army, and himself led the assault on the most difficult side of the position, by the river Anapus, ordering another body, under Isias the Corinthian, to attack from Achradina. A third corps, consisting of the newly arrived reinforcement under Deinarchus and Demaretus were to attack Epipolae. The assault took place simultaneously on all sides. The speedy rout of Hiketes and capture of the city may be justly ascribed to the skill of the General; but the fact that not one of the Corinthians was killed or wounded is due to Timoleon's good fortune, which seemed to vie with his courage and try to make those who read of his exploits wonder at their good luck more than their merit.

In a few days not only was all Sicily and Italy ringing with his fame, but throughout Greece his great successes were known, and the city of Corinth, which scarcely thought that the expedition had reached Sicily, heard at the same time that the troops were safe and victorious, so prosperously did affairs turn out, and with such speed did fortune publish the glory of his deeds.

XXII. Timoleon, having thus gained possession of the fortified citadel on the promontory, did not fall into the same snare as Dion, and was not moved to spare the place for the sake of its beautiful and costly architecture. Dion's jealousy of the people led him to distrust them, and proved his ruin; but Timoleon took a very different course. He made proclamation that any Syracusan who chose might come with a crowbar and take part in the destruction of the despot's castle. When they had all assembled, in order to mark that day and that proclamation as the real beginning of liberty, they not only destroyed and subverted the castle, but also the houses and tombs of the despots. Timoleon at once had the place levelled, and built upon it courts of justice, delighting the citizens by substituting a republic for a tyranny.

Having taken the city, he was now at a loss for citizens, for some had been killed in the wars and revolutions, and some had gone into exile to avoid the despots, so that the market-place of Syracuse was overrun with herbage so deep and thick that horses were pastured on it, while the grooms lay on the grass near them. The other cities, except a very few, had become the haunts of deer and wild boars, and persons at leisure used to hunt them with dogs in the suburbs and round the walls. None of those who had taken refuge in the various forts and castles would return to the city, as they all felt a dread and hatred of public assemblies and politics, which had produced the greater part of the tyrants under whom they had suffered. In this difficulty it occurred to Timoleon and the Syracusans to apply to the Corinthians, and ask them to send out fresh colonists from Greece. Otherwise, they said, the land must lie uncultivated, and, above all, they were looking forward to a great war with Africa, as they heard that on Mago's return the Carthaginians were so enraged at his failure, that, though he committed suicide to avoid a worse fate, they had crucified his dead body, and were collecting a great force, meaning next summer to invade Sicily.

XXIII. When these letters from Timoleon reached them, together with ambassadors from the Syracusans, who besought them to take upon them the care of this their poor city, and once again become the founders of it, the Corinthians were not tempted by greed to take unfair advantages and seize the city for themselves, but first sent heralds to all the games held in honour of the gods throughout Greece, and to all places where people assembled, to proclaim that the Corinthians, having abolished despotism at Syracuse and driven out the despot, invite all Syracusans and other Sicilian Greeks who choose to go and dwell in the city under free institutions, receiving an equal and just share of the land. Next they sent messengers to Asia Minor and the islands, wherever they heard that most of the scattered bands of exiles had settled, and invited them all to come to Corinth, as the Corinthians would at their own expense furnish them with vessels and commanders and a safe convoy to Syracuse.

By these proclamations Corinth gained great and well-deserved renown, seeing that she had forced Syracuse from its tyrants, saved it from the barbarians, and given back the country to its own citizens. The exiles, however, when assembled at Corinth found their numbers too small, and begged to be allowed to receive among them others from Corinth and the rest of Greece. When by this means they had raised their numbers to not less than ten thousand, they sailed to Syracuse. Many citizens from Italy and Sicily had already joined Timoleon, who, when he found their numbers (according to Athanis) amount to sixty thousand, divided the country among them, and sold the houses for a thousand talents, affording the original citizens the option of purchasing their own houses. At the same time, to relieve the financial distress of the State, with a view to the approaching war, he even sold all the statues. A vote of the assembly was taken about each one, and he was condemned, like a criminal on his trial. On this occasion they say that the Syracusans, though they condemned all the rest, decided on keeping that of the ancient prince Gelo, because they admired and respected him for his victory over the Carthaginians at Himera.

XXIV. The life of Syracuse being rekindled by this influx of citizens from all quarters, Timoleon determined to set free the other cities also, and to exterminate the despots in Sicily. In the course of his campaigns against them he compelled Hiketes to renounce his alliance with the Carthaginians, to demolish his castle, and to live in Leontini as a private citizen. Leptines, the despot of Apollonia and of several smaller towns, fearing to be taken by him, surrendered. Timoleon spared his life, and sent him to Corinth, as he thought that it reflected credit upon his native city, that the despots of Sicily should be seen by all Greece living there as humble exiles. As for the soldiers whom he had in his pay, he determined not to keep them idle, but to support them by the plunder of an enemy's country. So while he himself returned to Syracuse, to superintend the reconstruction of the constitution, and to assist the lawgivers Kephalus and Dionysius in framing the best form of polity, he sent the troops under Deinarchus and Demaretus to subdue the western portion of the island, which had fallen into the hands of the Carthaginians. Here they induced several cities to revolt from the barbarians, and not only gained abundant pay and plunder for themselves from their conquests, but were able to furnish funds for the approaching war.

XXV. During this time the Carthaginian forces sailed to Lilybaeum with seventy thousand men, two hundred ships of war, and a thousand transports carrying engines of war, four horse chariots, provisions, and other war material, as they meant no longer to use half measures, but at one swoop to drive the Greeks out of Sicily. Their force indeed was sufficient for the conquest of the Sikeliot Greeks even if they had not been weakened by their internal strife.

Hearing that their own part of the island was being ravaged, they at once in great anger marched to attack the Corinthians, under the command of Hasdrubal and Hamilcar. News of this quickly reached Syracuse, and the great numbers of the enemy caused such panic among the citizens, that, numerous as they were, Timoleon could only induce three thousand to get under arms and follow him. Besides these, there was the paid force, four thousand in number; and of these again about a thousand were overcome by their fears on the march, and went back, declaring that Timoleon could not be in his right senses, but must be insane to march with five thousand foot and a thousand horse to attack seventy thousand men, and to separate his force eight days' journey from Syracuse, in a place where there was no hope of shelter for the fugitives or of honourable burial for the dead. Timoleon treated it as an advantage that these men disclosed their cowardice before the day of battle. He encouraged the rest, and led them with all haste to the river Krimesus, where he heard that the Carthaginians were concentrating.

XXVI. As he was mounting a hill, beyond which he expected to see the camp and army of the enemy, there met him some mules loaded with parsley. It occurred to the soldiers that this was a bad omen, for we generally use parsley for wreathing tombs; indeed from this practice arises the proverb, when a man is dangerously ill, that he is ready for his parsley. Wishing to rid them from this superstition and to stop their fears, Timoleon halted them, and made a suitable speech, pointing out that their crown of victory had come of its own accord into their hands before the battle, for this is the herb with which the Corinthians crown the victors at the Isthmian games, accounting it sacred and peculiar to their own country. For then parsley was used for the crown at the Isthmian games, as it is even to this day at those of

Nemea, and the pine has only been lately introduced. So Timoleon, having addressed his soldiers, as has been said, first crowned himself with the parsley, and then his officers and men did so likewise. But the prophets perceiving two eagles flying towards them, one of whom carried a snake in its talons, while the other flew along with loud and inspiriting cries, pointed them out to the soldiers, who all began to pray and invoke the gods.

XXVII. The time of year was the beginning of summer, near the solstice at the end of the month Thargelion. A thick mist rose from the river, and all the plain was concealed in fog, so that nothing could be seen of the enemy, but only a confused murmur from the movement of that great host reached the hill. The Corinthians, when they had reached the summit, paused and piled their arms. Now the sun shone out, and the mist rose from the valley. Gathering together, it hung in clouds about the hill-tops, while below, the river Krimesus appeared, with the enemy crossing it.

First went the four-horse chariots in terrible pomp, all drawn up in battle array, while next to them followed ten thousand hoplites with white shields. These they conjectured to be native Carthaginians by the splendour of their equipments and their slow and orderly march. Following these came the other nations, turbulently and confusedly struggling across. Timoleon, seeing that the river kept off the mass of the enemy, and allowed them to fight with just so many as they chose, pointed out to his soldiers how the enemy's array was broken by the stream, some having crossed, and some being still crossing. He ordered Demaretus to take the cavalry and charge the Carthaginians, to prevent their having time to form in order of battle. But he himself marched down to the plain, having drawn up his force with the other Sicilian Greeks and a few strangers on each of the wings, but with his Syracusans and the best of the paid force under his own command in the centre.

For a short time he held back, watching the effect of the cavalry charge; but seeing that they were unable to come to blows with the Carthaginians because of the chariots which careered about in front of their ranks, and that they constantly had to fall back to avoid their array being broken, and then to make short rushes as occasion served, he himself took his shield, and called to the infantry to follow him and be of good cheer. It seemed to them that his voice was more than man's, and louder than was his wont, either from their faculties being strained by the excitement of the contest, or else because, as most of them believed, some god shouted with him. Quickly they raised their war-cry in answer, and begged him to lead them on and wait no longer. Ordering the cavalry to ride round the line of chariots and attack the infantry in flank, he closed up the foremost ranks, and with the trumpet sounding the charge, attacked the Carthaginians.

XXVIII. They manfully encountered his first assault, and being armed with iron cuirasses and brass helmets, and protected with large shields, they were able to withstand the thrust of the Greek spears. But when the struggle came to be decided with swords, where skill as well as strength was employed, there suddenly broke upon them from the mountains a terrible storm of thunder with vivid flashes of lightning. The mist, which had hitherto hung about the mountain peaks, now rolled down on to the field of battle, with violent gusts, hail, and rain. The Greeks received it on their backs, while the rain beat into the faces of the barbarians, and the lightning dazzled their eyes, as the storm swept violently along with frequent flashes from the clouds. These were great disadvantages, especially to inexperienced men, as the thunder and the pattering of the rain and hail on their armour prevented their hearing the commands of their officers. The Carthaginians, not being lightly equipped, but, as has been narrated, in complete armour, slipped on the muddy ground and were encumbered by the wet folds of their dress, which rendered them less active in the fight, and easily overcome by the Greeks, since when they fell in the slippery mud they could not rise again with their shields. The river Krimesus, which had been held up by the multitudes that were crossing it, was now swollen to a torrent by the rain, and the plain through which it runs, lying as it does under many steep glens and ravines, was now covered with streams not running in the ordinary channels, in which the Carthaginians stumbled and were hard bested.

At last, from the violence of the storm, and the Greeks having cut to pieces their front rank, a chosen body of four hundred men, the great mass turned and fled. Many were overtaken and slain on the plain, and many more perished in the river, while the light-armed troops prevented most of them from gaining the shelter of the mountains. It was said that among the myriads of slain there were three thousand citizens of Carthage—a great loss and grief to that city, for they belonged to the noblest and richest classes; nor do we ever hear of so many native Carthaginians having perished in any one battle before this, as they generally make use of Libyan, Spanish and Numidian troops, so that in case of defeat the loss falls upon other nations.

XXIX. The Greeks discovered the rank of the dead by the richness of their spoil; for when they collected the booty no account was taken of iron or brass, such an abundance was there of silver and gold; for they crossed the river and captured the enemy's camp. Of the captives, the greater part were stolen by the soldiers, and sold privately, but a body of five thousand was brought into the common stock. Two hundred chariots also were taken. The most glorious and magnificent spectacle of all was the tent of Timoleon, round which booty of every kind was piled up in heaps, among which were a thousand corslets of exquisite workmanship, and ten thousand shields. As they were but few to gather the plunder of so many, and as they fell in with such riches, it was only on the third day that they managed to erect a trophy of their victory. Together with the despatch announcing his success, Timoleon sent home to Corinth the finest of the arms and armour, desiring to make his country envied by all men, when they should see, in that alone of all Greek cities, that the most important shrines were not adorned with Grecian spoils, nor with offerings obtained by the slaughter of men of their own race and blood, dismal memorials at best, but with spoils of the barbarian, whose inscriptions bore noble testimony to the justice, as well as the courage of the victors, telling how the Corinthians and their general, Timoleon, having freed the Greeks who dwell in Sicily from the yoke of Carthage, set up these thank-offerings to the gods.

XXX. After the victory he left the paid force in the enemy's country, to ravage and plunder the Carthaginian dominions, and himself proceeded to Syracuse. He now ordered out of the island those mercenary troops by whom he had been deserted before the battle; and even forced them to quit Sicily before sunset. These men crossed into Italy and perished there at the hands of the Bruttians, who broke their word to them and betrayed them. This was the penalty which Heaven imposed on them for their desertion. But Mamercus, the despot of Catana, and Hiketes, either through disgust at Timoleon's successes, or else fearing him as a man not likely to keep faith with despots, made an alliance with Carthage, as they said that the Carthaginians, unless they wished to be utterly driven out of Sicily, must send a competent force and a general. Gisco the son of Hanno sailed thither with seventy ships, and also with a force of Greek mercenary soldiers, whom the Carthaginians had never used before; but now they were full of admiration for the Greeks, as being the most warlike and invincible of men. Having effected a junction of their forces in the territory of Messina, they cut to pieces a body of four hundred foreign soldiers whom Timoleon sent against them; and in the Carthaginian dominion they laid an ambush near the place called Hietae, and cut off the hired troops of Euthymus the Leukadian. Both these circumstances made the good fortune of Timoleon more renowned. For these were some of the men who under Philomelus of Phokis and Onomarchus sacrilegiously took Delphi, and shared in the plunder of the temple. As all men loathed them and shrank from them as from men under a curse, they wandered about Peloponnesus until Timoleon, being unable to get any other soldiers, enlisted them in his service. When they reached Sicily, they were victorious in every battle which they fought where he was present. After the most important struggles of the war were over, they were sent to reinforce others, and so perished and came to nought; and not all at once, but piecemeal, as if their avenging fate had given way to Timoleon's good fortune for a season, lest the good should suffer from the punishment of the wicked. Thus the kindness of the gods towards Timoleon was no less seen and wondered at in his failures than in his successes.

XXXI. The people of Syracuse were much nettled by the insulting jests passed upon them by the despots. Mamercus, who plumed himself on his poems and tragedies, gave himself great airs after conquering the mercenaries, and when he hung up their shields as offerings to the gods, he inscribed this insolent elegiac couplet upon them.

"These, with purple wrought, and ivory, gold, and amber, We with our simple shields conquered and laid in the dust."

After these events, while Timoleon was on a campaign in the direction of Kalauria, Hiketes invaded the Syracusan territory, did much damage and insult, and retired loaded with spoil, past the very walls of Kalauria, despising Timoleon, who had but a small force with him. He, however, let him pass, but then pursued with his cavalry and light troops. Hiketes, perceiving this, halted after crossing the river Damyrias, and drew up his troops along the farther bank to dispute the passage, encouraged to do so by the different nature of the ford, and the steepness of the hills on either hand. Now a strange rivalry and contest arose among Timoleon's captains, which delayed their onset. No one chose to let any one else lead the way against the enemy, but each man wished to be first; so that their crossing was conducted in a disorderly fashion, each man trying to push by and outstrip the rest. Hereupon Timoleon, wishing to choose the leaders by lot, took a ring from each. These he threw into his own cloak, mixed them up, and showed the first which he drew out, which happened to be engraved with the figure of a trophy of victory. When the young men saw this they raised a shout of joy, and would not wait for the rest to be drawn, but each man, as fast as he could, rode through the river and set upon the enemy. Their assault was irresistible; the enemy fled, all of them throwing away their shields, and with the loss of a hundred men.

XXXII. Soon after this, while Timoleon was campaigning in the Leontine country, he took Hiketes alive, with his son Eupolemus, and Euthymus, the commander of his cavalry. The soldiers seized and bound them, and led them into Timoleon's presence. Hiketes and his son were put to death as despots and traitors; nor did Euthymus meet with compassion, though he was a man of renown in athletic contest, and of great personal bravery, because of a scoffing speech of which he was accused against the Corinthians. The story goes that he was addressing the people of Leontini on the subject of the Corinthian invasion, and told them that there was nothing to be alarmed at if

"Corinthian ladies have come out from home."

Thus it is that most people seem to suffer more from hard words than hard deeds, and are more excited by insult than by actual hurt. What we do to our enemies in war is done of necessity, but the evil we say of them seems to spring from an excess of spite.

XXXIII. On Timoleon's return the Syracusans brought the family and daughters of Hiketes before the public assembly for trial, and condemned them to death. And this, methinks, is the most heartless of Timoleon's actions, that for want of a word from him these poor creatures should have perished. He seems not to have interfered, and to have let the people give full vent to their desire to avenge Dion, who dethroned Dionysius. For Hiketes was the man who threw Dion's wife Arete alive into the sea, with her sister Aristomache and her little son, as is told in the Life of Dion.

XXXIV. After this he marched against Mamercus at Catana. He beat him in a pitched battle near the river Abolus, routing him with a loss of two thousand men, no small part of whom belonged to the Phoenician contingent under Gisco. Hereupon, at the request of the Carthaginians, he made peace, stipulating that they should hold the country beyond the river Lykus, and that those who wished should be allowed to have it and go to reside at Syracuse, with their families and property, and also that they should give up their alliance with the despots. In despair at this Mamercus sailed to Italy, to try to bring the Lucanians against Timoleon and the Syracusans; but he was deserted by his followers, who turned their ships back, sailed to Syracuse, and surrendered Catana to Timoleon. Mamercus now was forced to take refuge in Messina with Hippo, the despot there. But Timoleon came and besieged it both by sea and land. Hippo endeavoured to escape on a ship, and was taken. The people of Messina, to whom he was delivered up, brought every one, even the boys from school, into the theatre, to witness that most salutary spectacle, a tyrant meeting with his deserts. He was put to death with torture; but Mamercus surrendered himself to Timoleon on condition that he should have a fair trial before the people of Syracuse, and that Timoleon should say nothing against him. When he was brought to Syracuse he was brought before the people, and tried to deliver a long premeditated speech to them, but meeting with interruptions and seeing that the assembly was inexorable he flung away his cloak and rushed across the theatre, striking his head against a stone step with the intention of killing himself. However he failed, and paid the penalty of his crimes by suffering the death of a pirate.

XXXV. In this fashion the despotisms were put down by Timoleon, and the wars finished. The whole island, which had become a mere wilderness through the constant wars, and was grown hateful to the very natives, under his administration became so civilized and desirable a country that colonists sailed to it from those very places to which its own citizens had formerly betaken themselves to escape from it. For Akragas and Gela, large cities, which after the war with Athens had been destroyed by the Carthaginians, were now repeopled; the former colonists led by Megellus and Pheristus, from Elea on the south coast of Italy, and the latter by a party led by Gorgus, who sailed from Keos and collected together the former citizens.

When these cities were being reorganised Timoleon not only afforded them peace and safety, but also gave them great assistance, and showed so great an interest in them as to be loved and respected by them as their real Founder. The other cities also all of them looked upon him with the same feelings, so that no peace could be made by them, no laws established, no country divided among settlers, no constitutional changes made that seemed satisfactory, unless he had a hand in them, and arranged them just as an architect, when a building is finished, gives some graceful touches which adorn the whole.

XXXVI. There were many Greeks, in his lifetime, who became great, and did great things, such as Timotheus, and Agesilaus, and Pelopidas, and Timoleon's great model, Epameinondas. But these men's actions produced a glory which was involved in much strain and toil, and some of their deeds have incurred censure, and even been repented of. Whereas those of Timoleon, if we except the terrible affair of his brother, have nothing in them to which we cannot apply, like Timaeus, that verse of Sophocles—
"Ye gods, what Venus or what grace divine Took part in this."

For as in the poetry of Antimachus, and the paintings of Dionysius, the Kolophonians, we find a certain vigour and power, yet think them forced in expression, and produced with much labour, while the paintings of Nikomachus and the verses of Homer, besides their other graces and merits, have the charm of seeming to have been composed easily and without effort, so also the campaigns of Timoleon, when compared with the laborious and hardly contested ones of Epameinondas or Agesilaus, seem to have, besides their glory, a wonderful ease, which property is not so much to be attributed to good luck as to prosperous valour. He, however, ascribed all his successes to Fortune, for in writing to his friends at home, and in his public speeches to the Syracusans, he frequently expressed his thankfulness to this goddess, who, having determined to save Sicily, had chosen to ascribe to him the credit of doing it. In his house he built a chapel to Automatia,—the goddess under whose auspices blessings and glory came as it were of themselves. To her he offered sacrifices, and consecrated his house to her. He lived in a house which the Syracusans had bestowed upon him as a special prize for his successes as general, and also the most beautiful and pleasant country seat, where indeed he spent most of his leisure time with his wife and children, whom he had sent for from Corinth. For he never returned to Corinth, nor mixed himself up in the troubles of Greece, nor did he expose himself to the hatred of political faction, which is the rock upon which great generals commonly split, in their insatiate thirst for honour and power; but he remained in Sicily, enjoying the blessings of which he was the author; the greatest of which was to see so many cities, and so many tens of thousands, all made happy and prosperous by his means.

XXXVII. But since, as Simonides says, all larks must have crests, and all republics sycophants, so two of the popular leaders, Laphystius and Demaenetus, attacked Timoleon. When Laphystius was insisting on his giving bail for some lawsuit, he would not permit the people to hoot at him or stop him; for he said that all his labours and dangers had been endured to obtain for every Syracusan the right of appealing to the laws. Demaenetus made many attacks in the public assembly on his generalship; but he made him no answer except to declare his thankfulness to the gods for having granted his prayer that he might see all Syracusans in possession of liberty of speech.

Though he confessedly had performed the greatest and most glorious actions of any Greek of his time, and though he had gained the glory of having alone done that which the orators in their speeches at great public meetings used to urge the entire nation to attempt, he was fortunately removed from the troubles which fell upon ancient Greece, and saved from defiling his hands with the blood of his countrymen. His courage and conduct were shown at the expense of barbarians and despots; his mildness of temper was experienced by Greeks; he was able to erect the trophies for most of his victories, without causing tears and mourning to the citizens; but nevertheless, within eight years, he restored Sicily to its native inhabitants, freed from the scourges which had afflicted it for so long a time and seemed so ineradicable. When advanced in years he suffered from a dimness of sight, which soon became total blindness. He had done nothing to cause it, and had met with no accident, but the disease was congenital, and in time produced a cataract. Many of his relatives are said in a similar fashion to have lost their sight when advanced in years. But Athanis tells us that during the war with Hippo and Mamercus, at the camp at Mylae, his eyesight became affected, and that this was noticed by all, but that he did not on that account desist from the siege, but persevered in the war, till he captured the two despots; but as soon as he returned to Syracuse he resigned his post of commander-in-chief, begging the citizens to allow him to do so, as the war had been brought to a happy conclusion.

XXXVIII. That he endured his misfortune without repining is not to be wondered at; but one must admire the respect and love shown him when blind by the people of Syracuse. They constantly visited him, and brought with them any strangers that might be staying with them, both to his town and country house, to show them their benefactor, glorying in the fact that he had chosen to spend his life amongst them, and had scorned the magnificent reception which his exploits would have ensured him, had he returned to Greece. Of the many important tributes to his worth none was greater than the decree of the Syracusans that whenever they should be engaged in war with foreign tribes, they would have a Corinthian for their general. Great honour was also reflected upon him by their conduct in the public assembly; for, though they managed ordinary business by themselves, on the occasion of any important debate they used to call him in. Then he would drive through the market-place into the theatre; and when the carriage in which he sat was brought in, the people would rise and salute him with one voice. Having returned their greeting, and allowed a short time for their cheers and blessings, he would hear the disputed point debated, and then give his opinion. When this had been voted upon his servants would lead his carriage out of the theatre, while the citizens, cheering and applauding him as he went, proceeded to despatch their other business without him.

XXXIX. Cherished in his old age with such respect and honour, as the common father of his country, Timoleon at length, after a slight illness, died. Some time was given for the Syracusans to prepare his funeral, and for neighbours and foreigners to assemble, so that the ceremony was performed with great splendour. The bier, magnificently adorned, and carried by young men chosen by lot, passed over the place where once the castle of Dionysius had been pulled down. The procession was joined by tens of thousands of men and women, whose appearance was gay enough for a festival, for they all wore garlands and white robes. Their lamentations and tears mingled with their praises of the deceased showed that they were not performing this as a matter of mere outward respect and compliance with a decree, but that they expressed real sorrow and loving gratitude. At last, when the bier was placed upon the pyre, Demetrius, the loudest voiced of the heralds at that time, read aloud the following:—

"The Syracusan people solemnise, at the cost of two hundred minae, the funeral of this man, the Corinthian Timoleon, son of Timodemus. They have passed a vote to honour him for all future time with festival matches in music, horse and chariot races, and gymnastics, because, after having put down the despots, subdued the foreign enemy, and recolonized the greatest among the ruined cities, he restored to the Sicilian Greeks their constitution and laws."

They buried him in the market-place, and afterwards surrounded the spot with a colonnade, and built a palastra in it for the young men to practise in, and called it the Timoleonteum; and, living under the constitution and laws which he established, they passed many years in prosperity.

Life of Aemilius.

II. Most writers agree that the Aemilian was one of the most noble and ancient of the patrician families of Rome. Those who tell us that King Numa was a pupil of Pythagoras, narrate also that Mamercus, the founder of this family, was a son of that philosopher, who for his singular grace and subtlety of speech was surnamed Aemilius. Most of the members of the family who gained distinction by their valour, were also fortunate, and even the mishap of Lucius Paullus at Cannae bore ample testimony to his prudence and valour. For since he could not prevail upon his colleague to refrain from battle, he, though against his better judgment, took part in it, and disdained to fly; but when he who had begun the contest fled from it, he stood firm, and died fighting the enemy. This Aemilius had a daughter, who married Scipio the Great, and a son who is the subject of this memoir. Born in an age which was rendered illustrious by the valour and wisdom of many distinguished men, he eclipsed them all, though he followed none of the studies by which young men were then gaining themselves a reputation, but chose a different path. He did not practise at the bar, nor could he bring himself to court the favour of the people by the greetings, embraces, and professions of friendship to which most men used to stoop to obtain popularity. Not that he was by nature unfitted for such pursuits; but he considered it better to gain a reputation for courage, justice, and truth, in which he soon outshone his contemporaries.

III. The first honourable office for which he was a candidate was that of aedile, for which he was elected against twelve others, who, they say, all afterwards became consuls. When chosen a priest of the college of Augurs, whom the Romans appoint to watch and register the omens derived from the flight of birds, or the signs of the heavens, he so carefully applied himself to learning the ancient customs and religion of his ancestors, that the priesthood, hitherto merely considered as an empty title of honour and sought after for that reason only, became regarded as the sublimest craft of all, confirming the saying of the philosophers, that holiness consists in a knowledge of how to serve the gods. Under him everything was done with both zeal and skill. He neglected all other duties, when engaged upon these, neither omitting any part nor adding any, arguing with his companions, when they blamed him for his care about trifles, that though a man might think that heaven was merciful and forgiving of negligences, yet that habitual disregard and overlooking of such points was dangerous for the state, seeing that no one ever begins till some flagrant breach of the law to disturb the constitution, but those who are careless of accuracy in small things soon begin to neglect the most important. He was no less severe in exacting and maintaining military discipline than with religious observances, never forgetting the general in the demagogue, nor, as many then did, endeavouring to make his first command lead to a second by indulgence and affability to his troops, but, like a priest expounding mysteries, he carefully taught them everything requisite for a campaign, and, by his severity to the careless and disobedient, restored the former glory to his country; for he seemed to think victory over the enemy was merely a subordinate incident in the great work of disciplining his fellow-citizens.

IV. When the Romans were at war with Antiochus the Great, and all their most experienced generals were employed against him, there arose another war in the west of Europe, in consequence of revolutionary movements in Spain. Aemilius was appointed commander to conduct this war, not with six lictors only, like ordinary generals, but twelve, so as to give him consular authority. He defeated the barbarians in two pitched battles, with a loss of nearly thirty thousand. The credit of this exploit belongs peculiarly to the general, who made such use of the advantage of the ground, and the ford over a certain river, as to render victory an easy matter for his soldiers. He also took two hundred and fifty cities, which opened their gates to him. Having established a lasting peace in his province he returned to Rome, not having gained a penny by his command. For he was careless of money-making, though he spent his fortune without stint; and it was so small, that after his death it hardly sufficed to make up the dower of his wife.

V. He married Papiria, the daughter of Papirius Maso, a consular; and after living with her for a considerable time, divorced her, though he had by her an illustrious family, for she was the mother of the renowned Scipio, and of Fabius Maximus. No reason for their separation has come down to us, but there is much truth in that other story about a divorce, that some Roman put away his wife; and his friends then blamed him, saying, "Is she not chaste? is she not beautiful? is she not fruitful?" He, stretching out his shoe, said, "Is it not beautiful? is it not new? But none of you can tell where it pinches me. In fact, some men divorce their wives for great and manifest faults, yet the little but constant irritation which proceeds from incompatible tempers and habits, though unnoticed by the world at large, does gradually produce between married people breaches which cannot be healed."

So Aemilius put away Papiria, and married again. By his second marriage he had two sons, whom he kept at home, but those by the former marriage he had adopted into the greatest and noblest families of Rome, the elder into that of Fabius Maximus, who had five times been consul, while the younger was treated by Scipio Africanus as his cousin, and took the name of Scipio.

Of his two daughters, one married a son of Cato, the other Aelius Tubero, an excellent man, who supported his poverty more gloriously than any other Roman. There were sixteen in the family, all Aelii; and one small house and estate sufficed for them all, with their numerous offspring and their wives, among whom was the daughter of our Aemilius, who, though her father had twice been consul and twice triumphed, was not ashamed of the poverty of her husband, but was proud of the virtue that kept him poor. But nowadays brothers and kinsmen, unless their inheritances be divided by mountain ranges, rivers, and walls like fortifications, with plenty of space between them, quarrel without ceasing. These are the materials for reflection which history affords to those who choose to make use of them.

VI. Aemilius, when elected consul, marched against the sub-Alpine Ligurians, called by some Ligustines, a brave and spirited nation, and from their nearness to Rome, skilled in the arts of war. Mixed with the Gauls, and the Iberians of the sea coast, they inhabit the extremity of Italy where it dies away into the Alps, and also that part of the Alps which is washed by the Tuscan Sea, opposite the Libyan coast. At this time they took also to seafaring, and, sailing forth in small piratical ships, they plundered and preyed upon commerce as far as the columns of Heracles. On Aemilius's approach they opposed him, forty thousand strong; but he, with only eight thousand, attacked five-fold his own numbers, put them to rout, and having chased them into their fastnesses, offered them reasonable and moderate terms; for it was not the Roman policy utterly to exterminate the Ligurian race, but to leave them as an outwork to protect Italy against the constant movements of the Gaulish tribes.

Trusting in Aemilius they surrendered all their ships and their cities into his hands. He did the cities no hurt, or at most destroyed the walls, and restored them to the owners, but he carried off all the ships, leaving them nothing larger than a six-oared boat; while he set free the numerous captives which they had taken both by sea and land, among whom were some Roman citizens. These were his glorious exploits in that consulship. Afterwards he frequently let his desire for re-election be seen, and once became a candidate, but as he failed and was passed over, he thenceforth remained in retirement, occupying himself with religious matters, and teaching his children not only the Roman education in which he himself had been brought up, but also the Greek, and that more carefully. For not only were the grammarians, philosophers, and orators Greek, but also the sculptors and painters, and the young men kept Greeks to manage their horses and hounds, and instruct them in hunting. Aemilius, unless hindered by public business, always was present at the exercises and studies of his sons, and was the kindest father in Rome.

VII. This was the period during which the Romans, who were at war with Perseus, King of Macedon, complained of their generals, whose ignorance and cowardice had led to the most disgraceful and ridiculous failure, and to the sustaining of much more loss than they inflicted. They, who had just driven Antiochus, called the Great, out of Asia Minor, beyond Taurus, and restricted him to Syria, making him glad to purchase peace at the price of fifteen thousand talents; who, a little before, had crushed Philip in Thessaly, and set free the Greeks from the power of Macedon; and who had also utterly subdued Hannibal himself, a man whose daring and immense resources rendered him far more dangerous an opponent than any king, thought that it was not to be borne that Perseus should wage war as if he were on equal terms with the Roman people, and that, too, with only the remnants of his father's routed forces; for they did not know that Philip, after his defeat, had greatly increased the power and efficiency of the Macedonian army. To explain which, I shall briefly relate the story from the beginning.

VIII. Antigonus, who was the most powerful of the generals and successors of Alexander, and who obtained for himself and his family the title of king, had a son named Demetrius, whose son was Antigonus, called Gonatas. His son again was named Demetrius, who, after reigning some short time, died, leaving a son Philip, a mere boy in years. Fearing disturbance during his minority, the Macedonian nobles made Antigonus, a cousin of the deceased, Regent and commander-in-chief, associating with him in this office the mother of Philip. Finding him a moderate and useful ruler, they soon gave him the title of king. He had the soubriquet of Doson, as though he were only a promiser, not a performer of his engagements. After this man, Philip came to the throne, and, while yet a boy, distinguished himself in all that becomes a king, so as to raise men's hopes that he might restore the empire of Macedon to its ancient glory, and be alone able to check the power of Rome, which now menaced the whole world. Defeated in a great battle at Scotussa by Titus Flamininus, he bent to the storm, surrendered all that he had to the Romans, and was thankful for mild treatment. Afterwards, chafing at his subordinate position, and thinking that to reign dependent on the pleasure of the Romans was more worthy of a slave who cares only for sensual pleasure, than of a man of spirit, he gave his whole mind up to preparations for war, and secretly and unscrupulously collected materials for it. Of the cities in his kingdom, he allowed those on the sea-coast and the main roads to fall into partial decay, so that his power might be despised, while he collected great forces in the interior. Here he filled all the outposts, fortresses, and cities with arms, money, and men fit for service, and thus trained the nation for war, yet kept his preparations secret. In his arsenals were arms for thirty thousand men; eight million medimni of corn were stored in his fortresses, and such a mass of treasure as would pay an army of ten thousand men for ten years. But before he could put all these forces in motion and begin the great struggle, he died of grief and remorse, for he had, as he admitted, unjustly put his other son Demetrius to death on the calumnies of one far worse than he was. Perseus, the survivor, inherited his father's hatred of the Romans with his kingdom, but was not of a calibre to carry out his designs, as his small and degraded mind was chiefly possessed by avarice. He is said not even to have been legitimate, but that Philip's wife obtained him when a baby from his real mother, a midwife of Argos, named Gnathaina, and palmed him off upon her husband. And this seems to have been one reason for her putting Demetrius to death, for fear that if the family had a legitimate heir, this one's bastardy would be discovered.

IX. However, low-born and low-minded though he was, yet having by the force of circumstances drifted into war, he held his own and maintained himself for a long time against the Romans, defeating generals of consular rank with great armies, and even capturing some of them. Publius Licinius, who first invaded Macedonia, was defeated in a cavalry engagement, with a loss of two thousand five hundred brave men killed, and six hundred prisoners. Perseus next by a sudden attack made himself master of the Roman naval station at Oreus, took twenty store ships, sunk the rest, which were loaded with grain, and took also four quinqueremes. He fought also a second battle, in which he drove back the consular general Hostilius, who was trying to invade Macedonia near Elimiae; and when he tried to steal in through Thessaly, he again offered battle, which the Roman declined. As an accessory to the war he now made a campaign against the Dardans, as if affecting to despise the Romans and to be at leisure. Here he cut to pieces ten thousand of the barbarians, and carried off much plunder. He also had secret negotiations with the Gauls who dwell near the Ister, called Basternae, a nation of warlike horsemen, and by means of Genthius their king he endeavoured to induce the Illyrians to take part in the war. There was even a report that the barbarians had been induced by his bribes to march through the southern part of Gaul beside the Adriatic, and so invade Italy.

X. The Romans, when they learnt all this, determined that they would disregard political influence in their choice of a general, and choose some man of sense and capable of undertaking great operations. Such a one was Paulus Aemilius, a man of advanced age, being about sixty years old, but still in full vigour of body, and surrounded by kinsmen, grown-up sons, and friends, who all urged him to listen to the appeal of his country and be consul. He at first treated the people with little respect, and shunned their eager professions of zeal, on the plea that he did not wish for the command; but as they waited on him daily, and called for him to come into the forum and shouted his name, he was at length prevailed upon. When a candidate, he seemed to enter the field not with a view to getting office, but to giving victory and strength in battle to his fellow-citizens; with such zeal and confidence did they unanimously elect him consul for the second time, not permitting lots to be cast for provinces by the two consuls, as is usual, but at once decreeing to him the management of the Macedonian war. It is said that when he was named general against Perseus, he was escorted home in triumph by the people en masse, and found his daughter Tertia, who was quite a little child, in tears. He embraced her, and asked her why she was crying; and she, throwing her arms round him and kissing him, said, "Do you not know, father, that our Perseus is dead?" meaning a little dog which she had brought up, which was so named. Aemilius said, "May this bring good luck, my daughter: I accept the omen." This story Cicero the orator tells in his book on Divination.

XI. It being the custom that the consuls-elect should return thanks, and make a gracious speech to the people from the rostrum, Aemilius called together the people and said that he had sought for his former consulship because he wanted office, but for this one because they wanted a general: wherefore he felt no gratitude towards them, but would lay down his consulship if they thought that they would succeed better in the war under some one else; but if they felt confidence in him, he asked them not to interfere with his acts as general, nor to gossip about him, but to furnish quietly what was wanted for the war; for if they tried to command their commander they would afford even a more sorry spectacle than they had already done. By these words he made the citizens stand greatly in awe of him, and gave them great expectations of what he would effect, while all rejoiced that they had passed over those who used to flatter them, and had chosen a general of independence and spirit. So much did the Roman people respect bravery and honour, because it led to conquests, and to making them masters of the world.

XII. I consider it to have been by divine favour that Aemilius Paulus on starting for his campaign met with such a fortunate and calm voyage, and so speedily and safely arrived at the camp; but as to the war itself, and his conduct of it, accomplished as it was partly by swift daring, partly by wise dispositions, by the valour of friends, confidence in the midst of dangers, and reliance on sound plans, I cannot tell of any glorious and distinguished exploit, which, as in the case of other generals, owed its success to his good fortune; unless, indeed, any one should count as good fortune for Aemilius the avarice of Perseus, which destroyed the great and well-founded hopes of the Macedonians in the war, and brought them to ruin by the meanness of their chief. At his request there came a force of Basternae, a thousand horse and ten thousand light troops who fought with them, all mercenary soldiers—men who knew nothing of tilling the soil, or of sailing the sea, who did not live from the produce of their flocks, but who studied one art and business solely, ever to fight and overcome their antagonists. So, when in the camp at Maedike, these men mixed with the king's troops, tall in their person, admirable in their drill, boastful and haughty in their defiance of the foe, they gave confidence to the Macedonians, and made them think that the Romans never could withstand their attack, but would be terrified at their appearance and march, outlandish and ferocious as it was. But Perseus, now that he had got such auxiliaries as these, and put his men into such heart, because he was asked for a thousand staters for each officer, became bewildered at the amount of the sum which he would have to pay, and his meanness prevailing over his reason, refused their offers, and broke off the alliance, as if he had been steward of his kingdom for the Romans rather than fighting against them, and had to give an exact account of his expenses in the war to his enemies; though he might have been taught by them, who had besides other war materials, a hundred thousand soldiers collected together ready for use. Yet he, when engaged in war with such a power as this, where such great forces were kept on foot to contend with him, kept doling out and sparing his money as if it were not his own. And still he was not a Lydian or Phoenician, but a man who from his descent ought to have had a share of the spirit of Philip and Alexander, who made all their conquests by the principle that empire may be gained by gold, not gold by empire. It used, indeed, to be a proverb that "It is not Philip, but Philip's gold that takes the cities of Greece." Alexander, too, when beginning his Indian campaign, seeing the Macedonians laboriously dragging along the rich and unwieldy plunder of the Persians, first burned all the royal carriages, and then persuaded the soldiers to do the like with their own, and start for the war as light as if they had shaken off a burden. But Perseus, when spending his own money to defend himself, his children, and his kingdom, rather than sacrifice a little and win, preferred to be taken to Rome with many others, a rich captive, and show the Romans how much he had saved for them.

XIII. For not only did he dismiss the Gauls and break his word to them, but after inducing Genthius the Illyrian to take part in the war for a bribe of three hundred talents, he lodged the money with that prince's envoys, all counted, and let them put their seals upon it. Genthius then thinking that he had got what he asked, did a wicked and impious deed in seizing and throwing into prison some Roman ambassadors who were sent to him. Perseus, thinking that Genthius no longer needed money to make him hostile to Rome, since he had given him such a pledge of his hatred of it, and had involved himself in war with it by such a crime, deprived the poor man of his three hundred talents, and shortly afterwards looked calmly on while he and his family were plucked out of their kingdom, like birds out of a nest, by Lucius Anicius, who was sent with an army against him. Aemilius, when he came to contend with such a rival as this, despised him as a man, but was surprised at the force which he had at his disposal. These were four thousand cavalry, and of infantry soldiers of the Macedonian phalanx nearly forty thousand. Encamped by the sea-shore, near the skirts of Mount Olympus, on ground nowhere accessible, and strongly fortified by himself with outworks and defences of wood, Perseus lived in careless security, thinking that by time and expense he should wear out Aemilius's attack. But he, while he busied his mind with every possible mode of assault, perceiving that his army in consequence of its past want of discipline was impatient, and usurped the general's province by proposing all sorts of wild schemes, severely reprimanded the soldiers, and ordered them not to meddle with what was not their concern, but only take care that they and their arms were ready, and to use their swords as Romans should when their general should give the word. He ordered the night sentries to go on guard without their spears, that they might be more attentive and less inclined to sleep, having no arms to defend themselves against the enemy.

XIV. The army was chiefly troubled by want of water; for only a very little bad water ran or rather dripped out of a spring near the sea. Aemilius perceiving that Olympus, immediately above him, was a large and well-wooded mountain, and guessing from the greenness of the foliage that it must contain some springs which had their courses underground, dug many pits and wells along the skirts of the mountain, which immediately were filled with pure water, which by the pressure above was driven into these vacant spaces. Yet some say that there are no hidden fountains of water, lying ready in such places as these, and say that it is not because they are dug out or broken into that they flow, but that they have their origin and cause in the saturation of the surrounding earth which becomes saturated by its close texture and coldness, acting upon the moist vapours, which when pressed together low down turn into water. For just as women's breasts are not receptacles full of milk ready to flow, but change the nutriment which is in them into milk, and so supply it, so also the cold places which are full of springs have no water concealed in them, nor any such reservoirs as would be needed to send out deep rivers from any fixed point, but by their pressure they convert the air and vapour which is in them into water. At any rate, those places which are dug over break more into springs and run more with water, in answer to this treatment of their surface, just as women's breasts respond to sucking, for it moistens and softens the vapour; whereas land which is not worked is incapable of producing water, not having the motion by which moisture is obtained. Those who argue thus have given sceptics the opportunity of saying, that if it be true, there can be no blood in animals, but that it gathers about wounds, and that the flow of blood is produced by the air, or some change which takes place in the flesh. They are proved to be wrong by those who sink shafts for mines, and meet with rivers in the depths of the earth, which have not collected themselves by degrees, as would be the case if they derived their origin from the sudden movements of the earth, but flow with a full stream. Also, when mountains and rocks are fissured by a blow, there springs out a gush of water, which afterwards ceases. But enough of this.

XV. Aemilius remained quiet for some days, and it is said two such great hosts never were so near together and so quiet. After exploring and trying every place he discovered that there was still one pass unguarded, that, namely, through Perrhaebae by Pythium and Petra. He called a council of war to consider this, being himself more hopeful of success that way, as the place was not watched, than alarmed at the precipices on account of which the enemy neglected it. First of those present, Scipio, surnamed Nasica, son-in-law to Scipio Africanus, afterwards a leading man in the Senate, volunteered to lead the party which was to make this circuitous attack. And next Fabius Maximus, the eldest of the sons of Aemilius, though still only a youth, rose and spiritedly offered his services. Aemilius, delighted, placed under their command not so many troops as Polybius says in his history, but so many as Nasica himself tells us that he had, in a letter which he wrote to one of the princes of that region about this affair. He had three thousand

Italians, besides his main body, and five thousand who composed the left wing. Besides these, Nasica took a hundred and twenty horse, and two hundred of Harpalus's light troops, Thracians and Cretans mixed. He began his march along the road towards the sea, and encamped near the temple of Herakles, as though he intended to sail round to the other side of the enemy's camp, and so surround him: but when the soldiers had supped, and it was dark, he explained his real plan to his officers, marched all night away from the sea, and halted his men for rest near the temple of Apollo. At this place Olympus is more than ten furlongs high: and this is proved by the epigram which the measurer wrote as follows:

"The height of Olympus' crest at the temple of Pythian Apollo consists of (measured by the plumb line) ten stades, and besides a hundred feet all but four. It was Xenagoras, the son of Eumelus, who discovered its height. King Apollo, hail to thee; be thou propitious to us."

And yet geometricians say that neither the height of any mountain nor the depth of any sea is above ten stades (furlongs). However, Xenophanes did not take its altitude conjecturally, but by a proper method with instruments.

XVI. Here then Nasica halted. Perseus in the morning saw Aemilius's army quiet in its place, and would have had no idea of what was going on had not a Cretan deserter come and told him of the flank march of the Romans. Then he became alarmed, but still did not disturb his camp, but, placing ten thousand foreign mercenaries and two thousand Macedonians under the command of Milo, ordered him to march swiftly and occupy the passes. Now Polybius says that the Romans fell upon these men when they were in their beds, but Nasica tells us that a sharp and dangerous conflict took place upon the heights. He himself was assailed by a Thracian, but struck him through the breast with his spear. However, the enemy were forced back; Milo most shamefully fled in his shirt, without his arms, and Scipio was able to follow, and at the same time lead his forces on to level ground. Perseus, terrified and despairing when he saw them, at once broke up his camp and retreated. But still he was obliged either to give battle before Pydna, or else to disperse his army among the various cities of the kingdom, and so to await the Romans, who, being once entered into his country, could not be driven out without much slaughter and bloodshed. It was urged by his friends that he had a great numerical superiority, and that the troops would fight desperately in defence of their wives and families, especially if their king took the command and shared their danger. He pitched his camp and prepared for battle, viewed the ground, and arranged the commands, intending to set upon the Romans as soon as they appeared. Now the position both possessed a flat plain for the manoeuvres of the phalanx, which requires level ground, and also hills rising one above another offered refuges and means for outflanking the enemy to his light troops. Also two rivers, the Aeson and Leukus, which ran across as it, though not very deep at that season (late autumn), were expected to give some trouble to the Romans.

XVII. Aemilius, on effecting a junction with Nasica, marched in battle array against the enemy. When, however, he saw their position and their numbers, he halted in surprise, considering within himself what he should do. His young officers, eager for battle, rode up to him and begged him not to delay. Conspicuous among these was Nasica, excited by his successful flank march round Olympus. Aemilius smiled at them and answered, "I would do so if I were of your age, but many victories have shown me the mistakes of the vanquished, and prevent my attacking a body of men drawn up in a chosen position with troops on the march and undeployed." He gave orders that those troops who were in front should gather together and appear to be forming in battle array, while those who were behind pitched their palisades and fortified a camp. Then by wheeling off men by degrees from the front line, he gradually broke up his line of battle, and quietly drew all his forces within the ramparts of his camp. When night fell, and after supper the army had betaken itself to sleep and rest, suddenly the moon, which was full and high in the heavens, became obscured, changed colour, and became totally eclipsed. The Romans, after their custom, called for her to shine again by clattering with brass vessels, and uplifting blazing faggots and torches. The Macedonians did nothing of the sort, but dismay spread over their camp, and they muttered under their breath that this portended the eclipse of their king. Now Aemilius was not unacquainted with the phenomena of eclipses, which result from the moon being at fixed periods brought into the shadow of the earth and darkened, until it passes the obscured tract and is again enlightened by the sun, yet being very devout and learned in divination, he offered to her a sacrifice of eleven calves. At daybreak he sacrificed twenty oxen to Herakles without obtaining a favourable response; but with the one-and-twentieth favourable signs appeared and portents of victory for them, provided they did not attack. He then vowed a hecatomb and sacred games in honour of the god, and ordered his officers to arrange the men in line of battle. But he waited till the sun declined and drew towards the west, that his troops might not fight with the morning sun in their eyes. He passed away the day sitting in his tent, which was pitched looking towards the flat country and the camp of the enemy.

XVIII. Some writers tell us, that about evening, by a device of Aemilius, the battle was begun by the enemy, the Romans having driven a horse without a bridle out of their camp and then tried to catch it, from which pursuit the battle began; but others say that Roman soldiers who were carrying fodder for the cattle were set upon by the Thracians under Alexander, and that to repel them a vigorous sortie was made with seven hundred Ligurians; that many on both sides came up to help their comrades, and so the battle began. Aemilius, like a pilot, seeing by the motion and disturbance of his camp that a storm was at hand, came out of his tent, and going along the lines of the infantry spoke encouraging words to them, while Nasica, riding up to the skirmishers, saw the whole army of the enemy just on the point of attacking. First marched the Thracians, whose aspect they saw was most terrible, as they were tall men, dressed in dark tunics, with large oblong shields and greaves of glittering white, brandishing aloft long heavy swords over their right shoulders. Next to the Thracians were the mercenaries, variously armed, and mixed with Paeonians. After these came a third corps, of Macedonians, picked men of proved courage, and in the flower of their age, glittering with gilded arms and new purple dresses. Behind them again came the phalanxes from the camp with their brazen shields, filling all the plain with the glittering of their armour, and making the hills ring with their shouts. So swiftly and boldly did they advance that those who were first slain fell two furlongs only from the Roman camp.

XIX. When the battle began, Aemilius came up, and found the front ranks of the Macedonians had struck their spear-heads into the Roman shields, so that they could not reach them with their swords. When also the other Macedonians took their shields off their shoulders and placed them in front, and then at the word of command all brought down their pikes, he, viewing the great strength of that serried mass of shields, and the menacing look of the spears that bristled before them, was amazed and terrified, having never seen a more imposing spectacle—and often afterwards he used to speak of that sight, and of his own feelings at it. At the time, however, he put on a cheerful and hopeful look, and rode along the ranks showing himself to the men without helmet or cuirass. But the Macedonian king, according to Polybius, having joined battle, was seized with a fit of cowardice, and rode off to the city on the pretext that he was going to sacrifice to Herakles, a god unlikely to receive the base offerings of cowards or to fulfil their unreasonable prayers; for it is not reasonable that he who does not shoot should hit the mark, nor that he who does not stand fast at his post should win the day, or that the helpless man should succeed or the coward prosper. But the god heard the prayers of Aemilius, for he prayed for victory whilst fighting, sword in hand, and invited the god into the battle to aid him. Not but what one Poseidonius, who says that he took part in these transactions, and wrote a history of Perseus in many volumes, says that it was not from cowardice, or on the pretext of offering sacrifice that he left the field, but that on the day before the battle he was kicked on the leg by a horse; that in the battle, though in great pain, and entreated by his friends to desist, he ordered a horse to be brought, and without armour rode up to the phalanx. Here as many missiles were flying about from both sides, an iron javelin struck him, not fairly with its point, but it ran obliquely down his left side, tearing his tunic, and causing a dark bruise on his flesh, the scar of which was long visible. This is what Poseidonius urges in defence of Perseus.

XX. Now as the Romans when they met the phalanx could make no impression upon it, Salovius, the leader of the Pelignians, seized the standard of his regiment and threw it among the enemy. The Pelignians, as the loss of a standard is thought to be a crime and an impiety by all Italians, rushed to the place, and a fierce conflict began there with terrible slaughter. The one party tried to dash aside the long spears with their swords, and to push them with their shields, and to seize them away with their very hands, while the Macedonians, wielding their spears with both hands, drove them through their opponents, armour and all: for no shield or corslet could resist their thrust. They then cast over their own heads the bodies of these Pelignians and Marrucini, who pressed madly like wild creatures up to the line of spears and certain death. When the first rank fell in this manner, those behind gave way: it cannot be said that they fled, but they retreated to a mountain called Olokrus. Poseidonius tells us that Aemilius tore his clothes in despair at seeing these men give ground, while the other Romans were confounded at the phalanx, which could not be assailed, but with its close line of spears, like a palisade, offered no point for attack. But when he saw that, from the inequalities of the ground, and the length of their line, the Macedonian phalanx did not preserve its alignment, and was breaking into gaps and breaches, as is natural should happen in a great army, according to the different attacks of the combatants, who made it bulge inwards in one place, and outward in another, then he came swiftly up, and dividing his men into companies, ordered them to force their way into the spaces and intervals of the enemy's line, and to make their attack, not in any one place all together, but in several, as they were broken up into several bodies. As soon as Aemilius had given these instructions to the officers, who communicated them to the men, they charged into the spaces, and at once some attacked the now helpless Macedonians in flank, while others got into their rear and cut them off. The phalanx dissolved immediately, and with it was lost all the power and mutual assistance which it gave. Fighting in single combats or small groups, the Macedonians struck in vain with their little daggers at the strong shields reaching to their feet carried by the Romans. Their light targets could ill ward off the blows of the Roman sword, which cut right through all their defensive armour. After a useless resistance they turned and fled.

XXI. But the fight was a sharp one. Here Marcus, the son of Cato, Aemilius's son-in-law, whilst fighting with great valour let fall his sword. Educated as he had been in the strictest principles of honour, and owing it to such a father to give extraordinary proofs of courage, he thought that life would be intolerable for him if he allowed an enemy to carry off such a trophy from him, and ran about calling upon every friend or acquaintance whom he saw to help him to recover it. Many brave men thus assembled, and with one accord left the rest of the army and followed him. After a sharp conflict and much slaughter, they succeeded in driving the enemy from the ground, and having thus chased it, they betook themselves to searching for the sword. When at last after much trouble it was found among the heaps of arms and corpses, they were overjoyed, and with a shout assailed those of the enemy who still resisted. At length the three thousand picked men were all slain fighting in their ranks. A great slaughter took place among the others as they fled, so that the plain and the skirts of the hills were covered with corpses, and the stream of the river Leukus ran red with blood even on the day after the battle; for, indeed, it is said that more than twenty-five thousand men perished. Of the Romans there fell a hundred, according to Poseidonius, but Nasica says only eighty.

XXII. This battle, fraught with such important issues, was decided in a remarkably short time; beginning to fight at the ninth hour, the Romans were victorious before the tenth. The remainder of the day was occupied in pursuit, which being pressed for some fifteen (English) miles, it was late before they returned to their camp. All the officers on their return were met by their servants with torches, and conducted with songs of triumph to their tents, which were illuminated and wreathed with ivy and laurel; but the general himself was deeply dejected. The youngest of the two sons who were serving under him—his own favourite, the noblest of all his children in character—was nowhere to be found; and it was feared that, being high-spirited and generous, though but a boy in years, he must have become mixed up with the enemy, and so perished. The whole army learned the cause of his sorrow and perplexity, and quitting their suppers, ran about with torches, some to the tent of Aemilius, and some outside the camp to look for him among the corpses. The whole camp was filled with sorrow, and all the plain with noise, covered as it was with men shouting for Scipio—for he had won all hearts from the very beginning, having beyond all his kinsfolk the power of commanding the affections of men. Very late at night, after he had been all but given up for lost, he came in with two or three comrades, covered with the blood of the enemies he had slain, having, like a well-bred hound, been thoughtlessly carried along by the joy of the chase. This was that Scipio who afterwards took by storm Carthage and Numantia, and became by far the most famous and powerful of all the Romans of his time. So fortune, deferring to another season the expression of her jealousy at his success, now permitted Aemilius to take an unalloyed pleasure in his victory.

XXIII. Perseus fled from Pydna to Pella, his cavalry having, as one would expect, all got safe out of the action. But when the infantry met them, they abused them as cowards and traitors, and began to push them from their horses and deal them blows, and so Perseus, terrified at the disturbance, forsook the main road, and to avoid detection took off his purple robe and laid it before him, and carried his crown in his hand; and, that he might talk to his friends as he walked, he got off his horse, and led him. But one of them made excuse that he must tie his shoes, another that he must water his horse, another that he must get himself a drink, and so they gradually fell off from him and left him, not fearing the rage of the enemy so much as his cruelty: for, exasperated by his defeat, he tried to fasten the blame of it upon others instead of himself. When he came to Pella, his treasurers Euktus and Eulaeus met him and blamed him for what had happened, and in an outspoken and unseasonable way gave him advice: at which he was so much enraged that he stabbed them both dead with his dagger. After this no one stayed with him except Evander a Cretan, Archedamus an Aetolian, and Neon a Boeotian. Of the common soldiers the Cretans followed him, not from any love they bore him, but being as eager for his riches as bees are for honey. For he carried great store of wealth with him, and out of it distributed among the Cretans cups and bowls and other gold and silver plate to the amount of fifty talents. But when he reached first Amphipolis, and then Galepsus, and had got a little the better of his fears, his old malady of meanness attacked him, and he would complain to his friends that he had flung some of the drinking cups of Alexander the Great to the Cretans by mistake, and entreated with tears those who had them to give back and take the value in money. Those who understood his character were not taken in by this attempt to play the Cretan with men of Crete, but some believed him and lost their cups for nothing. For he never paid the money, but having swindled his friends out of thirty talents, which soon fell into the hands of the enemy, he sailed with the money to Samothrace, and took sanctuary in the temple of the Dioskuri as a suppliant.

XXIV. The people of Macedon have always been thought to love their kings, but now, as if some main prop had broken, and the whole edifice of government fallen to the ground, they gave themselves up to Aemilius, and in two days constituted him master of the entire kingdom. This seems to confirm the opinion of those who say that these successes were owing to especial good fortune: and the incident of the sacrifice also was clearly sent from Heaven. For when Aemilius was offering sacrifice at Amphipolis, when the sacred rites had been performed, lightning came down upon the altar, and burned up the offering. But in its miraculous character and good luck the swiftness with which the news spread surpasses all these; for on the fourth day after Perseus had been vanquished at Pydna, while the people at Rome were assembled at a horse race, suddenly there arose amongst them a rumour that Aemilius had defeated Perseus in a great battle and had subdued all Macedonia. This report soon spread among the populace, who expressed their joy by applause and shouts throughout the city all that day. Afterwards, as the report could be traced to no trustworthy source, but was merely repeated among them vaguely, it was disbelieved and came to nothing; but in a few days they learned the real story, and wondered at the rumour which had preceded it, combining truth with falsehood.

XXV. There is a legend that the news of the battle on the river Sagra in Italy against the natives was carried the same day into Peloponnesus, and that of the battle of Mykale against the Medes was so carried to Plataea. The victory of the Romans over the Latins under the exiled Tarquins was reported at Rome a little after it took place, by two men, tall and fair, who came from the army. These men they conjectured to have been the Dioskuri (Castor and Pollux). The first man who fell in with them as they stood in the forum, near the fountain, found them washing their horses, which were covered with sweat. He marvelled much at their tale of the victory; and then they are said to have smiled serenely and stroked his beard, which instantly changed from black to yellow, thus causing his story to be believed, besides winning for him the soubriquet of Ahenobarbus, which means 'brazen beard.' But that which happened in our own time will make all these credible. When Antonius rebelled against Domitian, and a great war in Germany was expected, Rome was greatly disturbed till suddenly there arose among the people a rumour of victory, and a story ran through Rome that Antonius himself was killed, and that the army under him had been utterly exterminated. And this report was so clear and forcible, that many of the magistrates offered sacrifice for the victory. When the originator of it was sought for, as he could not be found, but the story when traced from one man to another was lost in the vast crowd as if in the sea, and appeared to have no solid foundation, all belief in it died away: but when Domitian set out with his forces to the war, he was met on the way by messengers with despatches describing the victory. The day of this success was the same as that stated by the rumours, though the places were more than two thousand five hundred (English) miles distant. All men of our own time know this to be true.

XXVI. Cnaeus Octavius, the admiral under Aemilius's orders, now cruised round Samothrace. He did not, from religious motives, violate Perseus's right of sanctuary, but prevented his leaving the island and escaping. But nevertheless Perseus somehow outwitted him so far as to bribe one Oroandes, a Cretan, who possessed a small vessel, to take him on board. But this man like a true Cretan took the money away by night, and bidding him come the next night with his family and attendants to the harbour near the temple of Demeter, as soon as evening fell, set sail. Now Perseus suffered pitiably in forcing himself, and his wife and children, who were unused to hardships, through a narrow window in the wall, and set up a most pitiful wailing when some one who met him wandering on the beach showed him the ship of Oroandes under sail far away at sea. Day was now breaking, and having lost his last hope, he made a hasty retreat to the town wall, and got into it with his wife, before the Romans, though they saw him, could prevent him. But his children he had entrusted to a man named Ion, who once had been a favourite of his, but now betrayed him, and delivered them up to the Romans, thus providing the chief means to compel him, like a wild animal, to come and surrender himself into the hands of those who had his children. He felt most confidence in Nasica, and inquired for him, but as he was not present, after lamenting his fate, and reflecting on the impossibility of acting otherwise, he surrendered himself to Cnaeus.

Now he was able to prove that he had a vice yet more sordid than avarice, namely, base love of life; by which he lost even his title to pity, the only consolation of which fortune does not deprive the fallen. He begged to be brought into the presence of Aemilius, who, to show respect to a great man who had met with a terrible misfortune, rose, and walked to meet him with his friends, with tears in his eyes. But Perseus offered a degrading spectacle by flinging himself down upon his face and embracing his knees, with unmanly cries and entreaties, which Aemilius could not endure to listen to; but looking on him with a pained and sad expression, said, "Wretched man: why do you by this conduct deprive fortune of all blame, by making yourself seem to deserve your mishaps, and to have been unworthy of your former prosperity, but worthy of your present misery? And why do you depreciate the value of my victory, and make my success a small one, by proving degenerate and an unworthy antagonist for Romans? Valour, however unfortunate, commands great respect even from enemies: but the Romans despise cowardice, even though it be prosperous."

XXVII. However, he raised him from the ground, and, having given him his hand, he entrusted him to Tubero, and then taking into his own tent his sons, sons-in-law, and most of the younger officers, he sat silent, wrapt in thought for some time, to their astonishment. Then he said, "Ought a man to be confident that he deserves his good fortune, and think much of himself when he has overcome a nation, or city, or empire; or does fortune give this as an example to the victor also of the uncertainty of human affairs, which never continue in one stay? For what time can there be for us mortals to feel confident, when our victories over others especially compel us to dread fortune, and while we are exulting, the reflection that the fatal day comes now to one, now to another, in regular succession, dashes our joy. Can we, who in less than an hour have trampled under our feet the successor of Alexander the Great, who was so powerful and mighty, and who see these kings who but lately were guarded by their tens of thousands of foot and thousands of horse, now receiving their daily bread from the hands of their foes, can we suppose that our present prosperity is likely to endure for all time? You, young men, be sure that you lay aside your haughty looks and vainglory in your victory, and await with humility what the future may bring forth, ever considering what form of retribution Heaven may have in store for us to set off against our present good fortune." They say that Aemilius spoke long in this strain, and sent away his young officers with their pride and boastfulness well curbed and restrained by his words, as though with a bridle.

XXVIII. After these events he sent the army into cantonments, to rest, and he himself set out to visit Greece, making a progress which was both glorious and beneficent; for in the cities to which he came he restored the popular constitutions, and bestowed on them presents, from the king's treasury, of corn and oil. For so much, they say, was found stored up, that all those who received it and asked for it, were satisfied before the mass could be exhausted. At Delphi, seeing a large square column of white marble, on which a golden statue of Perseus was to have been placed, he ordered his own to be placed there, as the vanquished ought to give place to the victors. At Olympia, as the story goes, he uttered that well-known saying, that Pheidias had carved the very Zeus of Homer.

When ten commissioners arrived from Rome, he restored to the Macedonians their country to dwell in, and their cities free and independent, imposing upon them a tribute of a hundred talents, only half what they used to pay to their kings. He exhibited gymnastic spectacles of every kind, and gave splendid sacrifices and feasts in honour of the gods, having boundless resources for the purpose in the king's treasury; and in ordering and arranging each man's place at table, and saluting him according to his merit and degree, he showed such a delicate perception of propriety, that the Greeks were astonished that he should carry his administrative talent even into his amusements, and be so business-like in trifles. But he was always delighted that though many splendid things were prepared, he himself was the chief object of interest to his guests, and when they expressed their surprise at his taking such pains, he would answer that the same mind can array an army for battle in the most terrific fashion, or a feast in the most acceptable one. All men praised to the skies his generous magnanimity, because, when a great mass of gold and silver was collected from the king's treasury, he would not so much as look at it, but handed it over to the quaestors to be put into the public treasury. Of all the spoil, he only allowed his sons, who were fond of reading, to take the king's books; and when distributing prizes for distinguished bravery in action, he gave Aelius Tubero, his son-in-law, a silver cup of five pounds' weight. This Tubero is he whom we said lived with fifteen other kinsfolk on a small farm, which supported them all. And that, they say, was the first piece of plate that ever was seen in the Aelian household, brought there by honourable valour; for before that neither they nor their wives used either gold or silver plate.

XXIX. When he had settled all things properly he took leave of the Greeks, and reminding the Macedonians to keep by orderly and unanimous conduct the liberty which the Romans had bestowed upon them, he started for Epirus, as the Senate had passed a decree that the soldiers who had been present in the battle against Perseus should be gratified with the spoil of the cities of Epirus. Desiring therefore to fall upon them all at once and unexpectedly, he sent for ten of the chief men from each city, and ordered them to bring together, on a fixed day, all the gold and silver which they had in their houses and temples. With each party he sent, as if for this purpose, a guard of soldiers and a captain, who was to pretend that he came to seek for and receive the money. But when day broke, they all at the same time fell to sacking and plundering the cities, so that, in one hour, a hundred and fifty thousand people were reduced to slavery, and seventy cities plundered; yet from such ruin and destruction as this, there resulted no more than eleven drachmae for each soldier, while all mankind shuddered at this termination of the war, that a whole nation should be cut to pieces to produce such a pitiful present.

XXX. Aemilius, having performed this work, greatly against his real nature, which was kind and gentle, proceeded to Oricum, and thence crossed to Italy with his army. He himself sailed up the river Tiber in the king's own ship of sixteen banks of oars, adorned with the arms of the vanquished, and crowns of victory and crimson flags, so that all the people of Rome came out in a body as if to a foretaste of the spectacle of his triumphal entry, and walked beside his ship as she was gently rowed up the river. But the soldiery, casting longing glances at the king's treasure, like men who had not met with their deserts, were angry and dissatisfied with Aemilius; for this reason really, though the charge they openly put forward was that he was a harsh and tyrannical ruler: so they showed no eagerness for the triumph.

Servius Galba, an enemy of Aemilius, who had once commanded a legion under him, hearing this, plucked up spirit to propose openly that he should not be allowed a triumph. He disseminated among the soldiers many calumnies against their general, and so still more exasperately their present temper; next he asked the tribunes of the plebs for another day, as that day would not suffice for his speech, only four hours remaining of it. However, the tribunes bade him speak, and he, beginning a long and abusive speech, consumed all the time. At nightfall the tribunes dismissed the assembly. But the soldiers, now grown bolder, assembled round Galba, and, forming themselves into an organized body, again at daybreak occupied the capitol; for it was thither that the tribunes had summoned the people.

XXXI. The voting began as soon as it was day, and the first tribe voted against the triumph. Soon the rumour of this spread to the rest of the people and to the Senate. Though the masses were grieved at the shameful treatment of Aemilius, they exhausted themselves in useless clamour, but the leading men of the Senate crying out one to another that what was going on was scandalous, encouraged each other to resist the licentious violence of the soldiers, who, if not restrained, were ready to use any kind of lawless violence to prevent Paulus Aemilius enjoying the reward of his victory. These men pushed the mob aside, and mounting to the capitol in a body, bade the tribunes stop the voting until they had said what they wished to the people. When voting ceased and silence was obtained, Marcus Servilius, a man of consular rank, who had challenged and slain twenty-three enemies in single combat, spoke as follows:—"What a commander Aemilius Paulus must be, you are now best able to judge, seeing with what a disobedient and worthless army he has succeeded in such great exploits; but I am surprised at the people's being proud of the triumphs over the Illyrians and Ligurians, and begrudging itself the sight of the king of Macedon brought alive, and all the glories of Philip and Alexander carried captive to the arms of Rome. Is it not a strange thing that on the unfounded rumour of this victory being circulated, you sacrificed to the gods, praying that you soon might behold this spectacle, yet now that the army has returned after a real victory, you refuse the gods the honour and yourself the pleasure of it, as if you feared to see the extent of your successes, or wished to spare the feelings of your captive enemy; though it would show a nobler feeling than pity for him, not to deprive your general of his triumph for a mean grudge. Your baseness has reached such a pitch that a man without a scar, with his body delicately nurtured in the shade, dares to speak about generalship and triumphs before us who have learned by so many wounds to judge of a general's vice and virtues." As he spoke, he opened his clothes, and showed his breast with an incredible number of scars upon it; then turning to Galba, who had made some remarks not very decent "You laugh," said he, "at these other marks: but I glory in them before my countrymen, for I got them by riding, night and day, in their service. But come, bring them to vote; I will go amongst them and follow them all to the poll, that I may know those who are cowardly and ungrateful, and like rather to be ruled by a demagogue than by a true general."

XXXII. These words are said to have caused such remorse and repentance among the soldiers, that all the tribes voted Aemilius his triumph. It is said to have been celebrated thus. The people, dressed in white robes, looked on from platforms erected in the horse course, which they call the Circus, and round the Forum, and in all other places which gave them a view of the procession. Every temple was open, and full of flowers and incense, and many officials with staves drove off people who formed disorderly mobs, and kept the way clear. The procession was divided into three days. The first scarcely sufficed for the display of the captured statues, sculptures, and paintings, which were carried on two hundred and fifty carriages. On the following day the finest and most costly of the Macedonian arms and armour were borne along in many waggons, glittering with newly burnished brass and iron, and arranged in a carefully studied disorder, helmets upon shields, and corslets upon greaves, with Cretan targets, Thracian wicker shields and quivers mixed with horses' bits, naked swords rising out of these, and the long spears of the phalanx ranged in order above them, making a harmonious clash of arms, as they were arranged to clatter when they were driven along, with a harsh and menacing sound, so that the sight of them even after victory was not without terror. After the waggons which bore the arms walked three thousand men, carrying the silver coin in seven hundred and fifty earthen vessels, each carrying three talents, and borne by four men. Others carried the silver drinking horns, and goblets and chalices, each of them disposed so that it could be well seen, and all remarkable for their size and the boldness of their carving.

XXXIII. On the third day, at earliest dawn, marched the trumpeters, not playing the music of a march, but sounding the notes which animate the Romans for a charge. After them were led along a hundred and twenty fat oxen with gilded horns, adorned with crowns and wreaths. They were led by youths clad in finely-fringed waistcloths in which to do the sacrifice, while boys carried the wine for the libations in gold and silver vessels. After these came men carrying the gold coin, divided into vessels of three talents each like the silver. The number of these vessels was eighty all but three. Then came those who carried the consecrated bowl which Aemilius had made of ten talents of gold adorned with jewels, and men carrying the plate of Antigonus and Seleukus, and cups of Therikles-ware, and all Perseus's own service of gold plate.

Next came the chariot of Perseus with his armour; and his crown set upon the top of his armour: and then after a little interval came the captive children of the king, and with them a tearful band of nurses and teachers, who held out their hands in supplication to the spectators, and taught the children to beg them for mercy. There were two boys and one girl, all too young to comprehend the extent of their misfortune. This carelessness made their fallen state all the more pitiable, so that Perseus himself walked almost unnoticed; for the Romans in their pity had eyes only for the children, and many shed tears, while all felt that the sight was more painful than pleasing till the children were gone by.

XXXIV. Behind the children and their attendants walked Perseus himself, dressed in a dark-coloured cloak with country boots, seeming to be dazed and stupefied by the greatness of his fall. A band of his friends and associates followed him with grief-laden countenances, and, by their constantly looking at Perseus, and weeping, gave the spectators the idea that they bewailed his fate without taking any thought about their own. However, Perseus had sent to Aemilius asking to be excused the walking in procession; but he, as it seems in mockery of his cowardice and love of life, answered, "That was formerly in his own hands, and is now if he pleases." Meaning that death was preferable to dishonour; but the dastard had not spirit enough for that, but buoyed up by some hope, became a part of his own spoils.

After these were borne golden crowns, four hundred in number, which the cities of Greece had sent to Aemilius with deputations, in recognition of his success. Next he came himself, sitting in a splendid chariot, a man worth looking upon even without his present grandeur, dressed in a purple robe sprinkled with gold, and holding a branch of laurel in his right hand. All the army was crowned with laurel and followed the car of the general in military array, at one time singing and laughing over old country songs, then raising in chorus the paean of victory and recital of their deeds, to the glory of Aemilius, who was gazed upon and envied by all, disliked by no good man. Yet it seems that some deity is charged with tempering these great and excessive pieces of good fortune, and skimming as it were the cream off human life, so that none may be absolutely without his ills in this life; but as Homer says, they may seem to fare best whose fortune partakes equally of good and evil.

XXXV. For he had four sons, two, as has been already related, adopted into other families, Scipio and Fabius; and two others who were still children, by his second wife, who lived in his own house. Of these, one died five days before Aemilius's triumph, at the age of fourteen, and the other, twelve years old, died three days after it; so that there was no Roman that did not grieve for him, and all trembled at the cruelty of fortune, which had burst into a house filled with joy and gladness, and mingled tears and funeral dirges with the triumphal paeans and songs of victory.

XXXVI. Yet Aemilius, rightly thinking that courage is as valuable in supporting misfortunes as it is against the Macedonian phalanx, so arranged matters as to show that for him the evil was overshadowed by the good, and that his private sorrows were eclipsed by the successes of the state, lest he should detract from the importance and glory of the victory. He buried the first child, and immediately afterwards triumphed, as we have said: and when the second died after the triumph, he assembled the people and addressed them, not so much in the words of one who needs consolation, as of one who would console his countrymen, who were grieved at his misfortunes. He said, that he never had feared what man could do to him, but always had feared Fortune, the most fickle and variable of all deities; and in the late war she had been so constantly present with him, like a favouring gale, that he expected now to meet with some reverse by way of retribution. "In one day," said he, "I crossed the Ionian sea from Brundisium to Corcyra; on the fifth day I sacrificed at Delphi; in five more I entered upon my command in Macedonia, performed the usual lustration of the army; and, at once beginning active operations, in fifteen days more I brought the war to a most glorious end. I did not trust in my good fortune as lasting, because every thing favoured me, and there was no danger to be feared from the enemy, but it was during my voyage that I especially feared that the change of fortune would befall me, after I had conquered so great a host, and was bearing with me such spoils and even kings as my captives. However, I reached you safe, and saw the city full of gladness and admiration and thanksgiving, but still I had my suspicions about Fortune, knowing that she never bestows any great kindness unalloyed and without exacting retribution for it. And no sooner had I dismissed this foreboding about some misfortune being about to happen to the state, than I met with this calamity in my own household, having during these holydays had to bury my noble sons, one after the other, who, had they lived, would alone have borne my name.

"Now therefore I fear no further great mischance, and am of good cheer; for a sufficient retribution has been exacted from me for my successes, and the triumpher has been made as notable an example of the uncertainty of human life as the victim; except that Perseus, though conquered, still has his children, while Aemilius, his conqueror, has lost his."

XXXVII. Such was the noble discourse which they say Aemilius from his simple and true heart pronounced before the people. As to Perseus, though he pitied his fallen fortunes and was most anxious to help him, all he could do was to get him removed from the common prison, called Carcer by the Romans, to a clean and habitable lodging, where, in confinement, according to most authors, he starved himself to death; but some give a strange and extraordinary account of how he died, saying that the soldiers who guarded him became angry with him, and not being able to vex him by any other means, they prevented his going to sleep, watching him by turns, and so carefully keeping him from rest by all manner of devices, that at last he was worn out and died. Two of his children died also; but the third, Alexander, they say became accomplished in repoussé work and other arts. He learned to speak and write the Roman language well, and was employed by the magistrates as a clerk, in which profession he was much esteemed.

XXXVIII. The most popular thing which Aemilius did in connection with Macedonia was that he brought back so much money that the people were not obliged to pay any taxes till the consulship of Hirtius and Pausa, during the first war between Antony and Augustus Caesar. This was remarkable about Aemilius, that he was peculiarly respected and loved by the people, though of the aristocratical party; and though he never said or did anything to make himself popular, but always in politics acted with the party of the nobles. Scipio Africanus was afterwards reproached with this by Appius. These were the leading men in the city, and were candidates for the office of Censor: the one with the Senate and nobles to support him, that being the hereditary party of the Appii; the other being a man of mark in himself, and one who ever enjoyed the greatest love and favour with the people. So when Appius saw Scipio coming into the forum surrounded by men of low birth and freed men, yet men who knew the forum, and who could collect a mob and by their influence and noise could get any measure passed, he called out, "O Paulus Aemilius, groan in your grave, at your son being brought into the Censorship by Aemilius the crier and Licinius Philonicus." But Scipio kept the people in good humour by constantly augmenting their privileges, whereas Aemilius, though of the aristocratic party, was no less loved by the people than those who courted their favour and caressed them. They showed this by electing him, amongst other dignities, to the Censorship; which office is most sacred, and confers great power, especially in examining men's lives; for the Censor can expel a senator of evil life from his place, and elect the President of the Senate, and punish licentious young men by taking away their horses. They also register the value of property, and the census of the people. In his time they amounted to three hundred and thirty-seven thousand four hundred and fifty-two. He appointed Marcus Aemilius Lepidus President of the Senate, who four times already had enjoyed that dignity, and he expelled three senators, not men of mark. With regard to the Equites, he and his colleague Marcius Philippus showed equal moderation.

XXXIX. After most of the labours of his life were accomplished, he fell sick of a disorder which at first seemed dangerous, but as time went on appeared not to be mortal, but wearisome and hard to cure.

At length he followed the advice of his physicians, and sailed to Paestum, in Italy. There he passed his time chiefly in the peaceful meadows near the sea-shore; but the people of Rome regretted his absence, and in the public theatre often would pray for his return, and speak of their longing to see him. When the time for some religious ceremony at which he had to be present approached, and he also considered himself sufficiently strong, he returned to Rome. He performed the sacrifice, with the other priests, the people surrounding him with congratulations. On the next day he again officiated, offering a thank-offering to the gods for his recovery. When this sacrifice was finished, he went home and lay down, and before any one noticed how changed he was, he fell into a delirious trance, and died in three days, having in his life wanted none of those things which are thought to render men happy. Even his funeral procession was admirable and enviable, and a noble tribute to his valour and goodness. I do not mean gold, ivory, and other expensive and vain-glorious apparatus, but love, honour, and respect, not only shown by his own countrymen, but also by foreigners. For of the Iberians, Ligurians, and Macedonians who happened to be in Rome, the strongest carried the bier, while the elder men followed after, praising Aemilius as the saviour and benefactor of their countries. For he not only during his period of conquest had treated them mildly and humanely, but throughout the rest of his life was always bestowing benefits upon them as persons peculiarly connected with himself. His estate, they say, scarcely amounted to three hundred and seventy thousand sesterces, which he left to be shared between his two sons; but Scipio, the younger, consented to give up his share to his brother, as he was a member of a rich family, that of Africanus. Such is said to have been the life and character of Aemilius Paulus.

Comparison of Paulus Aemilius and Timoleon.

I. The characters of these men being such as is shown in their histories, it is evident that in comparing them we shall find few differences and points of variance. Even their wars were in both cases waged against notable antagonists, the one with the Macedonians, the other with the Carthaginians: while their conquests were glorious, as the one took Macedonia, and crushed the dynasty of Antigonus in the person of its seventh king, while the other drove all the despots from Sicily and set the island free. Unless indeed any one should insinuate that Aemilius attacked Perseus when he was in great strength and had conquered the Romans before, whereas Timoleon fell upon Dionysius when he was quite worn out and helpless: though again it might be urged on behalf of Timoleon that he overcame many despots and the great power of Carthage, with an army hastily collected from all sources, not, like Aemilius, commanding men who were inured to war and knew how to obey, but making use of disorderly mercenary soldiers who only fought when it pleased them to do so. An equal success, gained with such unequal means, reflects the greater credit on the general.

II. Both were just and incorruptible in their conduct: but Aemilius seems to have had the advantage of the customs and state of feeling among his countrymen, by which he was trained to integrity, while Timoleon without any such encouragement acted virtuously, from his own nature. This is proved by the fact that the Romans of that period were all submissive to authority, and carried out the traditions of the state, respecting the laws and the opinions of their countrymen: whereas, except Dion, no Greek leader or general of that time had anything to do with Sicilian affairs who did not take bribes: though many suspected than Dion was meditating making himself king, and that he had dreams of an empire like that of Sparta.

Timaeus tells us that the Syracusans sent away Gylippus in disgrace for his insatiable covetousness, and the bribes which they discovered that he received when in command. And many writers had dwelt upon the wicked and treacherous acts which Pharax the Spartan and Kallippus the Athenian committed, when they were endeavouring to make themselves masters of Sicily. Yet, what were they, and what resources had they, that they conceived such great designs: the one being only a follower of Dionysius when he was banished from Syracuse, the other a captain of mercenaries under Dion? But

Timoleon, who was sent to the Syracusans as generalissimo at their own request and prayer, did not seek for command, but had a right to it. Yet when he received his power as general and ruler from them of their own free will, he voluntarily decided to hold it only till he should have expelled from Sicily all those who were reigning despotically. In Aemilius again we must admire this, that he subdued so great an empire and yet did not enrich himself by one drachma, and never even saw or touched the king's treasures, although he distributed much of them in presents to others. And still, I do not say that Timoleon is to be blamed for having received a fine house and estate; for there is no disgrace in receiving it by such means, though not to take it is better, and shows almost superhuman virtue, which cares not to take what is lawfully within its reach. Yet, as the strongest bodies are those which can equally well support the extremes of heat and cold, so the noblest minds are those which prosperity does not render insolent and overbearing, nor ill fortune depress: and here Aemilius appears more nearly to approach absolute perfection, as, when in great misfortune and grief for his children, he showed the same dignity and firmness as after the greatest success. Whereas Timoleon, though he acted towards his brother as became a noble nature, yet could not support himself against his sorrow by reason, but was so crushed by remorse and grief that for twenty years he could not appear or speak in the public assembly. We ought indeed to shrink from and feel shame at what is base; but the nature which is over-cautious to avoid blame may be gentle and kindly, but cannot be great.

Lightning Source UK Ltd.
Milton Keynes UK
UKOW05f2346230614

233938UK00002B/259/P